Motorcycle Journeys Through
Atlantic Canada

Rannie Gillis and Ken Aiken

D0878354

Whitehorse Press
Center Conway, New Hampshire

All photographs were taken by the authors unless otherwise noted.
The photo on page 209 was taken by Robin Taylor.

We recognize that some words, model names, and designations
mentioned herein are the property of the trademark holder. We use
them for identification purposes only.

Whitehorse Press books are also available at discounts in bulk
quantity for sales and promotional use. For details about special sales
or for a catalog of motorcycling books, videos, and gear write to the
publisher:

Whitehorse Press
107 East Conway Road
Center Conway, New Hampshire 03813
Phone: 603-356-6556 or 800-531-1133
E-mail: CustomerService@WhitehorsePress.com
Internet: www.WhitehorsePress.com

ISBN 978-1-884313-84-4

5 4 3 2

Printed in China

Contents

Acknowledgements

RANNIE GILLIS

I would like to dedicate my sections of this book to: the memory of Ann Marie MacLean, my partner and fellow riding enthusiast, and Maria Gillis, my niece, who is a student at St. Francis Xavier University, my alma mater.

I would also like to acknowledge the important contribution of our editor, Sarah Kimball, who has taken our rough drafts and turned them into the finished product that you read in this text. Over the last two years she has been encouraging, witty, and above all, patient, as she worked with two different authors, who live more than 1000 miles apart.

A final thank you to Judy and Dan Kennedy, and the wonderful staff of Whitehorse Press and Whitehorse Gear, who made my recent visit there such a memorable experience. A great bunch of Girls and Guys!

KEN AIKEN

Though authors get the credit, it is the efforts and contributions of numerous people that ensure the success of a project such as this one. This book would not have been written if not for the active support of Bard Nordby of Québec Tourisme, and a considerable amount of logistical work undertaken by representatives in regional tourism offices including Richard Ségin and Paule Bergeron in Québec City, Suzie Loiselle and Paule Côte of Québec Maritime, Nancy Donnelly in Saguenay–Lac-Saint-Jean, François Gariepy in the Charlevoix, and Julie Lamontagne in Bas-Saint-Laurent. Diane Rioux's assistance in creating the itinerary for my travels through New Brunswick and that of Judy Dougan in Moncton and Sally Cummings in Saint John are greatly appreciated.

The support of Rodd Hotels & Resorts and Karen McKay has, over the years, allowed me the opportunity to explore Nova Scotia and Prince Edward Island. Deeley Harley-Davidson in Toronto was gracious in lending me a Street Glide Trike to tour New Brunswick and Campagna Motors in Boucherville provided me with the Québec-made T-Rex with which to explore eastern Québec. I put many thousands of kilometers on these new vehicles and thank both companies for their support of this project.

So many people enhanced my travels by going out of their way to make

Atlantic Canada

100 km / 60 miles

my experience something beyond simply touring. I certainly can't mention them all, but Raynald, Ross, and Manon in the Saguenay; François in the Charlevoix; Christian in Franquelin; and Dale in Moncton spent their personal time to make portions of this book a success. I'd like to thank Ewa Spoczynska for her patience while I was away on extended trips, and the professional editing work of Sarah Kimball. I would especially like to thank Dan and Judy Kennedy for their friendship and professional support during the past 12 years.

Introduction to Atlantic Canada

For many people, especially those who arrive on a motorcycle, the main reason to come to Atlantic Canada is to experience Canada's most spectacular coastline, and to ride the breathtaking coastal highways that are found in each Atlantic Canadian province. Some of the best motorcycle touring in eastern North America is to be found in Canada. Furthermore, Atlantic Canada is more biker-friendly than most regions in the United States.

Canada's Atlantic provinces are New Brunswick, Prince Edward Island, Nova Scotia, and Newfoundland and Labrador. Although Québec is technically not one of the Atlantic provinces, we have included Québec's Gaspé Peninsula, and the north shore of the St. Lawrence River in this book, since

Touring Atlantic Canada will put you on roads that hug the coast, roam the hills, and swoop between the two.

both regions do border on the Atlantic Ocean, and many tourists often try to incorporate one or both of them in a visit to Atlantic Canada.

In contrast to the United States, which prides itself on being a "melting pot," Canada is more like a patchwork quilt of heritages—Acadian, Scottish, First Nations, British Loyalists, Québecois, Basque, and others. Certain regions are closely associated with particular cultural heritages, with differences reflected in local architecture, food, and language.

Diversity also applies to landscapes. The highest tides in the world occur in the Bay of Fundy and much of the Charlevoix is a giant meteorite crater. There are miles of long, perfect sand beaches in the Magdalen Islands; while rocky inlets and historic bays define the Atlantic coasts of Nova Scotia and Newfoundland. The vast ice-scoured landscape of southern Labrador contrasts vividly with the primeval forests of the central and northern regions, while the flat red soil of Prince Edward Island has produced one of the top potato-growing regions in the country. And to top it all off, the St. Lawrence River is the largest estuary in the world!

This varied landscape has defined the history and economies of these different regions to such an extent that even those settlements that rely on fishing are startlingly different. Along the Bay of Fundy fishing is directed by the forty-foot difference between low and high tide, which naturally requires special configurations for docking and lobster pounds. The rugged Atlantic Coast with its heavy fog limits maritime fishing ports to sheltered harbors while the protected bays of Prince Edward Island have led to the farming of the famous Malpeque oysters and blue mussels.

In attempting to describe Atlantic Canada one is reminded of the fable about the five blind men and the elephant. Each man experienced a portion of the great beast and each thought that they knew what an elephant was. One thought it was very much like a rope, another a tree, a wall, a snake, and a sail. Each portion of Atlantic Canada presents a different experience and the only way to understand it is to take all the journeys described in this book.

Fishing, forestry, and just a little bit of farming formed the economy of Atlantic Canada from its very beginning and set a pattern that's seen to this day. North America's fishing areas—Grand Banks and George's Banks—are located just off the coast of Nova Scotia and Newfoundland. Settlements had to be on the coast for fishing, shipbuilding, trade, and transportation. The interior forests supplied lumber, first for shipbuilding, then international trade, and finally pulp wood for paper production. The great schools of cod and herring are essentially gone and the main catch now is a mixture of lobster, crab, shrimp, and Atlantic salmon. Wooden ships are only

In Acadian communities the colors and gold star of the Stella Maris, *the Acadian flag, are often proudly incorporated into decorations.*

constructed in rare boatyards, but lumber is still a major industry. Farming, at least in the traditional sense, is commercially viable only along the St. John River in New Brunswick and on Prince Edward Island. Except for farming regions, settlements in these provinces are concentrated on the coastlines and very sparse in the forested interiors.

Prince Edward Island has a population of only 141,000 people and the amount of land that can be owned by one person is regulated. Except for the two cities—Summerside and Charlottetown—the island is fairly evenly settled. New Brunswick has a population of 750,000 but most people live along the coast and more than a third of the population lives in two cities—Saint John and Moncton. Except for the fertile Annapolis Valley, the same pattern is repeated in Nova Scotia with Halifax and Sydney being the principal urban centers. Québec is a huge chunk of land twice the size of Texas, and even with a population approaching eight million, it still has a density of less than six people per square kilometer. A quarter of these live on the Island of Montréal and another million reside just "off island."

Crossing the international border from the United States and Canada is not a problem as long as you have positive, official identification. To return to the United States though, you will need a passport.

Eastern Québec is mostly wilderness with a thin band of settlements along the St. Lawrence River and the coast of the Gaspé peninsula. This thin band of settlements extends into Labrador, with many of them accessible only by boat. Almost half the population of Newfoundland resides in the city of St. John's and the rest is scattered in small villages along the coast. Much of the interior and large sections of coastline are devoid of road access.

The genuine warmth and hospitality of the people cannot be understated. We both can tell of times when people have gone out of their way to guide us around their region. Fishermen have given us boat rides and taken the time to give us extensive tours of their operations. A shopkeeper in Charlottetown followed author Aiken up the street to return something he had left in her shop. Early one season, author Gillis stopped at an inn in St. Peters, PEI. Even though the restaurant had not yet opened, the proprietor kindly prepared lunch for him and his riding companions rather than send them away hungry. A motorcyclist stopped on the side of the road will invariably cause passers-by to slow down to make certain things are all right. Many times when author Aiken stopped to take photos he had to wave his camera as explanation. This willingness to bring a stranger into their lives has led to more stories than could be incorporated in this book and established a few lasting friendships.

The relatively small and dispersed populations of the Atlantic Provinces means that roads in Atlantic Canada do not have the large traffic volumes that are common in many parts of the United States. Although the Autoroutes in Québec and the Trans-Canada Highway in New Brunswick, along with sections of the Trans-Canada in Nova Scotia, are four-lane divided highways, most other highways are simple two-lane roads, usually without paved shoulders. One section of the Appalachian Range Drive in New Brunswick is gravel, but it's actually maintained in better condition than the asphalt that's been tortured by logging trucks. Basically, some stretches of pavement are quite rough, others are silky smooth, and which is which usually changes from year to year.

Three misconceptions about crossing the international border to travel in Canada need to be dispelled. First, there's no problem getting into the country—all you need is positive, official identification such as a driver's license with your photo. However, you need a valid passport or an augmented driver's license to return to the United States. The second myth is that French-speaking (Francophone) Québecers don't like English-speaking (Anglophone) visitors. Author Aiken does not speak French and has lived and traveled extensively throughout Québec for many years and yet has had only one negative experience related to language. The French vs. English conflict is simply internal politics. The third misconception is that it's more expensive to travel in Canada. Gasoline certainly is more expensive, but lodging and restaurants are, quality for quality, less. In the end, touring in Canada isn't going to cost any more, and often costs less, than most regions in the United States.

PROVINCIAL TOURISM OFFICES

Tourism offices in Canada are well organized and offer a considerable amount of information that will be of assistance in planning a trip. Some, like the office in the Magdalen Islands, will even book lodging for you. Nova Scotia has a guide written by Harold and Wendy Nesbitt especially for motorcyclists, the Gaspé offers a motorcycle-touring map, and author Aiken has developed maps and motorcycle touring information for the Charlevoix.

Each of the four Atlantic Provinces produces an extensive printed tourism guide, that is also available online. Profusely illustrated with photos and maps, they offer advice on accommodation, things to do and see, and information on various historic sites. Québec has informative guides published for each of their tourism regions. These guides, which are updated on a yearly basis, make planning a trip to this region very easy.

WEATHER AND RIDING SEASON

Touring on motorcycles depends to a great extent on the weather, and we are talking here about a five-month riding season that usually runs from the middle of May to the middle of October. However, as we all know, the weather can be variable from year to year. For example, 2010 was the warmest winter on record and in the oral history of the Innu people, yet there was snow in the Laurentian Mountains and the Chic Chocs in May. For certain areas, especially Cape Breton Island and Newfoundland and Labrador, the riding season may start early or late in June. It all depends on the spring ice conditions in the Gulf of St. Lawrence and the North Atlantic Ocean, which can vary considerably from year to year.

The island of Newfoundland has a temperate marine climate. Winters are usually mild with a normal temperature of 0 degrees Celsius (32 degrees Fahrenheit). Summer days range from cool to hot, with a normal temperature of 16 degrees C (61 degrees F). Good swimming weather generally begins at the end of June. Labrador winters are much colder than those on the island. While summers are shorter and generally cooler, extreme high temperatures are not uncommon in Labrador.

MEASUREMENT

Canada uses the metric system, which means that bikers from the States will have to do mental conversions. Even though your speedometer may read in miles, the highway signs are all in kilometers. Speed limits in Atlantic Canada, unless otherwise posted, permit a maximum speed of 110 km/h (65 mph) on four-lane provincial highways, 100 km/h (60 mph) or 80 km/h (50 mph) on two-lane

Metric conversions

1 kilometer (km) = 0.62 miles
1 mile (mi) = 1.6 kilometers
1 kilogram (kg) = 2.2 pounds.
1 meter (m) = 3.28 feet.
1 liter = 0.265 gallons
0° Celsius = 32° Fahrenheit
10° C = 50° F
20° C = 68° F
30° C = 86° F

Fishing has always formed a major part of the economy in Atlantic Canada. Now that the great schools of cod and herring are gone, the catch has become lobster, crab, shrimp and Atlantic salmon.

provincial highways and 50 km/h (30 mph) in urban areas.

Measurements in this book are given in both kilometers and miles. The distances given in the directions and the text are approximate and may differ from the distances shown on different odometers. The measurements are given to aid you in your trip planning. The maps in this book are included to highlight the location of each trip described. It is highly recommended that you use a more detailed road map for your on-the-road navigation.

TIME ZONES

Nova Scotia, New Brunswick, and Prince Edward Island are on Atlantic Standard, or Atlantic Daylight Time. If you enter the region from Maine or Québec, you should set your watch ahead one hour. The island of Newfoundland occupies its own time zone, known as Newfoundland Time. It is half an hour later than Atlantic Time, and a full hour and a half later than Eastern Time. Most of Labrador occupies the Atlantic Time Zone; however, the area from L'Anse-au-Claire to Black Tickle operates on Newfoundland Time. Confused?

CELL PHONE COVERAGE

As in many rural portions of the United States, cell phone coverage is spotty, and is most reliable near the more populated areas. Police carry radio-phones and even these don't always work. Remember "dial-up" Internet connections? You thought it was amazing just a few years ago and in many places you'll get to experience it again! However, in Moncton, New Brunswick, the entire downtown district and all of the bus lines are WiFi hotspots. The best advice is to inform people that you might be out of contact for a couple of days and pretend that you're back in 2000 when motorcyclists didn't carry cell phones, computers, or GPS.

Motorcycle helmets are mandatory in Atlantic Canada and Québec.

Firearms are strictly controlled in Canada, and fully automatic weapons are banned. Visitors may only bring firearms for a legitimate purpose, such as hunting or a target shooting competition. For more information contact the Canadian Firearms Centre at 800-731-4000.

Atlantic Canada offers miles of scenic coastline, a variety of cultures, a fascinating history, and of course, a healthy supply of exciting roads for motorcyclists. Welcome to Atlantic Canada, and we'll see you on the road!

ATLANTIC CANADA FERRIES

Visitors who plan to take one or more ferry rides should carry a good set of tie-down straps for their motorcycle, and know how to use them. Many local riders who frequent the Marine Atlantic ferries to and from Newfoundland and Labrador will carry two sets of tie-downs, one to secure the front of their motorcycle, and one to secure the rear. (See photo on page 344.)

Québec

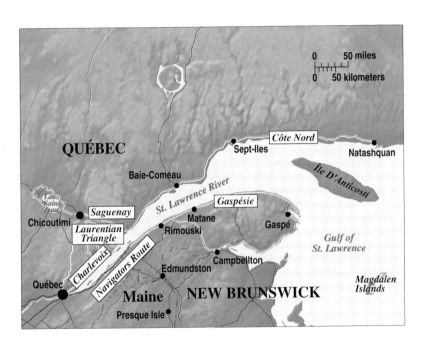

Québec *by Ken Aiken*

Québec is a vast province encompassing over a million-and-a-half square kilometers, or more than twice the size of Texas. It spans 1,355 kilometers (842 miles) east to west and 1,774 km (1,102 mi) south to north from the 45th parallel on the U.S. border at Vermont to beyond the 62nd. However, most of this is vast wilderness where no roads exist. This chapter encompasses only a comparatively thin sliver of territory east of Québec City, yet hundreds of miles of these roads are merely an asphalt thread connecting remote villages in an otherwise untamed environment.

On the north side of the St. Lawrence River are the billion-year-old Laurentian Mountains and the Canadian Shield; on the southern side the Appalachian Mountains that formed only 250 million years ago. Separating them is the largest estuary on the planet and where Blue, Fin, Humpback,

Looking downriver from the heights of the Citadel in Québec City, the port is visible in the lower right.

and Sperm whales can be observed in a river hundreds of miles from the Atlantic Ocean and an inland town can justifiably lay claim to being the Shrimp Capital of the World.

Québec is not like other places. It's New World French influenced by British colonization with the constant undercurrent of the First People nations who have called it home for thousands of years. You'll find vibrant international communities in Charlevoix, the heart of the Québecois nation in Saguenay, Innu settlements all along the Côte-Nord, and Acadian culture in the Magdalen Islands and the Gaspé coast. It's the only place in North America where the French language is the sole official language, but my lack of French hasn't limited my ability to live here six months a year. Try to speak French and you'll be embraced like a long-lost cousin.

Atlantic tides influence the daily rhythms north to Chicoutimi and west to Québec City, so although they are hundreds of miles from the ocean these cities are inarguably part of Atlantic Canada. However, Québec also has two percent of the world's available freshwater in a million lakes, 4,500 rivers, and 125,000 streams. Fresh water mixing with Atlantic tides creates the planet's largest estuary.

Rue St-Louis is one of the primary streets within the walls of old Québec.

There are cannon just about everywhere. These are on the ramparts of Port-Dauphin.

The first four trips described in this chapter are interconnected, as are the last three. Trip 1 provides the so-called base line that connects with Trips 2, 3, and 4. It's also a direct connection via ferry to Trips 5 and 6. Using Québec City as a destination or a base, a number of different popular touring loops can be configured, especially when utilizing ferry crossings *(traversiers)*. Trip 6, The Valley, also provides two gorgeous options for connecting to the New Brunswick rides outlined in another chapter.

QUÉBEC CITY

Founded in 1608 by Samuel de Champlain, Québec City (pop. 638,000) has since become the capital of the Province of Québec. "Kebec" is Algonquin for "where the river narrows" while "Canada" referred to the Iroquois settlement that existed at this spot prior to 1608. Surrounded by a fortified wall, the old city is a UNESCO World Heritage Site and it ranks as one of the world's top-20 tourist destinations.

Québec City's strategic location atop Cap-Diamant (Cape Diamond) at the place where the St. Lawrence River narrows, is apparent when traveling upriver. If you cross on the ferry from Lévis (on the south bank) to the old *(vieux)* port where the relentless river wrestles with powerful tides in the swirling narrows, the ramparts of the massive defensive wall are starkly visible on the heights. From an 18th-century perspective Québec appears to be nearly impregnable. However, from history we know that British General James Wolfe flanked the city and attacked from the west on the Plains of Abraham to capture it in 1759.

Château Frontenac is the landmark hotel within the walls of the old city of Québec.

Crossing the river on the Pont Pierre-Laporte, the eastern-most bridge over the St. Lawrence, provides two approaches to the walled city a few miles away. Route 175 leads east through the modern suburbs on an almost imperceptible slope and becomes La Grande-Allée as it runs across the Plains of Abraham. The other, Blvd. Champlain/Route 136, snakes between the north bank of the river and the ever-increasing height of the cape's escarpment to eventually end at the old port directly beneath the fortified wall.

The old city is a maze of narrow one-way streets and even finding its entrances tends to confuse first-time visitors. This is a city best explored on foot simply because there are so many pedestrians, visual distractions, and the cobblestones can be quite slippery when wet. Another problem is that motorcycles are banned inside the walls except for travel to reserved hotel accommodations.

This city is so rich in aesthetics and history that a comprehensive guide of what to see and where to eat will run several hundred pages. Vieux-Québec is not a large area, but every street is packed with things to see. Maps and extensive guides can be found at the information centers—one is located just off Grande-Allée on the edge of Battlefield Park a block from the Saint-Louis Gate and the other is on Rue Saint Anne next to Place d'Armes a block from Château Frontenac.

A minimum of two or three hours wandering around Lower Town is recommended. From Côte de la Montagne, the Breakneck Stairs leads down to Quartier Petit Champlain; or take the Funicular—the inclined rail system—from Terrasse Dufferin in front of the Château Frontenac. Place-Royale is a square, built on the site of the original 1608 settlement.

Secure Motorcycle Parking

If your bike isn't parked in a hotel garage the best space in town is beneath the Hôtel de Ville (town hall). Coming from Lower Town on Côte de la Montagne you'll make a sweeping left turn around the statue of François-Xavier de Montmorency-Laval (first bishop of Québec) onto Rue Port-Dauphin and immediately turn right onto Rue de Baude, always going uphill. Notre-Dame Basilica will be on your right along Rue de Baude and the street will end at Rue des Jardins in front of Hôtel de Ville (town hall). Left on Rue des Jardins and the next right on Rue Ste-Anne. The entry ramp to the underground parking will be on your immediate right and directly across the street from the landmark Art Deco skyscraper of the Hôtel Clarendon. Continue to the lowest level following the *SORTIE* (exit) signs. Motorcycle-only parking is by the tollbooth that is manned 24/7. Coming down Rue St-Louis (one way), simply turn left onto Rue des Jardins and left onto Rue Ste-Anne.

Another convenient parking area is next to the Québec Tourism Information Center on Place George-V in Upper Town. Located just off Grande-Allée (Route 175) on the edge of Battlefields Park and almost opposite the Québec Parliament, building it's only a block from the Saint-Louis Gate into Vieux-Québec and near popular restaurants. ∎

The St-Roch District lies outside the walls of Old Québec and, unfortunately, is too often overlooked by visitors to the city.

Art galleries line Rue St-Pierre and Rue du Sault-au-Matelot at the base of the fortified wall and numerous antique shops and cafés can be found along St-Paul.

Within the walls, Rue St-Louis is the main commercial street, and here the buildings that house boutiques, restaurants, and B&B inns are two- and three-hundred-years old. This is an UNESCO World Heritage Site and rightly so. The Citadelle commands the high ground and, despite being a historic site, this remains an active military installation and the official residence of the governor general. The Notre-Dame de Québec Basilica, the oldest parish in North America, is much like the great churches of Europe and is well worth a visit. Château Frontenac is the massive castle-like structure that dominates the skyline of Québec City. Built by Bruce Price for the Canadian Pacific Railroad, the Château Frontenac opened in 1893 and has since become the iconic symbol for this city and holds the Guinness World Record as "the most photographed hotel in the world." A stroll along the top of the wall along Rue des Remparts provides a sense of the commanding position of these fortifications—the emplaced cannons certainly enhance the experience.

Outside the walls in Upper Town lies the Plains of Abraham, and Battlefield Parks is the site of numerous festivals and mega-concerts during the year. La Grande-Allée/Route 175 has many fine restaurants, including the revolving L'Astral, high atop Loews le Concorde Hotel (418-647-2222, www.loewshotels.com). Rue St-Jean begins halfway down the hill at Avenue Honoré-Mercier and runs through the Saint-Jean-Baptiste District. This hip street has many fine restaurants and shops where prices are a bit more reasonable. The Saint-Roch District is nestled against the northern face of the bluff with Route 175 passing directly through the middle of it. It reminds me of the East Village in the late '60s, but in French.

Most fine-art galleries feature work done by Charlevoix artists.

The 360-degree view of the city from the top of the 727-foot Observatoire de la Capitale (525 Blvd. René-Lévesque Est, 418- 528-0773, www.ccnq.org) is a visual treat. This is the best way to get a sense of the layout of Québec prior to exploring it on foot.

Hôtel Clarendon (57 Rue Ste-Anne, 888-554-6001, www.dufour.ca.) This Art Deco skyscraper in the heart of the old city is a landmark. Parking next door in the garage beneath the Hôtel de Ville (city hall) is not terribly convenient, but bikes are supervised and secure. This is the oldest hotel in Québec and its Le Charles Baillairge restaurant is the oldest in Canada.

Le Château Frontenac (1 Rue Carrières, 800-441-1414). This is the uncontested symbol of Québec City, and to stay in any of its 618 guestrooms is an experience. Bikes have secure parking within the courtyard.

Auberge Saint-Antoine is located in Lower Town next to the Museum of Civilization. Probably unique in the world, with every room graced by archeological finds, it's essentially a museum coupled with five-star

Finding Your Way Around

Vieux-Québec is a maze of one-way streets running over and around the challenging topography of Cap Diamant. These are the basic, but by no means the only, routes through and around the walled city.

La Grande-Allée (Route 175) approaches the old city from the west and makes a 90-degree left becoming Ave. Honoré-Mercier. Going around the magnificent fountain the avenue becomes divided as it goes down the hill. At the bottom of the hill Route 175 makes a left turn; continuing straight leads directly onto Autoroute 440. Instead of making the turn onto Ave. Honoré-Mercier, continue straight onto Rue St-Louis (one way) and go through Porte (gate) St-Louis. It's downhill from here as Rue St-Louis becomes Côte de la Montagne to Rue Dalhousie in the Old Port.

The reverse is a more dramatic introduction to the old city and although it sounds complicated, it really isn't. If you arrive by the Lévis to Québec ferry or Blvd. Champlain/Route 136, you end up on Rue Dalhousie. A left turn onto Côte de la Montagne leads up the hill, a sweeping left turn around the statue of François-Xavier de Montmorency-Laval (first bishop of Québec) onto Rue Port-Dauphin and immediately turn right onto Rue de Baude, always going uphill. Notre-Dame Basilica will be on your right along Rue de Baude, and the street will end at Rue des Jardins in front of Hôtel de Ville. Left on Rue des Jardins

accommodations that has won countless awards and rates as one of the top two boutique hotels I've stayed at anywhere in the world. It's expensive, but has everything going for it, including secure parking.

Le Vincent (295 Rue St-Vallier Est, 418-523-5000, www.aubergele-vincent.com) is a delightful boutique hotel in the Saint-Roch District. It's easy to find if you are headed south on Route 175 since this area is a maze of one-way streets. Just so you know, it's half a block from the traffic light where Route 175 turns to follow Couronne. It *is* worth the extra effort, but since there are only 10 rooms it's best to make reservations in advance.

Château Laurier (1220 Place George-V Ouest, parking, four stars, 877-522-8108, www.hotelchateaulaurier.com) is located next to the ar-mory on Battlefield Park a block from the Saint-Louis Gate into the old city and across from the Parliament building. The information center is just a few meters away, as are the restaurants along Grand-Allée.

---

and the next right on Rue Ste-Anne. (The best public motorcycle park-ing in the city is located under the Hôtel de Ville and the entrance is on Rue Ste-Anne.) Rue Ste-Anne (one way) ends at Rue d'Auteuil. Turn right and then the next left onto Rue Dauphine. Alternately, continue straight from Rue Ste-Anne onto Rue Cook and the next left onto Rue Dauphine. Rue Dauphine goes through Porte Saint-Jean and ends at Ave. Honoré-Mercier/Route 175.

Vieux (old) Port runs around the base of Cap Diamant and be-tween Rue Dalhousie and the foot of the escarpment lie a series of narrow cobblestone streets hemmed in by 18th-century stone build-ings housing art galleries, choice boutiques, and fine restaurants. The original settlement was located here at Place-Royale and pedes-trian-only Rue du Petit Champlain is the oldest commercial street in North America. On the opposite side of Rue Dalhousie is the quay where blazingly white oceanic tour ships dock to discharge thousands of passengers. A left on Quai St-André (one way) leads along the har-bor to the train station (*gare* in French) onto Blvd. Jean-Lesage and across the bridge to the ramp for Autoroute 440 or Blvd. des Capucins and Chemin de la Canardiere to Route 138. Alternately, from Quai St-André bearing left on Rue St-Paul, which will become Blvd. Charest, leads to Rue de la Couronne/Route 175. Turn left and follow Route 175 to Parliament Hill. ∎

Trip 1 **Charlevoix**

Distance: *Approximately 200 km (125 mi) and theoretically only a couple of hours. The reality is that this is a day-long trip with stops, side trips, and loops. To make trip planning easier, this ride has been divided into five sections. Mix and match them with other Québec rides to structure your own tour.*

Terrain: *Riverside drive and roller coaster hills with a few tight corners in the mix. Dramatic views are the norm on most of these roads. Travel is through mostly deciduous forest and small villages. This ride is one of the premier motorcycle touring routes in Québec.*

Highlights: *Québec City is an experience in itself. Montmorency Falls, the Shrine of Ste-Anne, 19th-century gristmills and forges in the Charlevoix, art galleries and studios, food to die for, and outstanding scenic views are part and parcel for this ride. You will see more motorcyclists on Route 138/Route 362 than anywhere else in Atlantic Canada.*

Autoroute 440 follows the northern bank of the St. Lawrence River for 9 km (6 mi) and in many places the river meets the shoulder of the highway. The easiest way to gain access to both Routes 138 and 360 is by turning onto Blvd. François-de-Laval in the suburb of Giffard. The last exit before the autoroute becomes Route 138 is Exit 325. This affords a quick stop to take in Montmorency Falls or an 88-km (55 mi) side trip to explore Île d'Orléans.

The Route from Québec City to Baie-Saint-Paul on Route 138

0 km (0 mi) Begin on Autoroute 440 at Blvd. Honoré-Mercier in Québec City.

4 km (2.7 mi) On your left is Blvd. François-de-Laval for optional access to Routes 138 and 360.

9 km (6.0 mi) This exit ramp should be taken for the optional side trips to Montmorency Falls and/or Île d'Orléans.

10 km (6.5 mi) Autoroute 440 becomes Route 138.

15 km (9.8 mi) Arrive Sainte-Anne-de-Beaupré. Continue on Route 138.

35 km (21.7 mi) Optional left turn on Route 360 for Mont-Sainte-Anne ski area. (Route 360 rejoins Route 138 farther east.)

83 km (51.4 mi) Turn right on Chemin Du Belvédère to visit the Charlevoix Tourism Information Center.

86 km (53.4 mi) Turn right on Route 362/Rue de la Lumière in Baie-Saint-Paul.

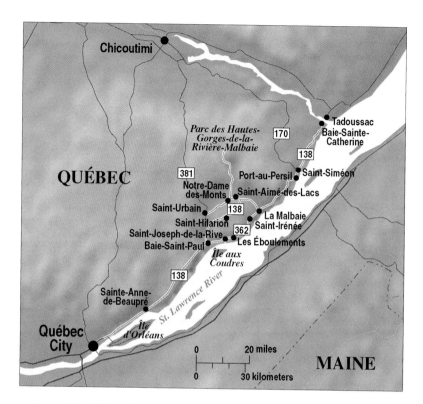

Route 360 follows high ground along the tops of the bluff that marks the ancient shore of this great river while Route 138 follows the current shoreline. Both come together in the town of Sainte-Anne-de-Beaupré (pop. 2,800).

The magnificent Sainte-Anne-de-Beaupré Shrine (10018 Ave. Royale, 418-827-3781, www.ssadb.qc.ca) is one of the most popular pilgrimage sites in North America and receives over a million visitors a year. Next door, the great cylindrical building is the Cyclorama of Jerusalem (8 Rue Regina, 418-827-3101, www.cyclorama.com) one of the last cycloramas in the world about the life of Jesus, is the largest panorama in the world. It was painted in Munich between1878 and 1882 and erected here in 1895. A more secular attraction is the Musée Edison du Phonographe (9812 Ave. Royale at Rue Regina, 418-827-5957, www.phono.org/beaupre.html). Alva Edison invented the phonograph in 1877 and the museum has three tinfoil phonographs dating back to 1878-1890. There are 200-plus phonographs in the collection, including a three-cylinder jukebox and a cylinder phonograph alarm clock. Here you can listen to recordings made by Teddy Roosevelt, Enrico Caruso, Sarah Bernhardt, and Alva Edison himself. The ski resort of Mont-Sainte-Anne is just outside the village on Route 360 and

The Cyclorama of Jerusalem with its panoramic depiction of the life of Jesus has been part of the Shrine of Sainte-Anne-de-Beaupré since 1895.

there is abundant affordable lodging to be found along Route 138.

The highway becomes more of a rollercoaster ride as it enters the Laurentian Mountains. The Charlevoix Tourism Information Center is located a couple of miles before and 1,000 feet above Baie-Saint-Paul. The observation deck offers a stunningly beautiful view of the only populated meteorite impact crater on the planet. In fact, the information center is built on its rim. This is a UNESCO World Biosphere Reserve and a region that's internationally recognized for its culinary and visual arts.

Baie-Saint-Paul (pop. 7,288) has the highest concentration of art galleries per capita of any town or city in North America. Bronze busts of artists on marble plinths grace public places instead of statues of military heroes or industrialists. It also has the distinction of being the birthplace of Cirque du Soleil in 1984. This is a place that attracts food aficionados from across North America and Europe and the region has an established Flavor Trail of specialty food producers. It has a single microbrewery that produces Belgian beers of very high caliber and sampling them on the patio of Le Saint Pub (2 Racine St., 418-240-2332, www.microbrasserie.com) is always on my agenda when visiting the region. Le Bouquet is an award-winning eco-café and La Muse a sweet romantic inn (39 Rue St-Jean-Baptiste, 418-435-6830, www.lamuse.com) in the heart of the village. There are so many choice places to eat and stay that you'll just have to "follow your nose" in this village. This is a major Québec motorcycle destination and even on a weekday you'll see hundreds of bikes rolling through or parked.

From Baie-Saint-Paul two primary highways and a secondary series of roads traverse the ancient crater to La Malbaie, while another leads north to La Baie on the Saguenay River.

Route du Fleuve—Baie-Saint-Paul to La Malbaie on Route 362

0 km (0 mi) Begin on Route 362 at Route 138 in Baie-Saint-Paul.

18 km (11.3 mi) In Les Éboulements, Route du Port leads down to Saint-Joseph-de-la-Rive and the ferry crossing to Île-aux-Coudres. A few meters farther is the driveway to the seigneurial gristmill.

18.7 km (11.71 mi) Rang Ste-Catherine is on your left (chocolatier, forge).

32 km (19.9 mi) Arrive in Saint-Irénée.

41 km (25.7 mi) Route 138 crosses Chemin des Falaises in La Malbaie (turn right for the casino and Le Manoir Richelieu; left for Auberge des Falaises; right into the parking lot for 3 Canards).

48 km (29.8 mi) Route 362 ends at Route 138 by the bridge over Malbaie River in downtown La Malbaie.

Route du Fleuve, the River Route (www.riverdrive.ca) is a bit of a misnomer since, except at Saint-Irénée—it runs inland and hundreds of feet above the St. Lawrence River. Also known as Route 362, it ranks as one of the top-10 scenic roads in Canada. From the village of Baie-Saint-Paul the highway climbs hundreds of feet in elevation along the side of the mountain overlooking the bay. The pull-off area offers a panoramic view of the village and river where landscape painters often set their easels and canvases.

Les Éboulements means "the landslide" and the town (pop. 1,242) is named after a massive one that took place during an earthquake in February of 1663. The last big one, the Charlevoix-Kamouraska Quake, took place on February 2, 1925, but there are literally hundreds of imperceptible tremors that take place each year. Mont Les Éboulements is the impact rebound at the center of the Charlevoix crater, a celestial impact that shattered the very crust of the planet. The St. Lawrence River flows over an ancient fault line that marks the original North American tectonic plate. Those who believe in earth energy and vortexes will notice the inordinate concentration of professional musicians, artists, artisans, and specialty food producers living in this area.

Anyone whose interest runs to mechanics, baking, or colonial history will want to stop and visit the Seigneurial Mill (Moulin Seigneurial des Éboulements, 418-635-2239, www.hcq-chq.org/mill.html). Built in 1790 at the top of a hundred-foot-high waterfall it has survived to the present era with very little change. The original wooden gear system was replaced by a "modern" system in the late 19th century, but it's still grinding flour for a local baker and the millwright still lives in the adjoining house.

Les Éboulements has an original 19th-century blacksmith shop and a first-class Belgian chocolatier (418-635-266, www.camplemanoir.qc.ca). Those looking for a sit-down meal should consider Les Saveurs Oubliées (350 Rang St-Godfrey, 418-635-9888), internationally renowned for the lamb it raises on its own farm next door. Roadside signs mark the *ateliers* (studios) of local artists all the way to Saint-Irénée (pop. 694), home to the internationally famous musicians' retreat of Le Domaine Forget (5 St-Antoine, 418-452-3535, www.domaineforget.com).

To visit L'Isle-aux-Coudres take the ferry from Saint-Joseph-de-la-Rive. In 1663 an earthquake caused a large portion of the shore to landslide into the St. Lawrence River. It doesn't seem like such a big deal until you ride down the hill from Les Éboulements to reach the port town of Saint-Joseph-de-la-Rive. The road descends 750 feet in elevation on grades that reach 18 percent, but the other road, Côte à Godin toward Baie-Saint-Paul,

Humberto Pinochet is one of the noted painters in the region—and that's saying a lot. His atelier (art studio) *is located on Route 362 in Les Éboulements.*

The beautiful little roadside chapel of Saint-Isidore was dedicated on November 13, 1736, but if you think this is old consider that the first mass held in Canada took place on Île aux Coudres on September 7, 1535.

seems even steeper. The Charlevoix Maritime Museum (Musée Maritime de Charlevoix, 305 Rue de L'Eglise, 418-635-1131, www.musee-maritime-charlevoix.com) and papermaking studio (Papeterie Saint-Gilles) are two of the local attractions in this small village.

Île aux Coudres was visited by Jacques Cartier during his explorations in 1535 and he named it for its stands of wild hazelnut bushes. The island was settled because of its convenient location for provisioning ships, but these days it's the splendid views that attracts wayfarers. The beautiful little roadside chapel of Saint-Isidore is more than 260 years old and its tiny doors are still open for travelers. There are two, early-19th-century gristmills on the island and they have been restored as working museums (Les Moulins de l'Isle aux Coudres, 36 Chemin du Moulin, 418-438-2184, lesmoulinsiac.com). The water mill was built in 1825 so local residents wouldn't have to make the arduous trek to the seigneurial mill in Les Éboulements. The other, powered by wind, was built in 1836 on the other side of the stream after a

The Restaurant L'Orange is one of several popular motorcycle destinations for lunch in Baie-Saint-Paul.

long period of drought. Enjoy the 24.4 km (15.2 mi) loop around the island and return on ferry.

La Malbaie (the bad bay, pop. 9,177), was so named by Samuel de Champlain when his ships ended up stranded on the mud flats when the tide went out. The British renamed it Murray Bay and modern French Québecois subsequently restored its original name. At one time it was called the "Newport of the North" and was the summer retreat of American society. The "cottage" that was owned by U. S. President William Howard Taft was known as "the summer White House."

Many of the summer "cottages" in the Pointe-au-Pic sector of town have been transformed into elegant B&B inns and the Fairmont Le Manoir Richelieu (181 Rue Richelieu, 418-665-3703, www.lfairmont.com) is five-star luxury. The Charlevoix Casino is located adjacent to this Fairmont hotel. Dinner at Auberge des 3 Canards (115 Côte Bellevue/Route 362, 418-665-3761, www.auberge3canards.com) is a culinary experience that I can't praise enough. The very epitome of fine dining will also be experienced at Le Charlevoix in Le Manoir Richelieu and at Auberge des Falaises (418-665-3731, www.aubergedesfalaise.com). There are so many good places to eat in this village and so many great places to stay that you're not likely to make a bad choice.

The River Route, Route 362, ends at Route 138 by the bridge over the Malbaie River in the downtown area. Rue St-Etienne is the main street in the village and runs roughly parallel to Blvd. de Comporté/Route 362.

Baie-Saint-Paul to La Malbaie on Route 138

0 km (0 mi) From the junction with Route 362 in Baie-Saint-Paul continue on Route 138 East.

9 km (5.9 mi) At the junction with Route 381 continue straight on Route 138.

20 km (12.3 mi) In Saint-Hilarion, Chemin Cartier on the right leads to Les Éboulements.

34 km (21.4 mi) Rue Principale on the right leads to the House of the Bootlegger.

36 km (22.8 mi) Rue Principale on the left, is the beginning of the Mountain Route.

41 km (25.8 mi) Route 138 continues across the bridge over Malbaie River in downtown La Malbaie.

The River Route is not the only highway leading from Baie-Saint-Paul to La Malbaie. Route 138 runs through the center of the region and anywhere else this would be considered a beautiful touring road, but here it is surpassed by the other two options.

In the village of Saint-Hilarion (pop. 1,200), 20 km (12 mi) from Baie-Saint-Paul, is an intersection with Chemin Cartier running north to connect with *Route des Montagnes,* the Mountain Route, and south to continue as Rang Ste-Catherine to Les Éboulements. "Rang" means "country road" and this sector of the Charlevoix region is crisscrossed with them. Route 138 reaches the Malbaie River in Clermont and becomes the commercial Blvd. de Comporté leading into the village of La Malbaie.

West of Clermont are signs denoting two turns: 2E RANG TO NOTRE-DAME-DES-MONTS (pop. 846) and RUE PRINCIPALE TO SAINT-AIMÉ-DES-LACS (pop. 996). The former is the beginning of the Mountain Route and the later road leads to Parc des Hautes-Gorges-de-la-Rivière-Malbaie.

The Upper Gorge (*Haute Gorges* in French) Route is paved all the way to the base lodge in the gorge. There is a modest entry fee for the park, but it's a small price to pay for these last few kilometers of road. The imposing cliffs mark the edge of the Charlevoix crater, and when you ride into the gorge, you've entered the oldest mountains on the planet. The cliffs are reputed to

The Bootlegger's House

It was once a hunting lodge but was reconstructed as a notorious speak-easy during the era of Canadian Prohibition. It has hidden doors and a secret room where the gaming table was painted on the floor and further hidden by a rug. An almost impossibly narrow, winding staircase leads to the extensive attic room with hidden windows and rough-hewn beams spanning the long room. This room is filled with wooden benches and tables where dinner guests are communally seated. The place is crammed with memorabilia and collectibles. There's no other place like it.

There's only one seating for dinner and after the plates and wine are cleared from the table the musicians plug in their amps and the place rocks until the proprietress decides to shut it down for the night. It seems apropos that this was one of Elvis Presley's favorite places, and it's one of mine.

La Maison du Bootlegger is located just off Route 138 west of Clermont on the east side of the highway (110 Rang Ruisseau-des-Frênes, 418-439-3711, www.maisondubootlegger.com). Turn onto Rue Principale toward Sainte-Agnès-de-Charlevoix and an immediate right on Rang Ruisseau-des-Frênes. The driveway and sign are on the left near the top of the hill. ∎

The road leading into the Parc des Hautes-Gorges-de-la-Rivière-Malbaie goes only as far as the base lodge, but what a road it is!

be the highest east of the Rocky Mountains and there are numerous hiking trails that wind to those lofty heights. The base lodge has facilities and parking, but any further exploration requires changing modes and continuing up the Malbaie River by kayak or canoe, or following the maintained trail on foot or mountain bike (reservations: 800-665-6527, www.parcsquebec .com). There's no choice but to return to Saint-Aimé-des-Lacs, but from there to continue west along the Mountain Route, turn left on Chemin du Lac-Nairne just before the village.

Route des Montagnes—Notre-Dame-des-Monts to Saint-Urbain

Follow the blue-and-white signs for this scenic route.
Begin at Route 138, 5 km (3 mi) west of La Malbaie.
Turn right on Rue Principale.
Turn left on Chemin du Lac-Nairne in Saint-Aimé-des-Lacs.
Turn left on Rue Principale to Rue de la Forêt in Notre-Dame-des-Monts.
Turn right on Rang Ste-Philomène.
Turn right, Rang St-Antonine to Rang St-Jean-Baptiste to Rue Ste-Anne.
29 km (18.2 mi) Arrive at Route 381/Rue St-Edouard in Saint-Urbain.

Route des Montagnes, the Mountain Route (www.mountainsdrive.com), is a series of narrow, twisting roads running from Notre-Dame-des-Monts to Saint-Urbain. It's well marked by blue-and-white signs and this route offers some exceptional panoramic views while passing small farms. Despite millions of years of natural erosion the jagged edge of this crater is strikingly evident from the vantage point of this road. It ends at Route 381 in Saint-Urbain only 4 km (2.5 mi) north of Route 138.

La Malbaie to the Saguenay River on Route 138

0 km (0 mi) From the bridge over the Malbaie River and junction with Route 362, take Route 138 east.
23 km (14.5 mi) A right turn on Chemin du Port-au-Persil takes you to the port in 4 km (2.5 mi) and back to Route 138 in 4 km (2.6 mi).
31 km (19.6 mi) Rue du Festival on right goes to Saint-Siméon ferry dock.
33 km (20.5 mi) Junction with Route 170 on left. Continue on Route 138.
64 km (39.7 mi) Enter Baie-Sainte-Catherine.
68 km (42.7 mi) The quay for whale-watching excursions on the left.
69 km (43.0 mi) Arrive at the Saguenay River and the ferry to Tadoussac.

Route 138 crosses the bridge over the Malbaie River in the town of La Malbaie and becomes Blvd. Malcolm-Fraser as it climbs the flank of the mountain above the bay. The picnic area overlook is a popular stopping place for both local and touring riders. Cap-à-l'Aigle is another sector in La Malbaie although it is located 5 km (3 mi) from the downtown area and just off the highway on Rue St-Raphael. This picturesque port could be a setting on the coast of Maine and the stone breakwater showing its high-tide mark belies the fact that this is a river still hundreds of miles from the sea.

The jagged edge of the Charlevoix crater is obvious to the eye. What other wall-like range of mountains are curved in an arc greater than 180 degrees?

A detour to Port-au-Persil rewards the riders with a spectacular view of the mountains coming down to the wide expanse of the great river in the region known as Parc Marin du Saguenay–Saint-Laurent. The small port area allows access to a popular recreational site of a long cascade of white water flowing over smooth bedrock. The road continues back up the hill to connect with Route 138.

Saint-Siméon marks another crossroad. Route 170 cuts through the forests of eastern Charlevoix and then parallels the Saguenay River to La Baie and Chicoutimi. Turning right leads to the all-important *traversier* (ferry) and the 65-minute trip to Rivière-du-Loup on the eastern shore (418-862-9545, www.traversedl.com). This is where you pick up Route 132 east to the Gaspé or west back to Québec City. Route 185/Trans-Canada Highway leads to Edmundston, New Brunswick and Madawaska, Maine.

Route 138 now moves inland and across the mountains to reach Baie-Sainte-Catherine (pop. 260) at the mouth of the Saguenay River. This bay is at the heart of the marine park and is the staging point for whale-watching excursions like Croisières AML (418-692-2634, www.croisieresaml.com). The mouth of the Saguenay is where the big whales—the Blue, Fin, and Humpback—come to feed on abundant krill.

Pavement ends at the Saguenay River, but Route 138 continues as a free ferry crossing to reach the continuation of the highway in Tadoussac. The river marks the eastern boundary of the Charlevoix and the beginning of the Manicouagan Region.

Trip 2 Saguenay

Distance: *323 km (201 mi) plus 318 km (199 mi) for Lac Saint-Jean loop. Allow a full day for the Québec through Chicoutimi to Tadoussac route and another day to circumnavigate Lac Saint-Jean.*
Terrain: *Mountain wilderness from Québec city to Chicoutimi on a beautiful four-lane and urban streets in Chicoutimi. Flat, rural roads run through villages around Lac Saint-Jean. Route 172 is a spectacular touring road with canyons, narrow side roads to the fjord, and very little traffic.*
Highlights *Route 175/Autoroute 73 will be the most scenic four-lane highway in eastern Canada when it is completed. The ghost town of Val-Jalbert, the aluminum bridge in Saguenay, numerous cascades, and Zoo Sauvage in Saint Félicien are the top spots when touring around Lac Saint-Jean. Picturesque views of the Saguenay fjord from the tiny village of Sainte-Rose-du-Nord and L'Anse-de-Roche and the canyon along Route 172 from a stunning touring road.*

Samuel de Champlain labeled the unknown upper reaches of the river as the Kingdom of Saguenay, and today this name refers to both the region and its major city. The city was formed in 2002 from the towns of Jonquière, Chicoutimi, and La Baie, which now constitute the three boroughs of Saguenay (pop. 146,332). Geologically this is a gouged glacial basin formed during the last ice age and Lac Saint-Jean is all that remains of a vast post-glacial lake.

People often refer to this region as the "heart of Québec" and joke that this is where they send people to learn Canadian French. A visit here is delving deep into Québecois culture. This is a place where outside activities are the prime attraction and there's an abundance of campgrounds, nature trails, canoe and kayak rentals, and fishing outfitters. There are parks and scenic walkways along the rivers and lakes in almost every village or city.

Québec City to Chicoutimi on Route 175

0 km (0 mi) Leave Québec City on Route 175/Blvd. Honoré-Mercier.
2 km (1.5 mi) Exit for Route 138 on the right. Continue on Autoroute 73.
128 km (80 mi) Junction with Route 169 on the left. Continue on Route 175.
206 km (129 mi) End of Route 175 at Route 372 in Chicoutimi.

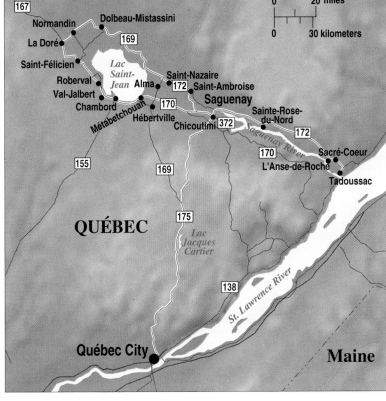

Ocean liners dock at the new facilities in La Baie and ocean freighters at Port Alfred in Ha! Ha! Bay.

The Saguenay fjord is the southern-most fjord in the Northern Hemisphere. The Saguenay–St. Lawrence Marine Park extends as far north as Ha! Ha! Bay and protects most of the land on both sides of the fjord. This is a major tourist attraction with both ocean cruise ships and local tour operators providing scenic trips up and down the river between Tadoussac and La Baie.

Route 175 is the primary highway going through Québec City. It runs east across the Plains of Abraham as La Grande-Allée, makes a 90-degree turn to become Ave. Honoré-Mercier between the National Assembly building and the western wall of the old city. The avenue, which looks more like a European boulevard, drops down the hill and at the bottom Route 175 takes a left turn at the traffic light to become Côte d'Abraham and continues going downhill. It cuts through the Saint-Roch District as the

An aluminum whale cavorts in the fountains of the park along the promenade in Chicoutimi.

one-way Rue de la Couronne going north (Rue Dorchester if heading south). A few blocks farther and it becomes Autoroute 73. It sounds confusing, but the flow of traffic and adequate signs makes it easy to follow.

There will be a few opportunities to fill your gas tank within the first few miles of Autoroute 73 and at Stoneham—the ski-resort town at the edge of the Laurentian Mountains—do so. There is only one gas stop between here and Chicoutimi.

The dangerous two-lane Route 175 from Québec City to Chicoutimi has been transformed into the divided four-lane Autoroute 73. It will be a beautiful road when completed, but now it's just 200 km (124 mi) of construction. I've noticed particular outcroppings and individual boulders that bulldozers and earthmoving equipment have carefully worked around and where streams have been channeled to form waterfalls. There's no hiding mile after mile of high fences built to deter moose, but then, nothing is perfect. I've seen moose in the meridian between the north and south lanes despite the fencing. Beware—if there are moose about during the day, this certainly is not a road to be traveled at night on a motorcycle.

The highway runs along the eastern edge of the Jacques Cartier Provincial Park and western shore of Jacques Cartier Lake. Make no mistake, this is boreal wilderness and there's only one stop where gasoline is available. Route 169 veers northwest to the left to the town of Alma and circumnavigates Lac Saint-Jean; Route 175 continues north to Chicoutimi.

The highway becomes a commercial strip when it enters Saguenay. It will cross Route 170/Autoroute 70 and then will make a 90-degree turn at the junction of Route 372 (to La Baie). Route 175 goes down the hill at Blvd. de l'Université and ends at Blvd. St-Paul. Right on St-Paul provides access to downtown Chicoutimi and crosses the Saguenay River on the Dubuc Bridge where it becomes Route 172. If this is your first time in Saguenay it might be easier to continue straight on Blvd. Talbot at the junction of Route 372. It ends at Route 372/Rue Jacques-Cartier Est, which is one of the main streets through downtown Chicoutimi.

Now a museum, the Little White House in Chicoutimi survived the devastating flood of 1996, which has been called a miracle considering the epic proportions of the torrent that cascaded around its foundation.

In Chicoutimi the biker-friendly hotel, *La Saguenéenne* (418-545-8326, www.lasagueneenne.com) is located just off the commercial strip of Route 175 on Rue des Saguenéenne. The hotel's director, Regis Nadeau, has been a presence at motorcycle shows in Montréal and Québec City long before most people even thought about motorcycle tourism.

Downtown Chicoutimi is lined with restaurants with their outside patios, retail stores, and an excellent waterfront park. The Chicoutimi Pulp Mill *(La Pulperie de Chicoutimi)* was an economic force in the early 20th century, but now it's a historic site and museum in the heart of the city. The Little White House *(Petite Maison Blanche)* is a minor miracle, the survivor of the great flood of 1996 *(Déluge du Saguenay)* when it stood alone in the middle of a raging torrent for days on end.

Lac-St-Jean Loop

0 km (0 mi) From Route 175 in Chicoutimi take Autoroute 70 west at Exit 47.

21 km (12.8 mi) Autoroute 70 becomes Route 170.

47 km (29.2 mi) Continue on Route 170 when it briefly merges with Route 169.

60 km (37.2 mi) Junction of Route 170 with Route 169. Turn right on Route 169.

81 km (50.3 mi) Junction with Route 155 on the left. Stay on Route 169.

89 km (55.3 mi) Turn left to visit Val-Jalbert.

120 km (74.5 mi) Enter Saint-Félicien.

125 km (78.1 mi) Turn left on Route 167.

146 km (91.2) In La Doré turn right onto Route St-Joseph-Nord, (becomes Chemin du Rocher).

166 km (103.7 mi) Arrive in Normandin. Take Route 169 toward Dolbeau-Mistassini.

263 km (164.4 mi) Turn left on Route 172.

288 km (180.2 mi) Bear right on Route Coulombe.

303 km (189.7 mi) Bear left on Route de la Dam Deux (just after the hydro dam).

306 km (191.4 mi) Bear right, crossing the Arvida Bridge.

308 km (192.9 mi) Turn left on Route 372/Blvd. du Saguenay.

318 km (198.7 mi) Arrive at Route 175 in downtown Chicoutimi.

Route 169 actually begins farther south at Route 175, but upon reaching the lake it makes a complete circle to join itself in Hébertville. Several highways lead to Lac Saint-Jean: Route 155 from Trois-Rivières, Route 175 and

La Vache Qui Rit at the harbor in Roberval is a popular stop for local riders. Yes, there is reserved moto parking.

169 from Québec City, Route 172 from Tadoussac, and Route 170 from Saint-Siméon. Then there's Route 167 to Chibougamau that combines with Route 113 to form what is known as "The Grand Loop." But beware—Route 167 runs through true wilderness and services are so far apart that an oversized gas tank is recommended for those who wish to ride this ribbon of asphalt across the Canadian Shield.

Lac Saint-Jean is, despite its size, a relatively shallow body of water with a maximum depth of 63 m (206 ft) and an average depth of 11.3 m (37 ft). It is 45 km (28 mi) long and 34 km (21 mi) wide. The *ouananiche,* a land-locked salmon that became isolated in the lake during the post-glacial era and adapted itself to fresh water, is the most sought-after fish in the lake, but it's illegal to sell it!

The easiest way to reach Lac Saint-Jean from Chicoutimi is to take Autoroute 70 west, which becomes Route 170. Route 170 briefly merges with Route 169 in St. Bruno and the option whether to follow the former or the later becomes a personal one. I prefer Route 170 to catch a glimpse of the lake, but even by doing so you will soon rejoin Route 169. There are other byways, notably 2 Rang from Route 169 in Hébertville to Route 169 in Métabetchouan, so don't hesitate to explore these paved country roads as an alternative to the main highway.

Route 169 rolls through the towns of Métabetchouan (pop. 4,277), Desbiens (pop. 1,082), and Chambord (pop. 1,718). Just west of Chambord

As you can see from the cycles parked at the Ouiathouan Falls, Québec riders are inclusive—it's not what you ride, but the fact you do ride that's important.

is the junction of Route 155 from Trois-Rivières and 8 km (5 mi) farther you'll see the turn to Val-Jalbert (888-675-3132, www.valjalbert.com).

The best-preserved ghost town in Canada is found in a blind valley, what would be called a "hollow," or "box canyon" in other places. Damase Jalbert built a pulp mill at the base of the 74-meter-high (242 ft) Ouiathouan Falls in 1901. The valley became a company town until the mill shut down at midnight on August 13, 1927. Residents drifted away, the government purchased the town in 1949 and closed the upper portion. Although it was open for visitors in 1960, restoration of this amazing ghost town didn't begin until the 1980s. The mill, general store, post office, convent, and numerous homes have been restored and visiting Val-Jalbert takes you back to the 1920s. It's quite an amazing place with limited accommodations and camping available.

For the next 5 km (3.5 mi) along Route 169 there will be glimpses of Lac Saint-Jean and even a couple of observation areas, but, for the most part, views of the lake can be had only by taking side roads. Point-de-la-Traverse and Pointe-Chambord are just off Route 169 on Route de la Pointe and both offer great views.

Saint Félicien (pop. 10,598) is 23 km (14.7 mi) from Roberval (pop. 10,512). It's most noted attraction is Zoo Sauvage (800-667-5687, www.zoosauvage.org) with its expansive enclosures for almost 1,000 animals. The junction with Route 167/Blvd. du Jardin is in downtown Saint Félicien and it offers a detour favored by local motorcyclists. La Doré (pop. 1,486) is 21 km (13 mi) from Saint-Félicien on Route 167 and Moulin des Pionniers (4201 Rue des Peupliers, La Doré, 418-256-8242, www.moulin-despionniers.qc.ca) is located just as you enter the village. Built in 1889, this water-powered sawmill is one of the last in existence. A forge, wood drivers' camp, residence, and a small farm are part of this historic site.

At the intersection in the center of La Doré make a right on Route St-Joseph-Nord. Following the obvious road, make a right turn onto Chemin du Rocher, which crosses the Ashuapmushuan River and goes to the town of Normandin (pop. 3,409) where it joins Route 169.

From Route 167 you can see the mountain ridges that mark the boundary of the Laflamme Sea that filled this basin a mere 12,000 years ago. Along this country road you will also notice sand dunes, now covered by pine trees, and billiard-table-flat fields of gray clay or blueberries. The sand dunes mark the ancient beaches of the post-glacial lake; the grayish-green clay soil is the fertile sediments of the former lake bottom; and the blueberries are the symbol of this region. More than 150,00 hectares (580 sq mi) of

Zoo Sauvage in Saint-Felicien draws visitors from as far away as Europe. Here a bighorn sheep peers over the crest of a hill.

The Aluminum Bridge in Saguenay is the only bridge in the world made entirely of aluminum.

commercial blueberry farms are situated around this lake and people from this region are known as "Bleuets."

The highway loops through Dolbeau-Mistassini (pop. 15,375) first crossing the Mistassini River and then the Mistassibi River. The first right, and immediate next right leads to a municipal park along a cascade, Chute des Pères, which only the world's best kayakers would dare to tackle. There are picnic tables and even tent sites on the southern extent of Île Talbot. By this time you've gone past several impressive waterfalls and a bit of exploring on side roads will reveal many more. In other places any of these would be a major tourism attraction, but here they're just accepted as a normal part of the landscape.

Beyond Dolbeau-Mistassini you will see signs for Parc de la Pointe-Taillon (800-665-6527, www.parcsquebec.com). There's 14 km (8.7 mi) of sand beach, but all of the great camping requires hiking or bicycles to reach the sites. It's a nice diversion and one of the touted features of the region, but unless you have time to lay in the sun or don't mind leaving your bike unattended it's best to keep riding on Route 169.

The highway will pass a "small" lake east of Saint-Henri-de-Taillon (pop. 750). This is actually the headwaters of the Saguenay River and is known as the Grand Discharge River.

Turning east on Route 172 you will ride through Saint-Nazaire and Saint-Ambroise before turning onto Route Coulombe to Shipshaw in the municipal city of Saguenay. The main road leads you across the narrow upper reaches of the Saguenay River by hydro dam 2. Take your second left onto Route de la Dam Deux and bear right to cross a remarkably ordinary looking bridge that spans a rocky gorge. Looks can be deceiving because this is the largest, and perhaps only, bridge in the world that's made entirely of aluminum. Built in 1950 it weighs a third that of a comparable steel bridge. Rio Tinto Alcan's most modern aluminum smelter in Alma has more than 6,000 employees, so this might explain why such a unique bridge was constructed.

A couple of kilometers past the bridge turn left on Route 372 (Blvd. du Saguenay). From here it's only 12 km (7.4 mi) to downtown Chicoutimi and the end of Route 175.

North side of the Saguenay Fjord—Chicoutimi to Tadoussac

0 km (0 mi) Start at the Dubuc Bridge in Chicoutimi.

0.5 km (0.3 mi) Exit right onto Blvd. Tadoussac (Route 172).

40 km (25.4 mi) On the right, Rue du Quai leads to Sainte-Rose-du-Nord.

97 km (60.7 mi) On the right, Chemin Traverse-de-Ligne-Anse-Saint-Jean leads to the fjord at Mill Bay.

104 km (65.2 mi) Chemin de l'Anse-de-Roche on the right leads to the village of L'Anse-de-Roche on the fjord.

108 km (67.8 mi) Enter Sacré-Coeur.

117 km (73.5 mi) Route 172 ends at Route 138 in Tadoussac.

The Saguenay River runs for 165 km (102 mi) from Lac-Saint-Jean to the St. Lawrence River along a fault line that formed 950 million years ago. Even after eons of erosion and at least four glacial periods it remains one of the world's longest fjords (100 km, 62 mi) and the most southerly in the Northern Hemisphere. Four- to six-meter (13 to 20 ft) tides flow up the river as far as Chicoutimi and since salt water is heavier than fresh, the river actually flows in two directions twice a day. The cold depths are patrolled by Greenland sharks, comparable to Great Whites in size, but fortunately not in aggressiveness. There are isolated populations of Arctic cod and Greenland halibut as well as Atlantic sturgeon, salmon, trout, mackerel, smelt, and some 68 other species of fish, 60 of which are found exclusively in the fjord. It's a unique ecosystem found nowhere else on earth. Fortunately the Saguenay–St. Lawrence Marine Park extends from the St. Lawrence River upstream to LaBaie while the Saguenay National Park protects the land along both sides of the fjord.

For the first 13.5 km (8.4 mi) the highway follows the north shore of the Saguenay River before moving inland. Until reaching Tadoussac Route 172 will usually be several kilometers from the fjord and outside of the Saguenay Park. Make sure you have a full tank of gasoline before leaving Saguenay. One stretch of this road has 74 km (46 mi) without any services and if you insist on premium-grade gasoline it's even farther.

There are a few roads that offer access to the river and these are the ones you should seek out while traveling. Rue de Quai, leads to the village of Sainte-Rose-du-Nord (pop. 409). This charming little village is crowded around a small bay on the fjord. The views are certainly worth the detour, but the road through the deep, narrow valley is as enjoyable as the destination.

Between Sainte-Rose-du-Nord and Sacré-Coeur Route 172 follows a glacially gouged valley and a famous salmon fishing river, the Sainte Marguerite. In other places this gorgeous valley would be called a "notch" or a "canyon" and would be considered a major tourist attraction. Here the fjord gets all the publicity. Route 170 on the west side of the river has the major truck traffic and Route 172 remains a touring secret to most of the world.

The majestic expanse of the Saguenay fjord can be seen in this view from L'Anse-de-Roche.

A Fin whale feeding in the turbulent waters at the mouth of the Saguenay River with Tadoussac in the background.

L'Anse-de-Roche is a tiny hamlet on the fjord downriver from Baie Sainte-Marguerite. East of the village of Rivière-Sainte-Marguerite you'll find a right turn onto Rang St-Joseph and this you'll follow until arriving at the dock on the Saguenay River. There's very limited parking, but lots of photo ops.

A pod of St. Lawrence Beluga whales live in the Saguenay and St. Lawrence Rivers all year. Endangered by pollution there are now less than 500 of these white cetaceans and they are listed as being endangered. During the summer a family of Belugas live at the mouth of the St. Marguerite River and often can be glimpsed from the shore. Other cetaceans—especially Fin, Humpback, Blue, and Minke whales—are found in the St. Lawrence River at the mouth of the Saguenay where they feed on an abundance of krill and shrimp during the summer months. There are numerous licensed operators in Tadoussac and Baie-Sainte-Catherine that offer whale-watching cruises.

Although the ferry between Tadoussac and Baie-Sainte-Catherine operates 24/7, there can be long lines at the ferry dock in Tadoussac. From here your options are to cross the Saguenay River to Baie-Sainte-Catherine (Trip 1) and return to Québec City, or take the ferry at Saint-Siméon to Rivière-du-Loup on the south shore in the Baie Saint-Laurent region (Trip 6). Another option is to continue east on Route 138 (Trip 4), either to Natashquan or one of the other ferries that cross the St. Lawrence River from Les Escoumins, Forestville, Baie-Comeau, or Godbout (Trip 5).

Trip 3 Laurentian Triangle

Distance: *240 km (150 mi)*
Terrain: *A scenic mountain road through forest interspersed with small lakes to the gorgeous Ha! Ha! Bay, followed by more deep forest. Optional side trips to the Saguenay fjord.*
Highlights: *Mountain views, twisting highway, and views of the fjord. Combined with the River Route/Route 362, this is the number-one touring route for Québec riders. The Bagotville Air Defence Museum, Pyramid de Ha! Ha!, the Saguenay Fjord Eco-center, and the site of Nouvelle France, are the primary man-made attractions.*

One of the most popular motorcycle touring loops in Québec runs through the Charlevoix and Saguenay regions. Whether it is ridden clockwise from Baie-Saint-Paul to La Baie to Saint-Siméon and back to Baie-Saint-Paul or counterclockwise is a matter of personal preference and each presents a different scenic view. The roads from Baie-Saint-Paul to Saint-Siméon are covered in Trip1 and the complete circuit of 328 km (205 mi) takes all day. These are not roads you want to travel at top speed, but rather to savor. Besides, with side trips to the fjord your travel distance will be closer to 350 km (217 mi) and factoring in lunch and photo stops, well, plan on a long day.

Ideally it won't be ridden in one day. Taking a day to explore Lac Saint-Jean (Trip 2) or one of the many festivals held in the Saguenay during the summer is highly recommended.

This ride starts where Route 381 branches off Route 138, 9 km (6 mi) north of Baie-Saint-Paul. Route 381 begins within the Charlevoix impact crater and follows the Gouffre River Valley—actually the outer annular ring of the crater—into the farming community of Saint-Urbain.

A few kilometers north, the highway cuts through the rim of the Charlevoix Crater as it enters Parc des Grands-Jardins (www.mountain-drive.com, 800-885-6527, www.parcsquebec.com). The scenery is

Saint-Urbain to La Baie on Route 381

0 km (0 mi) Take Route 381 from where it branches off Route 138 at 9 km (5.9 mi) north of the junction with Route 362 in Baie-Saint-Paul.
4.0 km (2.5 mi) In Saint-Urbain, Rue St-Anne (the western end of the Mountain Route) joins Route 381 on the right. Continue on Route 381.
25 km (15.4 mi) Entrance to Parc des Grands-Jardins.
113 km (70.6 mi) Route 381 ends at Route 170 in La Baie.

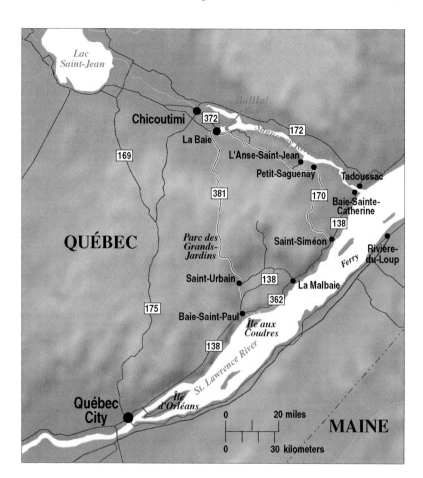

fantastic and just keeps getting better as the road continues to climb into the heights of the Laurentian Mountains.

La Baie (district pop. 19,639) is the easternmost sector of the amalgamated city of Saguenay (see Trip 2). Although it is hundreds of miles inland from the ocean, cruise ships from around the world dock at Ha! Ha! Bay while freighters haul aluminum to the Rio Tinto Alcan smelter's dock facilities in Port Alfred. Since it feels like you've climbed hundreds of feet in elevation to reach this bay, it seems rather strange to see these large trans-oceanic vessels sailing into port with the tide.

The summer calendar in Saguenay is filled with sporting events, art shows, and music and festivals. Outdoor performances take place at La Pyramide des Ha! Ha! in the public park on Rue Mgr Dufour at Route 170 (866-697-5077, www.restaurationdaa.com). The park has public restrooms and is along the pedestrian path that follows the shore of the bay.

Diagonally across the street from the pyramid on Route 170 is Le Musée du Fjord (418-697-5077, www.museedufjord.com), a modern interpretation center about the Saguenay marine ecosystem and the history of the city. Verrerie d'art Touverre (418-544-1660, www.touverre.com) is a glass-making workshop museum and in the same area will be found the Savonnerie Olivier Saguenay Workshop Museum where one can learn to make soap (418-544-8484, www.savonolivier.com).

The Bagotville Air Defence Museum (418-677-7159, www.bagotville.net) is located near the gate to the Canadian Air Force base on Route 170 between La Baie and Chicoutimi. The only MIG-23 jet fighter in the country is displayed as well as exhibits highlighting the only fighter base in eastern Canada.

The site created for the filming of Nouvelle-France is located on Vieux-Chemin off Route 170 near the head of the fjord (888-666-8027, www.sitenouvellefrance.com). After the production of the film it was transformed into a living history museum where people in costume go about daily life in 17th-century Québec City.

There are a dozen cheese producers in the Saguenay Region, but the one most popular with local motorcyclists is Fromagerie Boivin (2152 Chemin St-Joseph, 877-544-2622, wwww.fromagerieboivin.com). Their cheese curds are delicious and the perfect excuse to tour the beautiful countryside on roads seemingly made for motorcycles.

In the center of town at the intersection of Route 372 with Route 170 turn right (east) on Route de L'Anse and take the next left onto Chemin St-Joseph. At the intersection of St-Joseph and Chemin de la Grande-Anse you have three choices: 1) turn right and go directly to the Bagotville Air Defence Museum at Route 170; 2) turn left and follow the scenic

The Pyramid Ha! Ha! is built of aluminum panels and functions as the community's outdoor stage for a variety of events.

route back to downtown La Baie; or 3) to go straight on Rang St-Joseph where, at the T-intersection, you have the option of going right to loop back to downtown by riding along the Saguenay River or left to join Route 372 back to La Baie or on the main drag into downtown Chicoutimi.

There are numerous hotels located along the Baie des Ha! Ha! but if you like comfort and appreciate fine dining I recommend Auberge du Battures on Route 170 (6295 Blvd. de la Grande-Baie Sud, 418-544-9234, www.hotelsaguenay.com). Those who prefer B&B inns or camping sites have a very large number to choose from (www.saguenaylacsaintjean.ca).

It is 17.2 km (10.7 mi) from the junction of Route 381 in La Baie to Route 175 in Chicoutimi via Route 170. You might find Route 372 more pleasant if you plan to ride from La Baie to downtown Chicoutimi. If time permits, the scenic route (see directions for Fromagerie Boivin above) is the best choice from riding between the two downtown sectors of Saguenay.

La Baie to Saint-Siméon on Route 170

0 km (0 mi) Begin on Route 170 at the junction with Route 381 in La Baie.

9.0 km (5.8 mi) Chemin Vieux on the left leads to the Site of Nouvelle France in 17 km (10.3 mi) and then rejoins Route 170.

41 km (25.5 mi) Arrive Rivière-Éternité. Road on the left follows Rivière Éternité to fjord and Cap Trinité, (15 km/9.5 mi round trip).

55 km (34.8 mi) Rue St-Jean Baptise on left leads to L'Anse-Saint-Jean. (17 km/10.5 mi roundtrip).

126 km (78.7 mi) Route 170 ends at Route 138 in Saint-Siméon.

The ride to Saint-Siméon begins along Baie Ha! Ha! I was told that the name is from the French expression for surprise (ah! ha! in English) upon discovering that this bay was a cul-de-sac and not the continuation of the Saguenay River.

Chemin Vieux is an alternate route, but because kilometers of the road beyond the Site of Nouvelle-France are gravel, you have to make a decision whether to make a detour or stay on the main highway.

From here Route 170 moves away from the fjord and winds through the forested mountains. There are settlements like Saint-Félix-d'Otis and Hébert, and Rivière-Éternité. From the latter, a road, Rue Notre-Dame, follows the river to an observation point for the fjord. For the truly adventurous and those on dual-sport machines, there is a road that leads to one of the high points of the fjord, Cap Trinité, which is crowned by the Statue Notre-Dame-du-Saguenay. It's a rough gravel road that becomes quite steep in places. Take your first left off Rue Notre-Dame, then your second right, and second right again. If you think you're lost, you're probably on the right road (but maybe not). Cap Trinité is 348 to 411 meters (1142 to 1348 ft) high (depending upon the sources), but all agree that the statue of the Virgin Mary was erected here in 1881 and that it's 9 m (29 ft) high and weighs three tons. Remember, not only do you need to be comfortable going up this road, but also coming down.

At Le Portage the turn onto Rue St-Jean-Baptiste leads to the village of L'Anse-Saint-Jean (pop. 1,170). The simple covered bridge in L'Anse-Saint-Jean is famous for being on the back of an issue of $1,000 Canadian banknotes, but the major attraction is the road to the quay for the view of the Saguenay fjord. Another alternative is the road that goes through the bridge, Chemin de l'Anse, which follows along the bay and then climbs the mountain, passing beneath the power lines to an overlook.

Québec Ferry Crossings
(www.traversiers.gouv.qc.ca)

Lévis/Québec
Departure: every half hour during the day, operates 6 a.m. to 2 a.m.
Duration: 10 minutes. Distance: 1 km.
Cost: motorcycles $5.70; passengers $3.00
Reservations: N/A

L'Isle-aux-Coudres
Departure: Every hour May to October;
    every half hour July to August.
Duration: 15 minutes. Distance: 3.7 km
Cost: Free. Reservations: N/A

Saint-Siméon/Rivière-du-Loup
Departure: three times a day;
    four times a day from June 23 to August 22
Duration: 65 minutes
Cost: motorcycle $26; with trailer $40; passengers $15.80
Info: 418-862-5094, www.traverserdl.com
Arrival: 90 minutes prior to departure. Ferry capacity: 100 cars
Reservations: N/A

You'll also find a hotel and camping in this small village.

The next side trip is in Petit-Saguenay (pop. 850), which is the name of both the town and the river. The turn onto Chemin Vieux-Tremblay is just before reaching the village, but if you miss it just take the left turn onto Rue Tremblay in the center of town—they both lead to Rue du Quai and a view of the fjord.

It's another 42 km (26 mi) of beautiful riding through the forest to reach the junction at Route 138 in Saint-Siméon (pop. 1,360). There will be views of Lac Deschênes, craggy cliffs, and, if you're not alert, potential close encounters with the wildlife of the region. Upon reaching Saint-Siméon the question will be whether to head east to Tadoussac and then back to Chicoutimi and La Baie on Route 172; to cross on the ferry to Route 132 and Rivière-du Loop (Trips 5 and 6); or to ride west to La Malbaie or Baie-Saint-Paul.

Les Escoumins/Trois-Pistoles
Departure: two to three times a day end of May to November 1
Duration: 90 minutes
Cost: $17.75 pp; $25.50 motorcycle; $38.00 with trailer
Reservations: 877-851-4677 (www.traversiercnb.ca)

Baie-Sainte-Catherine/Tadoussac
Departure: Every 20 minutes during the day, but operates 24/7
Duration: 10 minutes. Distance: 1.6 km.
Cost: Free. Reservations: N/A

Forestville/Rimouski (CMN Évolution)
Departure: two or three times a day in summer
Duration: 60 minutes
Cost: $25 pp; $24 motorcycle; $32 trike or with trailer
Reservations: 800-973-2725, www.traversier.com

Baie-Comeau & Godbout/Matane
Departure: once or twice a day in the summer.
Duration: Matane/Godbout, 2 hours and 10 minutes (55.3km);
    Matane/Baie-Comeau, 10 minutes more (62.1 km).
Cost: motorcycle $26.25; with trailer/sidecar $35; passengers $15
Reservations: 877-562-6560; reservation.traversier.gouv.qc.ca
Arrival: 30 minutes prior to departure

Trip 4 Côte-Nord

Distance: *826 km (513 mi) one way. Allow two to three days. Total time and mileage will depend upon your return plans, but will be at least an additional 575 km (356.5 mi) and another two days to return to Godbout and the most eastern daily ferry crossing of the St. Lawrence to the Gaspé region.*

Terrain: *Boreal forest, taiga, peat bogs, and even tundra are ecosystems traveled through on a road that is filled with sweepers in some areas and runs so straight in others that it disappears in the imperceptible distance. There are industrial port cities, resort villages, tiny hamlets, and summer encampments strung along the north shore of the St. Lawrence River. An optional side trip to Labrador City is an expedition in itself.*

Highlights: *This is as much adventure as you'll find on a primary high-way. Whale sightings, Parc du Glacier, Manitou Falls, sand beaches, and wild rivers are coupled with views of the St. Lawrence and very little traffic.*

La Route des Baleines, The Whale Route, from Tadoussac to Natashquan on Route 138 is 808 km (502 mi) long. Whales that summer in the St. Lawrence River include the Blue, Fin, Humpback, Sperm, Beluga, Minke, and three species of dolphins. The Beluga lives in the river year-round and this is the only colony of Beluga that doesn't live in Arctic waters.

The Manicouagan region extends along the St. Lawrence River from Tadoussac to just north of Baie-Trinité; the Duplessis region continues to the Labrador border. The entire region of Manicouagan has been a

This sign marks the way from Tadoussac to Natashquan.

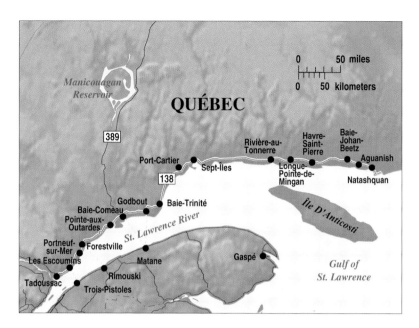

World Biosphere Reserve since 2007 and at 21,200 square miles it's one of the largest. Ironically, it also has the largest hydroelectric generating system east of James Bay (Hudson Bay).

The Gulf of St. Lawrence is the largest estuary in the world and the fresh water flow at the mouth of the St. Lawrence River is 367,273 cubic feet per second (3 million gallons per second). Yet this vast volume of water is overcome twice a day by ocean tides as far upriver as Québec City and La Baie in the city of Saguenay. Anticosti Island marks the western boundary of the gulf so the last 250 km (155 mi) of this ride are actually along the Gulf of St. Lawrence and the Jacques-Cartier Strait.

Gargantuan cruise ships and ocean freighters carrying aluminum travel the Saguenay River to La Baie (see Trip 2) so building a huge bridge across the Saguenay River to connect Baie-Sainte-Catherine with Tadoussac just isn't practical. Instead, ferries shuttle traffic from one shore to the other as a mobile portion of Route 138. One of the best views of the Saguenay fjord can be seen from the north side of the ferry during its crossing. The service is free and runs 24/7, but sometimes long lines form and you simply have to wait until your ship comes in.

Tadoussac (pop. 860) was the first North American town to be included in the "most beautiful bays in the world" club. It's a charming little village (www.tadoussac.com) with narrow, winding streets perched on a hillside at the mouth of the Saguenay River. A paved road, Rue des Pionniers, (2.5

The Route from Tadoussac to Natashquan on Route 138

0 km (0 mi) Depart fromTadoussac.

24 km (15 mi) Enter Les Bergeronnes.

40 km (25 mi) Enter Les Escoumins.

69 km (43 mi) Enter Longue-Rive.

98 km (61 mi) Enter Forestville.

195 km (121 mi) Enter Pointe-aux-Outardes.

200 km (124 mi) In Baie-Comeau, the ferry to Matane, and Route 389 to Labrador City.

255 km (158 mi) On your right, the road leads down to Godbout and the second ferry to Matane.

290 km (180 mi) Enter Baie-Trinité.

369 km (229 mi) Enter Port-Cartier.

430 km (267 mi) Enter Sept-Îles, the last city on the north coast and the ferry to Anticosti Island.

550 km (341 mi) Enter Rivière-au-Tonnerre.

602 km (374 mi) Enter Longue-Pointe-de-Mingan.

651 km (404 mi) Enter Havre-Saint-Pierre.

716 km (445 mi) Enter Baie-Johan-Beetz.

774 km (481 mi) Enter Aguanish.

808 km (502 mi) Enter Natashquan and Pointe-Parent.

826 km (513 mi) Arrive at the end of the road.

km,1.5 mi) leads into the dunes to wonderful beaches and overlooks of the St. Lawrence and the mouth of the Saguenay. Tracks in the sand prove that ATVs, and probably motorcycles, frequently tackle the deep sand in attempts to climb to the crest of these magnificent dunes. It's a premier whale-watching vantage point and it's free.

Tadoussac derives from the Innu word for "breasts." Jacques Cartier showed up here in 1535, Pierre de Chauvin de Tonnetuit arrived in 1599, and Samuel de Champlain didn't show up until 1603. Pierre gets extra points because he stayed, and in 1600 built the first fur trading post in Canada. A replica of his trading post called Poste de Traite Chauvin is located at 157 Rue du Bord-de-L'Eau (235-4657). The Petite Chapelle de Tadoussac, known as "the Indian chapel," was built in 1747 and is the oldest wooden church in Canada. There's plenty of history to be found in the oldest settlement in Québec.

Before getting on the highway you might consider stopping at *Centre d'Interprétation des Mammifères Marins* (Sea Mammal Interpretation Center, 108 Rue de la Cale-Sèche, Tadoussac, www.baleinesdirect.net) for a basic orientation on whales. This family-oriented, compact, ultra-modern nature museum has interactive displays explaining the whales and seals of the St. Lawrence River; a full-size model of a Sperm whale and actual skeleton of a Minke arc across the main room. Log onto www.whales-online.net for current information about whale sightings.

At the top of the hill in Tadoussac turn off the highway to the police station. Just beyond the station you'll find parking, a public restroom, and the best panoramic view of the river and town. If you haven't checked your fuel level, make sure to do so before leaving Tadoussac. Route 172 joins Route 138 just outside of town (see Trip 3) and there's a gas station, but it doesn't offer premium (super) octane. This will be normal along the entire Côte-Nord. If you absolutely require premium it would be best to carry three or four bottles of octane booster in your bags.

The road is wide and modern because of the Saguenay–St. Lawrence Marine Park and the tourism it attracts. There are several noted places where the great whales approach the shore during high tide. In Les Bergeronnes (pop. 690, www.bergeronnes.net) the Centre Archéo Topo (418-232-6286, www.archeotopo.com) features the archeological digs on the Côte-Nord, special exhibits, Internet access, and craft workshops. From the balcony tower whales can be observed. The premier site is the Cap-de-Bon-Désir Observation and Interpretation Centre (418-232-6751), and you'll also discover a lighthouse and a picnic area. Both sites are located off the main highway on paved roads and are well marked with directional signs.

A colorful mural graces the wall of the Marine Environment Discovery Centre in Les Escoumins.

The observation platform at the Marine Environment Discovery Centre in Les Escoumins is a comfortable place to watch for whales.

The next town is Les Escoumins (pop. 2,100) and this marks the northern and downstream extent of the marine park. Les Escoumins is an internationally acclaimed scuba diving site and the Marine Environment Discovery Centre (866-391-8835) is the place to learn about the marine environment and rent dive equipment. It's another land-based observation point with a great picnic area. During the summer months a ferry crosses the river to Trois-Pistoles and Route 132.

It's 50 km/hr through a long strip of residential development marked on the map as the settlements of Baie-des-Bacon, Sault-du-Mouton, and Saint-Paul-du-Nord, but are collectively known as Longue-Rive (pop. 1,300). The St. Lawrence River is now an estuary and the second-largest saltwater marsh in Québec is located here. The ecological importance of saltwater marshes cannot be understated, and this is one of the best bird-watching locations in the province.

Fortunately the posted speed limit increases and the condition of the pavement improves at Pointe-à-Boisvert. Brown-and-white signs stating HALTE MUNICIPALE give notice of roadside picnic areas, observation points, and restroom sites. These always offer scenic views, usually have paved parking, and are conveniently located along the entire length of Route 138 on the Côte-Nord.

Portneuf-sur-Mer (pop. 860) offers an excellent camping site near the Portneuf sandbar, another ecologically important site with 5 km (3 mi) of beaches! Actually you can camp just about anywhere because "crown land" is owned by Canada and available to anyone. Once you leave the highway it's wilderness, so don't leave food in or near your tent, pitch above high-tide and high-water marks, and follow proper procedures for campfires. Commercial camping areas are indicated by blue-and-white signs—a teepee indicates that tent sites are available, a camper trailer shows that hookups are offered.

Forestville (pop. 3,620) has at least five gas stations, including one that's open 24/7. There's an SAQ (liquor store), Provigo (grocery chain), McDonald's (you know), a few motels, some restaurants, and the seasonal ferry crossing to Rimouski.

You will see the tall obelisk before you reach Ragueneau (pop. 1,541). This marks the entry point to the Manicouagan Peninsula. A turn leads to the point where a scenic viewpoint with a large gazebo is situated in the shadow of this spire. Strange as it might seem, there's a life-size model of a brontosaurus and her baby at this site. The Rodéo Bike (www. rodeobike.ca), the only motorcycle rally on the Côte-Nord, takes place in Ragueneau at the end of July.

If you are touring in late June be sure to take in the Snow Crab Festival at Chûte-aux-Outardes (pop. 1,880). Snow crabs are one of the specialty catches and many consider them to be tastier than King crab. There's a campground near the Outardes-2 reservoir and more on the Manicouagan Peninsula, including one in the village of Baie-Saint-Ludger and another on the beach at Pointe-Lebel. Chemin Principale, the first right after crossing the Outardes River leads to Pointe-aux-Outardes (pop. 1,496) and the sand beaches of the nature park. The second right off Route 138 is Rue Granier that goes to Pointe-Lebel (pop. 1,980).

Baie-Comeau (pop. 23,000) is divided into two distinct sectors, Mingan on the east bank of

This tiny, elegant spire marks the gateway to the Manicouagan Peninsula in Ragueneau.

the Manicouagan River and Marquette on Pointe Saint-Gilles. Route 138 becomes Blvd. Pierre-Ouellet and it can be confusing unless you realize that several kilometers separates the two sectors of this consolidated city that's named for the naturalist Napoléon-Alexandre Comeau.

You can easily see Manic-1, the first of the great hydroelectric generating stations on the Manicouagan River, as you cross the bridge into Mingan. The exposed and weathered rock of the riverbed suggests how wild this river must have been before the four dams were built. Manic-2 and Manic-5 can be visited by following Route 389 north (see sidebar *The Road to Labrador City* at the end of this trip).

Route 138 actually avoids Marquette, and to reach the ferry dock you have to follow Boulevard la Salle through this industrial town to Parc des Pionniers (Pioneers Park). Located within sight of the ferry terminal and the hotel and restaurant Le Manoir de Baie-Comeau (8 Ave. Cabot, 418-296-3391), this park on the bay has ample parking, picnic tables, a *crème glacée* stand, bathrooms, and views and offers an excellent place to stop and take a break. Avenue Cartier leads directly to the quay for the Baie-Comeau/Matane ferry (two to six crossings daily, 418-562-2500, 877-562-6560, www.traversiers.gouv.qc.ca)

To visit award-winning Jardin des Glaciers (3 Avenue Denonville, 418-296-0182, www.jardindesglaciers.ca) just follow the blue-and-white signs. This world-class eco-museum focuses on the last ice age and climatology. It might sound boring, but the multi-media presentation is the best to be seen anywhere and streaking down the longest zip line in North America to view glacial gouging is an adrenaline rush. The Valley of Shells is the largest and best example of post-glacial inland seas to be found in the world. These banks of seashells are up to15 meters (50 ft) high, and many of these 8,000 year-old-plus shells look like they were left from yesterday's tide. Thematic reconstructions of Innu camps (yes, the whale bones and caribou hides are real) illustrate the great migration from Asia to North America that took place in the post-glacial era.

Route 389 goes north to the town of Manicouagan where it turns to gravel and continues to Labrador City. The "Eye of Québec" or the Manicouagan crater was formed 214 million years ago when a meteorite struck the planet. It's the fourth largest on earth and is easily seen from space thanks to the vast reservoir that encircles René-Levasseur Island and Mont Babel as a result of building the Manic-5 hydroelectric dam. The Manic-5 is the largest multiple-arch-and-buttress dam in the world and is a regional tourist attraction, as is Manic-2, which is much closer to Baie-Comeau (see sidebar *The Road to Labrador City* at the end of this trip).

The T-Rex is stalking a Brontosaurus in Ragueneau. Why? Because it is there.

East of Baie-Comeau there is an observation point marked with a brown sign with a white icon that's well worth the stop. From the gravel parking lot climb the wooden stairs to view the magnificent St-Pancrace Fjord that reaches the very edge of the highway. The Saguenay is still the southern-most fjord in the Northern Hemisphere, but it's not the only one in Québec that can be reached by road.

The highway now becomes a series of hills, valleys, and terrific sweeping curves. Although it's posted for 90 km/hr the flow of traffic is almost 30 km/hr faster. You can only glimpse the real Côte-Nord from the highway. To experience it you have to take one of the access roads to the shore (most are well-maintained gravel) or the almost 3,000 kilometers of forest roads that exist in the region. It's legally permissible to camp almost anywhere you're not intruding on people.

Franquelin (pop. 350) is named after Canada's first official cartographer, J. B. Franquelin. A land-based, whale-observation point and reconstructed forest village are the two tourist attractions in this small town. There's also a gas station, and if you didn't fill up in Baie-Comeau you better do so now. There are a sufficient number of gas stations along the Côte-Nord, but the distances between them are greater than most riders are accustomed to. Furthermore, if one is closed or out of fuel you want enough in your tank to make it to the next one.

Route 138 east of Baie-Comeau is a joy to ride. The fencing on the left is to protect the curious from falling hundreds of feet into a secret fjord.

Godbout (pop. 370) is 55 km (40 mi) east of Baie-Comeau and 480 km (300 mi) from Québec City. This is the easternmost ferry crossing of the St. Lawrence River and, like the one in Baie-Comeau, it docks at Matane on the southern shore. Unless you've booked passage on the Nordik Explorer to Labrador you'll have to backtrack from Natashquan to at least this point in order to cross to the Gaspé. The access road leads down from Route 138 to a beautiful bay lined with observation gazebos and picnic tables. Le Gîte aux Berges offers rooms and tent camping just a couple hundred meters from the ferry terminal and a good restaurant for breakfast can be found between the ferry terminal and the church. The village road is a cul-de-sac on both ends, with a salmon river bordering a sand beach at the west end, and the high cliffs to the east suggesting the existence of waterfalls.

Phare de Pointe-des-Monts (418-939-2400, www.pharepointe-des-monts.com) is located 11 km (6.8 mi) off Route 138 at the end of a paved road that crosses miles of sand dunes to reach the rocky point that juts into the river. This lighthouse was built in 1830 and designated a Québec historic monument in 1964. It's one of the oldest lighthouses in North America and was the home of eight successive keepers. It's been transformed into a B&B inn with seven different floors, each highlighting a different theme.

The balcony around the light offers spectacular views, and a restaurant is located in the keepers' cottage.

Baie-Trinité (pop. 530) has a gas station but only regular (*ordinaire*) gasoline. The next is at Pointe-aux-Anglais and then none for 80 km (50 mi) until reaching Port-Cartier. There's a very nice Provincial rest-stop with shaded picnic tables by the church and new information center. Behind the center is a 20 × 80 Kowa binocular spotting scope (free) that can be used to scan the St. Lawrence for whales or gaze at the Adirondack Mountains on the far shore. Hôtel Place Saint-Laurent (4 Rue Saint-Laurent, 418-939-2148) is located in the center of the village and has only four rooms, so make sure to make reservations in advance.

In 1711 British Admiral Walker commanded 60 warships and 12,000 men on a journey up the uncharted (for the British) St. Lawrence River to attack the French stronghold of Québec during the Hundred Years War. Eight ships and 900 men were lost on the rocky Egg Island off Pointe-aux-Anglais and the British turned back. These were not the first ships, nor the last, to flounder and sink along this coast that Jacques Cartier described as being "the land that God gave to Cain." The Centre National des Naufrages du Saint-Laurent (418-939-2679, www.centrenaufrages.ca) on the highway in Baie-Trinité displays artifacts from famous shipwrecks and documents these tragedies.

Phare de Pointe-des-Monts is now a B&B-inn-cum museum. This is one of the oldest lighthouses in Canada.

There's a *dépanneur* (mini-mart) and gas station at Pointe aux Anglais, but it's only 11 km (6.8 mi) to the next gas stations at the traffic light in Port-Cartier. Beautiful views of the river make this an especially nice ride.

Port-Cartier (pop. 6,830) is headquarters for the Iron Ore Company of Canada, the largest ore producer in the country with output going around the globe (see sidebar *The Road to Labrador City* at the end of this trip). More germane to this journey are the full-service gas stations, Tim Horton's, and fast-food restaurants located at the main intersection and traffic light. Turning right to follow the Whale Route through town leads past an IGA grocery store, Walmart, and other services. Continuing through the traffic light on Route 138 there are several small restaurants. The right turn for Rochers River Park is the first beyond the small bridge over the Trinité River (the falls can be seen on your left). The Salmon Interpretation Centre (24 Rue Luc-Mayrand, Port-Cartier, 418-766-2888) is located at the waterfall and apparently fish can be observed making their way up a salmon ladder during their annual run. Restrooms and picnic tables make this a spot to be noted on your map.

The Whale Route briefly leaves Route 138 in Port-Cartier. Right onto Rue de Shelter Bay, left on Chemin des Îles, which will cross Île Patterson and Île McCormick. Left on Blvd. Portage-des-Mousses. Right on Route 138 Est. Taking this route passes the turn to Rochers River Park, so a left turn onto Route 138 Ouest is required. The next left leads to the park.

Sept-Îles (pop. 25,865) is the commercial center of the Côte-Nord and home to the largest aluminum producer in the Americas, Aluminerie Alouette. Their refinery, which is the most technologically advanced in the world, is located on one of the seven islands for which the city is named. The main highway through town is lined with hotels, restaurants, grocery stores, and other services. Need chain lube, oil, or other motorcycle supplies? Better stop at Canadian Tire because it will be another 800 km (500 mi) before you return to this city. There are at least four campgrounds in the Port-Cartier/Sept-Îles area and several hotels. Do make reservations as contract workers for Hydro-Québec, Aluminerie Alouette, and other big corporations often book rooms for weeks at a time. Hôtel Gouverneur Sept-Îles (666 Blvd. Laure, 418-962-7071, www.quebecmaritime.ca/gouverneur7iles) is conveniently located along the main highway in the center of the shopping district.

The Whale Route leaves Route 138 through Sept-Îles but it might prove to be a disappointment except for one nice public park on the waterfront. Right on Blvd. des Montagnais, left on Rue de Quen, right on Rue Smith, left on Ave. Arnaud, left on Rue Monseigneur-Blanche, right on Route 138.

The saloon in the fishing camp at the mouth of the Moisie River is probably a center of social activity during the summer.

It's 223 km (139 mi) to Longue-Pointe-de-Mingan and there's a highway sign just outside of Sept-Îles advising that the gas station a few hundred meters up the road is the last for 101 km—it's not. Just so you'll know, the new Esso station at the junction of Moisie Road in De Grasse is the last station and it has premium octane fuel. Similar signs are posted all along the route, but this doesn't guarantee that the next station is open!

A side trip to Moisie at the mouth of the Moisie River requires negotiating rough pavement to reach the summer encampment of salmon fishing enthusiasts. It's a funky community, but there's probably room for a tent or two on an overnight stay. In 2003 the Moise River became the first in Québec to be named an aquatic reserve. The salmon fishing season is from June 1 to September 30, and both a permit and an access fee are required (www.salmonquebec.com).

After crossing Rivève Moisie the road, which has been rather mundane since leaving Sept-Îles, changes to one that is a joy to ride. It has the sweepers, the hills, and great views of the coastline. I say coastline because the St. Lawrence has now taken the appearance of being more ocean than river as it approaches the *Détroit de Jacques-Cartier* (Jacques-Cartier Strait) that separates the northern shore and Anticosti Island. The road soon becomes long, straight, and smooth with a few undulating hills thrown in. Views of the St. Lawrence are expansive. There are few vehicles on this highway, but it is

The awesome power of Manitou Falls can be glimpsed in this photo, but the sound was practically deafening.

patrolled—as I soon discover. The two officers had never seen a T-Rex and this, plus a clean license, saves my day. "Keep it down to 115 (km/h) and you'll have no trouble," I'm advised.

A Provincial information and rest-area (big brown sign) from which a path with wooden stairs leads to the 35-meter high (115 ft) Manitou Falls. This gorgeous woodland trail is flanked by deep beds of moss and the pink granite bedrock along the river is covered with day-glow green, orange, and red lichen in such profusion that it appears to be the work of a 1960s surrealist painter. This is a boreal cloud forest and I've never seen anything like it before. Forget about safety fencing at this or any other site—this is Canada and nobody is held liable for your own stupidity, so be careful! These rapids would be fatal for even a world-champion kayaker.

Sheldrake, blink and you miss it. Some place names on the map, like Pictou and Manitou Falls, don't really exist. Others, like Magpie (off Route 138), are just a few scattered homes along a bay. This one has a rest area near the harbor pier where a trail leads to a rock formation that is a lookout for whales. The economy of this town, like so many others on the north shore, was built on cod fishing, which no longer exists. Therefore, the population of most of these villages is in decline.

Rivière-au-Tonnerre (pop. 370) is reputed to be the most picturesque village on the Côte-Nord. There are motels and restaurants and a couple gas pumps at the garage. Although the village is situated on a tranquil bay it is named "Thunder River" because of the vibration from the 33-m falls (108 ft). Snow crab fishing is its primary industry, but there's a regional specialty that's found in very few other places: Cloudberries. They tend to grow in peat bogs and only one in eleven plants produce their single orange berry. If these berries are not picked when perfectly ripe the plant will take another seven years to flower! Obviously this is not a berry you'll find commercially grown and you have to be here in early June to experience this delicacy.

In the small village of Mingan there is a gas station that also is a 10-unit hotel (quite basic) and a seasonal grocery store. They also have a selection of gourmet coffees, ample medicine for a weary rider. There's a second gas station just 0.3 km beyond the first.

Longue-Pointe-de-Mingan (pop. 410) features a long beach with views of the first islands of the Mingan Archipelago. Whales often can be observed from the boardwalk that runs along the Promenade. A profusion of small cottages suggests that the population surges during the summer

The house of noted painter and sculptor Johan Beetz can be found in the village bearing his name.

season. The Longue-Pointe-de-Mingan Reception and Interpretation Centre (418-949-2126, www.parkscanada.gc.ca/mingan) and the Mingan Island Cetacean Study (MICS, 418-949-2845, www.rorqual.com) are both located at 625 Rue du Centre at Route 138, which is the entrance to the Mingan Archipelago. MICS is one of the leading whale research centers on the planet and on the back of their building there's an observation deck that provides a panoramic view. From here the Chic-Choc Mountains on the Gaspé are barely visible on the horizon.

There are several campgrounds along this stretch of Route 138, with the largest ones being in Longue-Pointe-de-Mingan and Natashquan. There are numerous *gîtes* (B&Bs) and *auberges* (hotels) on the north shore, but this is an outdoor paradise and camping seems to be the preferred lodging. Seasonal roadside fast-food trucks *(casse-croûte)* dot the highway and many of their offerings are quite good.

Untamed rivers the color of tea topped with white froth that run through dense forests of green so dark as to almost appear black have become common. However, the land changes after Mingan and the highway cuts through a vast plain dotted with countless small pools of dark water that reflect a big sky. This is where tundra mingles with taiga and the boreal forest and the few trees in existence are dwarf tamarack and black spruce. It's rather surreal, and some would even call it bleak, but this landscape has it's own unique beauty.

Havre-Saint-Pierre (pop. 3,170) was settled by six Acadian families from the Magdalen Islands in 1857 and it has since become a major port and industrial service center. A couple of gas stations are located on Blvd. de L'Escale, just off Route 138 and one even has high octane, but these are the last you'll encounter for 124 km (77 mi). The Whale Route leaves Route 138 (left on Blvd. de L'Escale) to an observation point at the marina, location of the Havre-Saint-Pierre Reception and Interpretation Center in the Portail Pélagie-Cormier (101 Promenade des Anciens, 418-538-3285, www.parkscanada.gc.ca/mingan). The Whale Route continues (left) on Promenade des Anciens, left on Blvd. du Cométique, right on Rue Boréale, left on Blvd. des Acadiens, and right onto Route 138.

Baie-Johan-Beetz (pop. 95) is a very small town situated on another pretty bay. The sidewalks are made of wood and curbed by stone. It's surprisingly quiet here and tranquil, which might be why painter and sculptor Johan Beetz built his house here. You might even hear seals barking somewhere beyond the concrete wharf. The rocky point beyond the wharf is reputed to be another whale-observation point.

Aguanish and L'Île-Michon (pop. 300) are two small hamlets separated by

Riding across tundra was a new experience. At the eastern end of Route 138 tundra intermingles with taiga and boreal forest.

several kilometers. L'Île-Michon is a cluster of homes on one side of a pretty little bay. Aguanish is a popular salmon-fishing location on the Rivière Aguanish that marks the eastern boundary of the Mingan Archipelago National Park. Aguanish means "small shelter" in Innu and First Peoples have been fishing here since time immemorial. There's a filling station-cum-liquor store (*ordinaire* only) and mini-mart in the middle of the village. The *Trait de Scie* (sawcut) is a geological phenomenon, a canyon, and the third waterfall on the river, but it requires an outfitting guide to visit it.

Many of the narrow one-lane bridges on this section of the highway are made of planked wood, often with a pavement dip on each end. I recommend approaching each with caution. If you stop along the highway expect that people will slow down to make sure you're okay. In remote rural areas such as this it becomes essential that one person is immediately ready to help another.

Natashquan (pop. 270) turns out to be a pretty little town on the Petite Rivière Natashquan with a number of B&B's (*gîtes*) and a restaurant. A

L'Île-Michon, this is it. All of it.

boardwalk runs from the new tourism center to the old general store that is now the Bord du Cap Interpretation Center, and passes a small café and ice cream stand that offers the best views in town. The town has miles of beautiful sand beach and reputedly the warmest water on the Côte-Nord. *La Vieille Ecole* (the old school—which is located behind the new school) is now a museum that pays homage to the iconic local poet and singer-songwriter Gilles Vigneault. Inside this museum are featured twelve of his famous songs that are represented by artifacts once belonging to the people who inspired them, and by donning headphones at each interpretive station you can experience his music.

Natashquan is a port-of-call for the MIV Nordik Express (800-463-0680, www.relaisnordik.com). a supply ship that has taken on the glamour of those days when passengers could board a "tramp steamer" for the far corners of the world. This is the secret backdoor to the Labrador Coastal Highway at Blanc-Sablon and Newfoundland (reservations are required 120 days in advance, but a year is recommended). The Nordik Express is the only public transportation from Havre-Saint-Pierre or Sept-Îles (depending upon which direction it is going) to Port-Menier on Anticosti Island. It docks in Natashquan on Sundays.

Just beyond the village can be found Auberge La Cache (183 Chemin d'en Haut, 418-726-3347, www.aubergelacache.com). Although quite basic, it's the last lodging on the road and a welcome respite after hundreds of kilometers of riding. Another option is the Innu camp, Campement Montagnais Mantèo Matikap, (418-726-3172, www.manteo-matikap.com) a reconstruction of a traditional meeting place where the Innu of *Nutashkuan* (this spelling is Innu) would come in the spring to fish for salmon and trade. Traditional meals can be arranged where visitors take part, starting with the making of the fire (which can take up to six hours). You can camp in a traditional or standard tent on the site.

The pavement ends at Pointe-Parent, but Route 138 continues as a well-maintained gravel road for another 18 km (11 mi) through First Nation territory. I wouldn't run my Ducati on such loose gravel and it would be a nerve-racking ride on my Beemer, but the three-wheeled T-Rex handled it with ease. Except for loose stones, the road is actually smoother than most of the pavement that's been ridden. The road ends just before the banks of the Natashquan River. The signs at the end of Route 138 bear the testimony of those who have made their mark to commemorate the accomplishment of riding to the end of the road.

The author and "The Beast" make it to the end of Route 138 in First Nation land on the west bank of the Natashquan River.

The Road to Labrador City

by Jeff Adams, Whitehorse Gear

The 583 km (362 mi) of Route 389 between Baie-Comeau, Québec and Labrador City take you through genuine wilderness with stunning views, past massive hydroelectric dams and mind-boggling iron mines. The road offers plenty of twisty pavement, miles of straight-aways through dense forest, and huge helpings of gravel.

This is one of the very few true wilderness motorcycle adventures remaining in North America. You are very much on your own. Be prepared for any eventuality including flat tires, high-speed tractor-trailer rigs flinging rocks and dust, extreme weather, wildlife, and deep, soft gravel roadways. Gravel roads in these parts are constantly being graded to make passage easy for the large, fast trucks that supply everything to Labrador West and beyond. Unfortunately that means the gravel could be hard packed and super-easy to ride, or freshly graded making your bike want to wallow like a hippo in mud. It just depends on how recently the graders have been working the road. You won't know until you get there. That being said, this is still one of the most exciting rides on the North American continent for those who love the great outdoors.

Before you leave Baie-Comeau make sure you have a full tank of gas. The next available fuel is more than 200 km (130 mi) away. Route 289 begins at Route 138 and is marked by a big, and slightly faded, sign. Almost immediately you and your motorcycle pull away from every sign of city life. This part of the road is fantastically hilly and curvy. Enjoy the ride but pay close attention to what's going on around you, as you could have a bit of traffic at this end of Route 389. Around 22 km (14 mi) into this roller coaster ride a huge concrete building comes

Baie-Comeau to Labrador City on Route 389

0 km (0 mi) Junction Routes 138 and 389.
211 km (131 mi) Arrive Hydroelectric Dam Manic-5.
316 km (196 mi) Arrive Relais-Gabriel.
570 km (354 mi) Enter Labrador. Road becomes Route 500 Trans-Labrador Highway.
583 km (362 mi) Arrive Labrador City, Labrador.

The grading never stops. Since you don't know how recently the grader has been by, be prepared for soft gravel.
©Adam Romanowicz, http://3scape.com

into view—Manic-2, one of several large hydroelectric dams on the Manicouagan River. Though a free 90-minute facility tour is available with information about Hydro-Québec, and hydroelectricity in general, you might want to save your time for Hydro-Québec's crown jewel, Manic-5, some 188 km (117 mi) north. Manic-5 is the world's largest arch-and-buttress dam, with the center arch being more than 213 m (700 ft) tall. This tour, also free, is a must see. Plan to spend at least two hours there. Across from Manic-2 is a good campground with showers, electricity, and food if it's time to pitch a tent.

Settling into the rhythm of the road moving north, you'll notice there's almost no traffic, or law enforcement present; it's an honest open road. A good paved one at that with endless forest, mighty rivers, and high-tension electric transmission lines and towers to accent the landscape. This is Hydro-Québec country. The people of Québec, the Québecois, are an industrious lot—very proud of their history, culture, language, and land. Not unlike the way Texans talk about everything being bigger in Texas, everything is also bigger and better in Québec. A perfect example is Hydro-Québec, one of the world's greatest dam builders and hydroelectric generators. The feats of civil engineering

*The massive dam at the Manic-5 power station at 214 m (700 ft)
high is the highest multiple-arch-and-buttress dam in the world and
contains 2.2 million cubic meters of concrete (enough to construct a
regular sidewalk from the North to the South pole).*

they've pulled off over the decades are almost too massive to compre-
hend. Take the tour at Manic-5 and you'll get the picture.

As you approach the mighty Manic-5, you'll see a fire-ravaged hillside on the west side of the road. Not so many years ago a forest fire
tore through this area. Had the fire gotten to the electricity transmission towers, it was thought it would weaken and collapse them, rendering the turbines of Manic-5 useless for a long while. Fortunately the
fires were extinguished. Just before arriving at the dam you'll find Motel Energy. This outpost in the forest is the only gas, food, and lodging
stop for a very long way. They have curious looking, tiny motel rooms
near the restaurant and store. But most likely if you're riding a motorcycle and you ask for lodging, they'll send you to the long-haul truck-
ers' dorm up on the hill behind the motel. It's very basic but it's a place
to clean up and sleep. Fill your gas tank here. The gas is expensive but
it's the only gas to be had. They actually have you over a barrel. (An oil
barrel?)

As you pass the stately arches of Manic-5, you get excellent views of the Manicouagan Reservoir, which stretches many miles to the north. Manic-5 created the fifth-largest body of fresh water on earth. In fact it includes the 200-million-year-old Manicouagan meteor impact site. Look at a map of Québec and in the center you'll see a do-nut-shaped lake some 44 miles across. Some call it the "eye of Québec."

After Manic-5 the pavement gives way to gravel, the typical road surface of interior Québec. On the gravel, surface conditions can vary tremendously from minute to minute, so take it easy for a while. It might be hard packed, just like pavement in places, but at the bottom of long downhill runs you may find lots of loose material that gets washed to the bottom in deep piles. If you see a small orange sign with a picture of a grader by the side of the road, you know you're in for some interesting conditions real soon. It's useful to have a good tire pump in case the road gets soft and deep, decreasing tire pressure just a bit can help a lot. Be sure to re-inflate properly once you're back on a sustained hard surface. "Your mileage may vary," as they say, so have fun—just be careful. There's no emergency room in the wilderness of interior Québec.

Relais-Gabriel (www.pourvoirierelaisgabriel.com) is 105 km (65 mi) north of Manic-5. "Relais" in French means transport café or truck stop, and this essential stop is anything but fancy. Two lonely gas pumps and a few small wooden structures with peeling paint is about it. The restaurant is . . . let's just say basic. But it'll do for sure. You thought gas was expensive at Motel Energy? If gasoline has never given you sticker shock, it just might here. Fill your tank anyhow as the next gas is in Fermont, just west of the Québec–Labrador bor-der—more than 250 km (150 mi) away. During our visit to Relais-Gabriel, we pulled up to the gas pumps and were mildly shocked to see the pump handles secured in place with giant zip ties. That did-n't look good. In the restaurant, the French-speaking grand-mother-type told us "No gaz! No gaz!" Now things looked less than good but we figured we'd eat. With gestures and pointing we man-aged to order up some microwave reheated spaghetti, a soft drink, and a good brownie. Only about $20 USD each! Such is travel in the wil-derness. Mercifully a pleasant English-speaking fellow on an ATV seemed to appear out of nowhere and was pumping fuel directly out of the underground tank through a small meter that measured liters of fuel dispensed. He helped us fill our tanks and then scribbled on some old-fashioned, carbon paper sales slips, which we brought to the restaurant and paid grandmother for our liters of gas. It was something like $2 per liter. Sure beats walking though.

The gravel road goes over rolling hills for about 80 km (50 mi) beyond Relais-Gabriel to the town of Gagnon. Once a thriving iron mining community, only a paved road, curbstones, storm drains, empty driveways, and a grassy median strip are left. Not a single building remains, as the mining company took everything when it pulled out. It's a little creepy, almost like the opening chapter of a Stephen King novel, but interesting in any event. At this point you can enjoy more than 80 km (50 mi) of pavement that once served the Gagnon mining operation. Just remember you could easily be the only person in Gagnon! Roll on the gas and bask in the beauty of the taiga—the boreal forest ecosystem of the northern latitudes. The taiga, which officially begins at the 52nd parallel (marked by a small metal sign), consists mostly of small black spruces, moss, and lichens. Not much else in the way of plant life can survive this far north. Broadleaf trees will be very rare from here on.

North of Gagnon, the pavement ends at Fire Lake, yet another closed iron mining operation. Two large silos still stand but as in Gagnon, the mining company took everything with them when they left. At this point the road changes character completely. Instead of long straight sections of either pavement or gravel surrounded by trees, the road snakes back and forth in an open, almost barren terrain. You will cross railroad tracks nine times. Without crossing signals, the tracks might seem abandoned, but beware—this is an active railroad line hauling ore from the Mount Wright iron mine. In addition, this part of the road is usually the most technically challenging. There are some blind corners, as well as endless soft gravel, and billions of loose stones. Mind the big trucks, especially up here. Unless you are comfortable riding very fast on this stuff, it's best to stop as close to the edge of the road as you can get, and let the trucks roll by. That's the bad news. The good news is this part of the road is only 61 km (38 mi) long.

As you approach the end of the gravel road, you'll see the Mount Wright mining operation. On your right is the mountain from which the ore is blasted. High on your left you'll see what looks like a

The Humphrey Pit at the Iron Ore Company of Canada's mine in Labrador City is more than 1,200 m deep (4,000 ft) and has yielded high-grade iron ore for more than 35 years.

strangely colored mountain with enormous heavy equipment trolling back and forth on its slopes like busy little ants. That's no mountain. It's the mountain-sized pile of tailings from the iron ore production process. As the years go by, Mount Wright is whittled away, getting smaller and smaller, while its mineral trash heap grows a new mountain directly across the road. It's incredible.

At the Mount Wright facility entrance the pavement begins again! Before you get to the Québec–Labrador border, you will see signs for the city of *Fermont* (iron mountain), Québec . This is another iron mining city but it's a bit unusual in that the entire city is under one roof. The mine workers' living quarters, the Hotel Fermont, grocery store, nightclub, movie theater, shops—everything in one giant Québec-sized building. And Texans think they know big! In a place with such brutal winter conditions this makes tremendous sense. Why would anyone want to go outside to drive to the grocery store at 50 below zero?

Just a few miles more and you'll see a huge blue sign reading: NEW-FOUNDLAND LABRADOR, WELCOME TO THE BIG LAND. This landmark sign features three flagpoles bearing the Canadian flag, the Newfoundland provincial flag, and the Union Jack. Only the most jaded traveler could

Welcome to Labrador West!

resist taking a photo at this spot. This is also the beginning of the Trans-Labrador Highway. Welcome to Labrador! Just up the road is Labrador City, population 7,200 hardy souls and its sister city, Wabush which is home to fewer than 2,000. Together, Labrador City and Wabush are known as Labrador West. Labrador City was built in the wilderness in the 1960s by the Iron Ore Company of Canada (www.ironore.ca) to house mine workers. If not for the iron ore rich Labrador Trough, there would be no Labrador City, Fermont, or Wabush.

The people of Labrador West are exceptionally friendly. They are eager to speak with visitors and are most helpful. At the Labrador City shopping center, you'll find an assortment of businesses including a Walmart without windows (due to the hard winter weather), and the always-busy Tim Horton's coffee shop (500 Vanier Ave., Labrador City NL, A2V 2W7, 709-944-2850). No matter the time of day or night, you'll find plenty of folks socializing at "Timmy Ho's." It's part of modern Canadian culture, even up here in the wilderness.

Directly on the Trans-Labrador Highway at the edge of town be sure to visit Gateway Labrador (www.gatewaylabrador.ca). This building is part museum of natural history, part gift shop, part chamber of commerce, and all-around visitor center. Ask about a tour of the Carol Lake Project Iron Mine. For $8 US at last check, you can climb aboard a tour bus and go right into the Lab City mine to get a thorough education of the iron ore industry. The size of this endeavor is staggering—you can easily become numb to the numbers they toss at you. How about a gargantuan ore-hauling truck (one of many) that works 24/7 and consumes a full 1,000-gallon tank of diesel fuel twice every day? Or the Humphrey Pit (one of several) at the mine which has to date, been excavated 1,220 m (4,000 ft) deep, more than a mile wide, and 4 km (2.5 mi) long and it's still yielding high-grade iron ore? You've really got to see it to believe it.

A few last tips for this ride. Beyond Baie-Comeau, cell phones will work almost nowhere. And should you get a cell signal, in either Fermont or Lab City, you could be paying many dollars per minute in local carrier charges. Also you will not find vacant hotel rooms in Labrador West without making reservations well in advance. The Two Seasons Inn (105 Hudson Dr., 800-670-7667, www.twoseasonsinn.com) is popular with motorcyclists, located right downtown. Just a few blocks away is the Carol Inn (215 Drake Ave., 709-944-7736, www.carol-inn.ca). In nearby Wabush you will find the Wabush Hotel Ltd. (9 Grenfell Drive, 709-282-3221, www.wabushhotel.com). The Labrador West Chamber of Commerce is located on 118 Humphrey Rd., (709-944-3723, www.labradorwestchamber.ca).

Labrador West is an excellent destination unto itself. Plenty of tourists on two wheels or more visit the area and return reversing their original route. But if you are heading east on the Trans-Labrador Highway, to Churchill Falls, Goose Bay–Happy Valley, or Cartwright Junction, take a little time to enjoy this pleasant town of accommodating frontier dwellers. Even if you, your bike, and gear are covered with dirt from the road, they'll come right up to you and offer, "Say, are you from around here?" They know you're not, but they're so polite. They've built a great life for themselves in The Big Land and are proud to share it with visitors. Have a chat with them; you'll be glad you did.   ■

Trip 5 **Gaspésie**

Distance: *The Route 132 loop is 861 km (540 mi) without side trips. Allow three to five days.*
Terrain: *Rocky coastal terrain that varies from red sandstone along Chaleur Bay to the gray metamorphic rock of Bon Ami. Sometimes the highway is hundreds of meters above the water and in one place highway signs warn of waves breaking across the pavement. Resort villages dot the bay coast, while mountain wilderness can be experienced on two side trips.*
Highlights: *The views are the main highlights of this ride and include Rocher Percé, Île Bonaventure, Forillon National Park, several lighthouses, the sandbar at Carleton, and the Chic-Choc Mountains. Miguasha National Park and the steam-powered sawmill in Rivière-au-Renard and the wind turbines in Cap-Chat should be added to a list of places to visit. This is one of the top motorcycle-touring destinations in eastern North America.*

There are five regions on the Gaspé peninsula: The Valley, The Coast, Upper Gaspé, Land's End, and The Bay, although I find these labels somewhat misleading because of their geographic extents. The Route 132 circuit of the Gaspé peninsula has been one of the most popular motorcycle-touring destinations in Atlantic Canada for decades. Allocating five days for riding the circuit is generally recommended, but this will depend on your style and the season. During the height of summer, advance reservations are necessary even for campsites.

How much of the 861 km (540 mi) Gaspé loop is traveled depends upon your entry and exit points. If you ride east on Route 132 from Lévis (Québec City) or take one of the ferries from the North Shore to Rivière-du-Loup, Trois-Pistoles, or Rimouski, then the logical beginning is in Sainte-Flavie where Route 132 joins itself to complete its loop of the

---

The Valley

Sainte-Flavie to Amqui is 73 km (45.3 mi)
Matane to Amqui is 65 km (40.3 mi)
Amqui to Matapédia is 77 km (47.8 mi)
Sainte-Flavie to Matapédia is 150 km (93.2 mi)

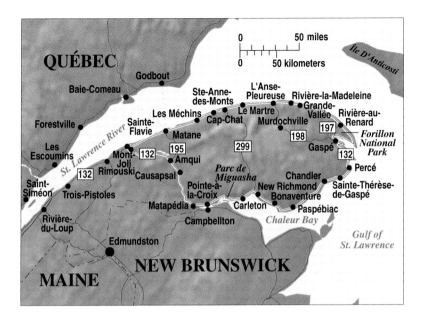

Gaspé peninsula. Coming north through New Brunswick on Route 17 or 11 you'll cross the bridge at Pointe-à-la-Croix. If you arrive from the Côte-Nord via ferry to Matane, then Route 195 will lead south to Route 132 in Amqui or east on Route 132 through the Upper Gaspé.

Route 195 follows the Matane River and the first spectacle is windmills on the ridge; the second is a pair of covered bridges less than 2 km apart. The road abruptly makes a 90-degree turn in the village of Rivière-Matane and climbs out of this valley before descending into "The Valley." It's 65 km (40.3 mi) south from Matane to Amqui and while the scenery is beautiful, the pavement is atrocious.

Route 132 forms a junction with itself in the tiny tourist town of Sainte-Flavie (pop. 937). Adjoining Mont-Joli (pop. 6,614) at Autoroute 20 has numerous gas stations, restaurants, grocery stores, and hotels. It's also known for the murals painted on the walls of commercial and municipal buildings throughout the town. Begun in 2002, this project has scheduled 35 murals to be painted by artists from around the world. They range from *trompe l'oeil* to canvas-like compositions with the theme of bridging the past to the future.

Lake Matapédia begins in Saybec and is the source of the Matapédia River, which Route 132 follows to the western end of the Chaleur Bay in the Restigouche Valley. The fame of this salmon-fishing stream is so great that most of its length is designated as the Matapédia River Nature Reserve.

The historic train station in Amqui, Québec, is still in service.

There are things worth seeing in Amqui (pop. 6,232). The Saint-Jean Covered Bridge is just off Route 132 on the edge of the village, but the Beauséjour Covered Bridge is accessible only by foot. The heritage train station with the oldest working Pullman car in North America is within sight of the junction of Route 195 in the center of town. You can even order your lunch served in the Pullman. You will find dealers for Can-Am, Honda, and Suzuki motorcycles plus several gas stations in the center of town. However, now that you're on Route 132 there won't be any lack of gas stations or camping areas from here to the town of Gaspé.

South of Amqui the highway runs along Lac au Saumon, which should require no translation, and into Causapscal (pop. 2,476). The town is best known for the fishing camp Matamajaw, which was established here in 1870 for British high society. This historic site overlooks the fork where the Causapscal River joins the Matapédia. Orvis, the famous fly-fishing outfitter from southern Vermont, has established a store in an old railway building just down the street. There's an abundance of camping and picnic areas along this route, but I opt for the comfort of Gîte des Tilleuls (418-794-2475, www.quebecmaritime.ca/gitetilleuls).

Matapédia (pop. 686), which means "where the rivers meet" in Mi'kmaq, is located at the confluence of the Matapédia and Restigouche Rivers, the latter being the border between Québec and New Brunswick. Going east you'll pass through a succession of small towns and scenic overlooks as the highway follows the Restigouche River estuary to Chaleur Bay.

The Bay

0 km (0 mi) From Matapédia continue on Route 132.
40 km (25.1 mi) Turn right onto Route d'Escuminac Flats.
45 km (28.2 mi) Turn left on Route de la Pointe-à-Fleurant.
52 km (32.9 mi) Stop at Parc National de Miguasha.
53.6 km (33.5 mi) Left on Route Water.
57 km (35.8 mi) Bear right on Route Water.
60 km (37.4 mi) Right on Route 132 in Nouvelle.
74 km (46.1 mi) Carleton Centre at Rue du Quai.
76 km (47.7 mi) Carleton at Avenue du Phare.
97 km (60.7 mi) Junction with Route 299.
134 km (84.0 mi) Enter Bonaventure.
185 km (115.8 mi) Enter Port Daniel.
215 km (134.5 mi) Arrive in Chandler.

The bridge that links Pointe-à-Croix and Campbellton, New Brunswick, is the primary entry point into the Gaspé so it is a logical spot to find a provincial rest area and tourist information center, which is located at the junction of Blvd. Interprovincial and Route 132.

From Pointe-à-Croix take Route 132 east. In about 21 km (13.4 mi) turn right on Route d'Escuminac Flats to Route de la Pointe-à-Fleurant and enjoy this delightful touring road as you follow the signs to Miguasha National Park. Back in 1842, a British geological survey discovered fossils in the stratified cliffs here, but the fossils were virtually ignored until the subsequent geological survey of 1879-1881 brought them to the attention of the world's paleontologists. The Miguasha fossils date back to the Devonian Era, 360 million years ago, also known as the Age of Fishes. This site is considered the world's best illustration of the Age of Fishes because five of the six fossil fish groups associated with the period are found here including the highest number and best preserved fossil specimens of the lobe-finned fishes that are thought to have given rise to the first four-legged, air-breathing terrestrial vertebrates. The first interpretation center wasn't built until 1978 and its protection as a provincial park came in 1985. Miguasha National Park became listed as the sixth UNESCO World Heritage Site in 1999.

In 22 km (14 mi) you will have the opportunity to search for natural treasures yourself by stopping at the beach at Carleton and doing a bit of beachcombing for agates. Whether the agates on the beach originated in the mountains to the north, or there is another source beneath the water of Chaleur Bay is open to question. Regardless, the sweeping spits of sand that

The Carleton lighthouse is situated at the end of a long sand bar that almost closes the bay. A gorgeous beach, the warmest water, great camping, and wonderful views make this a summer destination for thousands of people.

enclose this bay make this town a summer vacation destination and there's a choice campground at the far end of the sandbar by the lighthouse. Chaleur Bay (Warm Bay) has the warmest water in the Atlantic Maritimes and Carleton Bay the warmest on this coast.

The entire coastline of Chaleur Bay is dotted by small towns, villages, and residential homes, but the area is still scenic and traffic moves at a steady pace.

The Acadian Museum of Québec is located on the highway just east of the primary traffic light in Bonaventure (pop. 2,654), which has many services. The Riotel (by the traffic light, 98 Ave. Port-Royal/Route 132, 418-534-336) doesn't look like much from the outside, but situated on the beach it has a superb view of the bay, the rooms are spacious, and the bike can be parked just outside your door.

These bayside towns were settled by Basques, Jerseymen, Normans, Acadians, Loyalists, and even Scots and Irish. The immigration pattern to this portion of Canada was defined by geopolitical forces, but the history of the region was defined by economic ones. The first cod fishing port in Québec was established at Paspébiac (pop. 3,159) in 1767 by Charles Robin

(Banc-de-Pêche-de-Paspébiac, 418-752-6229, www.shbp.ca). Cod fishing became the mainstay of the peninsular economy for the next two centuries. Today, the only remaining place where codfish is still dried and salted for commercial sale is at the Lelièvre, Lelièvre & Lemoignan processing plant in Sainte-Thérèse-de-Gaspé (pop. 1,112).

Lands End

0 km (0 mi) Begin in Chandler.
39 km (24.5 mi) Arrive in Percé.
118 km (74 mi) The junction with Route 198 is on your left in Gaspé.
125 km (78.2 mi) Turn right to continue on Route 132; Route 197 bears to the left.
150 km (93.8 mi) On your right is the South Sector Road in Forillon National Park.
155 km (97.1 mi) On the right is the road to Cap-Bon-Ami.
159.5 km (99.7 mi) The Cap-des-Rosiers lighthouse.
182 km (114.2 mi) The junction of Route 197 in Rivière-au-Renard.
243 km (152 mi) Arrive in Grande-Vallée.

Chandler (pop. 7,893), is the economic hub of Chaldeur Bay and one of the ports for the AMTA ferry to the Magdalen Islands. There seems to be everything one needs in this city except a coin-operated laundromat.

Some roads, especially two that I wished to take in Port Daniel and one in Carleton, were closed due to erosion of cliffs caused by wave action. Depending upon the location, the coastline loss is 2 to 10 m (6 to 30 ft) a year. Observing how the sea undercuts the red sandstone cliffs I assume that some of this erosion occurs in rather dramatic fashion. In contrast, the lighthouse at Percé is situated on a narrow point of gray metamorphic rock that resists erosion. Eventually it will become an island as the surrounding sandstone disappears into the sea. The famous *Rocher Percé* (Pierced Rock) for which the town is named once had two eyes: since the era of the first European explorers one has collapsed. Fortunately—at least for modern tourism—nature has been gracious enough to leave the one remaining hole in the rock.

Percé (pop. 3,390) is actually a town encompassing ten villages and is best known for its famous rock, which is accessible during low tide. Photo ops can be found at various overlooks and one of the best is public. It's located at the top of the hill on a blind corner. Slow down after passing Lighthouse Camping—and the lighthouse—and approach with extreme caution. Another vantage point is the street immediately before the driveway to the *Hôtel de Ville* (town hall)—for obvious reasons it's not well

Through the Chic-Chocs on Route 299

Route 299 begins at Route 132 just east of the Gesgapegiag town limits in New Richmond on Chaleur Bay and runs 140 km (87 mi) north to Sainte-Anne-des-Monts on the St. Lawrence River. There are no gas stations on this highway and sections of the pavement are atrocious, but when the asphalt is smooth this becomes a top-notch touring road. It follows the Cascapédia River north into the Chic-Choc Mountains, climbing over the shoulder of Hog Back and arcing around the foot of Mont Albert. An interlocking series of wildlife reserves—Matane Nature Reserve, Gaspé Provincial Park, and Chic-Chocs Nature Reserve—that stretches from the Matapédia Valley to Route 198 in Murdochville, protects the Gaspé highlands from development. The park has the highest concentration of moose in Québec so caution is advised when touring on this road. If these huge creatures, with bodies of a Clydesdale and the brains of a chicken won't move at the blast of an air horn on a Peterbilt, a motorcycle isn't going to scare them.

Mont Lyall in the Chic-Chocs is noted for colorful agate geodes and there's a commercial operation that will allow (for a fee) people to "dig" for these treasures (Mine d'Agates du Mont Lyall, 418-786-2374, www.mont-lyall.com). It is located 85 km from New Richmond, 57 km from Sainte-Anne-des-Monts, and 1.5 km up a gravel road. Watch for the blue-and-white signs—since there's only one major gravel road in that vicinity it's easy to find. Acres of agates as thick as dandelions on an unkempt lawn, from marble to basketball size, are strewn across a mountainside. The views—when you look up from the ground—are awe inspiring.   ∎

marked. There are far too many restaurants, hotels, and boutiques to mention more than a couple. This is a major tourist town and the most difficult thing to find is parking. If you plan to book lodging in advance, fantastic views of the rock can be seen from Riôtel Percé in town (418-782-2166, www.riotel.com) or from the Au Pic de L'Aurore at the top of the hill beyond the village (418-782-2151, www.percechalet.com).

It's not known whether the name Gaspé (pop. 14,958) was derived from "gespey," Mi'kmaq for lands end or from "gerizpe," the Basque word for shelter. What is known is that Jacques Cartier planted a cross and claimed the land as the possession of the French king on July 24, 1534. What most school history books fail to mention is that native Mi'kmaqs spoke to Cartier in pidgin Basque, which implies that he wasn't the first French navigator to arrive in these lands. The municipality of Gaspé includes 17 towns and villages and covers 975 sq km— you'll see a number of villages with the surname Gaspé.

The famous Percé Rock with a weathered hole through it has become a world-famous tourist destination.

Anse-Blanchette was a typical fisherman-farmer's house of the early 19th century. It has been preserved and is staffed by costumed guides during the summer.

The southern junction of Route 198 is at the traffic light on the north side of the bridge over the York River. There's a series of boutiques and cafes on Rue de la Reine (parallel to, but elevated above, Route 198), a major hotel, and fine dining and lodging at biker-friendly Maison William Wakeham (186 Rue de la Reine, Gaspé, 418-368-5537). Gaspé will be the last large town you'll encounter for more than 200 km (125 mi). It's 171 km (106 mi) from Gaspé to L'Anse-Pleureuse by way of Route 132. Although Route 198 is a much faster road than Route 132, the 42 km (26 mi) saved will be a big loss to your experience of the Gaspé. Dramatic images of the region will be found along Route 132 between here and L'Anse-Pleureuse, so don't be seduced by this shortcut just because it's favored by the local residents.

Route 197 is a shortcut that follows the western edge of Forillon National Park to Rivière-au-Renard. You must make a right turn to continue on Route 132 around the cape through the national park and this turn comes as a bit of a surprise. No problem! Rather than risking a U-turn, just take the next right, which leads back to Route 132.

The Forillon National Park is on the north side of Gaspé Bay and extends to Cape Gaspé. There are three locations in the park worth visiting by motorcycle: Fort Péninsule on Route 132 just after entering the park, the road to Les Graves in the South Sector, and Cap-Bon-Ami in the North Sector. The first was the site of WWII gun placements to protect the bay. These bunkers are easily accessible and open to the public. The South Sector road follows the shoreline of Gaspé Bay. It's a beautiful road with access to beaches, a historic area with a general store and a homestead of the 1920s era, and finally a parking area near the end of Cap-Gaspé that offers a great view. There's a hiking trail that will take you from the parking lot to the very tip of Cape Gaspé, a place that truly is "lands end." The North Sector Road leads to Cap-Bon-Ami, the Gulf of St. Lawrence side of the cape. The sheer cliffs are absolutely dramatic. The three campgrounds in Forillon National Park have a total of 350 campsites (reservations: 877-737-3783, www.pccamping.ca) plus a few yurts (866-892-5873, www.gesmat.ca). The nearby Cap-Bon-Ami camping area is for tents only and has 41 sites.

Cap-des-Rosiers was named for the wild roses that used to grow here. The lighthouse is the tallest in Canada and is designated as a historic

Phare du Cap-des-Rosiers is the tallest lighthouse in Canada and has been designated a National Historic Site.

monument. There is another lighthouse to be found on Lands End, but Pointe-à-la-Renommée is 5 km (3 mi) off the highway near L'Anse-à-Valleau. This can be a nice detour and the views are awesome, but the road is a bit exposed so I'd recommend it only on days when the wind is less than a light gale and rain is not in the immediate forecast.

Be prepared for corners and changes in elevation. Route 132 becomes a roller-coaster ride along the coast and through the small villages that are clustered between the mountains and the sea. Fishing is the primary occupation in this area, so don't expect an abundance of B&Bs or fancy restaurants.

The junction of Route 197 is in Rivière-au-Renard. Across the bridge at the quay is Bardeau et Bateau, the last steam-powered sawmill in eastern Québec. All the equipment has been preserved in this early 20th-century mill that produced lumber for both shipbuilding and shingles for homes.

Upper Gaspé

0 km (0 mi) Continue from Grande-Vallée.
18 km (11.5 mi) Enter Rivière-la-Madeleine.
26 km (16.2 mi) The turn for the lighthouse, Rue du Phare, is on the right.
51 km (31.9 mi) Junction with Route 298 in L'Anse-Pleureuse.
112 km (70.3 mi) The northern end of Route 299 in Sainte-Anne-des-Monts.
133 km (83 mi) Enter Cap-Chat.
156 km (98.5 mi) Arrive in Les Méchins.

Continuing west from Grande-Vallée be prepared for tight corners, dramatic views from higher elevations only to plunge back to sea level. Little towns hugging stony points like tenacious starfish or clustered in sheltered coves like colorful sea anemones dot this famous coastline. There are observation areas with picnic tables in almost every small village and you might want to take advantage of these safe-parking havens to kick back and enjoy the essence of the Gaspé.

The Cap Madeleine Lighthouse is easily found 7 km (4 mi) west of Rivière-la-Madeleine. The very function of a lighthouse is to be as conspicuous as possible, so unless the coast is locked in by fog you'll see them long before you reach them. This lighthouse has a museum and you can climb to the light for an incredible view, but unlike others, it also features an Internet café. Have a coffee while e-mailing home—"you'll never guess where I am"—and keeping watch for whales.

The most dramatic section of Route 132 runs along the base of towering cliffs at the edge of the St. Lawrence between Manche-d'Épée and

Gros-Morne. Highway signs urge caution as waves sometimes break across the road. Being slapped by a rogue wave is not a situation I recall as having been covered in the Advance Motorcycle Safety Course.

Gaspé to L'Anse-Pleureuse on Route 198

Route 198 runs 96 km (60 mi) from Gaspé to L'Anse-Pleureuse. The junction of Routes 132 and 198 is at the traffic light in the village of Gaspé immediately after crossing the bridge over the York River. After a dozen kilometers you'll find yourself in wilderness and there are no gas stations until you reach Murdochville (84 km, 52 mi). The pavement alternates between smooth and quite rough, there is an abundance of wildlife (moose, deer, bear, and smaller creatures), and the temptation to wring that throttle has to be subdued to something less than 120 km/h (posted for 90 km/h, 56 mph, and generally ignored).

Murdochville (pop. 856) grew from the discovery of the mineral deposits in Mont Copper The underground mine closed in 1999 and the foundry in 2002, but you can experience the mine by taking a tour at the Centre d'Interpretation du Cuivre (800-487-8601, www.cicuivre.com) down into the depths of the Miller's Drift. There's also the Mont Miller windmill site, but you'll see dozens of these as you travel the highway.

The road reaches 660 m (2,165 feet) above sea level (Gaspé is at sea level) and you'll still see plenty of snow on the peaks and even alongside the road well into June.

Taking this highway saves about 42 km of travel, with fewer RV trailers slowing traffic. Unfortunately it also bypasses the most scenic portion of Route 132. ∎

Route 198 leaves the village of L'Anse-Pleureuse and cuts through the Chic-Chocs, but the next three towns—Mont-Louis, Mon-Sainte-Pierre, and Rivière-à-Claude—also have lesser-known roads that lead into these mountains. Those on dual-sport machines should consider them to be a challenge, but baggers beware.

Mont-Saint-Pierre (pop. 220) is the hang-gliding capital of eastern Canada, and with towering cliffs and hidden valleys it's easy to understand why. A string of funky-looking motels and restaurants curves around a beautiful crescent-shaped beach and give the appearance that this town has yet to be discovered by mainstream tourism. However, for 10 days in late July Icarusians take to the skies during the Festival du Vol Libre.

The survival of the wooden lighthouse at La Martre can be credited to the sheer stubbornness of the last keeper who refused to give it up and continued to maintain it even after it was decommissioned. It still has the original clockwork that rotates the working light! It's now an excellent museum (418-288-5698).

Sainte-Anne-des-Monts (pop. 6,765) marks the northern end of Route 299 and numerous restaurants and services can be found here. It is only 87 civilized kilometers (54 mi) to Matane, but if you plan to head south through the wilderness on Route 299 make certain that you have a full tank of gasoline: the next service station is 140 km (87 mi) away.

In Cap-Chat (pop. 2,721) windmills are everywhere! The tallest vertical-axis windmill in the world (110 m, 361 ft) is clearly visible from the highway and the visitor center is located practically beneath it. Over 76 are readily visible, but there are actually 133 wind generators in Le Nordais Windmill Park. The Capucins roadside rest area west of town provides the best view of the windmills.

The Coast

   0 km (0 mi) Continue from Les Méchins.
   43 km (27 mi) On the left is the junction with Route 195 in Matane.
   52 km (32.8 mi) The turn to the Matane/Baie-Comeau/Godbout ferry dock
   62 km (39.1 mi) Enter Saint-Ulric.
   79 km (49.7 mi) Enter Baie-des-Sables.
   99 km (61.9 mi) The junction of Route 234 in Grand-Métis.
   111 km (69.6 mi) Arrive in Sainte-Flavie at the division of Route 132.

At Les Méchins (pop. 1,182) just west of Capucins you enter the region known as The Coast. Route 132 follows the southern shore of the St. Lawrence River and it's only 111 km (69 mi) to Sainte-Flavie.

You'll feel that you've returned to civilization upon reaching Matane. Restaurants, box stores, motels, hotels, and traffic. The lighthouse along the busy highways houses the tourism center. The salmon run on the Matane River is a major attraction, as is the observation center at the Mathieu-D'Amours Dam (260 Ave. St-Jérôme, 418-562-7006). From Matane the ferry crosses the river to both Godbout and Baie-Comeau and Route 195 goes south to Route 132 in Amqui.

This region is aptly named. Route 132 runs along the southern shoreline of the St. Lawrence River with farms stretching across the littoral plain to the crumpled ridges that mark the edge of the Appalachian Mountains. Just

Shipyards are a common sight along the coast, but most are not as large as this one in Les Méchins.

outside the village of Saint-Ulric (pop. 1,691) is another Gaspé wind farm. Farmers are practical and they tend to like wind turbines on their land because it generates income while taking up very little space on fertile fields.

Every town has its treasures. Baie-des-Sables (pop. 616) has an old mill and great river views; Métis-sur-Mer (pop. 602) is an old resort village that has some interesting residential architecture; and Grand-Métis (pop. 270) features the Redford Garden, a National Historic Site of Canada where many festivals are held during the summer.

Autoroute 20 can be picked up in Grand-Métis as the shortest distance to Mont-Joli or you can continue for another 12 km (7.4 mi) on Route 132 and close the Gaspé loop.

Trip 6 Navigators Route

Distance: *331 km (205 mi) A one-day trip.*
Terrain: *Flat coastal road with nice views of the St. Lawrence River. The road runs along a littoral plain through farmland with a succession of villages that become larger towns when riding west.*
Highlights: *The Onondaga submarine, Empress of Ireland Exhibit, and the lighthouse in Pointe-au-Phare; art galleries and studios in Saint-Jean-Port Joli; and the ferry ride from Lévis to Québec City top my list of highlights.*

Most touring riders who travel to the Gaspé region are familiar with Route 132 along the southern shore of the St. Lawrence River. It also provides two vital segments for those who are returning from Trip 4, the Côte-Nord, and wish to travel to Edmundston, New Brunswick on Route 185 or back into New England on Autoroute 73.

For the most part, Route 132 follows an ancient littoral plain between the northern Adirondack Mountains and the southern shore, or bank, of the St. Lawrence River. This is fertile farmland and the cities and villages scattered along the South Coast tend to be small. The scenic Navigators Route pretty much follows Route 132, but often detours to follow the original coastal road.

The landmark Church of Sainte-Luce can be seen on Pointe-Anse-aux-Coques from Route 132 and the turn onto Route du Fleuve is only 9.8 km from the beginning of the Gaspé loop in Sainte-Flavie. This is the

The Route from Sainte-Flavie to Lévis on Route 132

0 km (0 mi) Begin in Sainte Flavie.
26 km (16.2 mi) Enter Pointe-au-Père.
28 km (14.8 mi) The right turn to the ferry dock in Rimouski.
93 km (57.7 mi) The right turn to the ferry dock in Trois-Pistoles.
133 km (82.8 mi) The right turn for the ferry at Pointe-Rivière-du-Loup.
135 km (83.7 mi) The left turn to go to Route 185 in Rivière-du-Loup.
164 km (101.6 mi) Junction with Route 289 on the left.
186 km (115.3 mi) Enter Kamouraska.
239 km (148 mi) Enter Saint-Jean-Port-Joli.
274 km (170 mi) Enter Montmagny.
331 km (205 mi) Arrive at the ferry dock in Lévis to cross to Québec City.

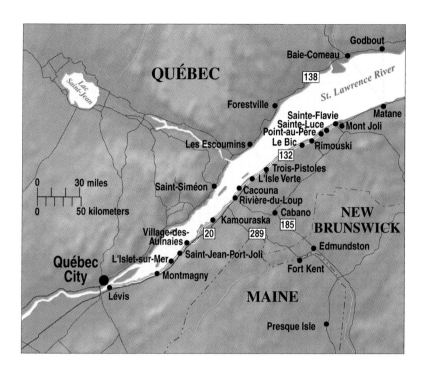

beginning of the Navigators Route, although it merely loops through Sainte-Luce (pop. 2,989) and returns to Route 132. Like so many other portions of the scenic drive this once was the main highway before Route 132 was constructed. It runs along a beautiful beach and past dozens of resort cottages so it can be a busy place during the summer.

Pointe-au-Père is a district of Rimouski and it's marked by one of the tallest lighthouses in Canada and directions are not required for this highly visible landmark. Open to the public, this concrete tower with buttress sides has 128 steps leading to the lamp and second-order Fresnel lens. If you think of lighthouse keepers as being old men sitting on the stoop smoking a pipe, you'll have a different vision after climbing and descending this tight spiral of stairs. This lighthouse keeper had to be fairly spry. The view from the top makes the climb worthwhile (418-724-6214, www.shmp.qc.ca).

The Treasures of the Empress of Ireland exhibit in the adjoining building tells the tale of the tragic sinking of this famous ocean liner off Pointe-Anse-aux-Coques as it departed from Pointe-au-Père on a voyage to Europe in 1914. The theater presentation is a must-see, and the museum houses artifacts recovered from the site.

The newest addition to the site is the HMCS Onondaga, a military submarine that operated from 1967 to 2000 and which is now in permanent dry dock. Audio tours in both English and French describe the various aspects of the submarine as you walk through the six watertight bulkhead compartments. Groups and individuals can make special reservations to stay overnight aboard the submarine. For those staying overnight: there will be emergency drills and other activities taking place under the captain's command.

For those who love to eat lobster, consider booking a room at Place Lemieux (866-440-2888, www.placelemieux.com). This complex includes a bar, restaurant, motel, fish market, and catering service. There's a tank holding four tons of live lobsters, so you can eat your fill while looking out across the St. Lawrence River. Ask to camp out back by the shore.

The Pointe-au-Père lighthouse is the last surviving example of the six that were built using this buttress design for a new building material—concrete.

Leaving the historic site of Pointe-au-Père you can continue straight through the intersection of Route 132 on Ave. du Père Nouvel Sud to Autoroute 20 Ouest. The Autoroute will bypass Rimouski and join Route 132 in Le Bic. Your other option is to turn right at the light and follow Route 132 as it sweeps into Rimouski (pop. 45,911) and along the bay.

On one side of the highway there is a promenade with distinctive observation centers and the quay for the ferry that makes the one-hour crossing to Forestville (418-725-2725, www.traversier.com). The quay is also the home port of Relais Nordik, Inc. (418-723-8787, www.relaisnordik.com) the operators of the Nordik Express, the ferry/freighter that services Anticosti Island and the ports along the Côte-Nord to Blanc-Sablon in Labrador. This is the secret "backdoor" approach to Labrador and Newfoundland that's being used by touring motorcyclists.

The Hôtel Rimouski is one of the hotels to be found along Route 132 (Blvd. René-Lepage, 800-463-0755, www.hotelrimouski.com) and I can vouch for their hospitality and excellent restaurant. Most hotels are located

The exhibition hall for the Empress of Ireland was designed to look like a listing ship.

between Pointe-au-Père and Rimouski, but this one is quite convenient. Good tent sites are available to the west of the city at Camping & Motel de l'Anse (1105 Blvd. St-Germain/Route 132, 418-721-0322, www.guide-camping.ca/anse). For good fast food it's worth seeking out La Station (hint: it's along the railroad tracks) on Rue St-Jean-Baptiste Est. Three kilometers past the dock, at the third traffic light west of Centre de Congrès and with the river on your right, make a left turn onto Ave. du la Cathédrale and ride several blocks until it crosses the railroad tracks at the third traffic light. This also is one of the best places to get a quick breakfast in the city.

Le Bic is not just a village: it's also a rocky outcrop and a national park located on the western edge of Rimouski. There's a beautiful road through the Bic National Park, but a couple of kilometers is gravel. Camping is in the southern sector of the park (418-736-5035, www.parcsquebec.com).

The topography of this area resembles a crumpled accordion with long parallel rock ridges alternating with narrow fertile valleys. About 350 million years ago the African tectonic plate, *Gondwana*, collided with the proto-North American plate, *Laurentia*, and these are the eroded remains of that titanic fender-bender. The valleys filled with nutrient-rich clay sediments during the recent post-glacial epoch, which is what makes the Bas-Saint-Laurent region such a farm rich area.

The Basque Cheese shop is popular with motorcyclists (and just about everyone else). This is a great deli stop.

The long, wall-like ridge and farm-filled valley extends southwest from Bic National Park through Saint-Fabien (pop. 1,959) and Saint-Simon (pop. 445) almost to Trois-Pistoles (pop. 3,465). The name is reputed to have originated in 1621 when a Basque sailor accidentally lost a silver goblet worth three gold coins, called *pistoles*. The name was given to the nearby river flowing into the St. Lawrence and subsequently the town when it was founded in 1693. This is also known as the Basque Coast.

From Trois-Pistoles, the ferry (877-851-4677, www.traversiercnb.ca) crosses the river to Les Ecoumins on the Côte-Nord, but there are other reasons to stop here. There's a municipal campground at the end of Chanoine-Côté along the coastal pedestrian path and two others—one just before town and another just after—that are also located along the shore. Rue Notre-Dame is the old road through the city, joining Route 132 on both ends. There are motels and gîtes in Trois-Pistoles and the outskirts. A maze of scenic roads and several small villages are also found south of this city, but it's best to pick up local maps from the information office on Route 132 first.

The Musée Saint-Laurent (552 Rue Notre-Dame West at Route 132, 418-815-2345) is the largest automobile museum east of Québec City, but being housed in an old barn it's easy to miss. The museum is only open from late June to Labour Day (same day as in the U.S.) but La Fromagerie des Basques (418-851-3576, www.fromageriedesbasques.ca) is open every day. This cheese factory and specialty food shop on Route 132 is almost a required stop for motorcyclists, so much so that bikes have reserved spaces in the front parking area. Food, food, food and outside picnic tables make this a stop for lunch and to stock up on goodies to munch on for the next couple of days.

Île-Verte is a long island that's just offshore from the mainland town of the same name. I've heard that it's a beautiful place, but since the ferry only makes the crossing during high tide it usually requires an overnight stay.

Route 20 begins again in Bois-des-Bel while Route 132 continues to hug the coast. The Navigators Route goes through Cacouna (pop. 1,897), a town that thrived during the era of grand hotels prior to the invention of air conditioning. Today it's most notable feature is that it is a deep-water port that seems to be bypassed by most shipping. However, those of you with a passion for ice cream shouldn't bypass Les Glaces Ali-Baba (1600 Rue du Patrimoine, 418-862-1976). Deviate from the main highway by turning right (north) on Rue du Quai and the second left onto Rue Desjardins. This residential road runs along the edge of the shore and offers stupendous views before ending back at the main highway.

Route 132 (Blvd. Cartier) passes Pointe-de-Rivière-du-Loup where the ferry is located for the 65-minute crossing to Saint-Siméon in the Charlevoix region. There are two primary roads that lead from the main highway to the ferry dock—Rue McKay and Rue de l'Ancrage—and both are well marked by signs.

The Museum of Miniature Boats and the Legends of the Bas-Saint-Laurent (80 Blvd. Cartier/Route 132, 866-868-0800) is located in a rather nondescript building that includes fast-food from Rôtisserie St-Hubert. Inside are 130 miniature boats that were made by 20 craftsmen in the region as well as related artwork. The tourism season is very short in this region, but fried chicken sells year-round.

After crossing the Rivière du Loup (River of Seals, *loup-marin* is French for seal) the highway then becomes Rue Fraser, the main drag through the city of Rivière-du-Loup (pop. 18,973). Autoroute 20 is actually more scenic than Route 132 within the city, but they soon switch positions and it's the old highway that runs along the shore. Autoroute 85/Route 185 is the primary road leading from the St. Lawrence River to Edmundston, New

Brunswick. As you can imagine, there is an abundance of hotels, motels, B&Bs, and campgrounds in and around this transportation center.

Parc des Chutes de Rivière-du-Loup (www.ville.riviere-du-loup.qc.ca) is a city park and hydroelectric station that features a 33-meter (106 ft) waterfall that can be viewed from two pedestrian suspension bridges. (From Route 132, turn left onto Rue Lafontaine and when it becomes a one-way street turn left on Rue Frontenac at 1.2 km (less than a mile) and ride to the park. This is also the beginning of Route 185 to Edmundston.)

Southwest of the city the highway is named Route des Montagnes, which might seem a little strange as you ride along the shoreline. Perhaps it's named for the narrow stony ridges that the road gently swerves to avoid or because the mountains of the Charlevoix region can be seen on the far side of the St. Lawrence River. For the most part this is a flat littoral plain where farms and residential homes line the highway.

This junction with Route 289 seems to be in the middle of nowhere. The village of Saint-Alexandre-de-Kamouraska is situated along Route 289 on the east side of Route 20, but the village of Kamouraska is another 20 km (12 mi) down Route 132 beyond the villages of Saint-André and Saint-Germain. All four of these villages, and others, lie within the township of Kamouraska.

Kamouraska (pop. 678) is touted as being one of the most beautiful

Express Route: Rivière-du-Loup to Edmundston, New Brunswick, on Route 185   112 km (70 mi)

The primary road from the St. Lawrence River to Edmundston is Route 185 (Autoroute 85). Sometimes this is a two-lane road and sometimes it's three or even a divided four-lane highway, but with posted speed up to 110 km/hr (68 mph) the traffic moves right along.

It's a little awkward to find from Route 132 in Rivière-du-Loup unless you're headed east on Autoroute 20. Turn left onto Rue Lafontaine in the middle of the city. You'll quickly pass the junction of Route 291, then the turn on Rue Frontenac to view the Chutes de Rivière-du-Loup (falls on the Rivière-du-Loup). The street name keeps changing but there's no confusion as to the proper one. There will be signs for Autoroute 85, but you can keep on following Chemin-Rivière-Verte until it ends at Autoroute 85 (Route 185).

The highway cuts through the Appalachian Mountains to reach

villages in the region, but such things tend to be highly subjective. It is a pretty little village and the brightly painted Kamouraska General Store (98 Ave. Morel/Route 132, 418-492-2882) has been restored to 1930s-era decor and features local products.

There are numerous camping areas in this region and signs make them easy to locate. After crossing the Ouelle River, Route 132 crosses to the east of Autoroute 20 for a few kilometers. When it veers back to the coast you've left the Bas-Saint-Laurent region and entered the Chaudière-Appalaches.

The stone mill in the center of Village-des-Aulnaies was built in 1842. The millers work in period costume, and it grinds organic flour to this day. There's a restaurant on site that is open for breakfast or lunch (418-354-2800, www.laseigneuriedesaulnaies.qc.ca). This village is the site of one of the oldest *seigneuries* (French, quasi-feudal-system land grants) on the south shore.

Three kilometers beyond the mill you'll see a gravel road that leads to an observation area on the river. Photo ops include the Laurentian Mountains on the opposite shore and the twin spires of the beautiful stone church in Saint-Roch-des-Aulnaies (pop. 959).

Saint-Jean-Port-Joli (pop. 3,407) is one of the gems you'll encounter on this ride. Even before you reach the town the number of *ateliers* (artist studios) along the road will catch your interest. This continues in the villages and for

---

Cabano (pop. 3,214) on Lac Témiscouata. This is a town that has just begun to embrace tourism, but the foremost B&B in the area is Auberge du Chemin Faisant (12 Vieux Chemin, 418-854-9342, www.cheminfaisant.qc.ca). If you like good food, Arts & Craft architecture, Art Deco interior design, or Scotch whiskey, this is the place for you. Route 232 briefly merges with Autoroute 85 for 6 km (3.8 mi).

You have to exit at Dégelis (pop. 3,220) for Route 295 or gasoline.

The Québec-New Brunswick border is almost 96 km (59.9 mi) from Route 132. Here you'll find the New Brunswick gateway information center and the Edmundston airport. The first has a wealth of brochures and maps; that latter has a WWII Lancaster bomber on display.

Exit 8 in Saint-Jacques is only 10.4 km (6.5 mi) from the border. The Antique Auto Museum and the botanical gardens are located here. In another 5 km (3.5 mi) is the exit onto Route 144 (Chemin Canada) to downtown Edmundston.   ∎

kilometers west of it. The majority of artists seem to favor sculpture over other forms of creative expression, but in a wide variety of styles, forms, and media. There are numerous cafes, restaurants, and lodging to be found in Port-Joli.

It's just a guess, but you might be interested in the great motorcycle museum they have here, Musée L'Épopée de la Moto (Route 132, www.epopeedelamoto.com). With more than 50 different marques and more than double that number of models there's probably something here that will intrigue you. A few buildings farther on the opposite side of the highway is Musée des Anciens Canadiens (418-598-3392, www.musee-desancienscanadiens.com) with its excellent wood carvings from the famed craftsmen of the region. A collection of vintage service station signs attached to the log building might catch your eye. This is La Bigorne (418-598-3887) and Clermont Guay is a *ferronnerie* (blacksmith). When he's not working the forge he's off exploring North American wilderness regions on his BMW GS. Just down the road is Sculptures Tremblay (418-247-5419, www.sculpturestremblay.com) and if birds or decoys are of any interest to you mark this as a stop.

You've just about had time to warm up the engine and reestablish your rhythm when it's time to stop at the Maritime Museum of Québec (55 Chemin des Pionniers/Route 132, 418-247-5001) in the small village of L'Islet-sur-Mer (pop. 3,799). Climb aboard the Ernest-Lapointe ice breaker, the Bras d'Or hydrofoil, or wander into the boat-building shop. FYI: there's a very nice camping area just a kilometer east of the junction of Route 285 in the village.

Small farms, residential homes, and views of L'Île-aux-Grues are what you can expect for the next 20 km (12 mi). There are several bird sanctuaries along this section of coastline so depending upon the season you can expect to see herons, ospreys, geese, and ducks in flight.

Montmagny (pop. 11,337) has what you need: fast food, gas stations, motels, restaurants, grocery stores, the SAQ liquor store, and much more. It's a city that's known for their international accordion festival and being a stopover for snow geese during their migrations.

The St. Lawrence River is dotted with 21 islands, but the dominant one is Île-d'Orléans. This is a beautiful place with specialty farms and American colonial-style homes. Some of this can be seen from the south shore, but the only access is from the opposite one (see Trip 1). This is still farmland, but the intrusion of residential homes upon prime agricultural property becomes more and more evident as you approach the city. There are things to see—mills, historic homes, and specialty food producers—but you'll be able to feel the pace of the city in the flow of traffic.

Route des Frontières: Kamouraska to Maine or New Brunswick via Route 289 134 km (84 mi)

This is the country route to Edmundston and is more suitable for motorcycle touring than the much faster Autoroute 85. It winds through woodlands and along lake shores to reach the St. John River and on a hot summer day is preferable to Autoroute 85 (Route 185).

It's 2 km (1.25 mi) from Route 132 to Route 20 and 5 km (3 mi) to Saint-Alexandre-de-Kamouraska (pop. 1,885). The road climbs into the mountains and along Lac Pohénégamook. For those traveling in a small group or wishing to make this area a base for exploring the region, renting a condo or cottage at Santé Plein Air on Lac Pohénégamook (800-463-1364, www.pohenegamook.com) would be advantageous.

The highway runs along Lac Long for 8 km (5 mi) before crossing to the opposite side of the lake in Saint-Marc-du-Lac-Long (pop. 459) and continuing for another 12 km (8 mi). The Québec-New Brunswick border is at 95 km (58.9 mi) and the route number changes from 289 to 120. This also is the beginning of Lac Baker, which can be seen on your left.

Turning left on Route 161 in Caron Brook at 108 km (67.8 mi) will take you to Fort Kent, Maine and the northern end of US Route 1.

Meanwhile Route 120 follows the northern bank of the St. John River, which is the international boundary between Canada and the U.S. The city limits of Edmundston are reached at 132 km (83 mi) and the highway ends 1,500 meters farther at Chemin Canada by the bridge in the downtown core. ■

The St. John River marks the international boundary between the United States and Canada. The United States is on the left.

Birds seem to be a specialty of Sculptures Tremblay in Saint-Jean-Port-Joli.

Lévis (pop. 133,074) is a major city formed by the merger of 10 smaller towns (www.tourismelevis.com). It's most noted aspect is the excellent views of Québec City at the point where the river narrows. Most of the city core is situated on the high bluffs or the steep slopes leading down to the river. The Lévis/Québec ferry (877-787-7483, www.travesiers.gouv.ca) is the best—and at this point, easiest—approach to the old port and Lower Town of Québec City. Traffic should occupy most of your attention, but there's much to see in the historic old town.

As you are leaving farmland and entering Lévis on Route 132/Blvd. de la Rive-Sud) be on the lookout for Rue St-Joseph bearing right. This will turn into Rue St-Laurent, which runs along the river to the ferry terminal. If you bypass Rue St-Joseph, turn around and don't attempt to look for a cross-over street. If you miss Rue St-Joseph, stay on Route 132 and follow the signs to the ferry. You'll make a right at a major intersection and ride down the hill on Côte du Passage. I encourage you to explore the city if you have the time. Should you decide to make the crossing on the bridges your best option will be the scenic Rue St-Laurent or the quicker Autoroute 20.

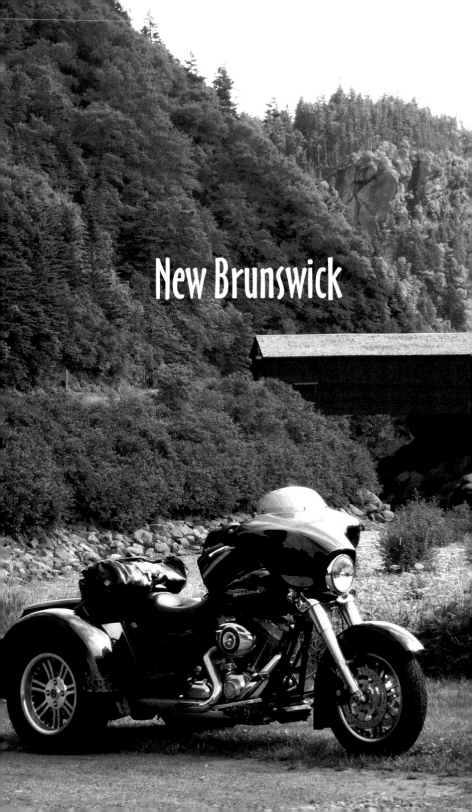

New Brunswick

New Brunswick *by Ken Aiken*

It's much easier to talk about particular regions than to describe the province as a whole. New Brunswick is 90 percent forested, and agricultural fields cover thousands of hectares in the Upper Saint John Valley, but the coastlines seem to define this province. Even so, there are three distinct coastlines—Chaleur Bay, the Gulf of St. Lawrence, and the Bay of Fundy—any one of which doesn't resemble either of the other two. When attempting to narrow this province down to a single, identifying coastline, I'm faced with describing the irreconcilable discrepancies of teeming metropolitan areas and wilderness regions that are inaccessible by road that somehow leave room for rural fishing harbors and pretty resort towns.

New Brunswick is the only Canadian province that is officially bi-lingual. This means that all public signs and documents are in both French and English. If you want to learn practical French nouns and prepare yourself for road signs in Québec you will appreciate the practicality of this policy. However, beyond officialdom, French is generally spoken in the north and English in the south. Just to make it a bit more interesting, Acadian is commonly spoken on the street in both the far northwestern and northeastern corners of the province.

In terms of road conditions, the best and worse pavement ridden during my recent journeys across Atlantic Canada were encountered here. Subjective as it might be, the most boring highway I rode and the most scenic road in Atlantic Canada were also in New Brunswick.

I had five-star culinary experiences and others I'd rather not talk about. I visited museums that were simply wild eclectic collections of stuff, to one whose interpretive displays are the equal to any in the world. I was moved by one of the natural wonders of the world and was merely left wondering about another as I quickly moved on. I rode across the longest covered bridge in the world and over others that, curiously enough, weren't even covered. This province is not one neat package that can be easily explained.

The one aspect of New Brunswick that proved to be consistent was the friendliness of the people. Many people went out of their way to make my travels just a little bit easier or to provide me with access to various places. These little random acts of kindness may be the thread that holds this province together. It may, in fact, be what defines New Brunswick.

Trip 7 Fundy Coastal Drive

Distance: *378 km (235 mi) not including side trips. Allow at least two days.*

Terrain: *This ride is mostly coastal terrain, but ranges from resort towns and fishing villages to the cities of Saint John and Moncton. Some locations are at sea level while others, most notably the Fundy Trail Parkway, are at elevation. Bays, inlets, salt marshes, upland forest, and rocky promontories contrast with the developed industries and cityscape of Saint John.*

Highlights: *This ride offers the most dramatic vistas of any ride in New Brunswick and some of its most interesting stops. St. Andrews is the prettiest resort town in the province and the attractions of Saint John include the Reversing Rapids, the New Brunswick Museum, restaurants, and boutiques. The sea caves of St. Martins and the "flower pots" of Hopewell Rocks are natural wonders that are augmented by the spectacular views on the Fundy Trail Parkway. The highest tides in the world make even the simplest fishing ports places of photographic interest at low tide.*

The Fundy Coastal Drive is the most popular touring highway in New Brunswick. Part of this is because of the destination cities of Saint John and Moncton and their respective connections to the rest of Atlantic Canada. Yet there is no denying that the dramatic Fundy tides, by far the highest in the world, create a coastline of visual delights. The Reversing Rapids in Saint John, the sculpted sandstone of Hopewell Rocks, and the tidal bore on the Petitcodiac River in Moncton are major tourist attractions based on these phenomenal tides. Other gems along this route include the historic town of St. Andrews and the rich heritage preserved in the New Brunswick Museum in Saint John. The Fundy Trail Parkway leads into previously

The Route from St. Stephen to St. Andrews

0 km (0 mi) Turn right in St. Stephen on Milltown Blvd.

0.5 km (0.3 mi) Turn left on Route 3/King Street.

2 km (1.3 mi) Turn right on Route 170 in St. Stephen. (Exit 9 of Route 1 is just ahead.)

14 km (9.1 mi) Turn right on Route 127 (just off Exit 25 of Route 1).

29 km (18.4 mi) Arrive at St. Andrews.

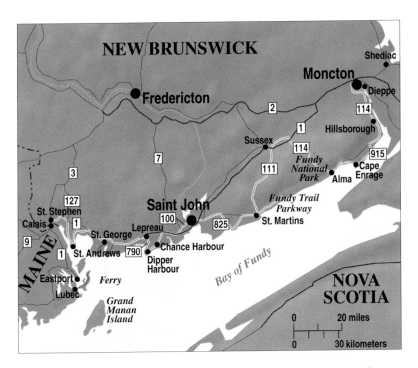

inaccessible wilderness along the Fundy escarpment to the east of Saint Martins. Although the entire parkway won't be completed until 2013, the 13 km (8 mi) now open are one of the highlights of this ride. The list goes on, but there's no doubt that this is a ride that should be on any motorcyclist's "must-do" list.

The primary gateways into the Canadian province of New Brunswick are on the southeastern border of Maine. There are numerous border posts along the Maine–New Brunswick border, and while some are little known, others, like at Houlton (I-95/ Route 2) and Calais (US Route 1/NB Route 1), handle a considerable amount of traffic. I usually cross at St. Stephen but there are two other options.

The first is Lubec, the easternmost town in the United States. From here the International Bridge crosses to Campobello Island, former summer home of Theodore Roosevelt, and a ferry crosses to Deer Island, New Brunswick, every hour. The second is Eastport, the easternmost city in the United States, and it too has a ferry to Deer Island every hour. Which route you take depends more upon what you wish to visit in the United States (see *Motorcycle Journeys Through New England*) although if you catch the tide right, the Eastport–Deer Island Ferry will provide an opportunity to view the Old Sow—the second-largest whirlpool in the world.

Bikes line up on Water Street during the annual Atlanticade rally in June in the biker-friendly town of St. Andrews.

After touring Deer Island, another (free) ferry makes a scenic crossing by winding through the lesser islands to reach Back Bay and Route 172 to St. George. These islands define the western boundary of the Bay of Fundy, while those that are located just a little farther from the coast—Grand Manan, The Wolves, and others—are called The Fundy Isles.

There are three border crossings between Calais, Maine, and St. Stephen, New Brunswick. If you are headed north on US Route 1, the first, or most eastern one, is the bridge that links the two downtown districts. The third or most western crossing that connects directly to New Brunswick is Autoroute 1 (a four-lane divided highway), and is best if you are arriving via US Route 9 and south on US Route 1. My personal choice is the first one through downtown St. Stephen because it's usually the quickest customs checkpoint. New Brunswick Route 3 leads to the beginning of Route 170 and Exit 9 of Route 1. The choice to take Autoroute 1, or the local highway Route 170, is a personal one, as both go around the head of Passamaquoddy Bay, both go to Route 127, and the mileage is the same either way. Take Route 127 to St. Andrews.

The tiny city of St. Andrews (pop. 1,798) can honestly lay claim to being the prettiest one to be found on the Fundy Coast and possibly even in the entire province. It's also the oldest seaside-resort town in Canada. There's a blockhouse at one end of Water Street that was built during the War of 1812 and a large campground on the other end at Indian Point. The

National Historic District is composed of street after street of beautiful homes and the Kingsbrae Gardens are gorgeous. Katy's Cove has a beach; Brandy Cove has the Huntsman Marine Science Centre and Aquarium. Minsters Island is accessible during low tide via a tidal road that crosses the ocean floor. This island was where Sir William Van Horne, the builder of the Canadian Pacific Railway, constructed his 50-room summer cottage from local sandstone as well as other outbuildings and a unique tidal swimming pool.

Restaurants, cafes, and unique boutiques line Water Street. Several tour operators offering whale-watching excursions are located on the Market Wharf. There are B&Bs, historic inns, and even a campground within a 15-minute walk of downtown. The Fairmont Algonquin is an elegant resort inn that is biker-friendly and becomes the headquarters for the annual Atlanticade motorcycle rally in June. In other words, this is a place that likes motorcyclists and offers an opportunity to spend a night and begin touring the Fundy Coast in the morning.

The Route from St. Andrews to Saint John

0 km (0 mi) Depart St. Andrews continuing on Route 127.

13 km (8.3 mi) Turn right on Exit 39, Route 1.

30 km (18.9 mi) On your right CR 770 leads to St. George and the Deer Island Ferry.

38 km (23.6 mi) On your right CR 176 at Pennfield Center leads to the ferry to Grand Manan Island.

58 km (36.5 mi) Turn right onto CR 795. (Missed it? Take CR 780 at 60 km, 37.9 mi)

60 km (37.5 mi) Turn right onto Lepreau Falls Rd. (Missed it? Continue to the intersection of 795 and 790 and turn right on CR 790 at 63 km/39.6 mi)

71 km (44.5 mi) Enter Dipper Harbour.

81 km (51 mi) Enter Chance Harbour.

86 km (54 mi) Continue as CR 790 merges with CR 795.

91 km (57 mi) Turn right (east) on Route 1.

105 km (65.8 mi) Take Exit 112 onto Route 100.

109 km (68.2 mi) The ramp for Route 7 north is on your left.

114 km (71.6 mi) Continue on Route 100 at Lancaster St. in West Saint John. (Follow Lancaster St. to reach the ferry dock to Nova Scotia.)

115 km (72 mi) Reversing Rapids (under the bridge on Route 100).

118 km (73.9 mi) Arrive in downtown Saint John, Union Street at Market Square.

The Reversing Rapids on the St. John River flow down to the ocean during low tide. However as the Fundy tides rise above the level of the river the rapids reverse and flow upstream.

The Fundy Coastal Drive is well-marked by blue-and-white signs with a lighthouse icon. Route 127 loops around the peninsula through St. Andrews and joins Route 1 at Exit 39. As previously mentioned, Route 172 through St. George goes to Deer Isle and Route 176 to Blacks Harbour for the ferry to Grand Manan Island. The Fundy Coastal Drive detours away from Route 1 in Lepreau to follow Route 790 through Dipper Harbour and Chance Harbour.

The exceptionally high tides on the Bay of Fundy require creative docking solutions. In Dipper Harbour the lobster sheds are built on floating rafts and the lobster pounds (where the lobster catch is stored) float. In Chance Harbour the concrete quay is flanked by docks and staircases that rise and fall with the tide. The best photo opportunities are at low tide.

SAINT JOHN

Saint John (metro pop. 122,389) is a transportation bottleneck and you have only three options: the fast and easy Route 1 expressway, the commercial main drag of Route 100, or taking the cable ferries on Kings County peninsula (see sidebar *Cable Ferry Alternate Route* at the end of Trip 8).

Commercial stores like Canadian Tire and the other chains can be found along Fairville Blvd./Route 100 (Take Exit 119 off Route 1) and Eldridge's Harley-Davidson/Honda at Exit 117—westbound only (1230 Fairville Blvd., 506-635-8707). The famous reversing falls—the correct name is Reversing Rapids—are west of downtown on Route 100 (Reversing Rapids Visitor Information Centre, 506-658-2937). The dock for the Princess of Acadia ferry to Digby, Nova Scotia, is in Saint John West (Route 1, Exit 120 or Lancaster Avenue just west of the Reversing Rapids on Route 100, 877-762-7245, www.bayferries.com) and is well-marked by signs. En route to the ferry you can easily find the Carleton Martello Tower (454 Whipple St., 888-773-888, www.pc.gc.ca/carletonmartellotower) that was built during the War of 1812, and which is now a National Historic Site. The Rockwood Park Campground is located on the northeastern edge of the city (Route 1, Exit 125) where tent sites are available.

Canada Day is July first, and one of the best places to celebrate is in the capital of New Brunswick.

The New Brunswick Museum

The New Brunswick Museum is located in the heart of Saint John at Market Square Wharf (506-643-2300, www.nbm-mnb.ca). It is the centerpiece of the convention center-shopping mall that includes the

hippest restaurants in town. Entrance to the museum is through a gift shop that appears to be an upscale boutique. Beyond the gift shop can be found the crème-de-la-crème of the province's diverse collections, including one of the most extensive geology and paleontology collections in Canada (www.nbm-mnb.ca/ stonehammer). Some exhibits are hands-on; some are hands-off, but all are of the highest quality. There's the study and workshop of William Turnbull, one of the pioneers of modern aviation, and so much shipbuilding history that it can only be exceeded by an active yard where wooden ships are still built. The Hall of Whales is a superlative presentation of cetaceans. The Ages of Earth exhibit is the finest educational presentation of the geologic time I've ever seen. This is *not* a run-of-the-mill provincial museum. If you are interested in geology or paleontology, ask about the Stone Hammer project and the walks around Saint John. ∎

Downtown is centered at the showcase Market Square. Exit 122 from Route 1, Route 100/Station Street, Union Street, and Patrick-Water Street all converge here. Obviously there are many lodging options in this city, but the Hilton Saint John (506-693-8484, www.hilton.com) sits on the North Market Wharf and is the most conveniently located hotel for all downtown activities. The restaurants along the wharf are slightly more expensive than those on Prince William, but they offer variety and expansive outdoor patios. The New Brunswick Museum is located at Market Square and Barbour's General Store Museum is literally across the street (506-632-6813, www.tourismsaintjohn.ca) at St. Andrews Park. The general store is quaint and authentic even though this small museum appears to

Chainsaw sculpture is ubiquitous in this province. This one is near Barbour's General Store Museum in downtown Saint John.

be a fabricated tourist attraction because of its location. There are other specialty museums in this city, but you'll want to start with these two.

Saint John is a deep-water port and shipping has always been at the heart of this city. There's the Seaman's Mission on Prince William Street and numerous other buildings that reflect the mercantile sea trade of the past and present. Giant gantry cranes along the wharfs of Saint John West testify that shipping remains a vital part of the local economy while ocean cruise ships moor at Pugsley Wharf along Water Street in the heart of downtown.

In Saint John East you'll discover the Irving oil refinery, source of the refined hydrocarbons that keep your motorcycle rolling, as well as other heavy industries. It's a very busy place. Loch Lomond Road is the direct shot between downtown and Route 111 at the Saint John airport. It begins as Thorne Ave. where it branches right from Route 100/Rothesay Avenue, and then changes to Loch Lomond Road to the Saint John Airport. The route I would recommend from downtown is to take Union Street east and over the Courtenay Bay Causeway to Bayside Drive. A left leads to Loch Lomond Rd. where you would turn right. A right turn on Bayside Drive takes you into the industrial sector with Grandview Avenue passing the oil refinery to

The Fundy Trail Parkway may be short, but it offers more stunning views than most top touring roads will in an entire day of traveling.

eventually become Latimore Lake Road. Turn left (north) on Eldersley Ave. (it's all quite obvious when riding it) to Loch Lomond Rd. where you'll turn right (east).

Whether you take Autoroute 1, Route 100, a Loch Lomon Road variation, or the cable ferry route, you'll end up on Route 111. Just beyond the Saint John Airport, the Fundy Coastal Drive takes another detour onto Route 825, although remaining on Route 111 is the shortest distance to St. Martins. Regardless of the choice you make, there are no accommodations or services along either route. Route 825 goes through the Garnet Settlement and then the road dips at Black River and Gardner Creek to offer ocean vistas and access to the coast. In the end, it returns inland to join Route 111 in Fairfield.

The Route from Saint John to St. Martins

0 km (0 mi) Depart from the entrance to Saint John Airport on Route 111 (Loch Lomond Road).

2 km (1.4 mi) Bear right onto CR 825 (Garnett Settlement Road).

28 km (17.76 mi) Turn right on Route 111.

39 km (24.3 mi) Right turn to St. Martins, sea caves, and the Fundy Trail.

With its deeply indented bay St. Martins (pop. 386) offers gorgeous beaches of orange sand, several attractive B&B inns, and a couple of restaurants. Two covered bridges cross Vaughan Creek near the harbor wharf where, at low tide, lobster boats rest on the sand meters below the dock. This is the only place in the world where two covered bridges and a lighthouse can be photographed together. Graceful arches can be seen in the pierced red sandstone rock near the harbor breakwater. The road twists up and around the corner to present the famous sea caves and a fascinating beach composed of highly polished rounded stones. The Caves Restaurant boldly advertises its "world-famous" chowder and lobster dinner. All of this is merely the gateway, the prelude, to the most scenic road in New Brunswick: the Fundy Trail Parkway (866-386-3987, www.fundytrailparkway.com).

This is the kind of road that touring motorcyclists dream about in the depths of winter. The parkway (for which there is a toll) is still under construction and won't be completed until 2013, but the existing 13 km (8 mi) of road is a rare example of a project where everything is being done right. This is one of the most beautiful and dramatic coastlines in all North America and the people involved in this project take this stewardship very

The Irish River bridges over Vaughan Creek in St. Martins were built in 1935, which is relatively late by U.S. standards, but not in New Brunswick.

seriously while developing public access through this remote area. The pavement is flawless and the road serpentine with grades up to 16 percent. Expect loose stone on the corners. You also need to be aware of hikers, bicyclists, and vehicles that turn in and out of amazing lookout points. This is not, nor ever will be, Deals Gap. This is for second- and third-gear cruising with frequent stops to admire stunning views.

The Route from St. Martins to Moncton

0 km (0 mi) Depart St. Martins, right (north) on Route 111.

37 km (23.3 mi) Enter Sussex Corner. (Take Route 121 into Sussex if you have less than a half tank of fuel.)

51 km (31.8 mi) Right ramp onto Route 1 or straight onto the beginning of Route 114.

(63 km) (39.7 mi) Right exit from Route 1, right on Route 114.

103 km (64.5 mi) Fundy National Park services.

106 km (66.6 mi) Enter Alma.

107 km (67.3 mi) Bear right onto CR 915 (Scenic Road).

121 km (75.61 mi) Cape Enrage Rd. is on your right.

131 km (82.1 mi) Mary's Point Rd. is on your right.

134 km (84.1 mi) Mary's Point Rd. in Harvey is on your right.

138 km (86.1 mi) Turn right onto Route 114 in Riverside-Albert.

153.6 km (96 mi) Entrance to The Rocks Provincial Park (Hopewell Rocks).

166.5 km (104.1 mi) The New Brunswick Railroad Museum in Hillsborough.

187 km (117.1 mi) Vaughan-Harvey Bridge to Moncton is on your right.

191.5 km (119.7 mi) Route 114 crosses the Causeway.

191.8 km (119.9 mi) Route 114 ends at the traffic circle in Moncton.

From here to Sussex Corner Route 111 is a ragged road that runs through rolling hills. It can only be described as rural/residential, with a few farms and numerous homes scattered along the highway. The only convenience store on the road appears to be a holdover from the 1950s. Route 121/Main Street goes into Sussex where all the amenities and services of a small city can be found, while Route 111 continues to Exit 198 of Route 1 and the beginning of Route 114 in Sussex Corner.

Route 114 intersects Route 1 at Exit 211 and then runs southeast through the middle of the 206-sq-km Fundy National Park (506-887-6000). As you might expect, there are more than 100 km (62 mi) of hiking trails through diverse environments, inexpensive camping, and scenic spots. The park contains 25 waterfalls, upland forest, bogs, coastal

At low tide on the Bay of Fundy you see
acres of chocolate-colored mud flats.

At high tide, the water from the Bay
rushes up-river as a tidal bore.

access, and three different camping areas. What you might not expect is a
nine-hole golf course and a heated saltwater pool. Many camping sites are
on a first-come-first-served basis, but a few can be reserved (877-737-3783,
www.pccamping.ca).

Just outside the park in the village of Alma is the junction with County
Route 915. Barn Marsh Island is plainly visible as you proceed along the
highway. It looks benign, but its southern tip has an ominous name—Cape
Enrage. Named by Acadians for the wave action over a treacherous reef that
extends into Chignecto Bay, it's a headland of towering cliffs. From the
highway an access road winds out to this rocky outcrop. Believe the signs
and keep your speed down while watching for loose gravel on the corners!
This site, with the oldest lighthouse on the New Brunswick mainland, was
saved from demolition in 1993 by a group of high school students from
Moncton. The Cape Enrage Interpretive Centre is a non-profit with a volunteer board of directors that has transformed the property. Besides an excellent restaurant in the keeper's cottage, students offer courses in rappelling
and kayaking. The views from the lighthouse are excellent.

There are some pretty vistas along Route 915, although the pavement is
a bit rough. The Mary's Point loop is clearly marked as a right off the county
road. The first couple of kilometers are orange dirt that becomes quite
greasy when it gets wet, but then it continues as asphalt. The Shipyard Park
commemorates the boatbuilding that took place here during the 19th century and the scenery is nothing short of idyllic. This short detour rejoins
Route 915 in Harvey, which is little more than a few houses and a place
name on the map. In turn, the county road ends at Route 114 in the small
village of Riverside Albert.

The posted speed limit is 80 km/hr (50 mph) as Route 114 undulates
along the coast. In Hopewell Hill you will discover the Broadleaf Guest

The Fundy tides have eroded the red sandstone on Hopewell Cape into fantastic shapes that you can walk among at low tide but are completely covered at high tide.

Ranch that offers horseback excursions. There also are a number of B&Bs, a couple of hotels, and at least one camping area. The covered bridge in Waterside-Albert marks where the road used to run. This is a beautiful highway, especially early on a Sunday morning in June. Since it is one of the most popular of the province's scenic roads I suspect that you'll encounter more than one or two RVs during your ride.

Some claim that Hopewell Rocks (877-734-3429, www.thehope-wellrocks.ca) is one of the seven wonders of the natural world. This might not be far off the mark. "The Rocks" are located on Hopewell Cape where the Fundy tides, which normally run 46 feet high at this location, surge into Shepody Bay. The action of moving water has sculpted the conglomerate sandstone into fantastic shapes, sometimes as freestanding towers and sometimes as caves and tunnels. The tumbled rocks in the orange sandstone are all that remains of the Caledonia Highland Mountains, a range more lofty and massive than today's Rocky Mountains that existed some 600 million years ago. It's as if these rocks were held in suspended animation and only now are being released to complete the cycle of erosion. Walking among these natural megaliths at low tide is awe inspiring and humbling. The Interpretive Centre, High Tide Café, and a gift shop are located at the upper site of the park (admission).

Route 114 continues along Shepody Bay, which narrows to become the mouth of the Petitcodiac River. This is the northeastern end of the Bay of Fundy. Due to the action of the tides, the concentration of suspended sediment in the Petitcodiac River is one of the highest found in North America. This has endowed it with the nickname Chocolate River.

Hillsborough (pop. 1,292) is a town with several attractive 19th-century commercial buildings and homes. The New Brunswick Railway Museum (506-734-3195, www.nbrm.ca) is established at the old depot and features a variety of rolling stock, including a restored steam engine built at the Montreal Locomotive Works in 1912. Grand Trunk passenger cars, a Jordan spreader, and 100-ton crane and crane idler car, and other artifacts are part of this collection. I don't know why the CF-101 Voodoo fighter jet is parked behind the post office and adjacent to the museum, but there it is.

Whether you call it Angel Mist Treasures, Johnson's Museum, or Johnson's Junk (506-387-6124) is unimportant. This place alongside the highway in Stoney Creek is a treasure trove stacked high and piled deep with stoves, typewriters, pocket watches, furniture, collectible toys, license plates, telephones, vintage jewelry, and even a couple cars and motorcycles.

The posted speed limit decreases as you enter Riverview (pop. 17,832). Gas stations, restaurants, and lodging are clustered along the highway.

On the opposite side of the Petitcodiac River lies the largest metropolitan center in the province, Moncton (pop. 126,424). From Riverview the Gunninsville Bridge (Vaughan Harvey Blvd.) leads to downtown Moncton. The Causeway/Route 114/Findlay Blvd. joins Route 106, the western end of Main Street, at the traffic circle that also includes the termination of Autoroute 15.

The Petitcodiac River marks one of the farthest extents of the Bay of Fundy. Despite being kilometers inland, Moncton experiences the ebb and flow of the great tides. At low tide the Petitcodiac River is a stream running along the bottom of an orange trough; six hours later it becomes a major river the color of light chocolate. The pressure of the incoming salt water from the bay actually pushes the flow of fresh water upstream in a phenomenon known as a tidal bore. Think of it as the opposite of a dam bursting and you'll get the idea. For many years the closing of the causeway dam diminished the bore to practically nothing since the size of the wave depends upon the volume of the river's flow as much as it does the height of the tide. In the spring of 2010 the causeway gates were opened and the size of the tidal bore has been increasing monthly. The best place to view the incoming bore will be along the boardwalk in downtown Moncton; the most convenient parking is at Bore Park and the information center on Main Street.

Trip 8 Down the Walloostok

Distance: *403 km (251 mi) Allow at least two days, but three is better.*
Terrain: *This is a ride along the banks of the St. John River through small towns, farms, and deciduous forests. It begins in the city of Edmundston, goes through the provincial capital of Fredericton, and ends in the city of Saint John. My chosen roads are not main transportation routes and in many places the pavement is only a few feet from the water.*
Highlights: *There's much to see along this route, beginning with the Lancaster bomber that's parked at the Québec–New Brunswick border and ending at the fantastic New Brunswick Museum in Saint John. The Antique Auto Museum and the blockhouse from the Aroostook War in Edmundston; the world's longest covered bridge and world's largest axe; and the historic British military buildings in downtown Fredericton are recommended stops. Natural wonders include the great gorge in Grand Falls/Grand-Sault and the Reversing Rapids in Saint John.*

From Québec, Edmundston can be reached by following Route 289 south from Route 132 or Autoroute 20. It becomes Route 120 at the New Brunswick border and follows the St. John River to become St. Francis Street in Edmundston. Route 185/Trans-Canada Highway/Autoroute 85 goes south from Rivière-du-Loup and becomes Route 2 upon entering New Brunswick. Route 144 begins at Exit 8 of the "T-Can" (Trans-Canada Highway) in Saint-Jacques and continues through downtown Edmundston. From US 1 in Maine, the primary crossing is at Madawaska to Route 144 in Edmundston, although there is another at the very end of Route 1 in Fort Kent that leads to Route 120. For the sake of brevity, this ride begins in downtown Edmundston on Route 144 at the junction of Route 120 by the Queen Street Bridge that crosses the Madawaska River. Those who wish to get to Fredericton in a hurry should take Trans-Canada Highway/Route 2, although it bypasses the beauty of the river.

From the Québec–New Brunswick border to Edmundston

0 km (0 mi) Begin on Route 2 at the Québec–New Brunswick border.
8.0 km (5.0 mi) Take Exit 8 for the Antique Car Museum.
13 km (7.7 mi) Bear right on Exit 3A to downtown Edmundston.
18 km (11.6 mi) Arrive at the Queen St. Bridge in Edmundston.

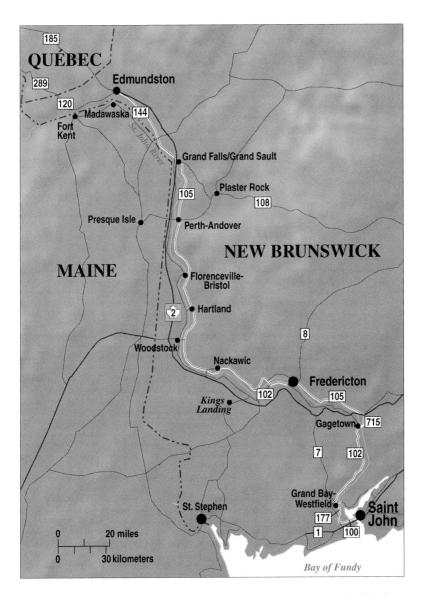

The St. John River is the second longest river system on the North Atlantic Coast and it has been a primary transportation route since the beginning days of the Wulustukieg Nation.

This was the territory of the Maliseet Indians, a branch of the Algonquin whose territory ran from the St. Lawrence River to the Bay of Fundy with the Wulustukieg (Walloostok) River in its center. Acadians settled the upper valley during the late 18th century and Edmundston was founded in 1784.

The Saint John Valley, especially the upper portion, is considered to be the most fertile agricultural land in the province and is checkered with potato, wheat, and clover fields.

The northwestern corner of New Brunswick was the center of the Aroostook War (1838–39)—that now-forgotten conflict between Great Britain and the United States over the boundary between Maine and Canada. The settlers on both sides of the St. John River were tired of the territorial conflict that had begun in 1825 over the vast stands of timber and declared the region to be the Independent Republic of Madawaska. As the situation escalated the Maine Militia built a blockhouse at Fort Kent, Maine, in 1839 and the British erected Fortin du Petit-Sault at Edmundston in 1841. The Webster-Ashburton Treaty of 1842 finally established the international boundary between Maine and New Brunswick. It also defined the northern boundaries of New Hampshire, Michigan, and

Minnesota! To this day, the mayor of Edmundston holds the honorary title of President of the Republic of Madawaska.

Edmundston (pop. 16,643) has the largest percentage Francophones of any city outside the Province of Québec, which isn't saying much since the border is only a few miles away. New Brunswick is a bilingual province with official signs and tourist information posted in both French and English. If you've ever wanted to learn to read French this is the province to visit. In reality some places, like Edmundston, the French language dominates while in others English is the primary language.

Museum of the Automobile (31 Principale St., Saint-Jacques [Exit 8 and turn left], 800-561-0123) is located at the entrance to the botanical gardens (www.jardinbotaniquenb.com) and the beginning of Route 144. This collection of vintage automobiles includes a Diamond "T" fire engine and several early bicycles. It features a 1905 REO (no, not the rock group), a 1910 Detroit Electric three-passenger coupe with a trunk full of 40-cell Edison batteries, and a few classics like 1928 Ford Model "A" and a 1933 Rolls-Royce Phantom. A 1976 Bricklin SV-1, an innovative design and the only automobile ever manufactured in New Brunswick, is also on display.

Edmundston sits on north bank of the St. John River and is split in half by the Madawaska River. The primary streets for navigating this city begin with Route 144/Chemin Canada that leads southeast to downtown, crosses the lower bridge over the Madawaska River and becomes Rue Queen. Chemin Rivière Madawaska begins on the east side of the Madawaska River at Chemin St-Joseph (just south of Route 2, Exit 8 at Route 144) and becomes Rue Victoria. This street intersects Route 2 and Boulevard to effectively end at the upper bridge at Route 120/Rue de l'Eglise. Route 120 follows the St. John River and becomes Rue St-Francis, which ends at Chemin Canada in downtown Edmundston.

The Railroad Interpretation and Tourist Information Centre (1091 Victoria St., 506-739-9644) is located in the Canadian Pacific Railway (CPR) depot on the east side of the Madawaska River just above the pedestrian park. To get there, follow Rue Victoria south or cross the bridge on Route 120/Rue de L'Eglise and take the first right to the end of Rue Victoria. You can also cross the lower bridge onto Route 144/Rue Queen, take the first left onto Ave. St-Jean, climb the hill and take your first left.

Fortin du Petit-Sault (14 Ave. St-Jean, 506-735-7237) is also located on the east side of the river a block south of the CPR depot. The easiest way to find it is to cross the Madawaska River onto Rue Queen and take your first left up the hill on Ave. St-Jean (ironically there is no access from Avenue Fort). The blockhouse is on the left. This one is a reconstruction, while the blockhouse in Fort Kent is a restored original. Both represent the forgotten Aroostook conflict over the vast wealth of timber, the early 19th-century equivalent of today's oil fields.

There seems to be an organized festival every weekend during the summer months. The season kicks off with the annual Jazz and Blues Festival in mid-June, followed by the Festival of Trucks the following weekend. For a complete list of events and information check with the local tourism office (866-737-6766, www.tourismedmundston.com). As you might infer, there is no shortage of lodging or restaurants in this city.

The Mototourism Association Madawaska County (www.umce.ca/clubvtnordouest) has organized rides departing from the NB Liquor store at 174 Rue Victoria on Wednesdays at 6:30 p.m. If you'd like to tour the area with local riders this would be your best opportunity.

The Route from Edmundston to Fredericton

0 km (0 mi) Take Route 144 south from the Queen St. Bridge in downtown Edmundston.

61 km (38.1 mi) The bridge in Grand Falls/Grand-Sault is on your right.

63 km (39.1 mi) Turn right onto Route 105/Undine Road.

101 km (62.9 mi) The bridge in Perth-Andover is on your right.

126 km (78.9 mi) Enter Bath.

134 km (83.6 mi) The Florenceville Bridge is on your right.

151 km (94.1 mi) The Hartland Covered Bridge is on your right.

165 km (102.9 mi) The Grafton Bridge is on your right.

192 km (119.7 mi) Continue straight through the Southampton intersection on Otis Drive.

195 km (122 mi) The world's largest axe is on your right next to the Nackawic Sports Arena.

197 km (122.7 mi) Turn right on Route 105 in Nackawic.

237 km (148 mi) Cross the Mactaquac Dam.

243 km (151.4 mi) Turn left onto Route 102.

261 km (162.7 mi) Arrive in downtown Fredericton.

Route 144 follows the New Brunswick side of the St. John River. On the opposite side is US Route 1 and the city of Madawaska, Maine. On the streets of this U.S. city you'll hear French, Acadian, and English spoken, so in one sense the Republic of Madawaska still exists despite an international boundary. Route 144 runs for 61 km (38 mi) through small towns and farmland along the river until it becomes Route 108 at Route 2/Trans-Canada Highway in Grand Falls/Grande-Sault.

Now tamed by the hydro-electric dam, Chicanekapeag, *The Great Destroyer, is but a trickle of its former self.*

Grand Falls/Grand-Sault (pop. 5,650) is the only town in Canada where the official name is in two languages. A deep gorge that's 70 meters (230 ft) deep is found in the center of town. The gorge actually encircles half the town and when the dam is open a 23-meter waterfall (75 ft) can be admired from the observation platform at the Malabeam Information Centre (admission). The native name for this torrent was Chicanekapeag, the Great Destroyer and during the spring freshet it's obvious why. The Ron Turcotte Bridge in the center of town offers a balcony view of the great gorge for pedestrians. There are several campgrounds in town, including La Rochelle Center that also offers a stairway into the gorge and rides through it on their pontoon boats. There are also numerous B&Bs, hotels, restaurants, and fast-food chains.

South of Grand Falls/Grand-Sault the St. John River no longer marks the international boundary and New Brunswick highways are on both sides

The chef at the Castle Inn in Perth-Andover specializes in British-Indian fusion cooking. Trust me, it works.

of the river. Route 130 begins at the bridge in the center of the city and follows the western side of the St. John Valley to Florenceville-Bristol where it becomes Route 103 to Woodstock and then a succession of other named routes to the city of Saint John. It has scenic sections and from Woodstock to Fredericton is designated as a portion of the scenic River Route. The west side of the river carries far more truck traffic than does Route 105. However, the road surface tends to be better maintained on these commercial highways than the residential Route 105.

Route 144 becomes Route 108 at Route 2/Trans-Canada Highway. Route 108 continues through Plaster Rock and heads to Derby Junction near Miramichi (see Trip 12 Appalachian Range Route), but this trip heads south by turning right on Route 105, only a mile from the bridge on the east side of Grand Falls/Grand-Sault. The turn comes up without warning and begins with a hard right corner as Undine Road. It follows a tributary gorge to reach the eastern bank of the St. John River. From here to Woodstock it's designated as the scenic River Route and is marked by a green sign with stylized, white, spiral question mark.

Route 105 is the old river road and despite segments of rather rough pavement it's a great touring road with very little traffic.

The road sometimes runs hundreds of feet above the river, yet alluvial sand and gravel deposits at these heights show how great this river was during the post-glacial epoch. The pavement is narrow and somewhat rough, but there's very little traffic and great views as it snakes along the banks of the St. John River. This is not a route where you'll make "good time," but one where you'll have a good time. At the Tobique Narrows the road even runs along the top of the hydroelectric dam.

It's 40 kilometers (25 mi) from Grand Falls/Grand-Sault to Perth-Andover (pop. 1,797) and the steel-girdle bridge that crosses the river. The Castle Inn, with its excellent restaurant and accommodations is on the bluff behind the post office. For the next 40 km (25 mi) the road goes through woodland and sometimes it runs beside the river. Fields of potatoes are becoming more frequent, although most farms are on the west side of the valley.

Florenceville-Bristol, (pop. 1,539) claims the title, "French Fry Capital of the World." This is the international headquarters for McCain Foods, Ltd., the largest producer of French fries in the world. If you've ever eaten fries at McDonald's, you've eaten potatoes grown in this valley. The Harvest Café—a far cry from McDonald's—specializes in dishes made from locally grown potatoes. This should come as no surprise since it resides at the New Brunswick Potato Museum (Potato World, 385 Centerville Rd., 506-392-1955, www.potatoworld.ca).

The Shogomoc Historical Railway Site on Route 105 (9189 Main St., 506-392-8226) is located on the north side of the village. There are three restored CPR cars and the first is the location of Fresh, a restaurant that features locally grown produce. You'd never know it, but the original Bristol

In Florenceville only one span of the covered bridge survived a flood and the rest was replaced by steel-girder trusses.

depot is long gone and the identical "sister" Florenceville depot was moved here in 2000 and placed on former depot's foundations.

One span of the Florenceville Bridge is a wooden covered bridge built in 1907. This Howe truss span is 47 meters (154 ft) long. Presumably the other spans were lost in a flood and replaced by the existing steel girdle bridge. Floods are nothing new to those who live along this river—the last great inundation was in 2008. In regard to floods, just outside of town there's a two-thirds-scale model of Noah's Ark that houses the offices and dormitories of Burnham Road Ministries. (South of the bridge turn left onto Burnham Road and continue east beyond the intersection of Route 130.)

The next stop is Hartland (pop. 902) where the world's longest covered bridge spans the St. John River to Somerville. Opened July 4, 1901 as an open-span bridge, it was covered in 1921 and the pedestrian walkway added in 1945. It is 390 m (1,282 ft) long and carries traffic on a daily basis. It's one-lane, so drivers politely take turns, eyeing the "light at the end of the tunnel" to determine if it's their turn to proceed.

The Covered Bridge Potato Chip Company is located in nearby Waterville (35 Alwright Ct., Route 2 Exit 172, 506-375-2447, www.coveredbridgechips.com) and is open for tours and product sampling.

Owned by a fourth-generation potato farmer the chips are gluten and trans-fat free. How many potato chip companies use potatoes grown on their own farm? (Go through the covered bridge and take a left onto Route 103 at the top of the hill. Bear right onto Somerville Road which will merge into the access road to the hospital and Trans-Canada Highway/Route 2. Go beneath Route 2 and turn left onto Alwright Court.)

The River Route and its corresponding marker signs hop the river in Upper Woodstock to continue along a succession of highways—Routes 103, 165, T-Can 2, and 102—to Fredericton. This leaves Route 105 practically deserted except for local residents, and your pace can become downright leisurely. The pavement might be rough, but this is compensated for being able to stop almost anywhere on the road to take photos. In many places only a few meters separate asphalt from the river.

At the four-way intersection in Southampton—don't look for a village, there isn't one—continue straight on Otis Drive instead of turning left to follow the new Route 105. Following the river is more scenic and leads to the Nackawic Arena (152 Otis Drive, Exit 231, www.nackawic.com) on the waterfront and the world's largest axe. Made of seven tons of stainless steel and measuring 20 m (66 ft) high it commemorates the importance of the forest industry to the city and province. Continuing to follow Otis Drive through Nackawic (pop. 977) leads to Route 105.

The world's longest covered bridge is in Hartland, New Brunswick, and it is the town's primary tourist attraction.

Kings Landing

If you wish to visit Kings Landing (506-363-4999, www.kingsland-ing.nb.ca), the number-one attraction in the province, it's best to turn right at the intersection in Southampton, cross the bridge onto Route 102, and proceed towards Fredericton. This living-history settlement is located on Route 102 just off Exit 253 of Trans-Canada High-way/Route 2. Encompassing acres of land along the river this settle-ment of original and reconstructed buildings is based in the mid-19th century. People in historically accurate attire perform daily tasks that were common a century-and-a-half ago.

Route 105 continues to follow the river to Fredericton, but another op-portunity to cross presents itself. The Mactaquac Dam is the largest power project in the province and the reservoir affects the river valley upstream as far as Woodstock. A road across the top of the dam connects Routes 105 and 102. On the right side the road is level with the reservoir and pleasure boaters, on the left side is a canyon-like 37.5-m (123 ft) drop to the rocks far below. Route 102/Woodstock Road is a faster-paced highway that leads di-rectly into the capital city and onto Brunswick Street. Route 105 becomes a ring road around the city of Nashwaaksis and then Westmorland Street crosses the St. John River into the downtown district. One route is not pref-erable to the other, but each is quite different.

Measuring 20 m (66 ft) high this axe in Nackawic is the largest in the world and there's not one mention of Paul Bunyan.

The York-Sunbury Museum, once the officers' quarters of the Fredericton garrison, presents the military history of Fredericton.

FREDERICTON

At the Crowne Plaza (659 Queen St., 866-444-1946, www.crowne-plaza.com) both the general manager and desk manager are former motorcyclists. Obviously this luxury hotel is biker friendly and I was encouraged to park on the sidewalk entrance. The menu developed by the executive chef is such that eating anywhere else is just out of the question, although there are numerous restaurants, cafes, and nightspots within a few blocks of the hotel.

The Lighthouse on the Green is essentially in the back parking lot of the hotel and the museum practically next door. The lighthouse is where tickets can be purchased for local events. The Garrison District, the original core of New Brunswick's capital city, is only a block away while the historic downtown district along Queen and King Street from Westmorland to Regents lies alongside it. One side of the hotel overlooks the 5-km Riverfront Walkway and the St. John River—this is about as central as you can get in the provincial capital.

The York-Sunbury Museum (506-455-6041, www.yorksunbury-museum.com) occupies the former officer's quarters for the garrison. Here you can learn about military history of the city and the surrounding area while outside on Officer's Square many outdoor activities and concerts take place. The museum is also the home to the world-famous Coleman Frog, a 42-lb bullfrog (now stuffed) that some say was real and others claim was a hoax. Artisans occupy the former barracks on Queen Street with workshops on the upper level and galleries on the lower. The New Brunswick College of Craft and Design will be found directly behind the barracks. The Guard House on Carleton Street is open to the public. This stone structure was re-built in 1828 after a fire, and the interior has been restored to that year. For more information about events and hours of operation, log onto www.historicgarrisondistrict.com (888-888-4768).

The Route from Fredericton to Saint John

0 km (0 mi) Depart Fredericton on Route 105/Riverside Dr. from Route 8 in St. Mary's First Nation. (This also is the beginning of Trip 3 Miramichi River Route.)

16 km (10.5 mi) The Burton Bridge crossing the St. John River to Coytown is on your right.

46 km (28.9 mi) Passing under Trans-Canada Highway/Route 2 for sec-ond time turn right (as if going onto Route 2).

48 km (30.4) Turn right onto CR 695.

49 km (30.8 mi) Turn left (you have no choice) onto CR 715.

55 km (34.9 mi) Turn right on Jemseg Ferry Rd. in Lower Jemseg.

59 km (37 mi) Cross the St. John River on the Jemseg ferry.

61 km (38 mi) Turn left on Route 102.

123 km (76.8 mi) Turn left on Route 177.

125 km (78.1 mi) Ferry Rd. to Westfield Ferry is on your left.

135 km (84.5 mi) Bear left onto Route 7 south.

139 km (86.8 mi) Exit 96 onto Route 100 east.

140 km (87.75 mi) Alternate turn onto Route 1.

140 km (87.9 mi) The intersection of Route 100 and Lancaster Ave. (straight on Route 100 to downtown Saint John; turn right on Lancas-ter Ave. for the ferry to Digby, Nova Scotia).

140 km (88 mi) Cross the bridge over the Reversing Rapids (parking for viewing the rapids in on your left).

142 km (88.7 mi) Arrive in downtown Saint John at Union St. and Mar-ket Square.

The River Route continues as Route 105. From Fredericton either Westmorland Street or the Princess Margaret Bridge (Route 8) will place you back on this highway in the city of St. Mary's First Nation. The distance is 5 km (3 mi) for the former, and the latter a mere 200 meters longer. Ten kilometers (6.5 mi) downriver from the Princess Margaret Bridge the

The Gageville ferry on the scenic River Route offers a free, quick, and efficient crossing of the St. John River.

highway returns to the banks of the St. John River with its scenic views. From here to the bridge at Coytown the river is dotted with islands and filled with recreational boaters. There's plenty of traffic due to the military base in Coytown and the road is well maintained. This is where you'll find a few motels, family restaurants, farm stands, and camping. Route 105 will go beneath T-Can Route 2 twice. The second time it does, take the first right (as if going onto Exit 339) and continue straight to the T-junction. Take a right onto Route 695 and then you have no choice but take a left onto Route 715.

The lower St. John River is a maze of islands, sand bars, and wetlands. Route 715 skirts some of these. In the tiny hamlet of Lower Jenseg you should turn onto the well-marked Jemseg Ferry Road. This scenic country road leads to the Gagetown cable ferry (free) for the crossing to Route 102. It's part of River Route so just follow the green-and-white signs with the funny spiral question mark.

Sometimes you'll not see the river for miles and sometimes you'll think you see the river when it's only a channel around an island or a huge setback formed by an extremely long sandbar. This is the largest wetlands area in the Maritimes—a haven for countless waterfowl, where you can expect to see bald eagles, ospreys, great blue herons, and any number of ducks and geese. Stop for a moment and you'll discover a world filled with birdsong in this bucolic landscape. There is very little traffic on this segment of Route 102. The reason lies to the west—Route 7, a highway with a posted speed limit

The vast wetlands along the St John River are a critically important ecological system that is home to eagles, osprey, herons, ducks, and geese.

20 km faster, which is 30 km (18.8 mi) shorter between Fredericton and Saint John.

Route 102 crosses the Nerepis River at Woodmans Point. Looking south from the bridge the Westfield Ferry can be seen making its crossing from Hardings Point to Westfield and the plume of the paper mill above the Reversing Rapids in Saint John might be visible. The quickest way to reach Saint John is to continue to the junction of Route 102 with Route 7 and go south on Route 7/Maritinon Bypass. However, Route 177/Nerepis Road goes south through Grand Bay-Westfield (pop. 4,981) and provides easy access to stores and restaurants before joining Route 7. It also provides access to the Westfield Ferry that crosses to King County peninsula and is an alternate way to reach Saint John, Rothesay, and Quispamsis (see sidebar *Cable Ferry Alternate Route*).

Exit 96 off Route 7 will place you on Route 100, Exit 97 puts you on Route 1. Going east both lead to downtown Saint John. Route 100 not only leads past the commercial plaza and Eldridge's Harley-Davidson/Honda dealership (1230 Fairville Blvd., 506-635-1223, www.eldridges.ca), but it's the easiest way to reach the Bay Ferries dock if you plan to cross to Digby, Nova Scotia (888-249-7245, www.nfl-bay.com). Lancaster Avenue is a major intersection by the Lancaster Mall and turning right will lead to the ferry dock and it passes close to the Carleton Martello Tower (454 Whipple St.,

506-636-4011). The way to both the dock and tower are well marked by signs. Just east of Lancaster Avenue, Route 100 crosses over the famous reversing falls. The proper name is Reversing Rapids (200 Bridge St., 506-658-2855) and this treacherous stretch of white water and whirlpools shifts and flows upstream twice a day when the great Fundy tide overpowers the St. John River. There's parking at the observation center and just above in Wolastoq Park (entrance is on Lancaster Ave).

Cable Ferry Alternate Route

The cable ferries provide an opportunity to bypass the congestion of Saint John and it's a scenic route. From Route 177 in Westfield Beach take a left (east) onto Ferry Road and ride to the dock of the Westfield Ferry. The crossing to Hardings Point is quick, easy, and free. You are now on Kingston Peninsula. Harding Point Road leads to County Route 845 where you take a right (not straight). The narrow road cuts across the tip of the peninsula, Lands End, winding through forested land. Route 845 makes a 90-degree left turn; on the right is Summerville Road, which leads to the Summerville-Saint John Ferry.

The ferry from Summerville to Saint John is the only one in the region that is not guided by a steel cable. It crosses Kennebecasis Bay to Millidgeville at the north end of the city. Take a left onto Kennebecasis Drive and at the T-junction go left on Foster Thurston Drive to Exit 128 of Route 1, or right onto Sandy Point Road along the border of Rockwood Park. From Sandy Point Rd., bear right onto Churchill Blvd. and left onto Somerset St. to go to Exit 123 of Route 1, Route 100, and downtown Saint John.

Instead of turning onto Summerville Road and taking the Summerville ferry to Saint John, follow Route 845, which often runs along the shore of the bay and offers beautiful views. It's a narrow road and rough in spots but the views make up for this. At Reeds Point the Gondola Point Ferry (actually these ferries run in pairs) makes the crossing and you'll be on Route 119/Gondola Point Arterial. It intersects Route 100 and joins the Trans-Canada Highway/Route 1 at Exit 141. The junction of Route 111, the Fundy Coastal Drive, is at Exit 137, which is to the west. Alternately, turning right (west) on Route 100/Hampton Rd. goes into Rothesay where you can fill your gas tank. A left onto Grove Avenue leads to Exit 137.   ■

Trip 9   Miramichi River Route

Distance: *178 km (111 mi) and an afternoon of travel without stops.*
Terrain: *The road is a straight shot across the forested interior inter-spersed with a town here and there. Signs warn about moose and this is not a highway that should be ridden at night due to the abundance of all types of wildlife.*
Highlights: *The beauty of this region is found off the main highway and along the most famous salmon river in eastern North America. The eclectic collection that is the Central New Brunswick Woodsmen's Mu-seum is worth a stop.*

Route 8 seems to lack personality. Its purpose is to go from point A to point B with ease. Still, there are gems along this route from Fredericton to Miramichi if you care to search for them. Such a dismissal will outrage any fly fisherman. Half of all Atlantic salmon caught on fly rods in North Amer-ica were landed from the Miramichi River, which makes it the primary sport-fishing river in Atlantic Canada. However, to savor the beauty of this river requires a slow pace and a willingness to venture up dead-end gravel roads.

From downtown Fredericton there are two ways to cross the St. John River to get onto Route 8. The first is to simply cross the Westmoreland Street bridge and follow Route 105 south to the junction of Route 8. The other is to loop up the hill to the University of New Brunswick at

The Route from Fredericton to Miramichi

0 km (0 mi) Begin on Route 8 at Route 105 in St. Mary's First Nation (Fredericton).

1.6 km (1 mi) Route 8 intersects Route 10.

33 km (21 mi) Enter Nashwaak Bridge.

53 km (33 mi) Enter McGivney.

66 km (41.5 mi) Enter Boiestown.

93 km (58 mi) Enter Doaktown.

124 km (77.4 mi) Enter Blackville.

137 km (85.8 mi) Route 108 crosses Route 8 at Exit 139.

160 km (100 mi) Route 108 ends at Exit 163 of Route 8.

170 km (106 mi) Cross the Miramichi Bridge.

178 km (111 mi) Arrive at the Centennial Bridge in Chatham.

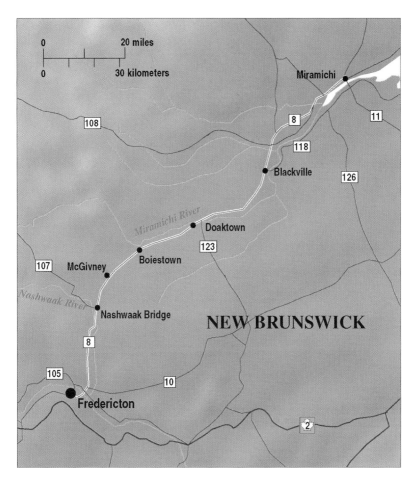

Fredericton and ride across the high Princess Margaret Bridge on Route 8. This will put you on the Barkers Point Bypass, which leads into the Maryville Bypass that's now under construction.

Initially the highway follows the Nashwaak River as it winds away from the capital region and into the vast forest of central New Brunswick. The highway leaves the river at the settlement of Nashwaak Bridge and somewhere near the hamlet of McGivney crosses the "height-of-the-land," that geological dividing line that separates watersheds. Everything on the south and east side of this division flows into the St. John River, while streams on the north drain into the Miramichi. It might not sound like a big deal, but the St. John has been industrialized and the Miramichi River system remains as one of the most important spawning areas for Atlantic salmon in North America.

This is moose country and highway signs have three levels of warnings. The first is the typical yellow-and-black diamond with a moose. The next is a larger sign stating ELEVATED RISK. The third is a big sign with flashing yellow lights. This one you definitely want to pay attention to.

There are only a few tourism highlights on Route 8 and the first is the Central New Brunswick Woodmen's Museum (506-369-7214) in Boiestown (pop. 349). Located at the geographic center of the province this sprawling property has an eclectic private collection of tools, artifacts, machinery, taxidermy, and much more. Across the road is displayed a historic TBM Avenger that was used as a tanker by the New Brunswick Forest Service after serving in the U.S. armed forces during WWII. Collections like these used to be one of the staples of regional tourism in the 1950s, but a half-century later they've all but disappeared in the United States.

Campsites—both official and impromptu—are plentiful, and there are a number of gîtes (B&Bs), but there's only one four-star lodging to be found along the Miramichi River and it's The Ledges (506-365-1820, www.ledgesinn.com) in Doaktown. During my stay the other guests were from the New York Athletic Club, but at other times they might be celebrities or even royalty. Some even fly in on their private jets. The fishing is that famous and the food, that good. Unlike the inn, most fishing cottages are extremely modest and some rather ramshackle, but a small piece of property with river frontage and a good salmon pool can sell for a million dollars.

Since it wasn't real, I initially ignored the mounted salmon on the wall of the Atlantic Salmon Museum (263 Main St., 866-725-6662) in Doaktown (pop. 888). It turns out that this is an exact replica of the largest salmon—72 lbs., 68.5 inches—ever caught with a fly rod in North America. Exact replica because this salmon was released after being landed, carefully weighed and measured. This is one of those quaint educational museums that is engaged in very important work. Their "Adopt A Salmon" campaign evokes an interest—especially in the schools—in learning about the lifecycle of this important fish. In the Miramichi area alone the sport of salmon fishing brings in 20 million dollars a year, so the ecology of these salmon streams is taken very seriously.

The highway crosses to the west side of the river in Doaktown and 19 km (12 mi) farther it makes a cross-country shortcut to Blackville (pop. 931) as the river begins to make giant serpentine curves. Route 8 eventually crosses back over to the eastern bank on the steel-trestle Miramichi Bridge from Newcastle to Chatham Head. Regardless of whether you chose to follow the river on Water Street or continue on Route 8 it's another 6 km (4 mi) to the next bridge.

Fly fishing is considered to be a sport, but the technique of casting is an art.

The Centennial Bridge is a magnificent steel arched bridge spanning the Miramichi River. Downtown Chatham is located on the east bank of the river at this bridge and Newcastle with its commercial strip development is on the west bank. Highway signs are confusing unless you happen to know that both Newscastle and Chatham are names for particular sectors of the incorporated city of Miramichi (pop. 18,129).

On January 1, 2000 the Water Street business district in Chatham became the first historic district in New Brunswick. The Rodd Miramichi Hotel (1809 Water St., 506-773-3111, www.Rodd-Miramichi.com) is located on the river in the heart of this small historic district. Ben's Lunch Room (280 Duke St. at the end of Water St., 506-778-2150) is a nondescript hole-in-the-wall, but this popular fast-food joint has been in operation since 1937 and you'll undoubtedly find a bike or two parked out front. A few buildings away is O'Donaghue's Pub (1696 Water St., 506-778-2150). With live music, good food, and cold beer this Irish pub seems to be the most popular place in town.

The big box stores and major services are located on the west bank of the river along King George Highway between the two bridges. The Centennial Bridge also marks the beginning Trip 10 south along the Acadian Coast to Moncton and Trip 11 north around the Acadian Peninsula to Campbellton.

Trip 10 Acadian Coast

Distance: *223 km (138 mi) A one-day trip.*
Terrain: *This coastal ride varies from cutting through peat bogs in the north and to cruising along sand bars and beaches in the south. Local roads follow the coastline, but keep looping back to Route 134 to cross major rivers.*
Highlights: *The cool refuge of Kouchibouguac National Park and beautiful views of the Gulf of St. Lawrence exemplify this ride. Those fascinated by folk art must put the workshop of the "Woodchuck Carver" on their itinerary, but be warned this personality can talk your ear off and you'll be lucky if your stop only lasts an hour. Wooden bridges—"naked" covered bridges if you will—are a unique aspect of this route.*

The Acadian Coastal Drive goes from Sackville on the Nova Scotia border to Campbellton on the Québec border. This trip generally follows the southern portion of the designated tourist route from Miramichi to Shediac

The Route from Miramichi to Shediac

0 km (0 mi) Depart from the Centennial Bridge in Chatham (Miramichi) on Route 117.
21 km (13 mi) Cross the Black River Bridge.
42 km (26 mi) Cross the Eel River Bridge.
54 km (33.5 mi) Enter Escuminac.
99 km (61.3 mi) Left turn onto Route 134.
107 km (66.7 mi) Enter Saint-Louis-de-Kent.
118 km (74 mi) Enter Richibucto.
123 km (76.8 mi) Cross the Richibucto River in Rexton.
124 km (77.5 mi) Turn left onto CR 505.
151 km (94.8 mi) A hard left turn onto CR 475.
165 km (103.5 mi) Left turn onto Route 134.
172 km (107.5 mi) Left turn onto CR 535 in Saint-Francois-de-Kent.
190 km (119 mi) Left onto Route 134.
191 km (119.8 mi) Left onto CR 530 in Cocagne.
195 km (120.9 mi) Hard left turn to stay on CR 530.
215 km (133.3 mi) Turn left onto Route 134.
221 km (137 mi) Continue straight on Route 133 in Gilberts Corner (Exit 2 of Route 11).
223 km (138.2 mi) End at Shediac (Exit 1 of Route 11).

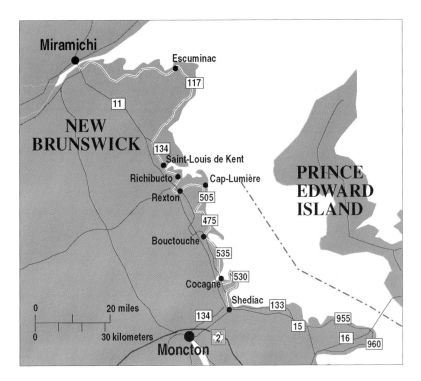

while the next trip covers the much different northern section from Miramichi to Campbellton. This southern portion goes through two very different types of terrain—the lush wetlands and peat bogs of the Kouchibouguac and sandy shoreline from Cap-Lumière to Shediac Bay. Much of this ride is on local roads, although they keep looping back to cross major rivers on Route 134 bridges.

Though the ride ends in Shediac, directions to Cape Tormentine and the Confederation Bridge are included as well as how to connect with Moncton. Both these extensions go through some pretty countryside but carry a considerable amount of traffic.

If you drew a direct line on a map from Miramichi to Richibucto you would be tracing Routes 11 and 134. To the east of that line would appear to be a large peninsula with Miramichi Bay to the north and Kouchibouguac Bay to the south. There's only one highway in this region and this is Route 117, a portion of the Acadian Coastal Drive. It's immediately obvious that anyone in a hurry as well as commercial trucks are going to travel on Route 11, leaving the meandering Route 117 to locals and tourists. In reality, there's not even much to attract the typical tourist, which leaves a delightful touring road to those of us on two wheels.

These poles are supporting a fishing weir, which is another method of catching salmon in the Miramichi River.

Heading east from the Chatham historic district in Miramichi Route 117 follows the mouth of the river to the bay of the same name. The small towns and hamlets along this road have names that include "Bay" or "Baie," "River" or "Rivière," and "Point" or "Pointe," which not only reflects the terrain, but also the mixed heritage of the area. There are very few places that provide a glimpse of the sea, but Escuminac and Pointe-Sapin are two of them. Between them and beyond are peat bogs, some which are commercially farmed for peat moss. In some places you'll ride past small farms while lush woods shade the pavement in others. Route 117 runs through the Kouchibouguac National Park. There are official campsites and hidden turnoffs—some are even paved—where you have to either cruise along in second gear or be prepared to make U-turns to access them. There's no drama here, just pleasurable cruising.

Route 117 intersects Route 134 on its way to join Route 11. Turning left (south) on Route 134 the first little delight to be discovered is the wooden bridge crossing the Kouchibouguacis River into Saint-Louis-de-Kent (pop. 960). This is what a covered bridge looks like without a protective roof and plank siding. Bridges, especially wooden ones, are a feature of this region. Although such bridges were once common most haven't survived the passage of time like the more noted covered ones. Parc des Forgerons is a pleasant municipal park along the north bank of the river that provides a safe vantage point for photographing the bridge. This town was the home of parish priest Marcel-Francois Richard who, besides his other accomplishments, proposed that Ave Maris Stella be adopted as the Acadian national anthem, that August 15 be designated as National Acadian Day, and also proposed the design for and had the first Acadian flag made in 1884. The huge Acadian flag flown over this town is in commemoration of the latter.

The Acadian Coast Drive intersects Route 11 in Richibucto (pop. 1,290). If you hop onto Route 11 to cross the Richibucto River instead of following Route 134 through Rexton you'll have to take Exit 53 and backtrack on Route 134 to the junction of Route 505. I suggest continuing on Route 134.

From the bridge in Rexton a small village can be seen in isolation on a small island or peninsula. This turns out to be the site of "Le Pays de la Sagouine." a "living theater," similar to an Acadian "living-history" museum, but is actually enactments based on the book "La Sagouine" by Antonine Maillet. Staged in a reconstructed Acadian village with costumed actors the fictional plays have a greater scope than a stage could possibly provide.

This is what a covered bridge looks like without a roof or plank siding.

If you want to carve a traditional figurehead for a sailing ship and don't have a ship on which to place it, what do you do? The Woodchuck Carver solved this problem by turning his shop into a ship.

County Route 505 joins Route 134 on the south bank of the Richibucto River and goes through Jardinville. It leads east to Cap-Lumière and then follows the shore for five kilometers (3 mi) before moving inland. Twenty-seven kilometers from the beginning of CR 505 (17.2 mi) make a hard left turn to continue on CR 475. Though county route signs seem to be absent, the red signs with the white starfish that mark this tourism route make it easy to follow. Beware—the turn comes up quickly. Don't try to make the

It looks like heaps of clutter, but in reality everything in and on this cabinet has been carved from blocks of wood, even the cup of Tim Horton's coffee.

It's not fancy, but the Rendez-vous on the bank of the Shediac River is a popular stop for motorcyclists.

turn if you're going too fast! There's usually gravel on this corner. Instead, make a U-turn and come back.

Searching for CR 475 I made a wrong turn. My map showed a local road, a shortcut, but the farther I rode the wider the expanse of water became to my right and the less optimistic I was about finding a bridge. It turned out to be a dead-end and I pulled into the parking lot of a commercial fish-processing plant. Suspecting that the floating platforms in the bay were for shellfish I wandered over to a pickup truck and asked the grizzled old-timer what they were. He turned out to be an encyclopedia on the commercial farming and production of oysters. I'll never eat another oyster without being reminded of him. Such is one of the rewards of random touring and not following a GPS screen.

County Route 475 is one of the touring gems of the Acadian Coastal Drive. The road follows the shore of Bouctouche Bay with views of a 10-km-long (6.2 mi) spit of sand dunes. There's a pedestrian boardwalk through the dunes with little gazebos and picnic tables along its length. One

The world's largest lobster can be found in Shediac, the "lobster capital of the world."

of the "must-see" stops along this road is the shop of Charles Bernard, the "woodchuck carver." This talented, self-taught, eccentric wood carver, former hardcore biker turned preacher will talk your ear off, but his work will fascinate anyone who appreciates folk art. One example of his work is the bow, stern, and masts that have been added to his workshop to transform it into a fantasy galleon. Why? Because he wanted to carve a ship's figurehead and didn't have an appropriate place for one. How about his carved coffin complete with his effigy on the lid and life story chiseled into the sides? There are theater seats positioned around it so visitors can settle in as he tells his story. The Woodchuck is a true eccentric and there are too few of them in the world.

Returning to Route 134 in Bouctouche (pop. 2,383), you cross two bridges and make a left turn onto Route 535. This road loops around Dixon Point and along the southern coast of the Bouctouche Bay and along the Northumberland Strait. There are some great views along CR 535 and, like all the others it eventually comes back to Route 134 to cross a major river, this time the Cocagne.

After crossing the bridge, either the first left on Chemin Lovers Lane or the second will put you onto CR 530. This county route loops around Cap-des-Caissie and offers more views of the strait while traveling through small farms, residential homes, and summer cottages. It's easy to miss most of CR 530 because Grande-Digue Road cuts across the loop and appears to be the primary road. This road is only 1.5 km long, but cuts 18 km from the Cap-des-Caissie loop.

Yes, CR 530 returns to Route 134. Directly across from this intersection is the Rendez-vous. It's typical fast food, but with a choice of outside patio or screened dining area it certainly is convenient. There's even a camping area and a laundromat! You now cross the Shediac River. Route 11 still runs parallel to Route 134 and most traffic is local until reaching Route 133. Shediac (pop. 5,497) is a major tourist destination so there are plenty of services, lodging, restaurants, and drivers trying to figure out where they are going.

Shediac claims the title of "Lobster Capital of the World" and its biggest tourist attraction is what I've come to see. The lobster sculpture in Rotary Park on the west side of the town was unveiled in 1990. It had taken Winston Bronnum three years to create the 50-ton crustacean (32 tons for the base). Measuring 10.7 m (135 feet) long, 5 m (16.4 ft) wide, and 4.9 m (16 ft) high, the lobster dwarfs the six-foot fisherman standing by one of its massive claws.

From Shediac Route 133 carries a considerable amount of traffic east and eventually joins Route 15. Except for the services and a photo of the "world's largest lobster" the major highway seems to be the better option for continuing to the Confederation Bridge to Prince Edward Island or Amherst, Nova Scotia. Even CR 950, which runs through farmland and rural residential areas, ends at Route 15.

The quickest way to reach Nova Scotia is to follow Route 15 to Port Elgin and then take Route 16/Trans-Canada Highway east. In Mates Corner, County Route 955 begins at Route 15 and will take you through beautiful farmland back to the Northumberland coast and east to intersect Route 16/Trans-Canada Highway just south of the Confederation Bridge. County Route 960 continues to follow the coast of Cape Tormentine to join Route 16 just east of Port Elgin.

From Shediac, Route 134 and Route 15 both go southwest to the city of Moncton (see Trip 7, Fundy Ride). Both roads are scenic and both go directly to downtown Moncton. Route 15 has a higher speed limit and carries more traffic, but this choice is more about time and your personal riding inclinations than distance or the condition of the pavement.

Trip 11 Acadian Peninsula

Distance: *374 km (234 mi) Allow a full day or a day and a half.*
Terrain: *The Acadian Peninsula is barely above sea level in contrast to the rugged Fundy coast with its dramatic elevation changes. A region of coves, islands, and beaches backed by peat moss bogs and scrubby trees, it has a beauty that differs from other parts of the province. The portion along the Chaleur Bay resembles the southern coast of the Gaspé and offers some beautiful panoramic views of the great bay.*
Highlights: *The northern tip of Miscou Island with its expansive peat bogs, beautiful beaches, and the second-oldest lighthouse on the Gulf of St. Lawrence is one of the highlights of this ride. On the peninsula and islands Acadians proudly proclaim their heritage with representations of the tricolor with its single gold star.*

The Route from Miramichi to Campbellton

0 km (0 mi) From the east side of the Centennial Bridge in Chatham (Miramichi) take Route 11 north.

70 km (44.1 mi) Turn right off Exit 192 into Tracadie-Sheila.

80 km (50.4) Turn right back onto Route 11.

91 km (56.9) Turn right onto CR 355/Chemin Pallot.

96 km (60 mi) Turn right on Route 113.

118 km (74.1 mi) Turn left CR 313 in Lamèque.

136 km (85 mi) Turn left on Route 113 in Little Shippagan.

139 km (87 mi) Enter Miscou Harbour.

153 km (95.6 mi) Arrive at the Miscou Lighthouse and end of Route 113. Turn around.

179 km (112 mi) Turn left onto CR 310.

190 km (118.6 mi) Turn right onto CR 305.

200 km (125 mi) Turn left onto Route 113.

220 km (137.8 mi) Turn right onto CR 345.

227 km (142.1 mi) Turn right onto CR 335/Chemin St-Siméon.

241 km (150.5 mi) Turn left on Route 145 in Le Bouthill.

243 km (152.2 mi) Continue straight onto Route 11.

283 km (177.1 mi) Turn right onto Cape Road in Janeville.

290 km (181.3 mi) Enter Salmon Beach.

299 km (186.9 mi) Bear right on Route 134 in East Bathurst.

300 km (187.4 mi) Enter West Bathurst.

353 km (221 mi) Enter Dalhousie.

374 km (234 mi) Arrive in downtown Campbellton.

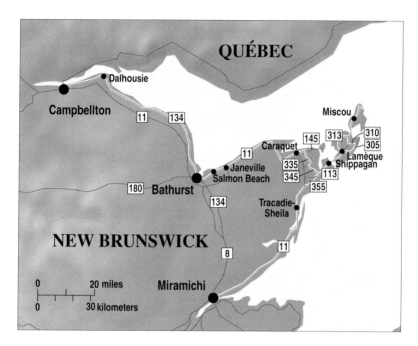

During the Seven Years War with France (1755–1763) the British deported more than 14,000 Acadians from Nova Scotia in what is now called Le Grand Dérangement, The Great Expulsion, or The Great Upheaval. Homes were burned, lands confiscated, and families split up. Approximately one-third of them died but many escaped from Nova Scotia and "hid" along the southern shore of Chaleur Bay. When the Treaty of Paris was signed in 1763 and Acadians were allowed to settle on land not occupied by the British subjects many of them chose the peninsula and islands that divide Chaleur Bay from the Gulf of St. Lawrence. This region is now known as the Acadian Peninsula.

The nature of both the coast and the small villages north of Miramichi Bay differ from those to the south. While the Acadian Coast runs from Dalhousie to Shediac, north of Miramichi the culture is primarily Francophone, while south of that city it becomes a mixture of Francophone and Anglophones.

The most direct route from Miramichi to Chaleur Bay is Route 8, and then Route 11 to Campbellton, which is the choice of those trying to make time and the bulk of the truck traffic. This trip will follow the coast on roads that have many more scenic qualities and much less traffic.

Officially New Brunswick is bilingual, but this region is 98 percent Francophone (French speaking) and a high proportion of this is

Acadian-French, which is quite different from Québec French. The good news is that road signs are in both French and English.

Route 11 between Miramichi and Tracadie-Sheila is a nondescript highway, but the smell of the sea is unmistakable. The shoreline is out of sight, but it's not far away and can be reached by various one-way roads that lead east from the highway. There are small towns, hamlets, and summer settlements strung

The three flags flown in this region are the gold-and-red provincial, the red-and-white Canadian, and the tri-color Stella Maris with the gold star—the Acadian flag.

along the northern side of Miramichi Bay and the Gulf of St. Lawrence. The road is relatively straight and there's not a trace of shade. In places large highway signs warn of "white-out" conditions due to high winds. Wind could become a factor that affects your ride, but I doubt you have to worry about snow during motorcycle touring season.

I can't tell the difference between an osprey nest and the trashy heap of sticks that great blue herons call home unless I spy one of the residents. In some places these big nests have been constructed on every second or third pair of electrical transmission poles.

It's not necessary to ride through Tracadie-Sheila (pop. 4,474), but temporarily leaving Route 11 provides an opportunity to fill up the gas tank, purchase some snacks, or catch an early lunch, and has psychological benefits that should not be ignored.

You're looking for Route 113, and though it branches directly off Route 11, a more interesting approach is to leave the main highway at County Route (CR) 355 (Chemin Pallot) and ride it along the coast and joining Route 113 at Inkerman. Route 113 is the primary road on the peninsula and continues across Lamèque and Miscou Islands to end at the Miscou Lighthouse. To get a real sense of Acadia, make looping detours on Routes 313, 310, and 305.

You will see the color combination of the Acadian flag, red, white, and blue with a yellow star (Stella Maris), presented in numerous ways and all announce that the residents of that property are Acadian. Telephone poles are painted in this motif, as are driveway markers and lawn ornaments. Another tradition, one rarely seen in other North American cultures, is the prominent posting of the family name on plaques or signs in front yards.

The peninsula ends at Shippagan (pop. 2,754), which proudly proclaims its Acadian heritage. As you might surmise, lobster and herring fishing are one of the primary occupations in the area, but an unexpected one is peat farming. Orange dust clouds mark the "fields" being harvested and signs along the highway warn about the danger of throwing cigarette butts out the window as peat bogs can burn underground and are almost impossible to extinguish. Huge vacuum-cleaner-like tractors work in tandem harvesting a product that is used in potted plants, wastewater purification, spa treatments, mushroom cultivation, and so much more. While almost half of Miscou Island is peat bog, none is harvested here. Most of the commercial operations are on Lamèque Island and around Shippagan.

The causeway across the "gut" puts you on Lamèque Island, one of the "Acadian Islands." County Route 313 loops around the western side of the island through a series of hamlets with the prefix "Petite," to return to Route 113 in Little Shippagan. On your return loop around the east side by way of CR 310 and 305 to rejoin the main highway in Haute-Lamèque. This island is more Acadian than any other place in Atlantic Canada and while these alternate routes are not the shortest way you should take advantage of the opportunity: you never know when you might pass this way again.

Basque, Norman, and Breton fishermen arrived in the 15th century and made Miscou a base of operations. Jacques Cartier arrived in 1534 and the

This miniature replica of a Mississippi paddlewheeler in Tracadie-Sheila might seem out of place until you realize that Louisiana Cajuns are of Acadian descent.

"Restigouche Sam," a 28-foot-tall (8.5 m), stainless-steel sculpture holds the title of "the world's largest salmon."

published account of his voyage gave him credit for "discovering" these islands. The bridge from Little Shippagan to Miscou Harbour replaced the cable ferry in 1996. The highway continues the length of the island, crossing the Miscou Plains, an extensive peat bog that is now a protected nature site, and winding out to the point on the north end where Chaleur Bay meets the Gulf of St. Lawrence. Here the attractions are beautiful sand beaches, bird watching, and the lighthouse. It's the prettiest stretch of road in the region offering great vistas and photo opportunities.

The Miscou Lighthouse is at the end of a very narrow winding Route 113. The heavy steel guide cables attached to the lighthouse tower imply that winds can become rather fierce on this island. When touring the interior of the lighthouse its massive post-and-beam construction looks strong enough to withstand a hurricane, so the anchoring cables make me wonder just how strong the wind becomes. Built in 1856 and originally named

Birch Point Light, it's been moved a couple of times, so obviously the cables are effective.

Retracing your path to Inkerman Ferry, take a right on CR 345, which leads directly to Route 11. Taking a right (north) on CR 335/Chemin St-Siméon will bring you to Le Bouthillier on Chaleur Bay where you will turn left on Route 145.

The town of Caraquet (pop. 4,156) is the unofficial capital of Acadia. From here Route 11 follows the coastline west along Chaleur Bay. The similarities to the coastline on the other side of the bay in the Gaspé region should come as no surprise, but the transition from the peat bogs and beaches of the Acadian Peninsula to that of farmland and red sandstone cliffs makes it surprising.

At Janeville the main highway goes inland, but the most scenic route is Cape Road that continues along the coast past Salmon Beach to East Bathurst. Streets in Bathurst (pop. 12,714) feel like a maze due to its topography as a peninsula formed by two rivers entering Bathurst Bay, the most southern point on Chaleur Bay. Although my hotel is just off Route 134, I find it only because it's located next to the hospital.

Route 11 is the quickest highway to Campbellton, but it's rather boring. Route 134 follows the coast through a series of small towns to loop through Dalhousie (pop. 3,676). This is the northernmost point on Chaleur Bay at the mouth of the Restigouche River. For decades the economy of the town was built around a major paper mill, but the only remaining heavy industry is the oil-fired electrical generating plant. I guess this explains why it looks like a cross between an old mill town and a commercial fishing port. The Inch Arran Park and Campground (506-684-7363) in Dalhousie is situated on the beach, has an adjacent laundry, and a convenience store, but it's best known for what it doesn't have. For some inexplicable reason this location doesn't have flies or mosquitoes.

West of Dalhousie Junction Route 134 is never far from Route 11 but since it's only a few minutes to downtown Campbellton (pop. 7,384) speed doesn't matter. The core of the city and the bridge to Gaspé are more easily reached by continuing on Route 134, which will become Water Street. Instead of turning left onto Water Street and slogging along this main street, consider continuing straight onto the new Salmon Boulevard for scenic views of the trans-provincial/J.C. Van Horne Bridge, the "world's largest salmon," and the Restigouche River. It loops back to Water Street for access to the bridge or to continue west on Route 134 to Tide Head (Trip 12 The Appalachian Range Route).

Trip 12 Appalachian Range Route

Distance: *374 km (233.5 mi) Allow one day.*

Terrain: *Highland terrain over the Appalachian Mountains and through extensive forests along the Mamozekel River and central New Brunswick.*

Highlights: *The woodlands of central New Brunswick and the highlands of the eastern Appalachian Mountain Range. Lots of miles without intersections or much traffic.*

Your choices are limited if you want to cross New Brunswick from east to west or take the shortest distance from southern Gaspé to Maine. Despite the best face put on by the tourism department these are transportation routes, ribbons of asphalt whose sole purpose is to connect point A to point B. Route 17 from Campbellton to Saint-Léonard is fine for all types of motorcycles, but Routes 385, 180, and 108 are best suited for the long suspension of dual-sport machines. However, if your goal is to get away from the bustle of civilization these roads are just what you are seeking.

The city of Campbellton (pop. 7,384) is often referred to as the "Gateway to the Gaspé," but traffic crosses the Transprovincial Bridge in both directions. Despite its strategic location there are only two primary New Brunswick highways leading to Campbellton: Route 17 and Route 11.

The Route from Campbellton to Miramichi

0 km (0 mi) Beginning at the trans-provincial/J.C. Van Horne Bridge in Campbellton take Route 134 to Tide Head.

8 km (4.9 mi) Turn left on Route 11 in Tide Head.

12 km (7.8 mi) Bear right onto Route 17.

69 km (43.3 mi) Enter Kedgwick.

95 km (59.3 mi) Turn left onto Route 180 in Saint-Quentin, (last gas station).

124 km (77.5 mi) Turn right onto CR 385.

134 km (83.8 mi) The entrance to Mt. Carleton Provincial Park is on your left.

210 km (131.4 mi) Enter Plaster Rock.

215 km (134.2 mi) Turn left onto Route 108 in Plaster Rock (last gas station).

348 km (217.8 mi) Route 108 crosses Route 8 at Exit 139 in Renous.

374 km (233.5 mi) Route 108 ends at Exit 163 of Route 8 in Miramichi.

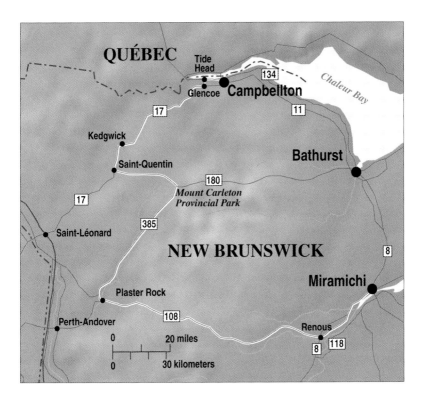

The Restigouche River is famous for Atlantic salmon fishing and therefore the salmon has an iconic status here. Murals on downtown buildings, a chainsaw sculpture of a fisherman with a fish on the line, and a beautiful metal sculpture of a salmon leaping from a pool are almost de rigor. This river valley is also famous for its fossils of fish that lived 400 million years ago, but this seems to be a dusty secret known only to paleontologists and rock collectors.

Tourists seem to quickly pass through this small city at just below the posted speed limit, which is too bad. Regardless of where you are headed this is an ideal place to stock up on provisions and prepare for the next day's adventures. There are a number of inexpensive hotels in the area, but the Howard Johnson Hotel (506-753-6386, hjmm@nb.aibn.com) is conveniently located at the foot of the bridge and attached to a small shopping mall.

Route 17 joins Route 11 in Glencoe, but whether you ride from downtown Campbellton to Tide Head on Route 134 or get onto Route 11 just outside of the city makes only a half-mile difference.

Tide Head (pop. 1,075) is so named because the ocean tides in Chaleur

The Restigouche River is famous for salmon fishing, as this chainsaw sculpture testifies. Behind it, the steel-truss bridge across the Restigouche River is known as the "Gateway to the Gaspé." The official name is the J. C. Van Horne Bridge, but everyone refers to it as the "Transprovincial."

Bay extend up the Restigouche River as far as Morrissey Rock. It's also known as the "Fiddlehead Capital of the World," which suggests that these steep mountainsides and wetlands have an abundance of ostrich ferns.

Route 17 climbs into the Appalachian Mountains and fortunately there are so many passing lanes that you don't have to worry about being stuck behind trucks or RV trailers. Views of endless mountain ridges don't provide a sense of elevation, but you climb 1,000 feet (305 m) above the Restigouche Valley.

The town of Saint-Quentin (pop. 2,250) is the "Maple Capital of Atlantic Canada" but it's also your last chance to fill the gas tank for more than 100 km (60 mi). Take Route 180, which cuts across northern New Brunswick from Saint-Quentin to Bathurst. "Can't see the forest for the trees" is an expression that doesn't apply in this region. Sectional clear cutting leaves a patchwork landscape that ranges from denuded to second-growth forests of different uniform heights. It provides variety, and, in places, expansive views.

Turn south onto Route 385 and in a few hundred yards the road turns to gravel. Actually this is not such a bad thing as this dirt road is in better shape than the kilometers of asphalt that have preceded it. It leads to the Mount Carleton Provincial Park, the highest point in Atlantic Canada. The park offers camping sites and hiking trails.

This sign in Saint-Quentin warns that there is no gas for 138 km. In fact, there aren't any services and this includes cell phone reception.

At the entrance to the park Route 385 changes from gravel to pavement, but don't get your hopes up. Despite the best efforts of the tourism department, this highway is nothing more than an access road for logging trucks. Scenic views are scarce and maintaining any speed requires a constant eye on the pavement. When you reach the Tobique River there are a few scattered hamlets, but you won't encounter any services until reaching Plaster Rock.

Plaster Rock (pop. 1,150) was named after the gypsum that was mined here, but it is best known for hosting the annual World Pond Hockey Championships. Located at the intersection of Route 108, the "World's Largest Fiddleheads" turns out to be a badly done chainsaw carving painted to look like sprouting ostrich ferns—it must be a local in-joke. Fill the gas tank and have something to eat. Heading east on Route 108 will take you through 137 km (85 mi) of uninhabited forest until reaching Route 8 in Renous.

The road runs through the heart of the forest and is a freeway for logging trucks. Regardless of how well maintained such roads might be, you can always expect parallel wheel ruts and broken pavement simply because logging trucks don't have weight limits. Log trucks blow by in pairs like comets with tails of dust and bark in their wake. This is where a full-face helmet becomes a blessing.

It comes without warning—construction. The asphalt is gone and the surface has been taken down to subsurface gravel. It's 50 kilometers back to Plaster Rock and an alternative route will add hundreds more to today's journey. The freshly graded dirt is soft and deep, but I'm fine on the Street Glide Trike borrowed from Deeley Harley-Davidson. I follow the weaving tracks of the two riders ahead of me on their dual-sport machines, thankful that I'm not on my Ducati or BMW. This would be a nightmare during a day of heavy rain. I should have checked with the highway department about road work (511 or 800-561-4053, www1.gnb.ca/cnb/transportation/index-e.asp) when planning my journey.

There are several gravel roads crisscrossing the Mount Carleton Provincial Park and while some are nice and wide, others leave little room for two vehicles to pass each other.

Route 108 intersects Route 8 at Exit 139 in Renous. From here it goes through a mix of woods and farmland along the Miramichi River while Route 8 cuts through mostly forested land. Route 8 is certainly the quickest highway with its higher speed limit, but it's only a kilometer shorter than Route 108.

Prince Edward Island

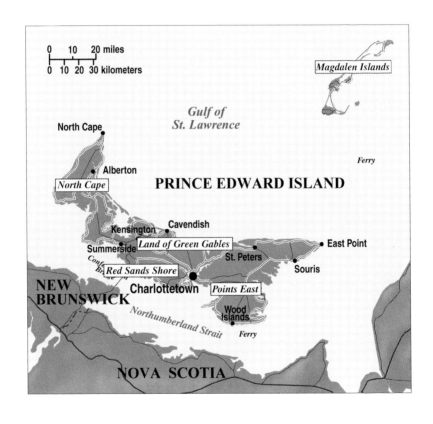

0 10 20 miles
0 10 20 30 kilometers

Magdalen Islands

Gulf of
St. Lawrence

Ferry

North Cape

Alberton

North Cape

PRINCE EDWARD ISLAND

Cavendish

Kensington

Land of Green Gables

East Point

Summerside

St. Peters

Souris

NEW
BRUNSWICK

Red Sands Shore

Charlottetown

Points East

Northumberland Strait

Wood
Islands

Ferry

NOVA SCOTIA

Prince Edward Island

By Ken Aiken and Rannie Gillis

The bridge stretches into the distance, a long grayish thread of concrete pillared across deep blue water to the island beyond. Long bridges, as tangible transitions from one land to another, define places. This is the Confederation Bridge, the longest bridge in Canada, and on the other side of the Northumberland Strait is Prince Edward Island.

The Mi'kmaq called the island *Abegweit* (Land Cradled on the Waves) but when Jacques Cartier "discovered" it in 1534, it was renamed Île Saint-Jean. The British took title in 1763 and changed it to Saint John's

Opened May 31, 1997, the Confederation Bridge is a 12.9 km (8 mi) long ribbon of concrete suspended 131 feet above the Northumberland Strait. Tolls are paid when leaving the island.

On Prince Edward Island, small farms are the norm and Victorian homes abound. Even the modern houses look like those found in villages throughout New England.

Island before finally deciding to rename it in honor of Queen Victoria's father, Prince Edward Augustus, in 1798. Most people simply refer to it as PEI.

The smallest of Canada's provinces at 5,660 sq km (2,184 sq mi) it ranks as the 104th-largest island in the world, and is just slightly larger than Rhode Island, the smallest American state. Its three counties—Prince, Queen, and King—roughly correspond to the three main geographic regions: North Cape, Central PEI, and Points East. Driving distance from one end to the other (North Cape to East Point) is a mere 273 km (170 mi) and can be ridden in less than four hours. On the other hand, you could spend a week, exploring all that the island has to offer, and enjoying it's many hidden charms, and the famous "laid-back" hospitality of its people.

For the most part the island is relatively flat, with small rolling hills mainly in the central region. It is indeed very pastoral, with beautiful farmland, miles and miles of sandy beaches, and some of the warmest water north of the Carolinas. Although there are woodlands, there is no wilderness on Prince Edward Island. No part of the island is more than 16 km (10 mi) from the sea.

Prince Edward Island has been described as "like Vermont, but with an ocean" and in many ways this seems apropos. There exists an honest neighborliness where Islanders are always helpful and there's time for spontaneous conversation with strangers. Stopping alongside the road to take a picture always requires giving the okay or thumbs up signal to passing motorists who slow down to make sure everything is fine. Doors to places like the fire department in Charlottetown are thrown wide open and any passersby can wander in and admire the old La France engine and memorabilia posted on the walls. There's a certain honest *naïveté* that exists throughout the island and it's a refreshing change from the pervasive urbanization found in so many places.

The province has only about 140,000 residents and the biggest city, the provincial capital of Charlottetown, has a population of just 32,000. The land is mostly agricultural with the famous Prince Edward Island potato topping the list of exports. In the bays along the coast the internationally renowned blue mussel and Malpeque oysters are farmed, while a full 80 percent of the lobster catch goes to market in the United States. Islanders are tied to the land and seduced by the sea, while visitors are enticed by both.

Motorcycle access to the province is either via the Confederation Bridge between Cape Jourimain, New Brunswick and Borden-Carleton, Prince Edward Island, the Northumberland Ferry sailing from Caribou, Nova Scotia or a little-known route by way of the Magdalen Islands. There's no charge for traveling to Prince Edward Island on either the Northumberland Ferry or the bridge, but there are fees for leaving the province (hum a few bars of "Hotel California" by the Eagles when contemplating this). The cost of the return trip (in 2009) to Nova Scotia by ferry is $79 compared to the $17 toll for crossing the bridge. For those who are fascinated by great bridges the 12.9-km (8 mi) ribbon of

The Rodd Charlottetown is a grand railway hotel built in 1927 in Charlottetown's historic downtown. Everything is within easy walking distance.

concrete that is elevated 40 m (131 ft) above the Northumberland Strait becomes a "must ride." The Trans-Canada Highway/Route 1 connects the Confederation Bridge to the ferry terminal at Wood Islands via Charlottetown. This is the only federal highway on the island and it's far more scenic than one might expect. There are no four-lane roads in the province.

Private campgrounds are scattered across the island, but those provincial parks that have campsites generally offer the most interesting settings. Lodging ranges from quaint roadside cottages to exquisite B&B inns and even a lighthouse. An extensive list of accommodations can be found on the Prince Edward Island tourism website (www.tourismpei.com). For those riders who want a hotel centrally located in Charlottetown, the Rodd Charlottetown on Kent Street (902-894-7371, www.roddcharlottetown.com) was originally built as one of the Canadian National Railway Hotels.

CHARLOTTETOWN

Charlottetown is the capital of Prince Edward Island and has the distinction of having held the first meeting that led to the confederation of the separate British provinces into the nation of Canada. The city occupies the peninsula at the confluence of the North and Hillsborough Rivers at the head of Hillsborough Bay with its historic center situated at the tip of the peninsula. The Trans-Canada Highway leads directly to Confederation Hall in the downtown area and the primary Provincial Highway Route 2, merges with it as University Avenue.

The downtown area is best explored on foot and this is one of my reasons for choosing the grand old railway hotel built in 1927 as my base. University Avenue forms a T-intersection with Grafton Street in front of Province House; Queen Street is one block southwest of University Avenue/Route 1. The Confederation Court Mall (902-894-9505, www.confedcourtmall.com) is bounded by University Avenue, Grafton Street, Queen Street, and Kent Street and is a convenient landmark since just about everyone on the island has been to this mall at one time or another. The Confederation Centre of the Arts (902-628-1864, www.confederationcentre.com) encompasses the next block from Grafton Street to Victoria Row, the block-long pedestrian section of Richmond Street. Another four short blocks downhill leads to Water Street and the restored buildings along the city's waterfront.

Most restaurants are located on the streets bordering the mall, on Victoria Row, and Sydney Street. Most stores and boutiques are along Queen Street. Water Street is a delight for photographers, but the buildings house professional offices. The waterfront is public and is where the annual Canada Day rock & roll bash takes place. Gahan House Pub & Brewery on

Victoria Row is a pedestrian-only, short section of Richmond Street that's touted for its outdoor café dining, where you can enjoy a beer and oysters while people-watching in the heart of historic downtown Charlottetown.

Sydney Street (902-626-2337, www.gahan.ca) is the only microbrewery on the island and they serve great food and stock a variety of Scotch whiskies. Fishbones Oyster Bar & Seafood Grill on Victoria Row (902-628-6569, www.fishbonespei.com) offers famous Malpeque oysters and other island fare. If you like ice cream, COWS (902-892-0247, www.cows.ca) is the place to visit.

The Confederation Court Mall is a touted shopping destination, but the reality is that the best shops are situated along Queen Street. The mall is a good place to catch a quick lunch or shop for essentials. The art center offers the perpetual running of *Anne of Green Gables—The Musical*, the longest running play in Canadian history. It's not listed on any tourism maps, but if you enjoy fine antique vehicles, stop by the fire station at city hall on Kent Street to check out their beautiful 1923 American La France engine.

Trip 13   The Land of Green Gables

Distance: *157 km (98 mi)*

Highlights: *The beaches of Prince Edward Island National Park explored via the Gulf shore Parkway. Green Gables National Park and other Lucy Montgomery sites for fans of children's literature. St. Mary's Church and its perfect acoustics juxtaposed to the Haunted Mansion and its subterranean secrets. Smooth, winding, coastal roads with a roller-coaster return to Charlottetown, all with scenic views.*

Lucy Maud Montgomery, the author of *Anne of Green Gables* and all its sequels, is the provincial heroine. When she published her novel about a young red-haired orphan girl in 1908, she had no idea that over the next 100 years her book would sell more than 50 million copies, and become an internationally acclaimed children's classic.

Based on the author's own childhood experiences on Prince Edward Island, the novel tells the story of an older couple (brother and sister) who

For anything remotely connected to Lucy M. Montgomery or Anne of Green Gables you can find it one of these stores. The boutiques on Queen Street are the place to shop.

offer to adopt a young child, and receive a rambunctious girl, Ann Shirley, instead of the rather sedate boy they had asked for.

Over the years Montgomery's book has been translated into 36 languages, and has been the inspiration for two feature movies, seven television movies, four television series, and a countless number of stage productions and musicals.

Sometimes it seems that everywhere you look there is a Green Gables store, motel, restaurant, or museum. There's no doubt that the most popular tourism region on Prince Edward Island is the Green Gables Shore, but the beautiful beaches and relatively warm waters of the Gulf of St. Lawrence seem to be the primary attraction.

Prince Edward Island National Park encompasses 60 km (37 mi) of shoreline along the province's north coast. Bordering on the Gulf of St. Lawrence, the park was established in 1937, and includes many of the island's best beaches, as well as an 18-hole golf course, and the Green Gables farmhouse that inspired the famous book.

From Charlottetown the most direct ride to the Prince Edward Island National Park is via Route 15, part of the Central Coastal Drive. However,

The Green Gables Loop from Charlottetown

0 km (0 mi) Leave Charlottetown on Route 2 east (Euston St. to Longworth Ave. to St. Peter's Rd.).

14 km (9.0 mi) Turn left onto Route 6.

24 km (15.1 mi) Continue straight on Gulf Shore Parkway.

36 km (22.6 mi) Bear left onto Route 15/Brackley Point Rd.

39 km (24.3 mi) Right, Route 6/Portage Rd.

61 km (38.3 mi) Arrive Cavendish, then continue on Route 6.

73 km (45.6 mi) Arrive New London. Turn right on Route 20.

95 km (59.0 mi) Arrive Malpeque. Continue on Route 20.

97 km (60.2 mi) Turn right onto Route 104.

104 km (65.0 mi) Turn right on Route 20.

109 km (68.0 mi) Arrive Kensington. Take Route 2 to Charlottetown.

157 km (98.0 mi) Arrive Charlottetown.

it is more scenic to follow Route 2 East (which actually goes north) for 14 km (9 mi) then turn left on Route 6 through Bedford, Mill Cove, and Grand Tracadie. These aren't villages, merely place names on the map with Grand Tracadie being a large potato field at the junction of Route 220. Approximately 24 km (15 mi) from downtown Charlottetown where Route 6 makes a dogleg corner to become Eastern Road simply continue straight on Gulf Shore Parkway.

The parkway runs along the shore through the national park about 12 km (7.5 mi) to the junction of Route 15 and in many places it is only a few

This is the landscape in which Lucy Maude Montgomery grew up and that became the setting for Anne of Green Gables. *Wild lupines abound and the rolling hills are dotted with small farms along Route 6 west of New London.*

Get an ice cream and go deep-sea fishing at Bob's in North Rustico. Summer is a short tourism season and you need to combine all the attractions you can into a single venue.

meters from the high-tide mark. This is not the quickest road and on those sunny mid-summer weekends when it's choked with family-filled SUVs this detour might not be the best choice, but if you're looking for paved parking adjacent to a magnificent sand beach this is the place to go. Since the parkway becomes a cul-de-sac ending at Robinson Island, turn inland on Route 15/Brackley Point Road and drive the 3 km (1.7 mi) to the junction with Route 6.

The biker-friendly Vacationland RV Park and Family Campground is located in Brackley Beach. Stay on Route 15 for a half-kilometer past its intersection with Route 6, turn left on Britain Shore Road and go to the end of the road. (800-529-0066, www.vacationlandrv.pe.ca) Owned by local rider Tom Nicholls, this is the site of the annual Island Rally on Labour Day.

Traveling west on Route 6 toward Cavendish places you on the well-marked Central Coastal Drive as it skirts the south side of Rustico Bay. The long lines of white buoys seen in the bays are not for Olympic swimming practice. These "backlines" are used for cultivation of the island's famous blue mussels and Malpeque oysters, which are considered to be the world's tastiest. The island's mollusks are famous gastronomic delicacies found on the menus of upscale restaurants throughout North America. Although some residents have licenses to harvest wild shellfish, most of the supply comes from aqua farms in the natural

Lobster boats docked in New London. More than 80 percent of the lobsters caught in Prince Edward Island are exported to the U.S. Unlike in Maine, the traditional arched-top wooden lobster traps are still used by fisherman in Prince Edward Island.

bays on the north shore. Fresh (caught or harvested that day) lobster, halibut, mussels, and oysters are offered in almost every restaurant at prices that would make a Bostonian envious.

The landscape around Cavendish and the Green Gables farm was the setting for Lucy Maud Montgomery's *Anne of Green Gables.* The continuing appeal of the story is evident in that *Anne of Green Gables—The Musical* is the longest running theatric musical production in Canada, and more than a quarter million people visit the Green Gables site (902-963-7874, pc.gc.ca/eng/lhn-nhs/pe/greengables/index.aspx) in Prince Edward Island National Park each year. Avonlea Village in Cavendish (902-963-3050,

Shortcuts

There are a number of shortcuts between Route 6 and Provincial Highway 2, and all are scenic.

- Route 13 from Cavendish 17 km (10.6 mi)
- Route 254 from Stanley Bridge 9 km (6.4 mi)
- Route 8 from New London 8 km (5.3 mi)

www.avonlea.ca), a "fictional living-history" museum, allows visitors to become a part of the Green Gables stories.

In Cavendish the touted Boardwalk is not anywhere near the coast or even along a river—it's simply a retail shopping attraction connecting several buildings. A fiberglass triceratops advertises Jurassic Bart's Dinosaur Museum and Petting Zoo while next door a silver geodesic dome and a shabby replica of a space shuttle are part of another venue. There are paintball arcades, miniature-golf courses, go-kart racing, a water slide, and other attractions. Quaint tourist cottages right out of the 1940s line the highway.

The house where Lucy Montgomery was born is located 11 km (7.3 mi) from Cavendish in New London on Route 6 at the junction of Routes 20 and 8 (902-886-2099 for hours). This might be a required stop if you're a fan of *Anne of Green Gables,* otherwise this is where you calculate how many hours of riding are left in the day and determine which road to take. Kensington to Charlottetown on Route 2 is a very quick 48 km (30 mi). Via

The island's trademark red soil and reddish sandstone cliffs contrast sharply with the beautiful sandy beaches along the Cavendish shore. These rust-colored sandstone cliffs would not be out of place in the red-rock canyons of Utah and Arizona...except for the presence of the Atlantic Ocean.

Shellfish Farming

by Ken Aiken

A boat was coming in to dock, so I stopped and asked about the lines of buoys in the bay. My questions led to an invitation to join the crew to harvest the next load of blue mussels *(Mytilus edulis)*. I spent the next three hours on Rustico Bay learning about mussel and oyster farming and we returned with four tons of shellfish.

PEI Aqua Farms (trademark "Island Gold") in Kensington holds shellfish until wholesale orders are placed. Even though I stopped by unannounced the general manager, Jerry Bidgood, found time to take me on a tour of the facility. The blue mussels, clams, quahogs, scallops, and Malpeque oysters are stored in stackable tanks through which seawater and nutrients are constantly circulated. When orders are placed, the shellfish are run through a shell-cleaning, sorting, and grading process; packaged in net bags that are tagged with information that traces the product back to the individual farmers; boxed on ice and shipped for delivery within 12 hours!

Approximately 38,000 tons of shellfish are harvested in PEI each year, which generates about 67 million dollars of income. ∎

Route 6 Kensington is only 11 km (6.8 mi) from New London. The longer Route 20 loops through Darnley and Malpeque covering 32 km (20 mi) before reaching Kensington. While it *could* be ridden in half an hour, photo ops will double, and even treble that time.

Route 20 crosses the Southwest River and cuts across kilometers of rich farmland. From New London Bay to Profitts Point the land along the coast is privately owned, but the beach is public property. The beautiful sand along Cousin's Shore is an attraction, and at least two roads—Cousins Shore Road and Branders Pond Road—still provide public access from Route 20. The dunes of Darnley Beach on Profitts Point are a draw and Cabot Beach Provincial Park in Malpeque has the most popular campsites on the island. Just 2 km (1.2 mi) beyond Malpeque Route 104 branches right from Route 20 and makes a C-shaped loop through Indian River then intersects Route 20 closer to Kensington.

The beautiful St. Mary's Church is located on Route 104 just west of Route 20. The acoustics are claimed to be so exceptional that it has gained an international reputation among professional musicians. I can only describe the architectural style of this church as post-modern neo-Gothic, but no matter what you call it, this is a definite photo op.

After 7 km (4.8 mi) Route 104 returns to Route 20 where you turn right and ride 5 km (3 mi) to Kensington.

The Haunted Mansion in downtown Kensington (81 Victoria Street, 902-836-3336, www.hauntedmansionpei.com) is an amazing piece of Victorian Tudor-style architecture built with secret doors and the twisting streets of London in the basement. The old railroad station near the intersection of Routes 6 and 2 will be of interest to railway buffs and it doubles as the official information center for the area. Route 20 can be ridden in half an hour, but an entire afternoon can easily be spent along this highway since time bears little relationship to distance on this island.

From Kensington take Route 2 east to return to Charlottetown in 48 km (30 mi).

Trip 14 North Cape

Distance: *301 km (186.9 mi)*

Highlights: *The College of Piping during concerts or practice. The Green Park Shipbuilding Museum for history buffs and chilling out. Lighthouses, wind farms, and expansive seascapes at the northern tip of the island. The Prince Edward Island Potato Museum for spuds and the eccentric bottle houses of E. Arsenault. Don't forget to try the local specialty—seaweed pie.*

The land bridge that connects central Prince Edward Island and Prince County is only 6 km wide between Malpeque Bay and Summerside Harbour. Route 2 cuts through the center of this region with Route 12 dodging around the numerous bays and inlets on the eastern shore and Route 14 following the low cliffs of the western side. The western portion of the province differs from both the eastern and central regions: it seems a bit rough

Two "old salts" (experienced sailors) take a break in the maintenance of their ocean-going tug, the Gulf Dianne. They had just delivered a barge to Summerside Harbour and are tied up next to the local yacht club.

around the edges, both in terms of landscape and the feeling the checker-board of fields and scruffy second-growth trees evoke. This rural landscape of the interior is reminiscent of northern Maine, which makes perfect sense considering the cash crop for both regions is potatoes.

Summerside is only 71 km (44.1 mi) from Charlottetown or 28 km (17.4 mi) from the Confederation Bridge; North Cape is another 97 km (60.2 mi) from Summerside and can be reached in another hour and a quarter by taking Route 2. The distance to North Cape by way of Route 12 is only 123 km (76.5 mi), but how long it takes depends upon how many stops and detours you decide to take.

The North Cape Loop from Summerside

0 km (0 mi) Starting in Summerside, go west on Route 11/Water St.

8 km (5.5 mi) Turn right on Route 12/Lady Slipper Dr.

40 km (24.7mi) Arrive in Port Hill. Continue north on Route 12.

44 km (27.5 mi) Turn right on Route 166/Bideford Rd.

48 km (29.9 mi) Arrive at the Ellerslie Shellfish Museum. Turn around and take first right to return to Route 12.

49 km (30.7 mi) Turn right on Route 12 to continue north.

67 km (41.7 mi) Turn right on Route 2 west in Portage.

70 km (43.4 mi) Turn right on Route 12/Cascumpec Rd.

90 km (55.8 mi) Arrive in Alberton. Continue on Route 12.

123 km (76.5 mi) Arrive in North Cape. Return on Route 12.

129 km (80.4 mi) Turn right on Route 161/Broderick Rd.

134 km (83.1 mi) Turn right on Route 14.

156 km (96.8 mi) Arrive Miminegash. Continue on Route 14.

190 km (118.4 mi) Arrive West Point, continue on Route 14

205 km (127.2 mi) Turn left on Route 148/Kennedy Rd.

209 km (130 mi) Turn right on Buchanan Rd.

210 km (130.4 mi) Turn left on Barclay Rd.

212 km (131.7 mi) Arrive O'Leary. Turn right on Route 142.

217 km (134.9 mi) Turn right on Route 2.

238 km (148.0 mi) Turn right on Route 11.

267 km (166.2 mi) Arrive Cap Egmont, continue on Route 11.

301 km (186.9 mi) Arrive Summerside.

Summerside is the second-largest city in the province with approximately 14,500 residents. This charming little city, which would be called a town in any other part of Canada, is best known for its heritage homes. The principal employers are several aerospace companies, various transportation firms, a large food-processing plant, and the provincial tax center for Revenue Canada.

A boardwalk along the waterfront makes it possible for visitors to explore Spinnaker's Landing. It has an information center, a few small boutiques, a café, and the intimate 527-seat Jubilee Theater that features local concerts and summer theater presentations. The International Fox Museum and Hall of Fame (236 Fitzroy St. just off Route 11, 902-436-2400, www.wyattheritage.com) is dedicated to the fur industry that flourished here at the beginning of the 20th century. Shipbuilding was another source of wealth for this small city and its beautiful Victorian homes are the heritage of those successful entrepreneurs. The College of Piping located on Water Street (902-436-5377, www.collegeofpiping.com) is the only college of Celtic performing arts in North America. Catching an impromptu rehearsal of drumming or pipes is a treat and there are several public performance held during the summer months.

Accommodations of all types can be found in Summerside, including camping at Linkletter Provincial Park, 8 km (5 mi) west of the city (902-888-8366).

Take Route 11 west out of Summerside (Water Street) then turn right (north) on Route 12 to explore the regions on the west side of Malpeque Bay. Compared to central Prince Edward Island this region seems practically devoid of tourist attractions. This is a region devoted to farming and fishing and seems a bit rough along the edges. The coastline from Malpeque to Alberton is protected by a chain of barrier islands, but there are very few roads that provide access to the Conway Narrows channel.

This colorful lighthouse marks the North Cape Coastal Drive. Each scenic drive has its own distinctive sign.

Just 40 km (24.7 mi) from Spinnaker's Landing in Port Hill the Green Park Shipbuilding Museum (902-831-7947, www.peimuseum.com) is located on the 219 acres of the provincial park. This was a 19th-century shipyard and the Interpretive Centre's exhibits presents the era when the region's forests were transformed into ships and fortunes were made. The site has a carpentry and blacksmith shop, and a recreated shipyard with the keel and stern of an uncompleted 200-ton brigantine. The Yeo House was the Victorian home of shipbuilder James Yeo, Jr, who was the richest man on the island. The Green Park Provincial Park also offers cabins, tent sites by the river, hot showers, a kitchen shelter, and laundry.

Return to Route 12 and continue north. To visit the Prince Edward Island Shellfish Museum (902-831-3225) in Bideford , travel a short distance beyond the junction of Routes 178 and 167 in Tyne Valley and bear right

Oyster fishing is done with two, long, rake-like tongs. Many Islanders have non-commercial permits to harvest shellfish for personal consumption.

on Route 166 (Bideford Road). Ride the 4 km (2.4 mi) to the end of the road. The shellfish museum is housed in a small clapboard building on an inlet in the "village" of Bideford. This tiny research station was where the commercial farming of the endangered Malpeque oyster was developed. The island's small museums tend to have a dusty, naïve charm reminiscent of local historical society exhibits that were tucked away in the upstairs room of public libraries during the 1960s, and this one is no exception.

To return to Route 12 simply turn around (you have no choice) and take the first right on Bideford Road, then right again in another kilometer on Route 12.

One has to keep a vigilant eye to the pavement, which can change from pristine to war-torn without warning. One particularly bad stretch of Route 12 raised the ire of residents to a sufficient degree that they posted a sign that reads RAGGED ASS RD.

In Portage, turn right as Route 12 joins Route 2, and then right again after 3 km (1.7 mi) as Route 12 heads toward Alberton.

There are several bridges that will be crossed in the vicinity of Alberton and here the fishing industry seems to intrude into farmland along estuaries that expand and contract with the tide.

The little town of Alberton (pop. 1081) is a regional service center for several fishing and farming communities located on the north side of Cascumpec Bay. Discovered by Jacques Cartier in 1534 it wasn't settled until 1788 by immigrants from Devonshire, England. Named after Albert Edward, Prince of Wales, it was established as a trading town. As in other settlements along the eastern shore of North Cape, Alberton's residents took advantage of the extensive natural forest cover and developed industries based on lumber and shipbuilding. By 1850, most of the forests were cleared and agriculture, especially potato farming, became the primary occupation in the region.

Another important industry was created in 1893 when Sir Charles Dalton and Robert Oulton established a farm to raise silver foxes. The industry brought increased prosperity to the North Cape region and commercial fur

The Shellfish Museum, located in Bideford, is housed in the same building where much of Dr. A.W. H. Needler's research was done for the domestic farming of Malpeque oysters.

farms continued to flourish until the 1940s, when the World War II reduced the demand for this "niche" product. The complete history is presented at the International Fox Museum and Hall of Fame in Summerside. The area's fine Victorian homes that were built with profits from the fur trade are still referred to as "Fox Houses" and a silver fox is still the central element in the town seal.

Route 12 offers only a few glimpses of the ocean until you reach Anglo Tignish, but from here to North Cape the horizon is filled with the blue waters of the Gulf of St. Lawrence.

The north tip of the island is one of the primary destinations for those touring Prince Edward Island. As you approach the end of the road you will hear the gentle whooshing sounds that the long blades of the Vestas wind turbines make in the nearly constant wind. This location is acknowledged as being one of the windiest in Canada and the federal government established the Atlantic Wind Test Site here in the late 1970s. The provincial government's wind farm has eight Vestas V-47-660 turbines and generates more than five megawatts of electricity annually. The nearby town of Norway has three turbines, with more planned; the big West Cape Wind Farm

The old wooden lighthouse at North Cape contrasts sharply with the starkly modern glass-walled visitors center.

Towering over the gentle landscape, the North Cape wind farm was one of the first in Atlantic Canada. The provincial government has made a commitment to the creation of renewable energy for the future.

along Route 142 in O'Leary has 55; and the city of Summerside is erecting four. The Prince Edward Island government's goal is to make the island energy independent by 2015.

Before the wind farm was operational in 2001, the North Cape was best known as the site of the longest natural rock reef in North America. At 3 km (2 mi) in length, the reef marks the point where the tides of the Gulf of St. Lawrence and the Northumberland Strait come together, to merge twice a day in a swirling mass of water and has been the site of countless shipwrecks through the centuries.

The sturdy North Cape lighthouse has dominated the skyline of this impressive cape since 1867. Now fully automated, the building is one of the last wooden lighthouses still operating in the Maritime Provinces.

On a nice day North Cape can be spectacular, however when wind or fog makes conditions less than ideal, sitting inside behind thermal pane windows with a hot cup of coffee or bowl of soup is a recommended option. The North Cape Interpretive Centre marks the end of the road and the Wind and Reef Restaurant & Lounge provides respite from the wind. The

Red-sand beaches, like this one at Cap Egmont, are a distinguishing feature of Prince Edward Island.

interpretive center has an exhibit explaining the Atlantic Wind Test Site, an aquarium, and displays about the history of the cape. While the North Cape Lighthouse is fenced off and not accessible to the public, walking trails follow the edge of the cliffs around the point.

The quickest way to reach Route 14 from North Cape is to return 6 km (3.9 mi) on Route 12 then turn right on Route 161/Broderick Rd. and follow it for another 4 km (2.7 mi). Make a right turn onto Route 14 and you're heading down the western coast of Prince Edward Island.

In the shallows along the west coast, men and horses can often be seen harvesting Irish Moss, a type of seaweed. From this is extracted a binding agent called *carrageenan,* which apparently we blithely consume in everything from toothpaste to ice cream and beer. There's an Irish Moss Festival, a Miss Irish Moss Pageant, and even Irish Moss soup, which I've been told can be found on the menu of the Seaweed Pie Café in Miminegash.

Route 14 is long and straight, but in places it offers you panoramic views of the sea while you travel down the coast. When a brisk wind is gusting eastward this might not be the best road to ride. Route 2 runs down the center of the island and provides a little more protection from the wind, but it's wide, straight, and there's not much to see other than potato fields and sometimes wind turbines silhouetted against the horizon.

The West Point Lighthouse and Museum is also an inn and restaurant. Only 67 km (41.9 mi) from North Cape and 1 km down the well-marked road to the Cedar Dunes Provincial Park, this black-and-white-striped lighthouse is the place to enjoy a bowl of tasty chowder on the patio deck (902-859-3605; www.westpointlighthouse.com). This provincial park offers both camping and beach access, but the rooms located in the lighthouse tower are worth making reservations for.

From West Point continue on Route 14 for 15 km (8.8 mi), then turn left on Route 148/Kennedy Road. In 4 km (2.8 mi) Route 148 takes a right on Buchanan Road, then in a half kilometer a left on Barclay Road. Ride 2 km (1.3 mi) to Route 142 in O'Leary.

Just off Route 142 in O'Leary on Parkview Drive is the Prince Edward Island Potato Museum (902-859-2039, www.peipotatomuseum.com). The potato deserves recognition as being the primary cash crop on the island, but here a person can learn about its history and view agricultural implements. Outside, the giant sculpted potato lends itself to photo ops, but it takes a real spud to become captivated by the Potato Hall of Fame exhibit. The Heritage Chapel and a one-room schoolhouse are worth a quick look.

Follow Route 142 for 5 km (3.2 mi), then turn right on Route 2. After riding 21 km (13.1 mi) turn right onto Route 11 to follow the coastline through Acadian country back to Summerside. The landscape seems softer on this protected southern coast and the road gently winds across the terrain. The red sand beach at Cap Egmont presents a colorful composition at low tide. The old concrete pier is an obvious vantage point to photograph the lighthouse, but it's also a tern colony. Trespass here during nesting season and these birds will actively defend their territory.

Pay attention on Route 11 just east of Cap Egmont and you might catch a glimpse of the bottle houses made by Edouard Arsenault (www.bottle-houses.com). When the lighthouse at Cap Egmont was automated he retired as the last resident keeper and began to build these houses from old bottles and concrete. They are open to the public, including the chapel, which is infused with spectacular light refracted through old wine and liquor bottles instead of the traditional stained glass.

It seems as quick to ride through Summerside on Route 11/Water St. as it does to return to Route 2 to bypass the city. From here Charlottetown is less than an hour away and the Confederation Bridge a mere 20 minutes.

Trip 15 Red Sands Shore

Distance: *150 km (93.4 mi) A half-day excursion.*
Highlights: *Fort Amherst and its views of Charlottetown Harbor, the New Englandesque village of Victoria-by-the-Sea, and Elvis's pink Cadillac at the Car Life Museum. In between its vivid green landscapes divided from the deep blue sea by a thin border of orange sandstone.*

This is what I call a sunny Sunday-afternoon type of ride, although you certainly don't have to wait until the end of the week to take this excursion. Vantage points for viewing the Charlottetown harbor, the beautiful open fields of the Argyle Shore, the tiny but charming village of Victoria-by-the-Sea, and the roller-coaster ride through the interior of the province back to the provincial capital makes this an enjoyable ride that can be taken at a leisurely pace.

The expansive landscape of Cape Traverse and the Argyle Shore are quite different than the coastline in other parts of Prince Edward Island. Despite its small size the province offers diverse landscapes for those touring the island.

This trip also details two scenic ways to reach the Confederation Bridge from Charlottetown other than the Trans-Canada Highway/Route 1. While it doesn't cost anything to get onto the island, there is a charge to leave. The cost to return to Nova Scotia on the Northumberland Ferry is $79; the toll for crossing to New Brunswick via the bridge is $17.

Take the Trans-Canada Highway west out of Charlottetown and cross the bridge into North River. Turn left onto Route 248/York Point Road. Red Rocks Harley-Davidson is located on the north side of this intersection (18 Warren Cove Road, 902-368-8324, www.redrockharleydavidson.com) and many of the scheduled poker runs and organized rides on the island begin at this location. Ride 5 km (3.2 mi) to the southern end of York Point Road where you get an excellent view of Charlottetown Harbour. You can see your next stop just across the river, but to reach it requires going west 4 km (2.4 mi) on Ferry Road to Route 19 and looping 15 km (9.6 mi) around Rocky Point. The old wharf, at the end of a short gravel road, provides an excellent vantage point for viewing the harbor, but so does Fort Amherst National Historic Site (902-672-6350). This was the location of the first Acadian French settlement on the island, Port-la-Joye, established in 1720. The rolling grassy mounds and ditches are the earthworks of the British fort built in 1758. The fort is long since gone, but the few cannon scattered about the grounds help to create the right atmosphere.

From Fort Amherst Route 19 travels 29 km (18.1 mi) through lush green farmland following the Argyle Shore before it reaches the junction with

The Route from Charlottetown

0 km (0 mi) Starting in Charlottetown, take the Trans-Canada Highway/Route 1 west.

7 km (4.6 mi) Turn left on Route 248/York Point Rd.

12 km (7.8 mi) Arrive York Point.

14 km (8.7 mi) Return on York Point Rd. and turn left on Ferry Rd.

18 km (11.1 mi) Turn left on Route 19/Meadowbank Rd. in Cornwall.

33 km (20.7 mi) Arrive Rocky Point, visit wharf at end of road, return to Route 19.

35 km (21.6 mi) Turn left on Blockhouse Rd.

36 km (22.3 mi) Visit Fort Amherst and return to Route 19.

65 km (40.4 mi) Turn left, on the Trans-Canada Highway/Route 1 West in DeSable.

69 km (42.9 mi) Turn left on Route 116/Shore Rd. to Causeway Rd.

72 km (44.8 mi) Arrive Victoria. Continue on Route 116.

78 km (48.7 mi) Turn left on Route 10.

90 km (56.2 mi) Turn left on the Trans-Canada Highway/Route 1 West.

93 km (57.8 mi) Arrive Gateway Village in Borden-Carleton. Turn around and go east on the Trans-Canada Highway.

100 km (62.3 mi) Exit on Route 1A.

106 km (66.1 mi) Arrive Middleton. Turn right on Route 225 east.

140 km (86.9 mi) Bear right on Route 248/North York River Rd.

143 km (89.0 mi) Turn left on the Trans-Canada Highway East in North River.

150 km (93.4 mi) Arrive Charlottetown.

Route 1 in DeSable. Turn left on Route 1 and ride 4 km (2.5 mi), then turn left onto Route 116, which is the most scenic road leading into the quaint village of Victoria-by-the-Sea. It feels like a small New England village and its approach to tourism is similar. There's a tiny museum located in the Palmer's Range Light, a couple of artisan boutiques, a chocolatier, and a summer theater.

Throughout this gentle province, you come face to face with the unique red-colored soil of Prince Edward Island. This is caused by the high iron content of the island's soft sandstone, which literally "rusts away" on exposure to the oxygen in the air. On a bright sunny day, the omnipresent rusty soil, the tidy green fields, and deep blue coastal waters merge together to create a captivating scene.

Continue west on Route 116 for 6 km (3.9 mi). Just before Route 116 reconnects with Route 1, turn left onto Route 10. Both highways cross Cape Traverse to reach Gateway Village at the end of the Confederation Bridge in

The best vantage point for photographing the long expanse of the Confederation Bridge is from the parking lot of St. Peter's Church in Chelton.

Borden-Carleton, but there's far less traffic on Route 10. The village has clean restrooms, souvenirs, island products, restaurants, and more tourist information than can be packed in a tank bag. The tourist shops are busy, but to tell the truth, I've never been in a single one of them. Don't bother trying to sneak out to the pier—the road is closed and off limits to tourists.

The Trans-Canada Highway/Route1 is a scenic two-lane highway and it's the quickest road from the bridge to Charlottetown, a mere 56 km (35 mi) that can be covered in 45 minutes. It makes sense to travel Route 1 when arriving in Prince Edward Island after a long day of riding or when departing the province en route to New Brunswick or Nova Scotia. When doing so, make certain to schedule a quick stop to view Elvis Presley's pink '59 Cadillac at the Car Life Museum in Bonshaw (902-675-3555). However, for this short afternoon excursion take Route 1A 6 km (3.8 mi) to Middleton and then turn right onto Route 225 to head east through the rolling heartland of Prince Edward Island to reconnect in 34 km (20.8 mi) with the Trans-Canada Highway at Red Rocks Harley-Davidson in North River. Although this distance is 7 km less than taking the Trans-Canada Highway, it's more leisurely and does take longer to cover.

Trip 16 Points East

Distance: *274 km (170 mi)*

Highlights: *The Orwell Corner Historical Museum and some of Atlantic Canada's finest lighthouses. The turbulent waters off East Point and the "singing sands" of Basin Head. Wind turbines against a big sky and sheltered fishing villages offer plenty of opportunities for photos.*

East of Hillsborough Bay and the Hillsborough River lies Kings County, a region that's known as Points East. It feels quite different from both central and western Prince Edward Island, but that is the beauty of touring this province. The eastern shore is cut with bays and inlets in which nestle fishing villages like Murray River, Montague, and Cardigan, while the interior is an expanse of fertile farmland. There are beaches, notably the Singing Sands at Basin Head and the Greenwich segment of the national park, but most of the coastline is red sandstone cliff.

The Northumberland Ferry carries travelers between Caribou, Nova Scotia and Wood Islands, Prince Edward Island.

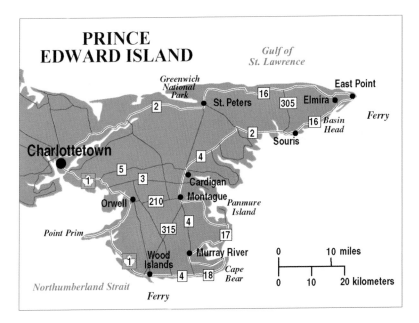

The extreme northeastern point of the island, East Point, is one of the primary destinations for touring riders. The ferry dock at Wood Islands marks the eastern end of Trans-Canadian Route 1. The dock for the CTMA Ferry to the Magdalen Islands is in Souris, only 26 km (16 mi) south of East Point.

With so many roads crisscrossing the county the variables for exploring the Points East region are usually dependent upon your chosen destination and the time available. Ferry schedules are absolute with six to eight (depending on the month) crossings to Nova Scotia and a single arrival and departure for the Magdalen Islands each day. These require reservations and arrival an hour prior to departure.

With a number of readily available shortcuts and the potential of several side excursions to places like Point Prim, Elmira, and the eastern section of the national park in St. Peters, total traveling distance becomes difficult to estimate. If you arrive at Wood Islands on the ferry in the morning you might wish to follow these directions to Charlottetown via East Point; if you arrive in the late afternoon heading west on Route 1 might be your choice. Then again, you might just decide to camp in one of several provincial parks along the eastern shore.

The Points East Coastal Drive is plainly marked by highway signs with a starfish logo and the first segment, the Trans-Canada Highway from Charlottetown to Wood Islands, is 61 km (38 mi) of cruising highway that can

The East Point Loop from Charlottetown

0 km (0 mi) Take the Trans-Canada Highway east from Charlottetown.

28 km (17.3 mi) Turn on MacPhail Road. Return to the Trans-Canada Highway and continue east.

39 km (24.0 mi) Turn on Prim Point Road.

49 km (30.7 mi) Arrive Prim Point return to Route 1.

60 km (37.4 mi) Turn right on the Trans-Canada Highway.

83 km (51.5 mi) Arrive Wood Islands. Leave Wood Islands, turn left on Route 4/Shore Rd.

103 km (63.3 mi) Turn right on to Route 18.

111 km (68.6 mi) Arrive Cape Bear. Continue on Route 18.

125 km (77.5 mi) Turn right on Route 4 to Murray River.

126 km (78.3 mi) In Murray River bear right on to Route 17/Point Pleasant Rd.

165 km (102.1mi) Arrive Montague. Continue straight on Route 4.

194 km (120.1 mi) Arrive Dingwells Mills. Bear right on Route 2.

210 km (129.8 mi) Arrive Souris. Take Route 16, East Point Rd. to East Point.

234 km (144.5 mi) Arrive East Point Lighthouse. Continue west on Route 16.

241 km (149.2 mi) Take Route 16A to Elmira.

259 km (159.8 mi) To the CTMA Ferry: Turn left on Route 305/Souris Line Rd. south

288 km (178.2 mi) Arrive St. Peters. Go right on Route 2 to Charlottetown.

342 km (211.5 mi) Arrive Charlottetown.

easily be covered in 45 minutes. Therein lies the problem—certain places are easily overlooked at highway speeds.

About 28 km (17.3 mi) from Charlottetown just off the Trans-Canada Highway on Macphail Park Road are the Orwell Corner Historical Village (902-651-8515, www.orwellcorner.ca) and the Sir Andrew Macphail Homestead (902-651-2789, www.macphailhomestead.ca). The living history village is comprised of the Prince Edward Island Agricultural Heritage Museum, D.E. Clarke's General Store with attached home, the Orwell Church, a blacksmith shop, the Orwell schoolhouse, E.D. Taylor's shingle mill, and a farmyard. The Macphail homestead and its furnishings are original and a visit is like stepping back a century in time.

Ride the Trans-Canada Highway another 11 km (6.7 mi) and turn right on Route 209, which leads to Point Prim Lighthouse (902-659-2768), the oldest (c. 1845) on Prince Edward Island and the only round lighthouse that's made of brick in Canada. The last kilometer or so of the road is gravel, but the panoramic vantage point of the lighthouse makes it worthwhile. Upon returning to the Trans-Canada Highway turn right and ride 23 km (14.1 mi) to Wood Islands.

The Wood Islands Lighthouse is located just east of the ferry terminal and just a mile (1.6 km) south of the junction of Route 4. One reason to stop is to sample the daily offering of traditional island food, whether it is ginger cookies, bannock, or local jellies. During the winter of 2009 the lighthouse was moved away from the crumbling cliff and placed on a new foundation. This is nothing new for lighthouses on an island whose sandstone cliffs can lose up to a meter a year to sea erosion.

The ferry passage from Nova Scotia to Prince Edward Island is free, but to get off the island and back to the mainland will cost $79 for a rider and motorcycle with or without a trailer or sidecar (reservations 877-635-7245, www.peiferry.com). It's a 75-minute ride, but those with reservations are still required to arrive an hour prior to departure or risk losing their place.

The fast highway to Souris—Route 315 to Route 4 in Montague—will get you there in just under an hour; following the Points East Coastal Drive will easily take four times that. Along Route 4, verdant fields run to the very edge of burnt-orange cliffs and the blue ocean water carries the eye to the distant horizon. The main highway, Route 4, cuts northwest to Murray

This tidy little marina is in Montague Harbour, a town that is considered to be one of the most beautiful on the island.

River, which is only 4.5 km (2.8 mi) away, but Route 18 continues to hug the coastline as it rounds the cape. There's no doubt that following the Lighthouse Route is far more scenic, but at 24 km it's five times as long. The choice is yours.

The Cape Bear Lighthouse (902-962-2917) was the first land station to receive distress calls from the Titanic and spread the news of its sinking. This lighthouse and the small Marconi museum will have to be moved in the near future as the edge of the crumbling cliffs advances toward its foundations. I doubt there is another region in North America where lighthouses have been moved as often as on Prince Edward Island.

Route 4 is the shortest distance between Murray River and Montague, but Route 17 is far more scenic. The first is only 16 km (9.84 mi); the loop on Route 17 is 38 km (23.8 mi). Those with available time should consider taking Route 347 to Panmure Island, perhaps one of the most beautiful spots on the east coast. The Points East Coastal Drive winds out to the tip of every peninsula, along estuary rivers, and through fishing villages, yet Route 4 plays an important role when weather and time are an issue.

The town of Souris (pop. 1300) received its unusual name (French for "mouse") after a short-lived plague of the rodents in the early 18th century. Today it's known as the "Gateway to the Îles de la Madeleine" (Magdalen Islands) and the CTMA Ferry (888-986-3278, www.ctma.ca) leaves the dock once a day: you either make it or you don't. Going to the Magdalen Islands requires at least three days and, if timed correctly, can provide a shortcut to the Gaspé Peninsula and even Québec City. Although it's only 81 km (50 mi) from Charlottetown on Route 2, we have covered far more territory to reach Souris by taking the scenic route.

Shortcuts Abound

Those with limited time and others trying to make it to the ferry dock at Souris will want to consider one of several readily available shortcuts between Route 1 and Route 4.

- The first is Route 5 from Mount Albion to just outside of Cardigan. While not as fast as Route 3, it has a more intimate quality of a road used by Islanders.
- Route 3 from Cherry Valley to Pooles Corner is the highway to take when time is of the essence.
- Route 210 from Orwell to Montague is a delightful local road and a nice alternative to Route 3 without adding much time.
- Route 315 goes north from Wood Islands to Montague. It's a relatively fast-paced road and direct route for those heading to East Point or Souris from the Wood Islands Ferry Terminal.

At Cape Bear, the exposed southeastern tip of the province, wave erosion of the coastline can be up to a meter (39 inches) a year.

The "singing sands" of Basin Head, halfway between Souris and East Point, are not so melodic. They squeak when walked on due to their abnormally high silica content. Unlike many beaches on this island, the sand is white instead of orange.

The primary destination for most riders is the lighthouse at East Point (902-357-2718, www.eastpointlighthouse.com) which is located 24 km (14 mi) northeast of Souris and approximately 2 km off Route 16 at the end of a paved road. The octagonal East Point Light is 20 meters (64 ft) tall, and was built in 1867, because of a real navigational hazard around this point of land. These coastal waters are very dangerous because of three offshore reefs and the presence of three major ocean currents that meet along this coast— the Atlantic Ocean, the Northumberland Strait, and the Gulf of St. Lawrence.

For some unfathomable reason the lighthouse was originally situated a half-mile inland from the eastern tip of the island. Naturally this caused some confusion among the local fishermen, but it wasn't until a British warship was wrecked in 1882, on an offshore reef, that remedial action was taken. Though the HMS Phoenix was lost, none of her crew of 100 was

Prince Edward Island bears a remarkable resemblance to rural New England in the landscape, the houses, and the character of the people.

injured. The lighthouse was hastily removed from its foundation, and relocated to a new position within 200 feet of the island's eastern tip. In 1908, due to severe coastal erosion, the lighthouse had to be moved a third time, to a position 200 feet back from the cliffs.

This is one of the last "manned" lights on the island and the views can be stupendous from the top of the tower. On a clear day you can see the Mabou Highlands and the Cape Breton Highlands across the 20 miles of the Northumberland Straits. (Prince Edward Island's East Point Light is visible from both the highlands.) There's a small gift shop where visitors can acquire the blue Tip-To-Tip ribbon for the East Point Light. If you also make it to the North Cape lighthouse at the other end of the island, you can receive a colorful Tip-to-Tip certificate, suitable for framing, from Prince Edward Island Tourism. A Prince Edward Island Lighthouse Lover's Certificate is also available.

Just a few miles down the road is the East Point Wind Farm, a series of 10 large Vestas V-90 wind turbines that started to produce electricity in January 2007. Owned and operated by the provincial government, these massive wind machines stand 81 meters (267 ft) above the surrounding

The historic East Point Lighthouse is a popular tourist destination especially with those who travel the length of the island visiting the North Cape Lighthouse as well.

countryside and each turbine has a rotor diameter of 90 meters (297 ft) — almost twice that of the turbines used on the North Cape Wind Farm. They now produce enough electricity for 12,000 homes, or 7.5 percent of the provincial energy requirement.

Continue west on Route 16. A short detour on Route 16A will take you to the town of Elmira, at one time the eastern end of the railroad on Prince Edward Island. When the railway was abandoned in 1989 several island social clubs turned the abandoned line into a multi-purpose recreational trail, suitable for walking, hiking, jogging, and cycling. Now known as the Confederation Trail, it extends for 270 km (169 mi) to the village of Tignish at the northern end of the island. The trail is off-limits to motorized vehicles, including ATVs and motorcycles, but the Elmira Depot with its restored stationmaster's office is worth visiting.

If you are taking the ferry to the Magdalen Islands, the CTMA Ferry leaves Souris at 2 p.m., but passengers still have to be at the dock by 1p.m. This means cutting south on Route 305. Riders with a different agenda should continue south toward St. Peters (pop. 248), which is 54 km (34 mi) from East Point.

The beautiful farms along this coast are interspersed with tracts of woodland, which makes for a great ride with little traffic and often quite amazing views out over the waters of the Gulf of St. Lawrence.

Before the arrival of European settlers the region around St. Peters, like most of the province, was covered with a thick primeval forest. Once settled the ample supplies of spruce, fir, birch, ash, and maple trees gave rise to a profitable overseas trade in lumber. The adjacent bay also offered a sheltered location in which shipbuilding developed.

These industries have long since disappeared, but the opening of a new national park in 1998 has brought renewed interest and seasonal visitors to this lovely part of Prince Edward Island's north shore. Greenwich National Park, located 9 km (5.5 mi) via Route 313 out on the peninsula west of St. Peters, is home to many unusual plants and flowers, and also to Prince Edward Island's only endangered species.

The Piping Plover is a sand-colored shorebird, much like a small sparrow, that lives along secluded coastal beaches throughout Atlantic Canada. Although tiny, it is a powerful flyer that migrates to warmer southern climates in late summer and early fall. It has been tracked to Cuba, Mexico, the Bahamas, and even to South America!

However, the new park's most significant feature is a rare system of parabolic sand dunes, which can move across the landscape at a rate of two to four meters each year. Propelled by prevailing winds, the migratory dunes have even destroyed local forests, leaving behind skeleton trees, some of which are only now being uncovered as the dunes move on. This strange phenomenon, which leaves behind a series of sand ridges called gegenwalle, is found nowhere else in North America.

From St. Peters take Route 2 for the final 54 km back to Charlottetown.

Prince Edward Island Motorcycle Shops

🏍 DBL Dear Machines: Honda dealer, but stocks parts for other makes.
1539 Linkletter Rd. (just before Linkletter Provincial Park), Linkletter,
902-436-2527, www.dbldreammachines.com

🏍 Centennial Auto Sports & Tire: Suzuki dealer, but has oil filters for
most makes.
616 South Dr., Summerside, 902-436-1022,
www.centennialast.com

🏍 Toy Master Motor Sports: Kawasaki dealer
5 Campbell Rd. (just off Rt. 2), Winsloe, 902-894-5287,
www.toymaster.com

🏍 Red Rock Harley-Davidson: Harley-Davidson dealer
18 Warren Grove Rd. (at Route 1/Trans-Canada Highway),
North River (just outside Charlottetown), 902-368.8324,
www.redrockharleydavidson.com

Prince Edward Island Touring Clubs

🏍 GWRRA Chapter "A" PEI
🏍 Steeletto Wheels (women's riding group)
🏍 PEI H.O.G. Chapter
🏍 Canadian Motorcycle Cruisers PEI Chapter   ■

Trip 17   The Magdalen Islands

Distance: *200 km (124 mi) Your timing will be driven by the ferry schedule.*

Highlights: *A magical place where every view is a photographer's dream. Endless perfect sand beaches, the freshest air you'll ever breathe, and a scenic sea cruise with your bike stowed below. Not many miles of road, but you just want to keep riding them over and over again.*

Once your bike is secured with tie-downs on the lower deck of the CTMA Traversier you can go up on deck. The upper stern area, sheltered from the wind by the big smokestack is a great place to enjoy the sunshine. It's a five-hour, 134 km (84 mi) sea cruise from Souris to the port of Cap-aux-Meules in the Magdalen Islands. Obviously this is more than a day trip and, due to ferry schedules (888-986-3278, www.ctma.ca) a minimum stay of two nights is recommended.

Traditional island homes in Old Harry with Mines Seleine on North Dune visible in the background. The roof gable is a feature of the traditional Madelinot house. Painting them a different color from their neighbors was adopted from Acadian culture.

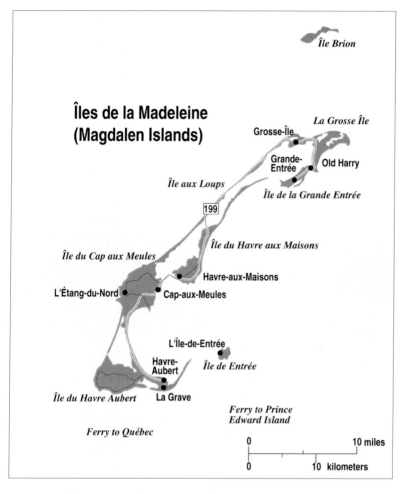

An unlikely segment of the Appalachian Mountains, this archipelago is located in the Gulf of St. Lawrence north of Prince Edward Island, west of Cape Breton Island, and east of the Gaspé. Part of the Province of Québec, it's the secret vacation getaway for Canadians seeking pristine white sand and crystal-clear water, including one of the top-ranked beaches in the world.

The ocean is really blue and emerald-green hills cap cliffs of vivid orange-red sandstone. There are 240 km (150 mi) of beautiful white sand beaches and the air is so fresh it's almost intoxicating. No two homes are painted the same color, an Acadian tradition that has been adopted by all Madelinots. A motorcycle can be parked and left for hours without fear of theft (Where would they take it? How could they hide it?) while its rider

Touring the Magdalen Islands

Start at the port in Cap-aux-Meules on Île du Cap aux Meules.

0 km (0 mi) Turn left on Route 199/Chemin Principale.

4 km (2.6 mi) Left on Route 199/Chemin de la Martinique.

26 km (16.5) Arrive La Grave on Île du Havre Aubert. Return on Route 199 North.

32 km (20 mi) Turn left on Chemin du Bassin, Chemin de l'Etang-des-Caps, and Chemin de la Montagne.

54 km (33.4 mi) Turn left on Chemin du Bassin.

56 km (34.4 mi) turn left on Route 199 north on Île du Havre Aubert.

70 km (43.7 mi) Turn left on Chemin de L'Etang-du-Nord on Île du Cap aux Meules.

75 km (46.3 mi) Turn right onto Chemin des Caps.

82 km (51.0 mi) Turn left on Route 199 north.

139 km (86.5 mi) Arrive Grande Entrée Harbor on Île de la Grande Entrée. Return Route 199 south.

200 km (124.4 mi) Arrive at the port in Cap-aux-Meules on Île du Cap aux Meules.

---

sunbathes nude on the face of some remote dune. The Magdalen Islands is not like other places.

Le bon goût frais des Îles, "the good fresh taste of the Islands," is an official designation for local produce. The microbrewery À l'abri de la Tempête in Cap-aux-Meules (418-986-5005, www.alabridelatempete.com) uses only locally grown barley and hops; La Fleur de Sable in Havre-Aubert (418-937-2224) bakes beer bread, smoked-herring foccacia, and more conventional loaves; Fromagerie du Pied-de-Vent (418-969-9292) crafts raw-milk cheeses; and Le Fumoir d'Antan (418-969-4907, www.fumoir-dantan.com) smokes fish in the traditional island fashion. *Bagosse* is the local home-brewed dandelion and berry wine, but berry liquors and ice cider are also produced here. The local veal is exquisite, seal sausage surprisingly good, and fresh lobster so inexpensive you wonder how the fishermen can afford to trap them.

Basque fishermen from Normandy were slaughtering walrus (known as "sea cows") to extinction in the islands since the early 1500s. Rendering their fat into lamp oil, a single barrel of such oil was worth an astronomical $1,000 in the mid-16th century. Jacques Cartier let the secret slip when he "discovered" the islands and published the account of his 1534 voyage to North America. Samuel de Champlain dropped anchor in here in 1626 and named the harbor Havre-Aubert. The name Îles de la Madeleine first appears on one of his maps dated 1632. The first Acadian

Herring is smoked in the traditional fashion at Fumoir d'Antan on l'Île-Havre-aux-Maisons. Saltier than Norwegian-style smoked herring, the small vacuum-packets purchased in the store provided road food for thousands of kilometers.

families arrived in 1762 fleeing the expulsion by the British in Nova Scotia and Madelinots lived here in relatively undisturbed isolation for the next couple of centuries. The first highway connecting these islands wasn't constructed until 1956.

The 88-km-long (54.6 mi) Route 199 is the only highway on the islands and the sum total of all streets and roads is less than 300 km (186 mi). Mileage is meaningless as you'll retrace your route numerous times for the sheer pleasure of the ride. The local roads, whether paved or gravel, are well-worth exploring and most lead to beautiful scenic vistas. Yet, there is only one place the journey can start and end: the port on Île du Cap aux Meules (*meule* is French for grindstone). From here Route 199 connects six of seven populated islands and a pedestrian ferry provides the link to Île de Entrée (Entry Island). The yellow information center at the end of the dock area has a staff of professionals who will assist with finding accommodations or any other questions relating to a visitor's stay.

The population of these islands totals less than 14,000 with more than half living on the island of Île du Cap aux Meules and Île de Entrée having a mere 130 residents. The town of Cap-aux-Meules (pop. 1,594) is the commercial center of the islands, site of the only shopping center, bank, two supermarkets, cinema, and the only place where premium-octane gasoline is available.

Located at the southern end of Route 199 on the island of Île du Havre Aubert (Albert's Harbor, pop. 2,516) and a mere 26 km (16 mi) from the ferry dock, the village of La Grave was established in 1762 as the first permanent settlement on the islands by Acadian families fleeing the "Great Upheaval" in Nova Scotia. Today it's a heritage site and artisan community where shops and boutiques occupy restored fishing sheds along the highway. Café de La Grave is in the old general store (418-937-5765). Its funky interior with mismatched chairs and tables and walls adorned with original art has made this the local hangout and the place to order the local specialty, a seafood pie called *pot-en-pot*. Sandy Hook is miles and miles of remote pristine beach where the international sand castle competition, the Concours de Châteaux de Sable, takes place every August. Anyone can enter, but the rules are specific: entrants must build a castle.

After exploring the island on local roads, take the highway back to Cap-aux-Meules along an 11 km (7 mi) strip of sand. In the town of L'Étang-du-Nord (The North Pond, pop. 3,047) a cluster of colorful clapboard-sided boutiques face the sea. The yellow one turns out to be Café la Côte (418-986-6412) where salt-cod pizza is the house specialty. From here, the angular hulk of *Duke of Connaught* can be seen resting against the rocks of Cap-au-Sauvage (Cape Savage). It's just one of more than 400 known shipwrecks scattered along these shores and also a reminder that many Madelinots are descendents of shipwreck survivors.

The main highway crosses the narrow bridge to the island of Île du Havre aux Maisons (House Harbor, pop. 2148). The local streets and roads that crisscross this island are a delight and I suggest taking the first right for a delightful 8 km (5 mi) alternate route. Chemin de la Pointe-Basse passes the local cheese maker *Pied-du-Vent* (Windfoot) and the eco-museum and traditional smokehouse of the Antan family, Le Fumoir d'Antan. The museum is interesting; the smokehouse offerings delicious. The road turns into Chemind des Échoueries, which becomes gravel just before the parking area and overlook of Cape Alright. Gravel or not, this is an awesome road (a short section beyond the parking area is closed to car traffic because of coastal erosion, but locals run scooters and motorcycles on it) and combined with Chemin des Montants (also gravel) it offers spectacular vistas. Chemin de la Dune-du-Sud leads to the beginning of 20 km (12 mi) of gorgeous sand beach known as the South Dune.

Cross the short causeway to Île aux Loups (Seal Island) where the highway runs along the dunes and ten continuous miles of beach that would make a Hawaiian jealous. There's plenty of parking, but carry a short piece of board for the kickstand—plastic kickstand cookies are insufficient and center stands are useless. Far beneath these sands lies a network of vast galleries *(Mines Seleine)* where men and machines mine the salt that's used on winter roads throughout much of eastern Canada and New England.

Route 199 then crosses to La Grosse Île (Fat Island, pop. 556) and onto Île de la Grande Entrée (pop. 646). Two exquisite beaches sweep around the East Point National Wildlife Reserve. One of these, the 10 kilometer-long, *Plage de la Grande Échouerie* (beach where walrus haul themselves out of the sea to sunbathe) is considered to be one of the best beaches in the world, yet it's rare to see anyone much beyond the very end by the village of Old Harry. It continues uninterrupted for another 11 km as the East Point Beach.

Route 199 ends at the fishing docks of Pointe de la Grande-Entrée and the village of Grande-Entrée. Now it's time to retrace the route, but a bit more leisurely. Exploring roads, visiting points of interest, watching windsurfers and parasail water skiers in the sheltered basins, or hanging out on a beach. It's only 58 km (36 mi) back to downtown Cap-aux-Meules.

An excursion to Île de Entrée is a must. There is a local ferry, but the 16 km (10 mi) trip across the open water and circumnavigating the island in a Zodiac (418-986-4745, excursionsenmer.com) is far more interesting. A climb to the top of Big Hill across pastures filled with wild iris and

The west end of Route 199 terminates at the docks of Grande-Entrée. There's a bit of tourism here, but this is a nitty-gritty fishing port, the mainstay of the island economy.

buttercups is truly a bucolic experience and the view of the islands from the summit is sublime.

All things must come to an end. The *Traversier* leaves daily at 8 a.m. for Prince Edward Island, but there is another option—the CTMA *Vacancier*. Having ridden Route 138 along the northern shore of the St. Lawrence River and followed the southern shore on Route 132, the final leg of author Aiken's journey is to cruise the 1190 km (790 mi) back home to Montréal on the river itself. This ship leaves the islands on Tuesday nights and docks in Montréal on Friday morning with stops at Chandler, New Brunswick, on Wednesday morning and in Québec City about noon on Thursday. On the outbound trip it anchors in Chandler on Saturday nights and arrives in Cap-aux-Meules on Sunday morning. This is the little-known "backdoor" route to Prince Edward Island from Gaspé.

Among the wide range of accommodations

Domaine du Vieux Couvent *(Old Convent Property)* on Île du Havre aux Maisons is a boutique motel and an aesthetic delight. Sensitivity to the heritage of this old convent, coupled with artisan woodworking, ultra-modern design, a view to die for, and an in-house restaurant with a locally renowned menu (which is a pretty high standard to begin with) makes this place special. (418-969-2233, www.domaineduvieuxcouvent.com)

La Maison des Falaises *(The House of Cliffs)* is a B&B on Île du Havre aux Maisons whose setting makes it the most-often-photographed house in the islands. It does have a shared bathroom, but with only three guest rooms (and one private apartment suite) it posed no problem. This is truly a fantasy setting. (418-969-4782)

Havre-sur-Mer *(Sea Cove)* is located between the South Point Lighthouse and the fishing docks on Île du Havre Aubert. With an expansive back lawn overlooking a private beach, this hand-built rambling B&B is the kind of place where one could spend an entire summer. (418-937-5675, www.havresurmer.com)

Auberge La Salicorne *(The Glasswort Hotel)* on Île de la Grande Entrée is the synthesis of a hostel and a hotel. With bicycle and kayak rentals, a seal-interpretation center, guided tours, and kilometers of hiking trails this makes a nice base from which to explore the island. There also is camping, showers, and meals. (418-985-2833, www.salicorne.ca) ■

Nova Scotia Mainland

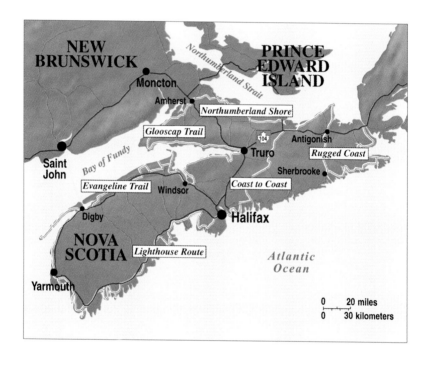

NEW
BRUNSWICK

Northumberland Strait

PRINCE
EDWARD
ISLAND

Moncton

Amherst

Northumberland Shore

Glooscap Trail

104

Antigonish

Rugged Coast

Saint
John

Bay of Fundy

Truro

Sherbrooke

Evangeline Trail

Windsor

Coast to Coast

Digby

Halifax

NOVA
SCOTIA

Lighthouse Route

*Atlantic
Ocean*

Yarmouth

0   20 miles

0   30 kilometers

Nova Scotia Mainland

by Rannie Gillis and Ken Aiken

The mainland portion of the province of Nova Scotia is actually a peninsula, joined to the rest of Canada by the 22-kilometer-wide (14 mi) Isthmus of Chignecto. Surrounded by several large bodies of water—Gulf of Maine, Bay of Fundy, Northumberland Strait, and the Atlantic Ocean—no point on the mainland is more than 45 miles from the sea. Prior to the Treaty of Utrecht in 1713, which ceded this area to British control, this region was considered the heart of French Acadia, and was referred to as The Acadian Peninsula.

Because of its strategic location, the mainland played an important role in the struggle between England and France for control of the lucrative fish and fur trade in eastern North America. The fortified port of Halifax became one of the great military outposts of the British Empire, and later played a significant part in both world wars. Today it remains the headquarters for the Royal Canadian Navy's Eastern Command.

Mainland Nova Scotia will enchant any visitor who will take the time to experience all that it has to offer. The secret is to leave the main highways, and follow the secondary roads, most of which are never far from the sea. The combination of charming coastal landscapes, dotted with picturesque fishing villages, and the gentle pastoral valleys and rolling forested uplands of the interior, makes for a wonderful touring experience.

Trip 18 The Evangeline Trail

Distance: *463 km (287.7 mi)*
Highlights: *Named after the fictional heroine of Longfellow's famous poem, this scenic ride follows the lower coast of the Bay of Fundy. Along the way you will pass through some of the earliest historical sites in North America, and get a chance to marvel at the Fundy tides, which can range as much as 16 m (54 feet) between high and low tide!*

This route through northwestern Nova Scotia starts in the town of Windsor on Minas Bay and ends in Yarmouth on the western edge of the province. We will visit the shore of the Bay of Fundy with the world's highest tides, travel through the fertile Annapolis valley, and learn about Acadian culture while riding along the Acadian Shore.

The small town of Windsor (pop. 3,709) is famous for two very different reasons. It is known as the Birthplace of Hockey, the Canadian national sport, and is the home of Howard Dill, whose giant pumpkins have been listed in the *Guinness Book of World Records*.

Cape Blomidon can be seen forming the distant shore on the other side of Minas Bay from the Grand-Pré National Historical Site.

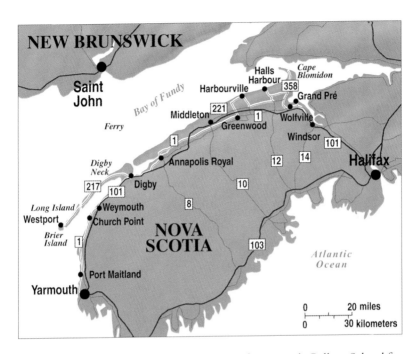

As early as the year 1800, young students from King's College School for Boys, were playing a primitive form of ice hockey, based on the Irish sport of hurley (field hockey). The Windsor Hockey Heritage Centre (128 Gerrish St., 902-798-1800) opened in 1994 and offers a nostalgic look at the origins of Canada's premier winter sport. On site you will find wooden pucks, skates made by local blacksmiths, and hand-carved hockey sticks made by Mi'kmaq natives.

Howard Dill amassed a fascinating collection of hockey memorabilia on his farm, but achieved international fame in the mid-1970s when he started growing the largest pumpkins in the world. In 1979 one of his giant gourds weighed in at 197 kilograms (433 pounds), and he was listed in *Ripley's Believe It or Not* and the *Guinness Book of World Records*. His Atlantic Giant Pumpkin Seeds became a best selling product, and his largest ever pumpkin topped the scales at an incredible 630 kg (1,386 lbs)! His farm, which is open to the public, is located at 400 College Road (902-798-2728).

From Windsor take Route 101 west toward Wolfville and take exit 10 onto Route 1 to visit the Grand-Pré National Historic Site. Turn right on Grand-Pré Road and the Grand-Pré National Historic Site Visitor Centre is a kilometer ahead on the left.

The Grand-Pré National Historic Site is located in an area that was a major center of Acadian activity from 1682 to 1755. It commemorates the

The route from Windsor to Yarmouth

0 km (0 mi) Start in Windsor. Take Route 101 west.

20 km (12.2 mi) Take Exit 10 to Route 1.

21 km (12.9 mi) Turn right on Grand-Pré Road.

22 km (13.5 mi) Arrive Grand-Pré National Historic Site, then return to Route 1.

23 km (14.1 mi) Turn right on Route 1.

31 km (19.3 mi) Arrive Wolfville. Continue on Route 1.

35 km (21.3 mi) Turn right on Route 358.

51 km (31.3 mi) Arrive Kings County Look-off. Turn right on Gospel Hill Road.

64 km (39.4 mi) Turn right on Route 359.

69 km (42.5 mi) Arrive Halls Harbour. Return on Route 359.

80 km (49.3 mi) Arrive Centreville. Turn right on Route 221.

99 km (61.4 mi) Turn right on Route 360.

108 km (67.0 mi) Arrive Harbourville. Take coastal road to Victoria Road.

113 km (70.1 mi) Turn left on Victoria Road.

120 km (74.6 mi) Arrive Dempseys Corner. Continue on Victoria Road.

122 km (75.8mi) Take 101 west.

125 km (77.7 mi) Take Exit 17 to Greenwood. Visit Greenwood Military Aviation Museum. Take Route 1 to Annapolis Royal.

184 km (113.9 mi) Arrive Annapolis Royal. Continue on Route 1.

216 km (133.8 mi) Arrive Digby. Take Route 217 down Digby Neck to Brier Island and return.

354 km (219.5 mi) From Digby take Route 1 to Weymouth.

387 km (240 mi) Arrive Weymouth. Continue on Route 1.

390 km (242.2 mi) Arrive St. Bernard. Continue on Route 1.

400 km (248.2 mi) Arrive Church Point. Continue on Route 1.

444 km (275.5 mi) Arrive Port Maitland. Turn right on Main Shore Drive.

463 km (287.7 mi) Arrive Yarmouth.

period of colonization and settlement of the area by Acadians as well as their deportation in 1755.

Grand-Pré is recognized internationally as the ancestral home of the Acadian people. In 1907 a memorial park was built at the site of a small Catholic church. By 1920 a statue of Evangeline was erected, and one year later a new church was built, with funds contributed by displaced Acadians from across North America. The Canadian government designated the location as a national historic site in 1961.

The Visitor Interpretation Centre opened in 2003. A large exhibit hall and multi-media theater, with a 22-minute film, explain the history of

The extensive scenic views of the surrounding countryside from the Kings County look-off are worth taking a detour to get there.

Grand-Pré (Great Meadow) and the Acadian people. The Visitor Centre is open daily from mid-May to mid-October.

An interesting side note is that the area surrounding the Grand-Pré National Historic Site was once below sea level, as part of a low-lying, salt-water marsh. The early Acadian settlers built an extensive series of dikes, and drained off the water to reclaim the land. The process continues today, with more than 8 km (5 mi) of dikes maintained by the Nova Scotia Department of Agriculture.

As you continue west on Route 1 to Wolfville, the massive outline of Cape Blomidon (from the nautical term "Blow Me Down") looms off to the right. This large promontory, with a lovely provincial park, separates the Bay of Fundy from the Minas Basin.

Wolfville (pop. 3,772) is the home of Acadia University, and a thriving tourist destination. Its Victorian architecture, historic inns and bed and breakfasts, and lively artistic and cultural life make it a popular place to visit year round.

Wolfville also marks the beginning of the Annapolis Valley, a fertile agricultural region known as Cradle of Acadie or the Bread Basket of Nova Scotia. About 150 km long (90 mi), it lies between two parallel mountain ranges, and has gained an international reputation for its delicious apples. (More than 3 million barrels of apples are produced in peak years.) The annual Apple Blossom Festival, held late each spring since 1933, is the most famous festival in the province, and marks the end of winter, the start of a new growing season, and the beginning of the summer tourist season. The unique scent of apple trees in bloom, along with the picture-perfect orchards, has long attracted visitors from near and far.

The Old Orchard Inn & Spa (902-542-5751, www.oldorchardinn.com) at Exit 11 of Route 101 in Wolfville is biker-friendly and serves the best meals in the area. The Greenwich Connector leads to the intersection with Route 1. Before continuing though, make sure you have close to a full tank of gasoline, as gas stations are scarce away from the main roads.

Take Route 358 north across the Black River into Port Williams. One of the best places to watch the Bay of Fundy tidal bore is from the parking lot on the northeast side of the bridge. The road goes through the village of Canning and then climbs the flank of North Mountain. The big corner comes just before reaching the summit and it's banked in the wrong direction! The Kings County look-off has an expansive pull-off area for parking.

At Halls Harbour on the Bay of Fundy coast boating schedules are determined by the tides, whose 12-meter (40 ft) range pull the water's edge far from the docks at low tide.

Chad restores vintage cars and has collected gas and oil signs, gas pumps, and even a vintage streetlight to complete the 1950s effect.

The panoramic views of Minas Basin and the Acadian lands of Gran- Pré are fantastic from this 600-meter-high (1970 ft) drop-off that marks the northern end of North Mountain. This ridge of basalt continues all the way to Brier Island and protects the Annapolis Valley from the radical atmospheric temperature changes associated with the tides in the Bay of Fundy.

For those interested in exploring Cape Blomidon, continue north on Route 358. There is a small provincial park in Scots Bay with picnic facilities and beach access. Blomidon Provincial Park is on the eastern shore with spectacular views of Midas Bay and offers camping facilities and a network of hiking trails.

From the look-off head back down the hill and immediately bear right onto Gospel Hill Road, which leads along the top of North Mountain and connects with West Halls Harbour Road. Descending the west side of North Mountain you get a fantastic view of the Minas Channel and Cape d'Or.

Halls Harbour is one those "must see" places, especially if the tide is out or is just coming in. With 12-meter (40 ft) tides being normal, the boats in the harbor are left high and dry at low tide. The cove is a popular site for mineral collectors and the Halls Harbour Lobster Pound is the place to indulge in fresh lobster. Their lobster rolls are reputed to be the best in Nova Scotia and this just might be true.

This military policeman, making his rounds of the Canadian Forces Base Greenwood, kindly agreed to be photographed in front of the Avro Lancaster bomber. This British-designed and Canadian-built plane was the most successful Allied bomber of World War II.

Take Route 359 over the mountain to Centerville. Turn right on Route 221, which merges from the left. Stay alert because Route 221 almost immediately makes a very sharp right turn. Slow down as soon as the highway reaches the foot of North Mountain, and enjoy the views of the fabulously lush farmland of the Annapolis Valley as Route 221 follows the base of North Mountain.

If you want to take a detour that involves twists, turns and gorgeous views of the Bay of Fundy and you don't mind riding on a section of gravel road, turn right on Route 360 and ride back over the North Mountain to Harbourville. The series of roads that run west from Harbourville along the Fundy coast include a few kilometers of well-maintained gravel, but are a delight on a motorcycle. Victoria Road takes you back over the mountain to intersect with Route 221 at Dempsey Corner. Continue on Victoria Road to Route 101.

To visit the Greenwood Military Aviation Museum go west on Route 101 and take the Greenwood Exit 17. Turn left and then right on Route 1. At the lights turn left onto Bridge Street. In 2.2 km (1.4 mi) turn left at the lights on to Central Ave. The museum is about a kilometer ahead on the left.

Note: If you decide to bypass the Greenwood Aviation Museum continue on Route 221 to Middleton. Route 221 turns into Route 362, which intersects Route 101 and then Route 1.

The Greenwood Aviation Military Museum is located at the entrance to the Canadian Forces Base Greenwood, the largest air base in Atlantic Canada, and is open year round.

When World War II started in 1939, England's Royal Air Force asked the Canadian government for permission to build a base in eastern Canada that would train aircrew for the coming air battles over Nazi-occupied Europe. Greenwood was chosen because of its relatively flat landscape, and its fog-free climate. At the end of the war the base reverted to the Royal Canadian Air Force.

During the Cold War the base was an essential part of integrated Canadian-American defense plans, especially with regard to long-range, anti-submarine patrols off the coast of northern Canada and the North Atlantic. At the present time, in addition to search and rescue aircraft, Canadian Forces Base Greenwood operates a fleet of maritime patrol aircraft, including long-range patrols over the Canadian Arctic.

The museum has several historical aircraft on permanent outdoor display, including the famous Avro Lancaster of Dambusters fame. An adjacent hangar, with much military memorabilia, houses exhibits that highlight the history of the base, as well as Canada's contribution to the war effort. There is also a cozy little gift shop, full of hard-to-find books and videos.

Continue west on Route 1, which follows the west side of the Annapolis River to Annapolis Royal, offering several views of the river. Prior to entering Annapolis Royal the information center provides a convenient rest stop.

On the causeway over the Annapolis River you will find the only tidal power generating station in North America, and it is well worth a visit. Harnessing the vast tidal resources of the Bay of Fundy (the greatest in the world), this facility opened in 1984 and produces enough electricity to power almost 5,000 homes. Built as an experiment, it has been so successful that it continues in operation, and draws environmentally conscious visitors (and politicians) from around the world. Its four-bladed turbine is the largest in the world, with a 7.6-meter (25 ft) diameter. At peak output it can generate 20 megawatts of electricity. The small Visitor Centre is open from mid-May to mid-October.

The most pleasant way into Annapolis Royal is by taking the first right past the tidal generating station, Saint Anthony St., and the second right onto Chapel St., which becomes the eastern end of Lower Saint George St.

First settled by Samuel de Champlain in 1605, the tiny hamlet of Port Royal and its close neighbor Annapolis Royal were the first established European settlements north of Florida. For the next 100 years this very fertile area passed back and forth between England and France, with the occasional raid by New England colonists.

In 1710 Annapolis Royal was named the first capital of the new Colony of Nova Scotia, and the British army built a small garrison (Fort Anne) to protect the region from seaborne attack. Much of the original fort remains, including stone buildings and ramparts. It is now a National Historic Site and located on the corner of Lower and Upper Saint George Streets.

Annapolis Royal, with its vibrant artists community and charming waterfront, is a lovely place to stop and relax. Have a bite to eat in any one of the numerous establishments along George Street and take a walk along the oldest street in Canada. Numerous early 19th- and 18th-century buildings line this street, including the home (c. 1869) built by Corey O'Dell, a former Nova Scotia Pony Express rider. The O'Dell House, formerly a tavern-inn on the waterfront, is now a museum (136 St. George St., 902-532-7754, www.annapolisheritagesociety.com). Two doors farther is the Bailey House (c1770) that is now a historic B&B. On Upper St. George Street is one of Annapolis Royal's best-kept secrets: the Historic Gardens, 10 acres of award-winning floral displays, including one of the best rose exhibits in all of Canada.

The futuristic design of the Annapolis Tidal Generating Station is rather appropriate, given the cutting-edge generating technology that is employed to harness the enormous tidal potential of the nearby Bay of Fundy.

Some of the historic houses in Annapolis Royale have been renovated and have been put to other uses such as the Bailey House, which is now a B&B inn.

Just a short distance away, on the other side of the Annapolis River Basin, is the Habitation at Port Royal, which dates back to 1605. (From Annapolis Royal take Route 1 past the Tidal Generating Station and turn left onto Granville Road to Port Royal.) Known as the Birthplace of Canada, the original fortified building was rectangular in shape, with a small interior courtyard. The Habitation was sacked and burned by American colonists from Virginia in 1613. By this time, however, most of the inhabitants had moved across the basin to Annapolis Royal. Rebuilt in 1939 by the Canadian government, the Habitation now stands as a monument to early French culture, colonization efforts, and the development of successful commercial relations with the local Mi'kmaq inhabitants. Although small in size, it proudly represents the European struggle for empire in the New World during the 17th and 18th centuries

From Annapolis Royal take Route 1 the 32 km (20 mi) to Digby. Where Annapolis Royal is located at the eastern end of the Annapolis Basin, the port of Digby is at the western end. A narrow gap through North Mountain allows easy access from this protected harbor to the Bay of Fundy. With a present-day population of 2,311, Digby was first settled in 1783 by a group of United Empire Loyalists from New England. Over the years its reputation was built on lumber and fishing, and it earned a distinction as the Scallop Capital of the World. The Fundy tides bring an inrush of cold water twice a day and the scallop fishing season is year-round instead of seasonal. Digby scallops are considered to be the tastiest scallops in the world. The difference between low tide and high tide in Digby Harbour ranges from 8.5 to 10.6 m (28 to 35 ft)!

Digby is also the Nova Scotia terminus for a year round ferry service across the Bay of Fundy to Saint John, New Brunswick. The three-hour crossing, on the Princess of Acadia, can save a long drive (615 km, 384 mi) between the two ports. (Reservations are required. Call Bay Ferries at 877-762-7245). The town also has abundant lodging, restaurants, gas stations, and even a Canadian Tire store where some motorcycle supplies are available. Local riders meet at Tim Horton's (the Canadian version of Dunkin' Donuts).

Digby is home to the largest motorcycle rally in Atlantic Canada. Held on the first weekend in September (Canada's Labour Day Weekend), the Wharf Rat Rally (love that name!) draws bikers from all over eastern Canada and the United States. In 2008 an estimated 17,000 bikes (and 50,000 people) participated in at least part of the four-day weekend! (For information, contact: The Wharf Rat Rally Motorcycle Association, P.O. Box 1200, Digby, Nova Scotia, Canada, B0V 1A0)

Digby Neck is the southwest end of North Mountain and this long, narrow strip of land divides St. Mary's Bay from the Bay of Fundy. Route 217 runs a leisurely 100 km (62 mi) down The Neck to the tiny fishing village of East Ferry. The road makes its way along the side of North Mountain, passing through thick deciduous forest, along Lake Midway and past Sandy Cove. There are few places that allow passing slower cars, but this road offers a delightful run when there's no traffic. (Hint: on the return trip, try to be the first off the ferry.)

A nice stop is at the Little River Trading Company, a century-old general store in the tiny community (pop. 220) of the same name. It is a great place to have an ice cream, and listen to the locals catch up on the latest news. The nearby fish plant also offers some interesting photo opportunities, especially when fishermen are off-loading their catch.

Take the small ferry to Tiverton on Long Island. Fifteen km (9 mi) long and only 5 km (3 mi) wide Long Island is surrounded by cliffs, higher on the south side than on the north, with several little coves. Those who don't mind a one-hour hike, with a steep descent by boardwalk at the ocean end, the famous Balancing Rock is well worth a visit. It is a narrow, 10-meter-high (33 ft) column of basalt, and is precariously balanced on its edge.

The Wharf Rat Motorcycle Rally is held on Canada's Labour Day Weekend, the first weekend in September.

Keep a sharp eye out for the small, handmade wooden sign that marks the inconspicuous dirt parking area.

Route 217 continues as a second ferry crossing from the village of Freeport across Grand Passage to Westport. Brier Island (pop. 188), is quite a bit smaller than Long Island. Once again the height of the Fundy tides is evident when piers and fishing shanties are left high above sea level and the long concrete ramp of the ferry landing is completely exposed. Whale-watching tours are offered by several different operators and sometimes when crossing Grand Passage during high tide these great cetaceans can be seen from the ferry. The island has several rare species of wildflowers and is considered to be the premier bird watching venue in Nova Scotia. Route 217 is paved from the ferry landing to where it ends in the village facing Peters Island, but the remaining roads are all crushed gravel. B&B accommodations are available on both islands and Brier Island has a lovely lodge perched on a cliff overlooking the Bay of Fundy. (Brier Island Lodge, 800-662-8355). Gas is available (regular only) at the general store.

The Acadians

Samuel de Champlain arrived with his company in 1604 to settle North America. After wintering at Île Sainte Croix (between Maine and New Brunswick at the mouth of the St. Croix River) they moved to the sheltered harbor of Port Royal in what is now Nova Scotia, but which they called La Cadie. About 60 French families settled the region in the 17th century and the first census in Port Royal lists 400 Acadian in 1671. Over the next century this population increased to more than 14,000.

The French settlers came from different regions in France, but their isolation in the Maritimes created a unique culture that differs from Québecois French. Acadian language incorporates Mi'kmaq and English words and the accent is markedly different from French or Québecois. The Acadian word *déjeuner* will be seen throughout Québec and it simply means breakfast. *Diner* is obviously lunchtime, and *souper* probably doesn't require translation. This isolation also resulted in the development of a unique culture and cuisine. Some, like *tête de violon* (fiddlehead ferns) have become New England traditional fare, and *pet-de-soeur* (a pastry made with pie dough, butter, and brown sugar) is obvious to anyone who has ever had dough left over from making a pie crust. *Râpure*, or rappie pie, takes on a bit more significance as a symbol of Acadian cuisine. Basically it's a seasoned potato pie with chicken or pork, but anything, even seafood, goes into family recipes along with a considerable amount of pride.

Unlike those who settled New France (Québec), the Acadians were politically neutral. This neutrality proved to be their undoing during the Seven Years' War when they refused to swear an absolute oath to the King of England out of moral consideration that they might be forced to take arms against French families or First Nations (Native Americans). This led to *Le Grand Dérangement* (The Great Expulsion) of 1755-63 that was ordered by Col. Charles Lawrence. Homes were burned, lands confiscated, and families split up. In what we now call "ethnic cleansing," 14,000 Acadians were deported and, as on the Trail of Tears for the Apache, a third of them died. Some escaped to the Magdalen Islands, others to Newfoundland, and still others to Louisiana (Cajun country) in 1763.

However, like the Amish or Mennonites, the Acadians survived in isolated, insular communities, many of them trickling back to the

Maritimes to establish themselves in places like Madawaska, Maine and Moncton, New Brunswick. Others eventually returned to the Pubnicos in Nova Scotia. It was the publication of an epic poem by Henry Wadsworth Longfellow in 1847 that provided the catalyst for the resurgence of Acadian culture. *Evangeline—A Tale of Acadie* was loosely based on the Great Expulsion, but it embodied the soul of a culture.

Today, Acadian culture and language is most evident in the vicinity of northern Maine, northeastern New Brunswick, Île du Havre Aubert in the Magdalen Islands, and southern Nova Scotia. The flag, a tri-color with the gold star that's known as Stella Maris, is flown alongside provincial and national flags in Acadian regions. ∎

These young Acadian lasses were tour guides in the Église Saint-Bernard.

For the 33 km (20.5 mi) from Digby to Weymouth Routes 1 and 101 are merged. Once past Weymouth, however, continue on Route 1 for a journey through the fascinating part of Nova Scotia known as The Acadian Shore.

From here to the Pubnicos you will find the province's largest Acadian population—more than 20,000 people—and the Stella Maris flag flying proudly beside those of Canada and Nova Scotia. It is a lovely ride through small rural villages and affords an opportunity to experience Acadian culture and cuisine. In this region the local Catholic Church, along with its associated activities, sets a pattern of daily life that has changed very little in the last 400 years.

About 3 km from Weymouth, you can't help but notice Église Saint-Bernard, an imposing stone church located near the village of Belliveau Cove that exemplifies the influence of the Catholic religion on Acadian culture. A truly majestic stone edifice with a seating capacity of 1,000 people, the church was built over a period of 32 years (1910 to 1942) of granite blocks quarried near Shelburne and transported by train and then ox cart to the site. Working almost entirely by hand, and with very few mechanical devices, local stonemasons patiently added a few rows of blocks each year until the building was completed.

The Église Sainte-Marie is just a short distance farther along the road at Church Point. It is the largest wooden church in North America and, somewhat incredibly, was built by 1,500 volunteers in only two years (1903 to 1905). The master carpenter could neither read nor write, but was able to follow the plans of a similar cathedral in France. There are 41 stained-glass windows (each was shipped from France in a crate of molasses to prevent breakage!) The 999-pipe church organ was built by the famous Casavant Brothers from Québec.

The steeple on top of the Église Sainte-Marie is exactly 56.4 m (185 ft) high.

The Cape Forchu Light guards the entrance into Yarmouth Harbour.

Church Point is also home to Université Sainte-Anne, the only French university in Nova Scotia. The archives on campus contain a vast amount of historical and genealogical information about the region's Acadian population.

As you make your way towards Yarmouth, several little communities like Metegan, Mavillette, Cape St. Marys, and Port Maitland, offer enchanting glimpses into the Acadian lifestyle, and the slow moving pace of the local inhabitants.

Route 1 goes directly to downtown Yarmouth, but Main Shore Drive from Port Maitland offers a scenic alternative route. Those who are fascinated by bridges might wish to stop at the harbor in Port Maitland to photograph the world's smallest wooden drawbridge (pedestrian only). Main Shore Road continues through a beautiful, rolling, rural landscape where lupines dominate the roadsides in season. It joins Route 304 at a dogleg. Turning right onto Route 304/Grove Rd. leads to the lighthouse on Cape Forchu. Continuing straight you are on Vancouver Street. The "horse monument," a gorgeous watering trough and fountain made of marble and topped by a gilded statue of a horse, is found at the junction of Vancouver Street and Route 1.

Yarmouth is the primary fishing harbor in the province and sees fog an average of 118 days a year. Most of the time it "burns off" by mid-morning.

Yarmouth

Don't be dismayed if you arrive in Yarmouth and find it enshrouded in fog. The town averages 118 days with fog each year, although it usually "burns off" by mid-morning. Consider the maritime fog to be an appropriate reception to one of the finest working seaports in the province.

This vibrant town is known as "The Gateway to Nova Scotia." With a population that slightly exceeds 7,000, Yarmouth is the closest Atlantic Canadian port to The Boston States, as Nova Scotians refer to their New England neighbors.

The month of April, 2010, saw the last fast ferry service between Yarmouth, Nova Scotia, and the Maine ports of Bar Harbor and Portland. This catamaran service had been in service for more than a decade, but rising costs and falling government subsidies brought it to an end. There are plans to bring in a replacement ferry service for 2011, but as we go to press the situation is still under consideration. Full ferry service to Maine should be restored by 2012 or 2013.

The sheltered harbor was visited by Samuel de Champlain during his first voyage to the New World in 1604, and it became a seasonal anchorage for French fishing fleets for the next 150 years. When a group

The Coffee Coach Express on Water Street was built from an old railway streetcar. Enjoy coffee and a lobster roll while watching the boats in the harbor.

of settlers arrived from Yarmouth, Massachusetts in 1759, they promptly named their new settlement after their former home.

Yarmouth is still the primary fishing harbor in the province because one of the world's most productive fishing sites, Georges Banks, lies just south of Nova Scotia. Over-fishing has resulted in a moratorium on cod, but mackerel, lobster, and crab are still important catches for the Nova Scotia fishing industry. It can be fascinating to sit along the waterfront, or while having lunch at the Coffee Coach Express, and watch the steady stream of local fishing boats as they go about their business, oblivious to the many seasonal visitors who observe and photograph them.

The many large and visually impressive Victorian homes in the town were built during the golden Age of Sail, when Yarmouth sea captains became wealthy through trade with the eastern United States and the various islands in the West Indies and the Caribbean. For almost two decades (1870–90) Yarmouth was considered to be the richest small town in North America. A brochure describing a walking tour of some of these lovely houses and various other heritage sights is available at the information center on Main Street. One of these—the home of Mrs. Alfred Fuller, wife of the founder and President of the Fuller Brush Company—is next door to the Yarmouth County Museum and is open to the public.

The Yarmouth County Museum (yarmouthcountymuseum.ednet-.ns.ca) has a number of fascinating exhibits and artifacts. The first-order Fresnel lens from the old Forchu Light, items from a 19th-century blacksmith shop, the largest collection of ship paintings in Canada, and much more are on display. The most controversial of these is the Runic Stone. Is it a hoax or did Vikings actually land in Yarmouth in 1007?

The Fire Fighters Museum of Nova Scotia (902-742-5525, www.firefighters.museum.gov.ns.ca) is fantastic and an Orient buckboard is part of the collection. The Killam Brother Shipping Office (Water St., 902-742-5539, yarmouuthcountymuseum.ednet.ns.ca) is a mid-1800s shipping office that is virtually unchanged since its operation during the great Age of Sail. The western branch of the Art Gallery of Nova Scotia (749-2248, www.artgalleryofnovascotia.ca/en/yarmouth-home) on Main St. has an excellent permanent collection and exhibitions. Those staying in Yarmouth for the night shouldn't miss the Dinner Theater at the Rodd Grand on Main Street. Dinner guests are entertained by a theater production that pulls them into the act. Verbal descriptions can't convey the atmosphere generated by the veteran actors of this summer theater. They may take your dinner order and serve your meal, but they'll not step out of character! There's plenty to see and do in Yarmouth. Coupled with one of the province's gateway information centers (corner of Main and Forest Streets) and all the services found in the malls along Starrs Road/Route 3 near the terminus of Routes 101 and 103, this is the perfect place to stop and take a breather.

If the weather is not foggy, you should consider a visit to the Cape Forchu Lightstation at the end of Route 304. The striking lighthouse is surrounded by three bodies of water—Yarmouth Harbour, the Atlantic Ocean, and the Bay of Fundy. Now reached by a causeway, the site offers a commanding view of the Gulf of Maine, and a panoramic view of the town itself.

Yarmouth is one place where room reservations are recommended, especially in the summer season. In addition to several Bed and Breakfasts, and cozy little inns, there are a number of motels offering a grand total of 408 rooms. These include: Comfort Inn (800-228-5150); Capri Motel (800-772-2774); Lakelawn Motel (877-664-0664); Midtown Motel (877-742-5600); biker-friendly Rodd Colony Harbour Inn (800-565-7633), the Rodd Grand Yarmouth (800-565-7633). ∎

Trip 19 Lighthouse Route

Distance: *522 km (323.8 mi) Allow one to two days.*
Highlights: *Gentle coastal scenery, pirates and privateers, and more than 20 lighthouses.*

Compared to the Evangeline Route along the southern part of the Bay of Fundy, the southwest coast of mainland Nova Scotia is markedly different. The red sandstone cliffs of the Minas Basin and the basalt cliffs of the Bay of Fundy give way to granite-strewn shores on the Atlantic coast. Deciduous trees on the western side give way to predominance of conifers on the east, and normal Atlantic tidal levels occur on this coast.

The Lighthouse Route begins as Route 3 in Yarmouth and follows the coast in an easterly direction around to Halifax. Route 103 is a provincial highway, the quickest way to reach the provincial capital, a three-hour ride. Route 3 follows the coastline of the many peninsulas and bays, although it often merges with the main highway. To allow plenty of time to explore the coast and its charming villages and towns, and to visit some of the many

These lobster boats moored at Cape Forchu head out to the primary lobster-fishing grounds, which are on Georges Banks just southeast of Yarmouth.

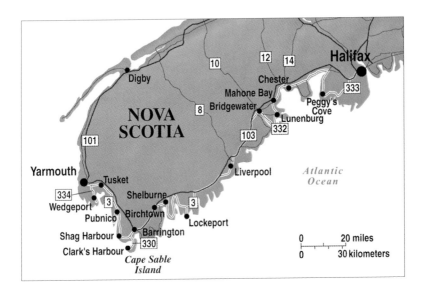

museums, plan to take an entire day or even two with an overnight stop in Liverpool or Lunenburg.

Wedgeport (pop. 1217) is an Acadian village located on Route 334 and was once known as the "Sport Tuna Fishing Capital of the World." During the mid-1930s to the 1980s, the village attracted many famous celebrities such as: President Franklin Roosevelt; heavy-weight boxing champion Gene Tunney; aviatrix Amelia Earhart; writer Ernest Hemingway; and Jean Beliveau, captain of the Montréal Canadiens hockey team.

The Sport Tuna Fishing Museum is located on the tip of the peninsula at the very end of Route 334. It chronicles the history of the International Tuna Cup Match, which started in 1937, and in its heyday drew teams from around the world. A record number of 1,780 Bluefin Tuna, the largest of the species, were landed during the Cup Match in 1949. These magnificent fighting fish can easily exceed 455 kg (1,000 lbs) in weight! The largest tuna ever recorded was an Atlantic bluefin caught off Nova Scotia that weighed 679 kg (1,496 lbs).

Returning to Route 3, it is only a short distance to Tusket (pop. 395), a village first settled in 1785 by refugees from the American Revolutionary War. The local courthouse and jail, with its small bell-tower, was built in 1805 and is the oldest surviving such structure in Canada. Tours are available in season.

The Pubnicos (Mi'kmaq for cleared land) were first settled in 1653, and are the oldest-existing Acadian communities in the world. The village of Pubnico is located at the head of Pubnico Harbour with the West Pubnicos

The Route from Yarmouth

0 km (0 mi) Take Route 3 from Yarmouth.

5 km (3.1 mi) Turn right on Route 334.

19 km (11.6 mi) Arrive Wedgeport. Return to Route 3.

32 km (20.1 mi) Turn right on Route 3.

81 km (50.5 mi) Arrive Pubnico. Continue on Route 3.

112 km (69.8 mi) Arrive Shag Harbour. Continue on Route 3.

121 km (75.1 mi) Turn right on Route 330.

134 km (82.5 mi) Arrive Clark's Harbour. Return to Route 3.

146 km (90.4 mi) Turn right on Route 3.

154 km (95.4 mi) Arrive Barrington. Continue on Route 3.

197 km (122.1 mi) Arrive Shelburne. Continue on Route 3.

228 km (141.2 mi) Arrive Lockeport. Continue on Route 3 and 103.

276 km (171.0 mi) Take Exit 20 to continue on Route 3.

292 km (180.8 mi) Arrive Liverpool. Continue on Route 103.

339 km (210mi) Arrive Bridgewater. Take Route 332 to Lunenburg.

376 km (233.2 mi) Arrive Lunenburg. Take Route 3 to Chester.

412 km (255.1 mi) Arrive Chester. Continue on Route 3.

450 km (278.9 mi) Turn right on Route 333.

478 km (296.5 mi) Arrive Peggy's Cove. Continue on Route 333 and Route 3.

522 km (323.8 mi) Arrive Halifax.

being on located on the western peninsula (Pubnico Point) and the East Pubnicos are the east side of the bay. West Pubnico, Middle West Pubnico, Lower West Pubnico, are active fishing villages, with much going on dockside. They are charming places to visit and experience the Acadian lifestyle. The Historic Acadien Village is located on School Street in Lower West Pubnico (888-381-8999, acadianvillage.museum.gov.ns.ca). This living history museum is a replica of an 1860s-era Acadian village complete with costumed interpreters. The Acadien Museum & Archives is located across from the fire station in West Pubnico (762-3380, www.museeacadien.ca). In addition to Acadian artifacts and display is an impressive collection of antique cameras.

The 17 turbines of the Pubnico Point Wind Farm generate a maximum of 30 megawatts, which is enough electricity to support 12,000 homes, but opponents claim they make too much noise and spoil the view. You be the judge. You can see them from the fishing dock of Lower East Pubnico and along Route 3.

Only a few miles farther on is the tiny fishing village of Shag Harbour (pop. 450), which is the site of one of the strangest, yet best documented,

This view of the docks in Lower East Pubnico has the Pubnico Point Wind Farm in the background. Opponents say the giant turbines spoil the view and make too much noise. However author Aiken could hear the "whoosh" only when directly beneath the blades.

UFO sightings in North America. On the night of October 4, 1967, several eyewitnesses observed a series of colored lights in the sky that appeared to crash into the nearby ocean. Thinking it was a downed aircraft, the Royal Canadian Mounted Police and local fishermen organized a rescue effort, but although lights were seen on the surface for a short while, nothing was ever found, either on or below the water. It has never been satisfactorily explained. The Shag Harbour Incident Society maintains the UFO Rest Stop and a local UFO Musuem and Family Research Centre. The post office uses a special UFO cancellation stamp and this provides an opportunity to send postcards to friends and family about your out-of-this-world travels.

At the very southwestern tip of Nova Scotia lies Cape Sable Island. Route 330 is a winding road along the shore and views of active boatyards make it well worth a visit, but not in one of its frequent fogs or high winds. It's famous for its distinctive inshore fishing boats, Cape Islanders, which first were built at Clark's Harbour in 1907 and are now in use all over Atlantic Canada. The island has also been the site of numerous shipwrecks, the worst being the *SS Hungarian* in 1860, with the loss of more than 200 lives.

Barrington proclaims itself as being the Lobster Capital of Canada. The stacks of lobster traps seen stacked in driveways makes one believe it's true. Cape Sable is the closest point of land to Georges Banks and this is one of the world's best lobster habitats. There are several points of historical

Seal Island Light Museum in Great Barrington allows visitors the opportunity to climb five stories to view the original Fresenel lens.

interest along Route 3 in this township. The Barrington Woolen Mill operated from 1882 to 1962 and is now a museum; The Old Meeting House (c. 1765) is the oldest non-conformist house of worship in Canada; and the Seal Island Light Museum is a conveniently located reconstruction with lens from the original light.

From Barrington the Lighthouse Route follows Route 309 along the coast. If you wish to take time out, enjoy a swim, and lie on a beautiful sand beach, then by all means visit Sand Hills Provincial Beach Park. For those concerned about time, it makes sense to continue on Route 3 as it merges with Provincial Highway 103, toward Shelburne.

Located on Route 3 just west of Shelburne, Birchtown was once the largest free black community in North America. Named after Brigadier General Samuel Birch, commander of New York and champion of the African Americans who supported the British forces during the American Revolution, it was settled in 1783 by five companies and at its peak had a population of 2,500 "free blacks." Two granite pedestals—one with a commemorative bronze plaque and the other with an interpretive map of the area—have been erected on land thought to have been a burial ground for Black Loyalists.

That same year, 1783, more than 3,000 (white) United Empire Loyalists, settled at what is considered to be one of the finest natural harbors in the world. Other Loyalists soon fled the United States and within a few years the population of Shelburne exceeded 10,000, the fourth-largest community in North America at that time.

Today Shelburne has an outstanding Heritage District on the waterfront, which was used as the setting for the 1994 movie *The Scarlet Letter* (set in puritan New England c. 1650), starring Robert Duvall and Demi Moore. Several museums are located in the Heritage District. The Ross-Thomson House is an original store restored as it appeared in 1820. The John C. Williams Dory Shop Museum (902-875-3219, doryshop.museum.gov.ns.ca), features a small boatyard displaying the art of building wooden boats. The Muir-Cox Shipyard, one of the oldest shipyards in the province, includes an interpretive center. The Shelburne County Museum features a number of historical exhibits including the oldest fire pumper in North America.

During American Revolutionary times, many African Americans and freed slaves came to Birchtown.

The view of this beautiful beach at White Point can be enjoyed from the vantage point of an Adirondack chair on the lawn of the White Point Resort.

Although not large, Shelburne has all the necessary facilities for visitors. There are cozy little inns and Bed and Breakfasts, along with several motels: MacKenzie's Motel & Cottages (866-875-0740); Wildwood Motel (800-565-5001); and the Loyalist Inn (888-253-1133), which first opened in the late 1800s.

The Lighthouse Route briefly joins Route 103, but continuing to follow Route 3 will take you to the busy fishing village of Lockeport (pop. 701). Originally settled by fishermen from Massachusetts in 1761, the little port soon became one of the wealthiest towns in Nova Scotia. Boasting Nova Scotia's first Registered Streetscape, it includes five historic homes, built in Colonial, Georgian, and Victorian styles, which overlook the harbor. The town is also known for Crescent Beach, a mile-long curve of hard, white sand that is a favorite picnic spot.

From Lockeport continue following the Lighthouse Route, which merges with Route 103. Taking Exit 20 onto Route 3 is not the quickest way into Liverpool but it's the most scenic. You will pass the White Point Resort, which is one of those places where riders can pamper themselves. Just make sure you don't run over any of the semi-tame rabbits that populate the resort: they're considered to be a trademark of the place.

Liverpool (pop. 3,295) started as a long-time seasonal camp of the Mi'kmaq. It later became an Acadian outpost, and then a full-time settlement of New England fishermen in 1759. They named it after Liverpool in England and even called the local river the Mersey.

Although sympathetic at first to the idea of American independence, the town was attacked by American privateers during the Revolution, and soon turned against the rebellion. The port became notorious for its privateers who preyed on American ships off the coast of Nova Scotia and New England during the Napoleonic Wars (1799–1815) and the War of 1812. The town later became a major seaport, as fishing, lumber, and ship building industries expanded rapidly in the 19th century. In the 1920s, in response to prohibition, Liverpool became a center for the "rum-running" trade between Nova Scotia and The Boston States.

If you like visiting museums plan to spend a full day in Liverpool. The Sherman Hines Museum of Photography is housed in the Town Hall (219 Main St., 394-2667, www.shermanhinesphotographymuseum.com) and the Queens County Museum with its historical collections is located just down the street (109 Main St., www.queenscountymuseum.com). The Hank Snow Country Music Centre (354-4675, www.aco.ca/hanksnow) is dedicated to the life of the local boy who became a country music legend and is housed with the Nova Scotia Country Music Hall of Fame in the old CN railway depot, a classic itself. The Perkins House Museum is a living history museum that is set in the mid-18th century in the household of judge and merchant Simeon Perkins. Haven't had enough? The Rossignol Cultural Centre at 205 Church Street (354-3067, www.rossignolcultural-centre.com) is a museum of museums. It includes the Museum of the Outhouse and the Apothecary Museum, the English Room, the Wildlife Art Gallery, and much more. It houses the Culture Village with tipis, a yurt, Mi'kmaq wigwam, log cabin, Acadian cottage, British block house, and others. These are full-sized, furnished dwellings—not models or panoramas. Oh yes, the Centre also includes libraries and other collections. There is also an interesting lighthouse museum at Fort Point, which contains the third-oldest lighthouse in the province and the ruins of the original French fort date back to 1632.

The town has a 27-unit motel (Lanes Privateer Inn, 800-794-3332), and within a 16-kilometer (10 mi) radius are several other small motels, inns, and B&Bs. Route 8 provides an opportunity to truncate this loop and head across the province, past the Kejimkujik National Park, to Annapolis Royal. Make sure you tank up with gasoline in Liverpool if you take Route 8.

From Liverpool Route 103 goes directly to Bridgewater. The Lighthouse Route makes a detour as Route 331 from Exit 17 to Bridgewater. From Bridgewater, Route 332 loops around past Rose Bay and along Lunenburg

Featured at the Fisheries Museum in Lunenburg is the Theresa E. Connor, a traditional Grand Banks schooner.

Harbour. This is the most scenic way to approach the experience of Lunenburg, although Route 3 is the more direct road. Named after a German medieval city and first settled by German immigrants in 1753, Lunenburg (pop. 2,317), quickly became an important port and commercial shipbuilding center.

Today the town with its original street plan is recognized as being the best-preserved example of a British colonial settlement in North America. In 1995 the United Nations Educational, Scientific, and Cultural Organization (UNESCO) designated this historic town a World Heritage Site. However, it is even more famous, at least among Canadians, as the homeport of the schooner Bluenose, and now the Bluenose II.

A highlight of any visit to Lunenburg is the Fisheries Museum of the Atlantic, a wonderful place to spend a few hours, if not an entire afternoon. Where else can you step aboard a traditional Grand Banks of Newfoundland schooner, the Theresa E. Connor, or the steel-sided trawler Cape Sable, the type of vessel that in the 1950s and '60s made the legendary wooden Grand Banks schooner obsolete. And if not on tour, the flagship of the Canadian tall-ship fleet, the Bluenose II, is open for visits dockside.

The bright-red buildings also house fresh- and salt-water aquaria and exhibits on the history of the east-coast fishery.

Docked at the Fisheries Museum is the Cape Sable, a steel-side trawler.

Daily demonstrations are offered on various topics, such as shipbuilding, rum-running, and how to make a lobster trap. Open from mid-May to mid-October the Fisheries Museum has a great nautical gift shop, a restaurant, with a superb view of the busy harbor, and offers guided tours on a regular basis.

The streets are narrow and, during the height of tourist season or when the tall ships are in port, parking can be a nightmare. Don't let this discourage you. Find a place to park and explore the heritage area on foot (it's small enough).

For a town with less than 2,500 inhabitants, Lunenburg has a wide range of accommodation, including 28 inns and B&Bs. The Lunenburg Inn is a Victorian-era Heritage Property (800-565-3963); the Rum Runner Inn, a former waterfront mansion that has been lovingly restored (888-778-6786); and the Lennox Tavern B&B is the oldest (1791) continuously operating Inn in Canada. The Bluenose Lodge (1863) offers 9 rooms (800-565-8851); the Lunenburg Arms Hotel has 24 rooms (800-679-4950); the Smuggler's Cove Inn has 17 rooms (888-777-8606); the 15-unit Topmast Motel (877-525-3222) has spectacular views of the harbor; and the Wheelhouse Motel has 18 drive-up units, for those who like to keep their bikes outside their door.

Route 3 is the most scenic road out of town, but if traffic is an issue, take the road that the locals use to reach the main highway, Route 324/Northwest Road, which begins at the port as both Green and Dufferin streets. Traveling along the southeast coast of the province one seems to be always deciding whether to take the "fast" road or the "scenic" one.

Between Lunenburg and Chester is the coastal town of Mahone Bay, a well-known artists' community with a number of cozy little shops and galleries. The charming setting of the town's three waterfront churches will have you pulling out your camera.

Among the several hundred small islands in scenic Mahone Bay is Oak Island (privately owned), site of the world's longest-running treasure hunt. For more than three centuries, various individuals and groups have tried to fathom the mystery and excavate past the booby-traps of its Money Pit. Some say it's the site of Bluebeard's treasure, but whatever is down there was hidden with a great deal of clever effort.

Less than 80 km (50 mi) from Nova Scotia's provincial capital of Halifax, is Chester, a small resort community full of "old homes and old money." At the beginning of the 20th century, it became a seasonal retreat for wealthy families from Halifax, or as far away as The Boston States, and retains this status still.

These two-men dories were used in the late 1800s to fish for cod on the Grand Banks of Newfoundland. Each man set long fishing lines, with upwards of 1,000 hooks per dory.

From Chester you have the option of taking Route 14 across the province to Windsor. By doing so you would be bypassing Halifax, the largest urban center in eastern Canada. If heading for Halifax, you must once again choose between the faster Route 103 and the scenic Route 333 through Peggy's Cove.

The Lighthouse Route continues on Route 333. However, during the tourist season this route has a well-deserved reputation as being a "slow road" because the narrow, winding, secondary highway is usually crowded with cars, camper trailers, and tour buses. The reason for such heavy traffic is that the little fishing village of Peggy's Cove at the very tip of the headland has gained a reputation as one of the most photographed places in Canada.

As you make your way towards the Atlantic Ocean, the scenery becomes quite barren, with large granite outcroppings along the shore. Peggy's Cove (pop. 50) is known for its rugged coastal scenery, weathered fishing shacks, and a photogenic lighthouse. The lighthouse contains a post office, the only post office in the country, if not North America, that is housed in a lighthouse. Be attentive to the posted warning signs: the exposed granite rocks along the shore present a real danger in periods of heavy weather and unwary individuals have been washed out to sea by large breaking waves that seem to come from nowhere.

During the months of July and August the site can be too crowded, too commercialized, and far too difficult to access—especially by motorcycle. There is even a monetary charge just to get off your bike and take a photograph! However, in the off-season it does make for a pleasant excursion, though not on a foggy day.

Just over a kilometer from the lighthouse is a poignant tribute to the 229 victims of Swissair Flight 111 that crashed into the nearby ocean on the night of September 2, 1998. The isolation of the monument, and its stark design with sight holes for marking the crash site, make for a moving memorial.

Route 333 bears right onto Route 3 and it's a short, direct ride to downtown Halifax. Those whose destination is Dartmouth should bear left and onto Route 103 at Exit 2B, which quickly ends at Route 102. Stay in the right lane to go east into the city; left lane for Route 102 north, which will intersect Route 101. Route 102 east will end as Bayers Road at Connaught Avenue. Turn left on Connaught Ave. and left on Windsor Ave. (it's simpler than it sounds, just go with the flow of traffic). Windsor Avenue becomes Route 2, which is the road that follows the waterfront and will lead back to Route 3. However, bear right onto the Route 111 ramp and over the A. Murray McKay Bridge to Exit 1 and Princess Margaret Blvd. Turn left and the next street is Route 7/Windmill Road: right (south) goes to downtown Dartmouth, and the left eventually becomes Route 101. Good luck!

Though a major port and the hub of Nova Scotia, Halifax is a very biker-friendly city. Photo by Robin Taylor

Halifax

It can be a little bit confusing when you say that you're going to Halifax—the capital of Nova Scotia with a population of about 380,000. In 1996 the original city was amalgamated with its suburbs and neighboring cities to create the Halifax Regional Municipality (HRM). You could be 180 kilometers offshore on Sable Island and you'd still be in Halifax! The downtown historic core—what locals call "Halifax metro centre"—with it's vibrant waterfront is what most of us think of as being "Halifax."

On June 21, 1749 Halifax was founded at the foot of what would later become Citadel Hill on Halifax Peninsula, which in turn is on Chebuto Peninsula. These peninsulas had been the summer encampments for First Nations people long before Basque sailors used the sheltered harbor as a temporary refuge from North Atlantic storms on the offshore fishing banks. These land protrusions create the second-largest natural harbor in the world and this, along with its geographic location, defines the history of this city to the present day.

This is the largest naval dockyard north of Norfolk, Virginia, and historically it played a crucial role for the British navy in its colonial struggle with both France and the United States. As a Canadian navy port its role in WWI and WWII was crucial to Allied efforts in Europe. Such a port is more than just the military. Both the Grand Banks and Georges Banks, the most productive fishing areas in the world, are offshore. In other eras it was involved in the Caribbean trade and even today it remains one of the closest North American ports to Europe. Halifax's historic buildings and sites are the heritage of both military and commercial activity.

The Halifax Citadel, a fort built on top of a glacial drumlin, dominates the city's skyline, and is the most popular National Historic Site in Canada. Established by the British in 1749, to counteract the massive French Fortress of Louisbourg on Cape Breton Island, it has had a strategic military presence ever since, and today serves as the main east coast port for the Royal Canadian Navy. The 78th Highland Regiment and Royal Artillery, or at least actors and students portraying them, still perform ceremonial duties on the hill. The star-shaped Halifax Citadel (www.pc.qc.ca/eng/lhn-nhs/ns/halifax) is perpetually fixed in the year 1869 and this is the fourth fortress to command the heights above the city and harbor.

The citadel is the best landmark for orienting yourself in touring the city. This is an extremely biker-friendly city, but this doesn't mean that it's easy maneuvering around the hilly one-way streets on Citadel Hill. It's best to park and explore on foot. The Halifax Common is adjacent to the Citadel on its northwestern side; the Halifax Public Gardens on the southwestern; and the site of the Royal Nova Scotia International Tattoo (www.nstattoo.ca) that takes place the first week in July is on the southeastern side by the Citadel parking area on Sackville Street. With more than 2,000 performers this is the largest annual indoor show in the world. Full of pomp and pageantry, it combines military and civilian performers to present an unforgettable evening of ceremony and spectacle. Spring Garden Road is the southern boundary of the gardens and the hippest boutiques in the city are along this street going east towards St. Mary's Cathedral. To the east lies the historic city center. The Neptune Theatre (1593 Argyle Street, 902-429-7070, www.neptunetheatre.com) is three blocks east of the Citadel just off Sackville St. and another five blocks will bring you to Lower Water

Motorcycle Journeys Through Atlantic Canada

Street. The Halifax Argyle Information Center is located directly across the street from the theater. From here the Alexander Keith Brewery is one block south; the Maritime Museum of the Atlantic one block north. The famous waterfront restaurants and the ferries to Dartmouth and Woodside are on Cable Wharf east of the Citadel and just one long block north of the Maritime Museum. Casino Nova Scotia (1919 Upper Water Street, 902-425-777 www.casinonovascotia.com) is the next building north of the historic waterfront, Privateer's Wharf. This outlines the relatively small rectangular area that you might consider exploring as a pedestrian.

Depending upon your inclinations, there are a number of places to put on your visitor list, but the history of this city is so dense that it seems you can't walk five minutes without stopping for a photo or to read a plaque. The tower clock on Citadel Hill at the head of Carmichael Street has been keeping accurate time since 1803, with weights that have to be winched (wound) every week and a 4-me-ter (13 ft) pendulum. The clock was ordered by Edward, Duke of Kent (Queen Victoria's father) when he was stationed at the garrison.

An iron bar can be seen protruding from one side of the oldest building in the city, St. Paul's Church (three blocks east of the Citadel and one north of Sackville St.) on George Street. It's a piece of shrapnel from the Dec. 6, 1917 explosion of a munitions ship in Halifax Harbor. During WWI the harbor was a very crowded place, when a Belgian re-lief ship struck a French munitions carrier. Unfortunately the unfolding drama attracted a large crowd, because just after 9 a.m. the munitions ship ignited, causing the largest manmade explosion in history prior to the dropping of the atomic bomb on Hiroshima. On that side of Citadel Hill buildings were leveled, more than 1,600 people died instantly, and thousands more were seriously injured. Windows were shattered within a 50-mile radius of the city, and the powerful shock wave was felt in Sydney, on Cape Breton Island, 250 miles from Halifax Harbour. Along with disaster relief from several nations, emergency trains were dis-patched from Boston the next morning. As a token of thanks, every year the province of Nova Scotia sends Boston the huge Christmas tree that is erected on the Boston Common.

More details about the Halifax Explosion can learned at the Maritime Museum of the Atlantic, which also has exhibits on the Battle of the Atlantic (1939 to 1945), and artifacts recovered from the Titanic. The 1913 Canadian hydrographic research vessel, Acadia, is permanently moored outside the museum and about 20 small craft grace the interior with another 50 in the museum's boat sheds. Samuel Cunard of Halifax founded the famous shipping line (1838 to 1840) that bears his name, so it seems natural to find exhibits about Cunard Lines in the museum. Anyone who is interested in model ships or shipwrecks will have a great time here.

The Public Gardens were established in 1836 and these 17 acres are considered one of the finest Victorian-era formal gardens in North America. The wrought-iron fence that encloses the garden and the main gates are exquisite. Halifax also created the first zoo in North America in 1847, but sold it in 1863. You can still view the zoo, but you now have to go to Central Park in New York City to do so.

A large number of "firsts" are associated with this city, but the one you might be most interested in is the world's longest downtown boardwalk. It runs more than four kilometers along the harbor and provides a great way to explore the vibrant nightlife of the city.

Halifax is known for its restaurants as well as its wonderful bars and brewpubs, which can be found from the waterfront to the edge of the Citadel grounds. The Granite Brewery (1662 Barrington St., 422-4954) specializes in English ales and the Split Crow Pub (1855 Granville St., 422-4366) has been serving sailors and travelers for 250 years. The one that should not be missed is the Red Stag Tavern, located in the heart of Alexander Keith's Brewery (1496 Lower Water St., 902-455-1474), one of the oldest working breweries in North America.

Thursday is officially "bike night" in Halifax with a number of places offering specials and free parking in designated areas. The main action takes place at Perk's on the waterfront across from Alexander Keith's and at Cable Wharf (the ferry dock). What other city do you know of that has an official "bike night," and where most hotels offers discounts to motorcyclists? Halifax just might be the most biker-friendly city in Atlantic Canada. ∎

Trip 20 The Glooscap Trail

Distance: *347 km (215 mi)*
Highlights: *Following the shore of the Bay of Fundy you pass several viewpoints where you can watch the tidal bore move relentlessly up-stream. The road around Cape d'Or is exceptionally thrilling to ride on a motorcycle.*

Like something out of a Stephen King novel, the bone-chilling fog rides the tidal bore as it rushes across the vast plain of red mud. Advancing faster than a person can run is a volume of seawater equaling that of all fresh water rivers in the world. In six hours this land will be 12 meters (40 ft) beneath the sea. It's the flood epic as described by the ancient Sumerians and retold in the Bible, and it happens every 12 hours and 26 minutes.

The Minas Basin lies at the end of the Bay of Fundy and the highest tides on the planet occur here. The Glooscap Trail, which is currently being relabeled as The Fundy Shore Ecotour, follows the shore of the Minas Basin from Windsor to Joggins. Some of the best motorcycle touring on mainland Nova Scotia will be found between Truro and Cape d'Or.

The Route from Windsor to Amherst

0 km (0 mi) Beginning at Exit 5 of Route 101 east of Windsor take Route 14 east.
6 km (3.7 mi) Turn left on Avondale Rd.
7 km (4.6 mi) Turn right on Lawrence Rd.
10 km (6.2 mi) Turn left on Route 215.
104 km (64.4 mi) Turn left on Route 236 in South Maitland.
126 km (78.1 mi) Turn left on ramp onto Route 102.
127 km (78.8 mi) Take the next exit 14A onto Route 2.
166 km (103.3 mi) Arrive Bass River. Continue on Route 2.
178 km (110.6 mi) Arrive Economy. Continue on Route 2.
214 km (132.9 mi) Just past Parrsboro, turn left on Route 209.
257 km (159.8 mi) Arrive Advocate Harbour. Continue on Route 209.
314 km (195.4 mi) Turn right on Route 242 in Joggins.
333 km (206.8 mi) Turn left on Route 302 in Maccan.
342 km (212.3 mi) Turn left on Route 2.
347 km (215.5 mi) Arrive Amherst.

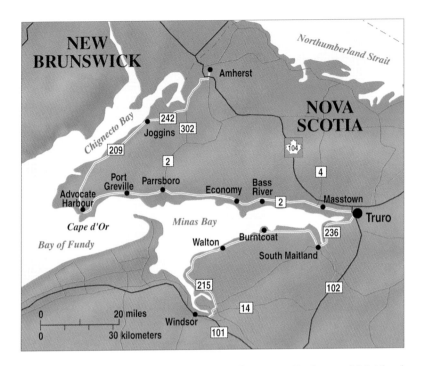

Be advised that there are no gas stations between Windsor and Maitland or between Parrsboro and Joggins. Expect foggy conditions along the coastline when the tide rolls in.

No matter whether your day begins in Halifax or somewhere in the Annapolis Valley, this ride begins just east of the city of Windsor, among farmland cut through by reddish clay tributaries of the Avon River. Route 101 and Route 1 (Trip 18 The Evangeline Trail) traverse this region and are intersected by Route 14 (The Glooscap Trail). There are shortcuts, notably the junction of Route 215 in Newport Corner for those traveling Route 1 from Halifax or Wentworth Road between Route 101 and Route 14, but for the sake of clarity kilometer 0 (mile 0) is at Exit 5 of Route 101 onto Route 14.

The first stop is dictated by the time of day. A couple of hundred meters off Route 14 on Avondale Road there is a concrete bridge with a walkway that crosses the Herbert River. The "Bridge to Mantua" is just one of several vantage points along the Glooscap Trail from which the famous tidal bore can be viewed. When the force of the incoming tide rushes up the rivers and streams that flow into the Minas Basin it collides with their opposing flow and forms a wave that churns its way upstream. The size of the tidal bore wave will depend upon variable factors such as the height of the tide and

The Bridge to Mantua is just one of many vantage points to witness the famous tidal bore rushing upstream. The size of the cresting wave depends upon a number of factors including the phase of the moon and amount of recent rainfall.

amount of water flowing downstream in the watercourse but, in some places and at certain times, the wave can crest at 3 m (10 ft). (www.central-novascotia.com/tides.php)

The next vantage point is at the bridge spanning the Kennetcook River and the best place to view the phenomenon is at the boat launch on the southwest side. The tidal bore arrives here about 20 minutes after the one at the Bridge to Mantua. I suggest continuing on Avondale Road and taking the first right onto Lawrence Road. This scenic road leads directly to Route 215, where you turn left to continue on the Glooscap Trail. The distance between these two sites can be easily ridden in 12 to 15 minutes.

Route 215 makes a dogleg after crossing the Walton River. Slow down and continue straight onto Lorne Smith Road instead of negotiating the next 90-degree corner. The Walton Lighthouse is found at the end of the road on the cliffs above the Minas Basin. It was constructed in 1873 to guide ships to the still visible docks in the river estuary. Visitors can climb the narrow stairs into the lighthouse or simply take in the views from several vantage points along the fenced-off cliffs.

This portion of the Glooscap Trail is a rather sedate road with very little traffic that doesn't offer dramatic vistas or challenging curves. A slight detour onto Burntcoat Road leads to the sweet, low-key Burntcoat Provincial Park. Picnic tables, washrooms, and a lighthouse are reason enough to visit, but there is a stairway down the cliffs that provides access to the sea floor at low tide. At high tide the sea floor will be 12 m (40 ft) beneath the waves, so don't venture too far from the cliffs until you know the timing of the tides for that particular day! In 1869 the highest tide recorded on earth measured 54.6 ft (16.8 m) at Burntcoat Head. Gazing across the expansive mud flats at low tide it's almost inconceivable that they will be covered by this much water in a mere six hours time.

The Glooscap trail turns onto Route 236 in South Maitland and intersects Route 2 in Truro. The tidal bore on the Salmon River is the most dramatic of all. The best two viewing areas are adjacent to the Route 2 bridge. Take South Tidal Bore Road off Route 236 and Tidal Bore Road on the north bank just off Route 2/Route 4. However, if you don't plan to stop in Truro the easiest route is to take the Trans-Canada Highway/Route 104 West and then exit onto Route 2 near Masstown.

Truro is called the Hub of Nova Scotia and is the third-largest city in the province. Those who are always seeking the finest barbeque a region can offer will

Though Walton Light is now privately owned, visitors can still climb the narrow stairs to the lamp.

When the tide rushes up the Shubenacadie River at South Maitland, the water rises a foot every four minutes. These two photos were taken about 15 minutes apart.

want to head over to Roadside Willies (902-843-3486; 27 Jennifer Drive, Bible Hill just off Route 4). Slow cooked at low temperature over apple or hickory-wood fires, this BBQ is the real deal.

When the city lost its elm trees to Dutch elm disease they had sections of the trunks carved into unique sculptures than can be seen through the downtown area. Another odd point of interest is the six sections of the Berlin Wall that somehow found their way across the ocean to be erected in a vacant lot next to a car dealership on Prince Street. Spaced like monolithic concrete tombstones they look more like an uncompleted demolition site than pieces of history, but perhaps they will soon be moved to a more suitable location at the Cold-War survival bunker in nearby Debert.

Route 2 is an ideal cruising road as it follows Cobequid Bay and the Minas Basin to Parrsboro. The Trans-Canada Highway handles the majority of traffic between Truro and Amherst leaving this highway to locals, tourists, and motorcycle riders.

Bass River is noted for two things—a style of chair once made by the Dominion Chair Company, and bass fishing. One time, author Aiken took Wharf Road, which leads to the mouth of the Bass River and found the end of the potholed pavement jammed with parked cars on both sides. People lined the shore fishing with rods the size of small saplings. Earlier in the day there would have been a trickle of water from Bass River flowing onto the red mud flats and disappearing, now people were pulling meter-long striped bass and dogfish from Cobequid Bay!

Riding from Upper Economy to Lower Economy may sound like the story of life, but here these are pleasant rural towns. Adrian's Lunch in Economy is reputed to serve the best lobster rolls in all Nova Scotia. The Five Islands Provincial Park (902-254-2980, www.novascotiaparks.ca/brochures/fiveislands.pdf) offers campgrounds, a picnic area, a beach, hiking trails, and a lighthouse. This is a beautiful area named for the offshore islands Moose, Diamond, Long, Egg, and Pinnacle. Mi'kmaq legend says the Kluscap (Glooscap) created the Five Islands when he threw handfuls of sod at Beaver. Why this god was throwing clumps of earth at a poor beaver has never been explained to me.

Parrsboro is a required stop, if only to fill up the gas tank. This village is famous for rock-hounding and The Nova Scotia Gem & Mineral Show takes place here every August. The famous fossil discovery at nearby Wasson's Bluff in 1984 is critically important as the fossils date from the Triassic-Jurassic mass-extinction boundary and is one of the largest finds of vertebrate fossils in North America. (To reach the access point to Wasson's

A few hours earlier Cobequid Bay was nothing but a vast mud flat. Now fishermen are pulling striped bass a meter long from the incoming water.

Charles Lyell published Principles of Geology *in 1830 and he further refined his theories on evolutionary geology after visiting Joggins in 1842 and 1852. Lyell's discoveries at Joggins were a major influence on Charles Darwin as he developed his theory of evolution.*

Bluff from Parrsboro, take Swan Creek Rd. to Greenhill, then onto Two Islands Road for 2 km (1.3 mi) The fabulous Fundy Geological Museum (162 Two Islands Rd., museum.gov.ns.ca/fgm/en/home/default.aspx) is located on the eastern side of the harbor, while the Parrsboro Rock & Mineral Shop (39 Whitehall Rd.) is located on the western. The shop exhibits the world's smallest dinosaur footprint and both the shop and museum display local gemstones, minerals, and fossils.

Route 2 is the highway most touring riders tend to follow when visiting Nova Scotia and Amherst is only 56 km (34 mi) from Parrsboro by this route. When time is of the essence or the weather is terrible this makes perfect sense, but the best motorcycling road on mainland Nova Scotia is undoubtedly Route 209 from Parrsboro to Advocate Harbour and Cape d'Or.

From the junction at Route 2 to Port Greville the highway is deceptively sedate and quite scenic. Every inlet on the "Parrsboro Shore" once held a shipyard during the Age of Sail and for almost two centuries shipbuilders created mast schooners that plied the oceans of the world. The Age of Sail Heritage Museum (902-348-2030, www.ageofsailmuseum.ca) documents that history. Shaw's Market is the last opportunity to pick up snacks or groceries between Port Greville and Joggins.

Immediately west of Port Greville the road gets interesting and road signs should be heeded. The first wake-up call is a radical corner with a steep descent to a narrow hairpin on a very narrow bridge and an immediate ascent up the other side to another sharp turn. The corners get tighter when approaching Cape d'Or and in places the road is notched into the side of the mountain. Gravel-strewn corners are the norm and drifting into the oncoming lane on these blind curves is like playing Russian roulette. The views would be stupendous, but there's no place to pull off and taking your eyes from the road is not advised. Still, this section of highway is a thrill to ride.

Advocate Harbour is best known for The Lighthouse on Cape d'Or. Situated on top of dramatic cliffs at the very tip of the cape, the lighthouse offers awe-inspiring views of the Bay of Fundy and Cape Split. The light and lightkeeper's house were built in the 1960s and have since been converted into a four-bedroom guest house and a separate restaurant that serves lunch and dinner (902-670-0534, www.capedor.ca). The 5.5-km (3.4 mi) gravel road leading down to the light is quite steep and narrow in places, so caution is advised.

Route 209 continues up the east side of Chignecto Bay, but there are no panoramic views to be seen as the narrow asphalt cuts through the remote forest. There are private summer camps, but no villages or side roads until reaching Joggins. The area teems with wildlife that has had little experience with traffic and the woods come right to the very edge of the pavement. Deer and moose use the road as a convenient trail while quail, grouse, and pheasant tend to sunbathe on it.

At the very end of the Bay of Fundy the great tides have opened the vault of time. This is where Charles Lyell's discoveries in 1842 and 1852 proved growing evidence to support the concept of evolution and inspired Charles Darwin's *Origin of Species*. The cliffs at Joggins are now designated a UNESCO World Heritage Site and the Joggins Fossil Centre attracts visitors from around the world.

Route 242 goes east from Joggins to Route 302 that, in turn, leads to Route 2. The city of Amherst is the "Gateway to Nova Scotia" and here choices need to be made. From Amherst to Truro on the Trans-Canada Highway (Route 104) is about 100 km (62 mi); Halifax is another 100 km from Truro. From Amherst to Moncton, New Brunswick is about 65 km (40 mi). Amherst to New Glasgow on Route 6 along the Northumberland Strait is 158 km (98 mi). The route to Charlottetown on Prince Edward Island, taking Route 16/Trans-Canada Highway in New Brunswick and across the Confederation Bridge would take about two hours.

Trip 21 Northumberland Shore

Distance: *137 km (85 mi) Allow a leisurely day.*
Highlights: *A scenic drive along the southern coast of the Northumberland Strait with a detour to visit both a water-powered grist-mill and a steam-powered one.*

The Isthmus of Chignecto is the narrow neck of land that prevents "mainland" Nova Scotia from becoming an island. Amherst is positioned on the isthmus at Chignecto Bay, the very end of the Bay of Fundy and just a short distance from the New Brunswick–Nova Scotia border, and calls itself the "Gateway to Nova Scotia."

It is 137 km (85 mi) from Amherst to Pictou, but Route 6 is the scenic road and it might take all day to cover this short distance. The Northumberland Ferry crosses from Caribou, just north of Pictou, to Woods Island on PEI.

Blueberries and maple syrup are two products closely associated with this region, but the Northumberland Shore also has the greatest number of warm-water beaches in the province. Nova Scotia's premier winery is located here as well. During July and August there seems to be a festival taking place every week whether it be the Gathering of the Clans in Pugwash, the Highland Games in Antigonish, or the Festival of Tartans in New Glasgow. This province isn't called New Scotland simply by chance.

Acadians were the first European settlers, but their expulsion by the British in 1755 left the land open to colonization by English. However, it was yet another deportation, part of the "Highland Clearances" that forced (figuratively and literally) Scots to emigrate to the Americas and from 1773 many settled on the Northumberland shore.

The Route from Amherst

0 km (0 mi) Begin at the junction of Route 6/Victoria St. and Route 104/Trans-Canada Highway west of Amherst.

3 km (1.8 mi) Arrive downtown Amherst. Continue on Route 6.

7 km (4.2 mi) Junction with Route 366. Continue on Route 6.

42 km (26.1 mi) Junction with Route 366. Continue on Route 6.

51 km (31.8 mi) Arrive Pugwash. Continue on Route 6.

87 km (54.1 mi) Arrive Tatamagouche. Continue on Route 6.

88 km (54.8 mi) Junction with Route 311. Continue on Route 6.

137 km (85 mi) Arrive Pictou.

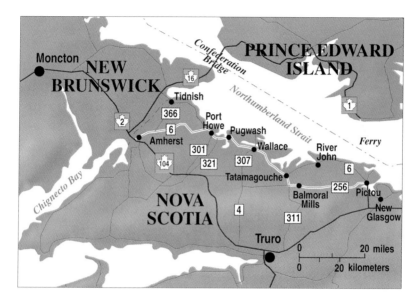

Head out of Amherst on Route 6. At the fork with Route 366 you can choose between the left fork onto Route 366 to Tidnish or the right fork, which keeps you on Route 6. Upon reaching Tidnish you could either head north on New Brunswick Route 970 to the Trans-Canada Highway and the Confederation Bridge or continue to follow Nova Scotia Route 366 along the Northumberland Strait to Port Howe. Route 6 goes directly from Amherst to Port Howe, cutting across the gentle agricultural landscape and past deciduous forests where maples predominate. From here the scenic road crosses the Philip River and through West Pugwash.

In Pugwash (pop. 784) the street signs are bilingual, posted in both English and Gaelic. This is one unusual aspect of the town. The other is the largest underground salt mine in Atlantic Canada lies beneath it. The Pugwash Conference on Science and World Affairs began in 1957 at the height of the Cold War. Bertrand Russell organized a convention of scholars and scientists—from both east and west—who were opposed to nuclear weapons. It still meets on an annual basis, and the political implications are not on the scale of those at the first session in 1957, yet the 1995 Nobel Peace Prize was awarded to the Pugwash Conference.

A scenic detour begins in downtown Pugwash. Turn left (north) on Gulf Shore Road. This will offer you expansive views of the Northumberland Strait and leads past the Gulf Shore Provincial Park. It becomes Ferry Road as it turns and goes south across the peninsula to rejoin Route 6 just west of Wallace.

The accommodations at the Tatamagouche Train Station Inn are in cabooses. When the middle caboose in the photo was purchased—a unique design with bay windows on the side instead of a cupola on top—it took eight months to make the 1,200-mile journey from Toronto. Apparently it was hidden by railway workers who did not want to part with it, and had to be retrieved by railway police.

About 16 km (10 mi) beyond Pugwash, the highway begins to run along the shore of Wallace Bay. Most of the panoramic views will be discovered by exploring local side roads, simply because most settlements originated in the sheltered harbors of the coastal inlets and bays. We leave you to explore such roads as those leading to Malagash Point and Sandville on your own. At the innermost inlet on Tatamagouche Bay is the town of Tatamagouche.

There is a famous person in the annals of almost every town and this one is no exception. Anna Swan of Tatamagouche was born in 1846 and grew to be 7-ft,11-in tall. She found fame and fortune touring with P.T. Barnum and Tom Thumb when she was only 17 years old. She married the "Kentucky Giant"—7-ft, 9-in tall Martin Van Buren Oaks—and they became an internationally famous couple. The Anna Swan Museum & Exhibit (39 Creamery Square, 902-657-2086) has some interesting photos and artifacts.

Shortcuts:
🏍 From Port Howe both Route 301and 321 go south to Oxford and Exit 6 of Route 104/Trans-Canada Highway.

🏍 Route 307 goes south from Wallace (it's quicker than Route 368) to Route 4 at Wentworth Centre. Route 4 goes west to Exit 7 of the Trans-Canada Highway or south to Exit 11.

🏍 From Tatamagouche those who wish to return to Amherst can take Route 246 to Route 4 and ride west to Exit 7 of the Trans-Canada Highway. Those who wish to shortcut to Truro should take Route 311.

In a region noted for fossils, Tatamagouche Fossil Trackways, (3971 Highway 6) is one of the most important sites for dinosaur tracks in the world. Hundreds of footprints made by reptiles and amphibians that predate the dinosaurs can be viewed here.

The Train Station in Tatamagouche is a bit different from most—this one is a B&B (21 Station Drive, 902-657-3222, www.trainstation.ca). The restored depot has a museum, gift shop, and café on the first floor, while the former station master's residence on the second floor has been transformed into an apartment suite. Seven cabooses, ranging in date from 1911 to 1978, have been converted to deluxe accommodations and each are furnished according to the era of the railway car. Dining is in a 1928 Canadian National Railway dining car.

The sea is never far away and even when it can't be seen, it can be felt. The highway runs along Tatamagouche Bay in Brule, and cuts across the Cape John peninsula at River John. Just after passing through the village an intersection provides two options. The first is a left (north) on Cape John Road, a 14-km (9 mi) round trip to the vantage point by the fishing wharf at the tip of the cape. Here you'll have a sweeping view of the bay and across to Malagash Point. The second is a right (south) on River John Road, a 26-km (16 mi) shortcut through bucolic farmland that ends just a mile west of the traffic circle at Pictou. It comes in handy if you get stuck behind a caravan of RV travelers.

The vivid blue sea and the verdant green fields are a mirror image of PEI, which can now be glimpsed as the strait narrows between Caribou Island and Wood Islands. A left turn onto Three Brooks Road is a shortcut to the ferry to Prince Edward Island, otherwise you should ride for another 5 km (3.5 mi) along the main road. Route 6 ends at the Route 106 traffic circle.

From the Route 6/Route 106 traffic circle Route 106 north goes directly to the Northumberland Ferry dock in Caribou. Route 106 south crosses Pictou Harbour and connects to Route 104 at Mount William west of New Glasgow. West River Road leads into downtown Pictou. From Pictou to New Glasgow is a mere 15 kilometers on the Trans-Canada Highway, which is the fastest route to Truro or Cape Breton Island. Exit 2 onto Abercrombie Road is the best way to enter New Glasgow from Pictou; continuing to Route 104/Trans-Canada Highway is the best way to bypass the city. This is also where you can connect with Trip 22.

From the traffic circle the way to Pictou (pop. 3,813) on West River Road is easy to find. The first wave of Scottish immigrants to Nova Scotia arrived at this sheltered harbor aboard the Hector on September 15, 1773. A replica of this ship can be found moored at the Hector Heritage Quay by

The Hector brought the first group of Scottish settlers to Nova Scotia. They were the vanguard of many thousands of Highlanders who would later add a distinctive Scottish flavor to New Scotland.

the Hector Exhibit Centre. The center presents the story of the Scottish immigration, but to truly experience this culture you want to arrive during mid-August when the Hector Festival brings Celtic and Highland heritage to life.

The only knife factory in Canada is Grohmann Knives (116 Water St., 902-485-4224, www.grohmann.com). Their signature D.H. Russell belt knives are world famous and all their knives are handcrafted. You can tour the factory and watch these knives being made.

There are numerous restaurants and lodging to be found in this area, which makes it a logical overnight stop if you plan to cross to PEI. New Glasgow offers much, but this town feels a bit more laid back.

Inland Route

Just east of Tatamagouche is the junction of Route 311. Take this alternate route away from the coast, and turn right (west) on Route 256. If the wind is blowing strong off the Northumberland Strait the hills and forests along Route 256 offer protection and there's far less traffic than on Route 6.

It's not exactly Zen and motorcycles, but Dorje Denma Ling does add to the "flavor" to Tatamagouche. This is the only Shambala Buddhist center in eastern Canada, which is based on the teachings of Chögyam Trungpa Rimpoche, a monk who brought Tibetan Buddhism to North America. It's located on Route 256, less than a mile west of Route 311.

A turn to the east on Route 256 will take you to Balmoral Grist Mill Museum (660 Matheson Brook Rd., www.museum.gov.ns.ca/bgm/en). Built in 1874, this water-powered grist mill is one of the last examples of the type of mills that were cornerstone of American colonial settlements. Still in operation it grinds oats and barley between its Scottish granite millstones. In contrast, the Sutherland Steam Mill Museum, (3169 Denmark—just off Route 326, 902-657-3016) is an example of the era in the late 19th century when waterpower gave way to steam. This carriage shop and lumber mill that was built in 1890 by Alexander Sutherland is a fine example of a local factory prior to electrification.

The decision whether to return to Route 6 via Route 326 or continue on Route 256 to Pictou is an entirely personal one. Pictou is 40 km (25 mi) by way of Route 256 and just a few miles longer via Brule. One is not better than the other, merely different. ∎

New Glasglow is split in half by the East River of Pictou with the Kempt Bridge (George St.) connecting the two halves of downtown. Routes 289 and 374 merge just three blocks south of the bridge on the west side; Routes 289, 348, 347, and 4 are on the east side. If you are thinking that this sounds like a scenario for traffic congestion you would be right, especially when an event or festival is taking place. One solution is the Trenton Connector. From Abercrombie Road it crosses the river on the northern edge of town and connects with Route 348. The road to take if you plan to visit Powells Point Provincial Park or Melmery Beach Provincial Park is Route 348, but unfortunately it offers no convenient shortcut to Route 4.

Trip 22 From Coast to Coast

Distance: *271 km (168.4 mi)*
Highlights: *A relaxing drive inland from the province's Atlantic coast, which follows an ancient Mi'kmaq waterway, and passes through a picturesque valley before reaching the Northumberland Strait and the Gulf of St. Lawrence. You will then follow the Gulf coast to one of Nova Scotia's hidden gems, Cape George and the tranquil shoreline of St. Georges Bay.*

Although just about every serious biker has heard about the world-famous Cabot Trail, on Cape Breton Island, very few have ever heard of mainland Nova Scotia's mini-Cabot Trail. Even riders from the mainland would probably not be able to identify its exact location, or give you directions on how to find it. But this daylong tour, starting across the harbor from Nova Scotia's capital city, will end in a coastal excursion that will only serve to whet your appetite for the real Cabot Trail, on the other side of the Canso Causeway.

The Route from Dartmouth to Antigonish

0 km (0 mi) Start in Dartmouth going east on Route 7.
6 km (3.8 mi) Join Route 107 East.
35 km (22.1 mi) Turn right on Route 7.
38 km (23.7 mi) Arrive Musquodoboit Harbour. Turn left on Route 357.
77 km (47.9 mi) Arrive Middle Musquodoboit. Continue on Route 224.
87 km (54.1 mi) Arrive Centre Musquodoboit. Continue on Route 224.
96 km (59.7 mi) Arrive Upper Musquodoboit. Continue on Route 336.
118 km (73.5 mi) Turn right on Route 289 in Eastville.
156 km (97.3 mi) Arrive Westville. Continue on Route 289.
160 km (99.6 mi) Take ramp onto Trans-Canada Highway104 east.
175 km (109.0 mi) Turn left on to Route 245.
183 km (113.7 mi) Arrive Merigomish. Continue on Route 245.
201 km (124.8 mi) Arrive Knoydart. Continue on Route 245.
209 km (129.7 mi) Arrive Arisaig. Continue on Route 245.
216 km (134.4 mi) Arrive Malignant Cove. Bear left on Route 337 north.
226 km (140.6 mi) Arrive Morar. Continue on Route 337.
234 km (145.7 mi) Arrive Cape George Point. Continue on Route 337.
237 km (147.6 mi) Arrive Ballantynes Cove. Continue on Route 337.
271 km (168.4 mi) Arrive Antigonish.

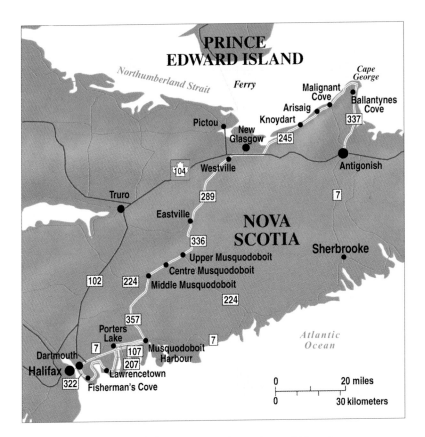

Before leaving the Halifax–Dartmouth area it would be wise to gas up, as your next gas station is 160 km (100 mi) away, on the Trans-Canada Highway.

Take Route 7 out of Dartmouth and go east on Route 107, a controlled-access, two-lane highway.

For most of the first 100 km, this tour follows the right-of-way of the former Musquodoboit Railway. For a period of 66 years, from 1916 to 1982, freight and passenger trains followed the coast east from Dartmouth to Musquodoboit Harbour, before turning inland, and following the river of the same name north into the unspoiled countryside of the Musquodoboit Valley. Although only a short-line system, there were few routes anywhere in eastern Canada that offered such a variety of scenic beauty. In the first 40 km (25 mi) you will encounter extensive salt-water bogs, numerous lakes peppered with tiny islands, deserted beaches, and several small fishing villages. In less than an hour you will arrive in downtown Musquodoboit Harbour (pop. 2,139).

Alternative Route to Musquodoboit Harbour 68 km (42 mi)

Leave Dartmouth on Route 322. The first stop is the Shearwater Aviation Museum, located on the Canadian Air Force Base. The entrance is at the main gate by the traffic lights. A Grumman TBM-3 Avenger from WWII, a more modern McDonnell F-101 Voodoo jet fighter, an interesting Canadair Tutor CT-114 painted in the colors of the elite Canadian Royal Air Force (CRAF) acrobatic Snowbird team, and various other fixed-wing and rotor aircraft are on display. Check out a flight simulator or fit into a jet cockpit trainer.

Fisherman's Cove (902-465-6093) is located just south of Route 322 along Shore Road. This sheltered inlet is a working fishing port, but in 1996 it was transformed into a tourist attraction with the addition of craft shops, boutiques, and restaurants. With tourism in decline the commercial longevity of this location is uncertain at the time of writing. The McCormick's Beach Provincial Park is just south of Fisherman's Cove and it is extremely busy on summer weekends.

Connector Route 322/Cow Bay Road cuts across the peninsula. At one point Cow Bay Road turns right and Connector Route 322 continues straight as Dyke Road. Follow Cow Bay Road for the ocean views across Cow Bay. This road returns to the eastern end of Dyke Road to continue as Route 322/Cow Bay Road to Rainbow Haven Beach P.P. and Bissett Road to Route 207 at the eastern edge of Cole Harbour.

Route 328 begins east of Cole Harbour and goes north to Routes 107 and 7 which divide less than a mile (1.46 km) west of the Route 328 junction. Route 207 continues east winding around tidal wetlands to reach Lawrencetown Beach P.P., a noted surfing area and gorgeous sand beach.

Just beyond the park is a left turn (north) onto Crowell Road. This scenic local road follows Porter Lake—a 24 km (15 mi) long, 1 km (.6 mi) wide body of water that is fresh at its northern end and saline on the southern—passing the Porter's Lake Provincial Park, and the west end of Bellefontaine Road to end at Route 7 in the town of Porters Lake (pop. 3,217). Route 207 crosses the outlet of Porters Lake and turns north on a long peninsula that takes you past more tidal flats and wetlands to intersect Route 107 and end at Route 7. Bellefontaine Road crosses the islands of Porters Lake to meet Route 207 in West Chezzetcook. Don't bother looking for a village, but there is an interesting attraction—the Acadian House Museum (79 Hill Road, 902-827-5992). This small cedar-shingled house presents what life was like for an Acadian family in the mid-19th century on the remote, eastern coast of Nova Scotia. Routes 207 and 7 rejoin near the head of Chezzetcook Inlet. ■

A motorcyclist contemplates a different mode of touring at the Musquodoboit Railway Museum in Musquodoboit Harbour.

The original settlers of Musquodoboit Harbour (pop. 2,139) were United Empire Loyalists who were later joined—after the American Revolution—by immigrants from Scotland, England, and Germany. As soon as you drive into town you will notice the Musquodoboit Railway Museum (902-889-2689, www.novascotiarailwayheritage.com/musquodoboit) on your left, which is also the local visitor information center. The original 1918 station makes a great stop, and is a charming example of Canadian railway architecture at the end of World War I. On site are a caboose, a snowplow, various baggage wagons, an interesting collection of vintage photographs, and other railway memorabilia.

Musquodoboit is a Mi'kmaq name, which means "rolling out in foam," a reference to the local waterway meeting the ocean. From Musquodoboit Harbour, you take Route 357 north. You'll follow the river as it passes through thick forest, large swaths of which were devastated by Hurricane Juan, which hit Halifax and central Nova Scotia in September, 2003.

The narrow river valley soon opens out, offering lovely pastoral views out over the surrounding farmland. At one point, in a distance of less than 20 km, you will pass through Middle Musquodoboit, Centre Musquodoboit, and Upper Musquodoboit, each of which had it's own railway station! In Middle Musquodoboit, Route 357 ends and you continue northeastward on Route 224. In Upper Musquodoboit, Route 224 turns southeast and you take Route 336 northward. After 22 km (13.8 mi) you turn right on Route 289 in Eastville.

This very scenic road, well off the normal tourist track, takes you through a series of charming little communities, where the traffic is light, and the unspoiled countryside gives you a chance to recharge your mental batteries. There are no shopping malls, no high-rise apartment blocks, and only one large industrial site—a former pulp mill that has been forced to close due to the recent recession.

As you reach the upper end of the Musquodoboit valley, the pastoral farmland and rolling hills give way to thickly forested uplands, with little in the way of human habitation. This is one of the best woodlands in the province for pulp and paper products. So, even though the local mills may be closed, this valuable forest resource is still shipped to other companies around the province. Be very careful and vigilant, as you may meet a large pulp truck coming around a turn, and they tend not to slow down!

You gradually return to civilization as you approach the little town of Westville (pop. 3,805), and its close neighbor Stellarton (pop. 4,717). This region used to be famous for its coal mines, and was known internationally for having the thickest coal seam in the world, up to 14 m (46 ft) in some places! In 1992, however, the area attracted worldwide attention, but for the wrong reasons.

The Salmon River House Country Inn & Restaurant, located on Route 7 just 15 minutes east of Musquodoboit Harbour is a charming and relaxing place to stay.

The Musquodoboit Valley has supplied wood for lumber, paper pulp and wood products for many years.

An early morning explosion at the Westray Mine, caused by methane gas and coal dust, trapped 26 miners underground. Despite a valiant rescue effort, it was obvious that there would be no survivors. After 15 bodies had been recovered, the decision was made to seal the mine, because conditions underground were just too dangerous for rescue work to continue. This disaster brought an end to two centuries of underground coal mining, dating back to 1790.

It is only a short 4 km (2.3 mi) from Westville to Route 104 east (Trans-Canada Highway), and a mere 15 km (9.4 mi) to Exit 27 at Sutherlands River, where you pick up Route 245 east.

From here you head for the Northumberland Strait, the body of water that separates northern Nova Scotia from Prince Edward Island.

This section of the tour starts out at sea-level, but the elevation slowly changes as you follow this coastal road along the northern shore of the Antigonish Highlands. As you climb, the scenery becomes ever more dramatic, with inspiring views out over the Gulf of St. Lawrence, and the western shoreline of Cape Breton Island.

The upper portion of this tour takes you through the Highland Heart of northern Nova Scotia. Tiny coastal communities like Knoydart, Arisaig, and Morar, were all named after places in Scotland, and reflect the homesickness felt by the first trans-oceanic immigrants to this area. In fact, Morar is that part of western Scotland from which author Gillis' ancestors emigrated.

The look-off as you approach Arisaig provides a panoramic view of the town and its adjacent coastline.

Arisaig, about two-thirds of the way along this coast, is a very interesting place to take a rest break. There is a lovely look-off, as you approach the village, which gives an excellent view of the snug little harbor, and the surrounding countryside. The tiny lighthouse is a charming replica, where you can purchase a delicious ice cream cone, in the summer months.

This fishing village was the first Highland Scots settlement in Antigonish county, and St. Margaret's Church (1792) was the first Roman Catholic mission in the province of Nova Scotia. The present church is the third on the site, and dates from 1878.

Arisaig has also gained a reputation for its fascinating geological history, which dates back some 450 million years! A 4-km-long (2.5 mi) stretch of coastline, on both sides of the local fishing wharf, contains an amazing range of fossils, as well as some exposed volcanic lava flows. These cliffs, and the fossils they continuously produce, thanks to coastal erosion, have been explored and catalogued by international geologists for more than 150 years.

Malignant Cove is 7 km (4.7 mi) up the road, and is named after a Royal Navy warship that ran aground in a vicious winter storm in 1779. *HMS Malignant* was transporting British soldiers to Québec, who were destined to take part in the American Revolutionary Wars. Although most on board reached the shore, the vast majority of those perished in the extreme weather conditions before they could be rescued.

(At Malignant Cove, Route 245 turns inland, and for those who are running short of time, this paved detour offers a short 20 km (12.7 mi) run into the town of Antigonish.)

At this junction bear left on Route 337, and continue on, climbing steadily for another 18 km (11.3 mi) until you reach Cape George Point. At the Point itself there are magnificent views across the waters of St. Georges Bay to the west coast of Cape Breton Island, and the far reaches of the Gulf of St. Lawrence.

At the very tip of the Point is a gravel road (0.7 km) that leads to the Cape George Lighthouse. The present structure stands 110 m (360 ft) above the bay, and was built in 1968. It is the third lighthouse on this site. This road, although hilly, can be negotiated by a touring motorcycle.

Route 337 now turns south, and begins a steep descent, with several switchbacks, into Ballantynes Cove. Named after a British soldier who received a land grant after military service in the American Revolution, this picture-perfect little harbor boasts a 40-slip marina, and is a focal point for Japanese fish brokers who look to buy sushi-grade tuna from the nearby fishing grounds.

The Ballantynes Cove Bluefin Tuna Interpretive Centre is located right on the main wharf, and offers various displays about the life cycle of this very valuable delicacy, along with the colorful history of tuna fishing in the offshore waters. The center, with free admission, is open from mid-June to mid-September.

From Ballantynes Cove to the college town of Antigonish is a leisurely 34-km (20.8 mi) ride, through rolling hills and fertile farmland, with great panoramic views over St. Georges Bay and the inner reaches of Antigonish Harbour. It makes a fitting finale to a daylong tour that has taken you from the south coast of Nova Scotia to the resource-rich waters of the province's northern coast.

270 Motorcycle Journeys Through Atlantic Canada

Trip 23 Follow the Rugged Coast

Distance: *296 km (184 mi). Allow at least a day and a half, or two days.*
Highlights: *A gentle coastal drive with a stop in Canso, the oldest (1604) seaport in mainland North America. The road from Canso to Sherbrooke follows a rugged and indented coastline, passing through several small Acadian communities, until you reach Sherbrooke Village, the largest museum complex in the province of Nova Scotia. Then a lovely ride north, along one of Atlantic Canada's finest salmon rivers, to the Highland Heart of mainland Nova Scotia.*

We start our tour of the rugged coast of northeastern Nova Scotia where Route 344 takes off from the Trans-Canada Highway just before it crosses the Canso Causeway in Auld's Cove. Our first stop is Mulgrave (pop. 879), just a few kilometers down from the Trans-Canada Highway. Prior to the opening of the Canso Causeway in 1955, Mulgrave was the mainland terminus for the ferries that carried rail and passenger cars across the Strait of Canso to Cape Breton Island. Today the small town has a new life as a marine service center.

The Route from Auld's Cove

0 km (0 mi) Take Route 344 south from Route 104 (Trans-Canada Highway) in Auld's Cove.
6 km (3.8 mi) Arrive Mulgrave. Continue on Route 344.
50 km (31.4 mi) Arrive Boyleston. Turn left on Route 16 south.
60 km (37.2 mi) Arrive Guysborough. Continue on Route 16.
74 km (45.8 mi) Arrive Halfway Cove. Continue on Route 16.
85 km (53.1 mi) Arrive Queensport. Continue on Route 16.
109 km (67.7 mi) Arrive Canso. Take Route 16 back to Route 316.
125 km (77.9 mi) Turn left on Route 316.
140 km (87.2 mi) Arrive Port Felix. Continue on Route 316.
190 km (118.0 mi) Arrive Goldboro. Continue on Route 316.
195 km (121.2 mi) Arrive Isaac's Harbour North. Turn left on Route 211.
198 km (123.2 mi) Take Country Harbour cable ferry.
231 km (143.8 mi) Turn left on Route 7.
236 km (146.5 mi) Arrive Sherbrooke. Turn around and go north on Route 7.
296 km (184.2 mi) Arrive Antigonish.

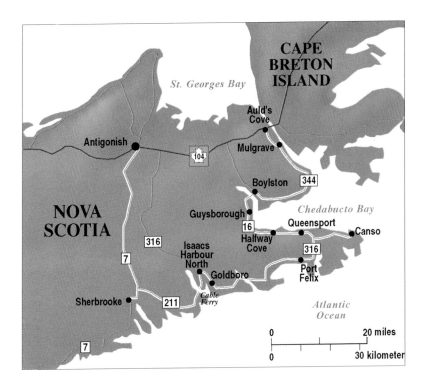

Just on your left, as you enter the town, is a new tourist information center in Venus Cove Marine Park. This rather striking center is located in a full-size replica of one of the ferries that used to travel back and forth across the Strait of Canso.

From this Marine Park you get an excellent view of Point Tupper, on the other side of the Strait. At one time Point Tupper was the Cape Breton terminus for the ferry service; today it is the site of a large industrial park, which includes an oil refinery, a power-generating station, and one of the largest pulp and paper mills in North America!

From Mulgrave to the town of Canso is only 103 km (63.9 mi). For the most part this is a lovely coastal drive, where you play hide and seek with the Strait of Canso (Route 344), and later follow the north shore of Chedabucto Bay (Route 16). Along the way you pass through the charming village of Boylston on one side of Guysborough Harbour, and the town of Guysborough on the other.

Should you be ready to take a break, Guysborough (pop. 922) is a delightful place to park your bike and take a short walk around. With a restored waterfront area that includes a small marina, and several refurbished mercantile establishments, which have been converted into pubs and

When author Gillis stopped to see the Mulgrave Road Theatre, he met a young cousin of his from rural Cape Breton whom he had not seen for several years. She had recently been awarded a Protégé Prize to develop a new screenplay.

boutiques, the town has become a center for creative and artistic endeavor in eastern Nova Scotia.

This is best exemplified by the Mulgrave Road Theatre, a small regional cultural organization that, in the last 30 years, has developed a national following for its innovative promotion and development of Atlantic Canadian writers and dramatists. Housed in a former general store, which contains offices, technical production facilities, and rehearsal space, the company's productions tour all over the Atlantic region, and have even been featured in central and western Canada.

Guysborough offers two accommodation options, for those who might want to spend the night. The DesBarres Manor Inn, an 1837 vintage seaside mansion, offers 10 luxury rooms, with complimentary gourmet breakfast (90 Church St., 902-533-2099); and the Osprey Shores Golf Resort has 10 units, with continental breakfast (119 Ferry Lane, 800-909-3904).

Large sections of Route 16, from Guysborough to Canso town, have recently been upgraded, which makes for a relaxed drive along this interesting coast. Many turns have been eliminated, or shortened, and the highway has been widened and newly paved. This makes for an easy, 13-km (8.6 mi) drive to the scenic look-off at the appropriately named Halfway Cove. Here, in addition to the lovely view, is a large stone monument that commemorates the visit of Prince Henry Sinclair from Scotland's Orkney Islands. He supposedly visited Nova Scotia in 1398, almost 100 years before either Columbus or John Cabot reached the new world. Whether or not you agree with this theory—and there are many (especially in Scotland) who do—the plaque attached to the monument will give you a brief history of this historical curiosity.

Not too far away is the tiny hamlet of Queensport, with a lovely little lighthouse situated on a small offshore island. Built in 1882 and automated in 1980, the building was later saved from demolition when members of the community offered to take over ownership of the structure from the Department of Transportation. They plan to restore the building and offer boat tours to the island during the summer months.

Route 16 soon swings inland, away from the coast, and continues on to the small town of Canso (pop. 1,250). Situated at the end of a peninsula, Canso can trace its origins back to 1604, which makes it the oldest seaport on mainland North America.

Since the collapse of the Atlantic Ground Fishery and the Cod Moratorium in the early 1990s, the town has struggled to retain its identity. When the local fish plant closed, hundreds of well-paying jobs—both ashore and on the fishing fleet—suddenly disappeared. Today, most residents find seasonal work in central or western Canada.

On the way into town you will pass a large, elongated structure that seems totally out of place in this remote location. Made of cut stone and bricks, this now-shuttered facility was once the home of the Commercial Cable Company, an American firm that specialized in underwater telegraphy. From 1884 to 1962, telegraph cables ran from here, under the Atlantic Ocean, to the British Isles, and the town of Canso found itself at the forefront of Trans-Atlantic telecommunications technology. The company was largely staffed by British telegraphers, who with their families enjoyed a lifestyle that was totally foreign to the small fishing community. They had electric lights, running water, and indoor toilets, when most Nova Scotians were still using oil lamps and outdoor privies. They were also very well paid, and lived in their own little enclave, which they called Hazel Hill. Plans are underway to restore the building, and open it during the tourist season.

Canso is a pleasant little town, with two interesting museums, and a number of old heritage homes that date back to the golden age of the fishery. At the Whitman House Museum (1297 Union St., 902-366-2170), you can explore the fascinating history of Canso Town, and the Commercial Cable Company. The roof of the museum has a lovely example of a traditional widow's walk, a rooftop observation point from which fishermen's wives could scan the horizon while waiting for the return of their husbands and sons from the Grand Banks. Admission is free, although donations are accepted to help defray operating costs, and the museum is open from June 1 to September 30.

Just a short distance away, on the waterfront, is the Canso Islands National Historic Site. Here, thanks to a short film and life-size dioramas, you can learn of the rivalry that existed between England and France during colonial times, especially with regard to the lucrative fishing grounds off the east coast.

Although Canso was first settled in 1604 by Basque fishermen from France, by the early 1700s boats and crews from New England had forced them to leave. By 1740 the town and nearby Grassy Island had a population of almost 2,000. However, when England and France went to war in 1744, the town and island were captured by French forces from Louisbourg, and the settlement was destroyed. The following spring, New England militia forces used Grassy Island as a staging point to launch a successful siege on the Fortress of Louisbourg on Cape Breton Island.

The Canso Islands National Historic Site is open from June 1 to September 15. There is no admission fee, although donations are accepted. A 15-minute boat ride, weather permitting, is available to Grassy Island, where an interpretative trail allows visitors to examine some of the historic sites.

Canso is also home to the annual Stan Rogers Folk Festival, a three-day musical event held on the first weekend in July. The festival started in 1997, to honor the memory of this prolific Canadian singer and songwriter, who lost his life in a tragic plane crash. This popular event brings more than 10,000 fans to the quiet town, which has only one motel. The appropriately named Last Port Motel & Restaurant (902-366-2400) has only 13 units, and during the festival these are usually reserved for guest artists. Four local campgrounds do their best to provide basic facilities for the thousands of visitors, who come from all parts of Atlantic Canada and New England.

Head back on Route 16 for 16 km (10.2 mi) to the junction with Route 316 (with gas facilities). Turn left to go west along the rugged coast toward the town of Sherbrooke. Although the distance from Canso town to

The Commercial Cable Company in Canso was once the launching point for messages on the underwater telegraph cable that ran between North America and Great Britain.

Sherbrooke is only 125 km (78 mi), plan on a slow ride of about two hours because of the nature of the road. Not that Route 316, along Nova Scotia's eastern shore, is not a good highway. It is, but it is also an old highway, first paved in the early 1960s. Although sections of it have been recently upgraded, for the most part it is a slow road that basically follows the contours of the former wagon road that once connected the small communities along this rugged coast.

Port Felix, one of three little Acadian communities located along this section of Nova Scotia's Marine Drive, is about 31 km (19.5 mi) from Canso. Although the modern concrete span of the bridge at the entrance to Port Felix is only 130 feet long, it stands apart from the surrounding countryside, somewhat like a mirage. This effect is all the more striking because the state of the rural highway leading up to the bridge is anything but modern.

Port Felix was originally known as Molasses Harbour. According to a local lore, the first Acadian settlers to arrive in the vicinity had found a barrel of molasses washed up on the shore. It had probably come from a passing ship, and was more than likely washed overboard in heavy weather. Then, around 1870, the name was changed to Port Felix, to honor a Belgian priest who had served the several small Catholic parishes along this shore.

When the nice new bridge at the entrance to town was mentioned, Port Felix resident Enos Greencorn's comment was, "A million-dollar bridge and a hundred-dollar road."

Several small islands, with rather unique names, are located offshore directly in front of St. Joseph's Church. Hog Island and Sheep Island were used as summer pasture for pigs and sheep; Goat Burying Island was a place to bury diseased animals; while the appropriately named Potato Island, with its fertile soil, was used to grow vegetables that could not be grown elsewhere.

Continue along Route 316 which passes through several small Acadian villages in the 50 km (30.8 mi) between Port Felix and the tiny hamlet of Goldboro (pop. 450), site of the eastern terminus of a natural gas pipeline from the Sable Offshore Energy Project.

Since early 2000, gas from several offshore wells near Sable Island has flowed through an undersea pipeline for a distance of 225 km (140 mi) until it reaches Goldboro. It is then transmitted by pipeline through mainland Nova Scotia and New Brunswick to markets in Maine, Massachusetts, and New Hampshire. A short, paved road leads to the production facility, but no tours are available.

Route 316 continues for about 5 km (3.2 mi) to Issac's Harbour North, a scenic village nestled at the head of a narrow coastal inlet. Turn left at the junction with Route 211, and ride another 3 km (2 mi) to the Country Harbour cable ferry. A short wait, and a $5 fee will get you to the other side. From there it is a 33 km (20.6 mi) ride to Route 7, where a left turn and another 5 km (2.7 mi) will take you to the charming little village of Sherbrooke (pop. 400).

This community is the location of the largest museum complex in the province, which recreates a period of time around the year 1900, when Sherbrooke was the hub of a regional shipbuilding and lumbering industry. With a total of 80 buildings—25 of which are preserved on their original foundations and open to the public—this is a wonderful place to spend a morning or afternoon.

Many of the buildings have been in continuous use for more than 100 years. These include the courthouse (1858–2000), the jail (1862–1965), the Sherbrooke Hotel (1860s–1918), a blacksmith shop and general store (1870s), and the temperance hall (1892), later used as an elementary school, and now used by the Royal Canadian Legion. In respect for its origin, it remains one of the few "dry" legions in Canada. The village also houses a reconstruction of a water-powered, up-and-down sawmill that first operated in 1826. The Historic Sherbrooke Village is located at 42 Main Street, and is open from June 1 to October 15 (888-743-7845). Adult admission in 2010 was $10.

From Sherbrooke take Route 7 back north and continue on it the 60 km (37.7 mi) to Antigonish. For the first 20 km or so this very scenic highway follows the picturesque St. Mary's River, one of eastern Canada's finest salmon rivers. Just north of Sherbrooke on Route 7 is the St. Mary's River

To cross to the other side and continue on Route 211 you must ride the Country Harbour cable ferry.

Two costumed interpreters stand in front to the Courthouse in historic Sherbrooke Village. With 25 of the 80 buildings open to the public, Sherbrooke Village depicts a typical Nova Scotian Village in the late 1800s.

Education and Interpretive Centre, where you can find a large collection of historical photos, artifacts, and other memorabilia. Open from June 1 - October 15, there is no admission fee, although donations are accepted. This is a must-stop for anyone interested in the sport of salmon fishing. Back in 1936 the legendary Babe Ruth, newly retired and inducted into baseball's Hall of Fame, was fishing on this river, when he encountered some rough water, and fell out of the small boat. His quick-thinking guide fished him out of the river just as he was about to disappear into some rapids.

Antigonish (pop. 4,236) is the home of St. Francis Xavier University, a small university with 4,000 full-time students, and author Gillis' alma mater. Antigonish is also home to the oldest continuous Highland Games in North America, held each summer in early July. Starting in 1863, this annual celebration of all things Scottish has brought together athletes and musicians from all parts of Nova Scotia and the rest of Atlantic Canada. Traditional events like the Caber Toss and Hammer Throw, as well as a wide range of other sporting and musical events make this one of the premier tourist attractions in the province.

From Antigonish you can take the Trans-Canada Highway east toward Cape Breton, or west to New Glasgow and Pictou if you wish to connect with the ferry to Prince Edward Island.

Cape Breton

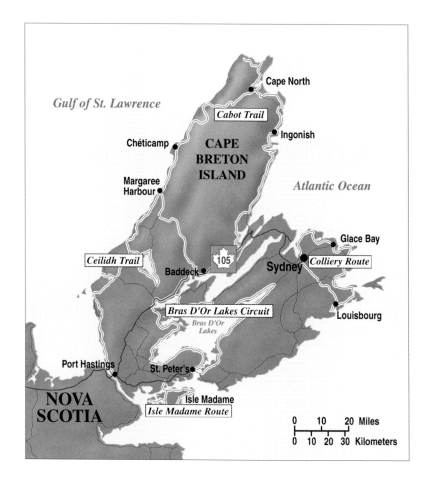

Cape North

Gulf of St. Lawrence

Cabot Trail

Ingonish

Chéticamp

CAPE BRETON ISLAND

Margaree Harbour

Atlantic Ocean

Glace Bay

Ceilidh Trail

105

Baddeck

Sydney

Colliery Route

Bras D'Or Lakes Circuit

Bras D'Or Lakes

Louisbourg

Port Hastings

St. Peter's

NOVA SCOTIA

Isle Madame

Isle Madame Route

0   10   20 Miles
0 10 20 30 Kilometers

Cape Breton *By Rannie Gillis*

"Canada is a large body of land off the coast of Cape Breton!"

This answer to an exam question, by one of my former high school students, sums up in one simple sentence the outlook of Cape Bretonners with regard to this island's place in the Canadian scheme of things. We are a distinct society, proud and defiant (like Newfoundland), and until quite recently isolated from the mainstream of Canadian life and culture. As our unofficial Cape Breton anthem states: "We are an island, a rock in the stream!"

Cape Breton is not a large island. It is only 177 km (110 mi) long and 140 km (87 mi) wide, with an area of 3,981 sq mi. But it looms large in Canadian history because of its strategic location at the entrance to the Gulf of St. Lawrence, and its primary role in the centuries-long rivalry between England and France for control of the fish and fur trade in eastern North America.

Over the last 400 years, the original Mi'kmaq inhabitants have been joined by settlers from France, England, the Channel Islands, the Highlands and Islands of Scotland, and United Empire Loyalists from the American colonies. The rise of the steel and coal industry in the early 20th century brought an additional influx of people from central and eastern Europe, as well as from the islands of the Caribbean. By 1950 Sydney was a much more cosmopolitan city—based on ethnicity—than either Toronto, Montréal, or Vancouver!

The island is famous for its spectacular coastal scenery, especially on the north and west coasts. However, that large body of inland water known as the Bras d'Or Lakes, and the pastoral beauty of the interior hills and small lochs along the eastern and southern side of the island, would easily rival that to be found in most other Canadian provinces.

Trip 24 Ceilidh Trail & Lake Ainslie

Distance: *Ceilidh Trail: 117 km (73 mi)*
Lake Ainslie Loop: 59 km (36 mi)

Highlights: *Lovely coastal scenery, gentle mountains with charming little villages and hidden glens, and a captivating little loch.*

Ceilidh (pronounced kay-lee) is a Scots Gaelic word for a kitchen party, or a spontaneous musical gathering. A ride along the island's beautiful west coast will take you through the heart and soul of Cape Breton's Celtic experience. All along this shore, especially from May to October, the hills come alive with the sound of music—Celtic music. Fiddles, bagpipes, square dances, and Gaelic song, can all be found at church halls, community centers, and charming little pubs along the way. Several of the villages also hold annual Scotch concerts, featuring the best local musicians, dancers, and singers.

Leaving the Canso Causeway at Port Hastings you make your way left, around a small traffic circle, and head down Route 19 in the direction of Troy, a small village that is the birthplace of one of the brightest stars in

The Canso Causeway, which opened in 1955, is the deepest man-made causeway in the world. More than a mile in length, with an average depth of 67 m (220 ft), it created one of the deepest ice-free harbors in the world, The Canso Canal allows small vessels to pass between the Gulf of St. Lawrence to the north, and the Strait of Canso and Atlantic Ocean on the south.

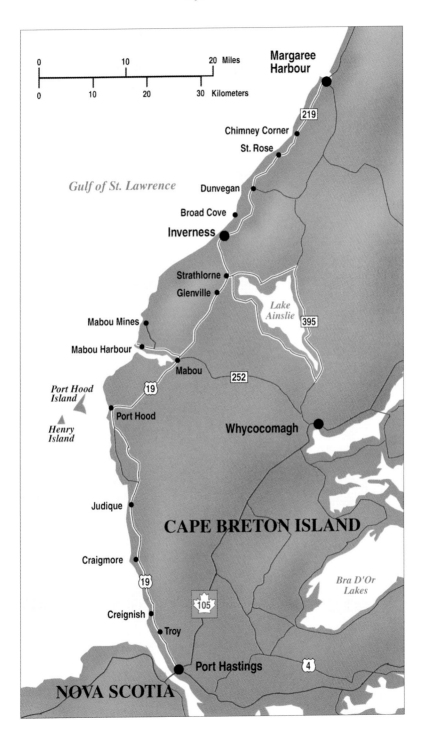

Margaree
Harbour

219

Chimney Corner
St. Rose

Gulf of St. Lawrence   Dunvegan

Broad Cove
Inverness

Strathlorne
Glenville

Lake Ainslie   395

Mabou Mines

Mabou Harbour

Mabou   252

Port Hood
Island   19

Henry
Island   Port Hood

Whycocomagh

Judique

CAPE BRETON ISLAND

Craigmore

19

Bra D'Or Lakes

105

Creignish
Troy

Port Hastings   4

NOVA SCOTIA

0   10   20 Miles

0   10   20   30 Kilometers

The Route from the Canso Causeway

0 km (0 mi) From Canso Causeway take Route 19 north.
45 km (28.1 mi) Arrive Port Hood.
60 km (37.1 mi) Arrive Mabou.
72 km (44.5 mi) Arrive Glenville.
76 km (47.3 mi) Arrive Strathlorne.
  Lake Ainslie circuit 59 km (36.6 mi)
84 km (52.1 mi) Arrive Inverness.
97 km (60.5 mi) Arrive Dunvegan. Turn left on Route 219.
117 km (72.8 mi) Arrive Margaree Harbour.

Canada's Celtic world—Natalie MacMaster, an internationally recognized virtuoso of the Celtic fiddle.

This two-lane highway soon offers wonderful coastal panoramas, as it makes its way through several little villages that look out over St. George's Bay and the Gulf of St. Lawrence. Places like Creignish and Craigmore reflect the Scottish ancestry of the original settlers, while Judique, 28 km (17.2 mi) from the Causeway, denotes an Acadian French origin. About half-way along is Christy's Look-off, a delightful place to stop and take a few pictures.

In spite of Judique's French name, the approximately 700 people who live there today are primarily of Highland-Scots background. A post office, gas station, general store and liquor outlet, are found in the community, as is St. Andrews Catholic Church, built of stone from a nearby island. Judique is perhaps best known for its annual Celtic summer festival called Judique On The Floor Days, usually held in mid-July. It is also the location of the Celtic Music Interpretive Center, a relatively new structure devoted to the preservation and promotion of Cape Breton style Celtic music. During the tourist season the Center offers musical demonstrations, fiddle and guitar master classes, regular concerts, along with an in-house archive holding historic audio and visual components.

Port Hood, a fishing-farming community with two offshore islands, is 17 km (10.9 mi) down the road and is home to about 1,400 people. With miles of pristine sandy beaches, and the warmest water north of the Carolinas, it is a great place to rest for a few days, with several restaurants and places to stay.

Port Hood Island, which provides a natural breakwater to the tidy little harbor, used to have about 30 families living on it, with a little one-room school. Today the island is home to about a dozen families, but only during the summer months. Boat trips can usually be arranged to the island, which

Port Hood Island (with Henry Island hidden behind) forms the backdrop for this lovely pastoral view from the village of Port Hood.

has a lovely secluded beach, and a 300-year-old quarry that once provided stone for the construction of the great French fortress of Louisbourg, on the east side of Cape Breton. Henry Island, which is much smaller and hidden away behind Port Hood Island, has a 16-meter-high (53 ft) wooden lighthouse. The 150-acre island is privately owned and used as a summer retreat.

At Port Hood Route 19 turns inland, and heads for the charming village of Mabou, only 15 km (9 mi) away. However, for those who would prefer to follow the coast, and who do not mind traveling on a well-kept gravel road, the Colindale Road offers a visually stunning alternative to the main highway. Be aware, however, that this road is really not suitable for fully laden touring bikes. If you are on a dual-sport bike, go for it!

Mabou has about 1,300 inhabitants, and is situated on the river of the same name. It is nestled in the lee of the Mabou Highlands, which contain some of the most spectacular hiking trails in the province of Nova Scotia. Mabou is also known as the home of The Rankin Family, five immensely gifted siblings who have taken their Celtic musical heritage and transformed it into a national treasure. Beginning in 1989, the group went on to win numerous music awards, sell several multi-platinum record albums, and are still touring internationally. The Rankins never forgot where they grew up, and in the spring of 2005 took over operation of the Red Shoe Pub, located in a 100-year-old former general store in the center of the village. With their extensive musical connections, the place has become one of the hotbeds of Celtic music on the west side of the island, and a must-stop

Haymaking is just one of the chores on this family farm near Lake Ainslie, a region containing some of the finest agricultural land in Nova Scotia.

for any one passing through. Live Celtic music can be heard every supper hour in July and August, and the place really gets rocking on the weekends.

From the village center a 5-km (3 mi), paved road leads to Mabou Harbour, which offers beautiful views out over the Gulf of St. Lawrence. The looming bulk of the southern flank of the Mabou Highlands provide a stunning backdrop. Part way along, a 5-km (3 mi), gravel road leads to Mabou Coal Mines, a picture-postcard-perfect little cove that was the site of three undersea coal mines in the period before World War I. A very slow—and cautious—ride on a touring bike!

As you leave the quaint little village of Mabou, the road swings around the eastern flank of the majestic Mabou Highlands. Here you enter a realm of special beauty, not unlike that to be found in the Highlands of Scotland.

In the years before World War I, the broad upland plains of the Mabou Highlands were home to several enterprising families. Today, however, the upland farms are deserted and abandoned. The prairie-like grasslands, hidden away on the tops of the mountains, are still in use as community pastures during the summer months.

At scenic Glenville, 12 km (7.4 mi) farther up the road, you may well be forgiven for rubbing your eyes in disbelief. Tucked away in the shadow of the mountains is The Glenora Distillery and Inn, the only single-malt whisky distillery in North America. The buildings were constructed in the traditional Post-and-Beam style found in traditional Scottish distilleries, and as such are quite unlike typical Cape Breton architecture. Here you will find afternoon ceilidhs, fine dining and a Celtic pub, and fascinating tours of the whisky-distilling process, with an opportunity to try a "drop of the hard stuff" before you leave. The Inn has nine tastefully appointed rooms, and six wooden chalets located on the nearby mountain.

Another 4 km (2.8 mi) takes you to Strathlorne, where with a right turn you can begin a wonderful circuit of Lake Ainslie, the largest fresh water lake in Nova Scotia. The road down the west side, and up the east side of this scenic gem, is one of the best-kept secrets in the province. For 59 km (36.6 mi) you will pass through some of the most fertile farmland on Cape Breton Island, in a rolling landscape that—without the trees—could easily pass for the famous Loch Lomond in Scotland.

Glenora Distillery is an interesting place to take a break. I wonder if this happy couple have bought some of the product to taste in their room tonight. As the locals say, "have a drop of the hard stuff!"

Returning to Route 19 at Strathlorne, a right turn will take you on to Inverness, the largest community on the Ceilidh Trail, where you will find an excellent supervised beach, as well as the usual tourist facilities. Inverness, with a population of about 2,000, has a traditional harness-racing season during the summer months. It also has an interesting little museum that gives the history of the undersea coal mining that took place in the town during and after World War I.

A few miles north of Inverness is Broad Cove, home of the oldest annual Scotch Concert held in Cape Breton. Held on the last Sunday in July, it is the largest event of its kind in the province and draws as many as 7,000 people who are treated to a remarkable exhibition of Celtic music and dance, as well as traditional Gaelic singing.

As an alternative route from Broad Cove to Dunvegan, serious dual-sport riders might enjoy the 9 km (5 mi) of rough gravel road that skirts the shore along high cliffs.

At Dunvegan the Ceilidh Trail makes a left turn onto Route 219, which leads for the next 20 km (12 mi) through the lovely coastal communities of St. Rose and Chimney Corner. Whale Cove has a charming little sandy beach, with campgrounds and rental cottages just across the road. A gem of a place!

The Ceilidh Trail comes to an end at picturesque Margaree Harbour, an idyllic little village that is one of my favourite places on Cape Breton Island. With one church, and about a dozen homes, the road ends at Lawrence's General Store, which is also the local post office. This charming, family-run business, has been in operation for well over 100 years.

The view up the coast to Chéticamp from the store's tiny parking lot has to be one of the most spectacular in Nova Scotia. Directly in front of you is the bustling little harbor, with its imposing little breakwater. Off in the distance is the western flank of the Cape Breton Highlands, and to the left the open waters of the Gulf of St. Lawrence. Magnificent!

Although there is no accommodation in Margaree Harbour, less than one kilometer away is the Duck Cove Inn (800-565-9993), known locally as the "Inn with a View." With a panoramic view of the Margaree River and the Gulf of St. Lawrence, the 24-unit motel and restaurant is a great place to spend the night. By doing so you can spend an entire day exploring the Cabot Trail, including my three recommended side trips, and be back in Baddeck or North Sydney that same evening.

For those staying in Baddeck, it is a 62 km (39 mi) drive back up the Cabot Trail. Another route to Baddeck would be to take the Ceilidh Trail to Strathlorne, and follow the west side of Lake Ainslie to the village of

A lobster boat returns to the snug little anchorage at Margaree Harbour, with the western flank of the Cape Breton Highlands as a scenic backdrop.

Whycocomagh, where you can take the Trans-Canada Highway to Baddeck.

To spend the night in an Acadian setting, travel the 25 km (16 mi) north to the charming village of Chéticamp. Located right on the Cabot Trail there are several places to stay, including the Chéticamp Motel (866-721-2711), L'Auberge Doucet Inn (800-646-8668), Laurie's Motor Inn (800-959-4253), the Ocean View Motel & Chalets (877-743-4404), and the Parkview Motel & Restaurant (902-224-3232).

Trip 25 The Cabot Trail

Distance: *302 km (186 mi)*

Highlights: *Spectacular mountain roads and sub-Arctic plateaus, bordered by steep cliffs, offering superb panoramic views out over the surrounding ocean, and interspersed with lush lowland valleys carved by the glaciers of the last ice age. The Cape Breton Highlands National Park, the largest protected wilderness region in the province of Nova Scotia; arctic-alpine plants left over from the last Ice Age; rare plant and animal species found nowhere else in Canada; lovely little fishing villages, Celtic and Acadian cultures and traditions.*

It may sound a little prejudiced, but for me and many motorcycle enthusiasts in eastern Canada it is generally agreed that the Cabot Trail is the most breathtaking one-day touring experience in eastern North America. No

From a scenic look-off on the appropriately named French Mountain you can look back at the Acadian village of Chéticamp, and Chéticamp Island.

0   10   20 Miles
0 10 20 30 Kilometers

Meat Cove
Bay St. Lawrence
Capstick
Dingwall
Cape North
White Point
Pleasant Bay
New Haven
Neils Harbour
Gulf of St. Lawrence

CAPE BRETON ISLAND

Ingonish
Chéticamp
Cape Smokey
Grand-Étang
Wreck Cove
St. Joseph du Moine
Cap Le Moine
Terre Noir
Atlantic Ocean
Margaree Harbour
Belle Côte
Margaree Forks
North East Margaree
Tarbot
312
Goose Cove
Englishtown Ferry
St. Anns
19
Sydney
Middle River
105
Lake Ainslie
Baddeck
Bras D'Or Lakes

other stretch of highway, whether in Canada or the United States, even comes close! Approximately 300 km (186 mi) long, the Cabot Trail winds its way around the mountainous northern peninsula of Cape Breton Island. Nowhere else will you find such a combination of serpentine road, steep ascents and descents, sudden and unexpected switchbacks, and picturesque little fishing villages nestled between the mountains and the sea. As if all this were not enough, there is above all the dominating presence of the Atlantic Ocean on one side, and the Gulf of St. Lawrence on the other. The distant horizon line of these vast bodies of water seems to expand your field of

The Route from Baddeck

0 km (0 mi) From Baddeck take the Trans-Canada Highway west.
10 km (6.5 mi) Turn right on the Cabot Trail.
63 km (39.2 mi) Arrive Margaree Harbour.
90 km (55.5 mi) Arrive Chéticamp.
161 km (100 mi) Arrive Cape North.
  Take side trip to Bay St. Lawrence and Meat Cove: 63 km (39.1 mi)
  round trip.
  Take side trip to Dingwall: 6 km (3.9 mi) round trip.
Continue on Cabot Trail.
164 km (102.0 mi) Turn off to White Point.
182 km (113.3 mi) Return to Cabot Trail.
200 km (124.2 mi) Arrive Ingonish.
256 km (159.1 mi) A left on Route 312 takes you to the ferry.
272 km (169.1 mi) Arrive St. Anns.
284 km (176.4 mi) Turn right on the Trans-Canada Highway.
300 km (186 mi) Arrive Baddeck.

vision, and places everything in a different perspective.

Named after John Cabot, who became the first European to visit mainland North America in 1497 (Columbus never made it beyond the Caribbean), the Cabot Trail is definitely not the place for high-speed touring. However, it can still provide a challenging test of your driving skills. Even for those familiar with it, the Cabot Trail demands respect.

With reference to a map, there are two ways to travel the Cabot Trail—clockwise or counter-clockwise. In the old days, before pavement was laid and guardrails installed, it was common knowledge among the locals that it was best to travel the Trail in a clockwise direction. By doing this, you remained on the inside, and away from the cliffs! Today it doesn't really matter, as you are completely safe in either direction. However, the clockwise tour is still superior, because it offers the most striking scenic views.

Starting in Baddeck head west for 10 km (6.5 mi) along the Trans-Canada Highway /Route 105, until you reach a very prominent local landmark known as The Red Barn. A right turn at this colorful restaurant and gift shop (Exit 7), leads up and over Hunters Mountain, and down into the lovely, sheltered valley that is home to the little farming community of Middle River.

Here you will find a former service station that is the only motorcycle repair shop on the Cabot Trail. Gasit Enterprises Ltd., which is open year round, offers replacement tires, oil changes, and an emergency pickup

From the last week in September to the middle of October, the Margaree Valley comes alive with the many colorful hues of the annual autumn foliage.

service (902-295-3221). It is also a great place to stop for a visit, or to check out the used motorcycles and ATVs that are for sale.

The road continues through fertile farms and gentle pastures until the valley narrows, the mountains close in on both sides, and you suddenly find yourself sweeping through a series of lazy turns. You have reached three small bodies of water known as Lake O'Law, and on your right loom three graceful, thickly forested mountains, that are known locally as "The Three Sisters."

Before long you break out into another valley, where the northeast branch of the Margaree River flows down from the surrounding mountains. One of the most famous salmon rivers in eastern Canada, the Margaree was the first river in the Maritime Provinces to be designated a Canadian Heritage River.

The village of North East Margaree is also home to a lovely little salmon museum, located in a former one-room schoolhouse. There is a connection between this charming place, with its collection of regional fishing

Young Celtic musicians and step dancers carry on a centuries-old tradition at the Saturday afternoon ceilidh at the Doryman Tavern in Chéticamp.

mementos, and the infamous Field Marshall Herman Goering, head of the German Luftwaffe (Air Force) in the World War II. (If you want to find out what it is, you will have to visit!)

Only a few kilometers away, at the north end of the valley, is the Margaree Fish Hatchery and Visitor Centre, which offers self-guided tours, and a fascinating illustrated history of the Atlantic salmon industry. Opened in 1902, this was the first hatchery in the province, and it still plays a vital role in maintaining healthy fish stocks in the various branches of this renowned river.

At Margaree Forks, the Cabot Trail turns north and follows the west side of the Margaree River until it reaches the Gulf of St. Lawrence at Margaree Harbour, which is where the Ceilidh Trail and the Cabot Trail meet. Here, and just across the new bridge at Belle Cote, the Celtic culture of the Highland Scots comes face-to-face with the proud tradition of French settlement on the west coast of Cape Breton Island. As you travel along this exposed coast, you immediately become aware this is an Acadian Region, and it is very different from where you have just come.

From Margaree Harbour to Chéticamp is 27 km (16.3 mi). Along the way you pass through a sequence of small villages, all situated on a broad coastal plain overlooking the Gulf of St. Lawrence. Their names give them away: *Belle Côte* (pretty hillside), *Terre Noire* (black or dark earth), *Cap Le Moine* (friar or monk's cape—after a rocky promontory or cliff), *Saint-Joseph-du-Moine* (Saint Joseph the monk), and *Grand Étang* (big pond). These are French-speaking communities, places that for more than two hundred years have lived in harmony with their Celtic neighbors, along this spectacular coast. All along this shore, the sharp-eyed visitor will notice a distinctive form of local architecture—houses and barns that are physically joined together. This unusual feature enabled farmers to feed their livestock without venturing outdoors, an important detail given the extreme weather conditions that occur here in the winter, and the awesome power of on-shore winds that often reach speeds of 150 km/h (93 mph)!

As you arrive on the outskirts of Chéticamp (poor campground), the dramatic contours of the Cape Breton Highlands provide a spectacular backdrop for this little Acadian village, a scene quite unlike any other in the Maritime provinces. With its bilingual population of less than 2,000 people, the village lies on a fertile coastal plain, situated between the mountains and the shimmering waters of the Gulf of St. Lawrence. First settled in the mid-1700s, as a fishing station, the town today offers such a wide variety of visitor services that it has become the tourist center of western Cape Breton Island. Other attractions include an information and genealogical center, a waterfront boardwalk, whale-watching cruises, and deep-sea fishing charters.

At one time, not that long ago, Chéticamp was an isolated area, cut off from the rest of Cape Breton for the most part. Because of this isolation, the small village was able to retain its unique French-Acadian language, culture, and music. Yet it maintained a close connection with its Gaelic-speaking Scottish neighbors, a fact that is reflected today in Chéticamp's lively Celtic music scene. (If you arrive in Chéticamp on a Saturday afternoon, be sure to take in the Celtic fiddle music at the Doryman Tavern and Restaurant. Every Saturday, from mid-May to mid-October, you have a chance to hear the best Celtic musicians on Cape Breton Island. Where else can you hear a four-hour concert, 2–6 p.m., for only $6!)

As you leave the village, with those majestic mountains looming all around, you cross the Chéticamp River and enter the Cape Breton Highlands National Park, one of the most spectacular national parks in all of Canada. On your right, a wonderful visitor center beckons, and is well worth a visit. Not only can you pay your park entrance fee, you can also view a very large, wall-sized diorama that vividly illustrates the topographic nature of the terrain that you will soon pass over. Other displays highlight the various species of plants and animals that inhabit this special place, and give a short history of the park itself. A large picnic area, rest rooms, and a small gift shop with a great selection of books and maps about the park complete the complex.

A lovely hiking trail leads down to Fishing Cove, a former summer fishing station between Chéticamp and Pleasant Bay. It is an easy walk down, but a very strenuous climb back up!

Before modern navigational aids, offshore fishermen would locate the entrance to Chéticamp Harbour by the nearby presence of the sheer, red-tinted cliffs of Cap Rouge.

Then the fun begins! Within minutes of leaving the visitor Center you start to climb up the appropriately named French Mountain, with the sheer precipice of Cap Rouge (Red Cape) on your right. It is the first of five mountains that you will climb, and descend, in the next 100 km (62 mi). The steep ascent brings a feeling of euphoria, followed by a sense of disbelief, as one magnificent vista after another comes into view. The Gulf of St. Lawrence is on your left, while the mountains on the right seem close enough to reach out and touch.

For about 6 km (3.7 mi) the road twists and turns back upon itself, until it reaches an immense plateau. Here the road turns inland, away from the Gulf, but only for a distance of about 30 km (18 mi). On this plateau you will find yourself in a sub-Arctic terrain of bogs, barrens, and stunted trees. Moose can often be seen in the small lakes that border the highway, or even on the road itself. Should you come upon one, they should best be viewed from a distance, preferably through a telephoto lens.

At strategic intervals along this highland plateau you will notice small, white, emergency cabins. In addition to a telephone, they contain beds, food, firewood, and a stove. Although usually locked for the summer months, they have saved more than one stranded motorist from almost certain death, when sudden winter storms roar in off the surrounding waters.

At the other side of the plateau you will travel across a most unusual geographical feature known as The Boar's Back. This section of highway, which takes you from French Mountain to MacKenzie Mountain, travels along the top of a narrow ridge, with near-vertical drops of about 450 m (1,500 ft) on one side and 335 m (1,100 ft) on the other. From the top of MacKenzie Mountain the road begins a steep descent, in a series of sweeping, 180-degree, hairpin turns. The view is awesome and quite overwhelming. In front of you is the vast expanse of the Gulf of St. Lawrence and the entire west flank of the mountainous northern peninsula.

At the tiny village of Pleasant Bay the Cabot Trail cuts inland, and after a few kilometers, it climbs again—this time up the side of North Mountain. This section of highway takes you through the only untouched Acadian hardwood forest still standing in the Maritime Provinces. It has never been cut, and remains much the same as when John Cabot arrived.

Before you climb North mountain you can visit The Lone Shieling, a reconstruction of a typical crofter's cottage found in the Highlands of

Scotland more than 200 years ago. This area was one of the first parts of *Nova Scotia* (Latin for New Scotland) to be settled by immigrants from Scotland in the early 1800s, and their descendants are still found here today.

At Cape North village, 71 km (44.5 mi) north of Chéticamp, you are about halfway around the Cabot Trail (without detours). Gas is sometimes available, but I always prefer to gas up before leaving Chéticamp, just in case. Here you will also find the first of three short side trips, off the "official" Cabot Trail, that I strongly recommend.

The first is a 18 km (11.1 mi) paved road leading to the fishing village of Bay St. Lawrence (pop. 350), a scenic drive that will take you to the northern tip of Cape Breton (and Nova Scotia). This charming detour is dominated by the massive presence of Sugarloaf and Cape North mountains. About 8 km (5 mi) along is Cabot Landing, a gorgeous provincial park that has a 7 km (4 mi) sand beach, the longest in the province. There is also a fine little monument to John Cabot that marks the site of his first landfall in North America. This spot has magnificent views out over the ocean.

From Bay St. Lawrence a short detour leads to Capstick, and the end of the pavement. For those of you with a sense of adventure, the next 8 km (5 mi) of dirt road leading to Meat Cove could well be the highlight of your Cabot Trail tour. Considered to be one of the 10 most-beautiful locations in Canada, the panoramic views on the way in, and on the way back, will take your breath away! Be aware, however, that guardrails are few, the cliffs are

Riders admire the spectacular view from the top of MacKenzie Mountain, before starting down the series of hairpin turns leading to the little village of Pleasant Bay.

sheer, and the road is quite steep in places. It is not really suitable for a fully loaded touring bike.

When you return to Cape North village, a left turn will take you down a hill, past the local fire hall, to the turnoff for Dingwall (pop. 613). This little detour is well worth the effort, for you will end up at the Markland Resort, an up-scale lodge and restaurant, with a magnificent view over the ocean. On your left, the massive eastern flank of Cape North Mountain extends as far as Money Point, the northeastern tip of the province, and the location of more than 200 shipwrecks. In the center, 24 km (15 mi) offshore, the outline of St. Paul Island dominates the horizon. Known as the "Graveyard of the Gulf," over the centuries more than 300 ships have come to grief on this 5 km (3 mi) long piece of primeval rock!

After returning to the Cabot Trail, another few kilometers brings you to a sign for White Point, and my third recommended and not to be missed diversion. For the next several kilometers this narrow paved road closely follows the contours of this remarkable stretch of coastline, sweeping up and down the side of the mountain, and through the tiny fishing village of Smelt Brook. At one point you come upon an amazing panorama, with a series of

Old-style lobster traps, in the foreground, reflect the seasonal nature of White Point's main economic activity. Haddock, mackerel, and crab, also play a part in the offshore fishery.

"The Wreck of the Jessie"

In the early morning hours of January 1, 1825, a three-masted sailing ship was driven ashore near the southwest tip of St. Paul Island during a raging snowstorm. On board the barque Jessie, from Prince Edward Island, were her owner Donald MacKay and 27 other crew members. Miraculously, all survived and were able to scale the rocky cliffs, taking with them whatever food they could carry, along with a few other supplies.

Over the next few weeks the survivors lit several huge bonfires, using material from the wrecked vessel. Although the fires were easily seen by residents of northern Cape Breton, they had no way of reaching the stranded men, because the seasonal pack ice had moved into the Cabot Strait just a few days after the ship went aground.

Later that spring, after the ice had dispersed, sailors from Chéticamp arrived at St. Paul and discovered the remains of the marooned mariners. On the owner's body they found a diary, with the last entry dated March 17th. He had been the last to die, from starvation. Incredibly, in spite of the isolation, the freezing temperatures, and the lack of food, a few of the crew had managed to survive for more than 10 weeks!

A short while later, in Charlottetown, the owner's wife happened to notice a man wearing the same coat that she had made for her husband, Donald, one year earlier. She confronted him, and with the proof of her husband's initials sewn into the lining, he was forced to admit that he had removed the heavy coat from Donald's frozen body, along with a sum of money. Both the coat and the money were returned to Mrs. MacKay! ■

sheer cliffs in the foreground, and mysterious outline of St. Paul Island off on the horizon.

The last kilometer to White Point (pop. 75) is very steep, with some sharp turns, but you can easily follow the pavement down to the local wharf. Here you can park your bike, climb on the breakwater for a better view (if you're careful), and take some time to appreciate the sheer beauty of this snug little harbor. Should you be so inclined, and if you have the proper footwear, you can even hike out to the end of the point itself. If you do, an easy 20-minute hike will take you to a lonely little graveyard, at the site of the original village. This cemetery, with a large white cross, holds the remains of many individuals, adults as well as children, who have perished in

The small cable ferry at Englishtown will save a 40-minute drive around the perimeter of St. Ann's Bay. Giant McAskill's grave is just to the right of this pastoral scene.

shipwrecks along this perilous coast. Whether you remain at the wharf, or hike to the point, you will be rewarded with a splendid view of lovely Aspy Bay and the Cape North escarpment.

When you return to the stop sign, just above White Point, you have the option of returning to the Cabot Trail the way you came, or making a left turn. I always go left, and take a paved side road through the woods for about 6 km (3.7 mi) to the charming little fishing village of New Haven. Its close neighbor Neil's Harbour also has a lovely little lighthouse, in a very picturesque setting.

Rejoining the Cabot Trail, you turn left, and head for the resort area of Ingonish (pop. 1,250), the service center for the eastern side of the Cabot Trail. Here you will find two gas stations, several restaurants, and a wide variety of accommodation including the renowned, and quite expensive, Keltic Lodge (800-565-0444), which is situated on a point of land that juts out into the ocean. Nearby is the Highland Links Golf Course, a spectacular combination of mountains and sea that *Golf Digest* ranked as the best public golf course in Canada in 2005.

Beyond Ingonish, you play hide-and-seek with the Atlantic as you climb up the thickly forested slope of Cape Smokey Mountain. As you approach the summit, the view over the ocean becomes increasingly dramatic and spectacular. Suddenly, and without warning, the road drops away, and you find yourself staring directly down at the ocean, with nothing but sheer cliffs and a narrow guardrail between you and a long, long, fall!

In the next two kilometers you'll twist and turn in full view of the sea, while the road continues to drop away in front of you. I usually put my Yamaha Venture into second gear, and let the braking power of the engine take me down. Often, when we reach the bottom, we turn around and head back up, just for the sheer exhilaration of it all. To many, the descent of Cape Smoky is the highlight of their Cabot Trail tour.

For the next 50 km (30 mi), the Cabot Trail follows the ocean as you make your way to the little village of St. Anns. Here you will find the only Gaelic College in North America, where those with a Scottish background may spend a fascinating afternoon enjoying the culture and music of their Celtic ancestors.

Along the way, and just a short distance from the foot of Cape Smoky, is the Wreck Cove General Store, and I never pass by without stopping in. Gas

The imposing visitor center at the Gaelic College of Arts & Crafts will entice all those with a trace of Scottish blood in them. Outdoor concerts are held on a regular basis throughout the summer and fall.

is available, as well as basic groceries and a variety of snacks, and the conversation is always enjoyable. The real reason I stop, however, is to buy one of their world-famous lobster sandwiches, made with home-baked bread, and a special secret sauce, the ingredients of which are known by only two people. I usually take it home, and have it before bedtime. Delicious!

By the way, if you plan to take the ferry at Englishtown, and if you buy a snack or an ice cream, the friendly staff at the General Store will sell you a ferry ticket for $1.25, instead of the $5 fee you will be charged at the ferry.

Twenty minutes farther on you come to a junction. The Cabot Trail turns to the right, and continues on through the tiny hamlets of Tarbot and Goose Cove, to the Gaelic College at St. Ann's. Route 312 is to the left and leads directly to the Englishtown cable ferry. Though the route with the

Giant McAskill

Angus McAskill, known as the Cape Breton Giant, was born in 1825, on the Isle of Bernera in the Outer Hebrides, Scotland. While he was still a young child, his family left Scotland and emigrated to Cape Breton, where they settled on the south shore of St. Ann's Bay in an area now known as Englishtown. He was normal in size until the age of 16, then he started to grow. By the time he was 21, he stood 7 feet, 9 inches tall, and weighed 425 pounds! At this age some of his other vital statistics were as follows: chest measurement, 80 inches; width of shoulders, 44 inches; length of his hand, 12 inches; length of his boot, 14.5 inches!

Despite his imposing height, he was perfectly proportioned with—needless to say—a very muscular physique. He had deep-set blue eyes, curly black hair, a musical-sounding voice, and a great sense of humor. Fortunately, for a man his size, he was a very kind and compassionate individual, who—by all accounts—fully deserved his nickname, "The Gentle Giant."

Hard times in Cape Breton forced Angus to leave the island in 1848, at the age of 23. He embarked on a series of tours throughout Canada, the United States, the West Indies, and Europe, where he amazed and delighted thousands with his feats of strength, and his gentle personality. While in London, England, he had a private audience with Queen Victoria.

ferry is 10.6 km (6.6 mi) shorter than going around the bay, there is often an extended waiting period before you get across especially on weekends in the summer season

Should you take the ferry, and if you have the time, you might want to stop at the Giant McAskill Museum, also on Route 312.

No matter which way you come, around the bay or by the ferry, you rejoin the Trans-Canada Highway at St. Ann's. A short drive of 16 km (9.6 mi) brings you back to Baddeck, where the Cabot Trail officially begins and ends.

Shortly before he died, in 1922, Alexander Graham Bell wrote in his diary: "I have traveled around the globe. I have seen the Canadian and American Rockies, the Andes and the Alps, and the Highlands of Scotland; but for simple beauty the Cape Breton Highlands outrivals them all!"

The same could be said of the Cabot Trail. Ride it and understand why!

Stories of his incredible strength are legendary. Like the time he and his brother were plowing their father's field with a pair of oxen. When the oxen tired, Angus unhooked their harness, put it over his shoulder, and finished the job with his younger brother guiding the plow!

By the age of 26, Angus was again touring the United States, this time with the Barnum and Bailey Circus. As part of his strongman act, he would let the celebrated midget Tom Thumb dance on the palm of his hand. Angus would end the show by putting the midget in his jacket pocket, and walking off the stage!

During a visit to New Orleans he was told of a certain ship's anchor that a number of American strongmen had tried, unsuccessfully, to lift from a wharf. With a large crowd watching, Angus picked up the one-ton anchor and put it on his shoulder. However, one of the anchor flukes hit his shoulder when he went to put it down. He was never the same after that. He returned to Englishtown, bought farms for his brothers and sisters, and opened a general store. At the young age of 28 Angus, the tallest, non-pathological giant ever medically recorded, died from a severe fever. He is buried in the local cemetery.

(The 1981 *Guinness Book of World Records* claimed that he was the tallest natural giant who ever lived, the strongest man who ever lived, and the man having the largest chest measurements of any non-obese man!)   ■

Trip 26 Baddeck & Bras d'Or Lakes Circuit

Distance: *300 km (186 mi)*
Highlights: *Gentle rolling hills and small mountains, many quaint little villages, and a relaxing daylong ride around Canada's Inland Sea.*

Alexander Graham Bell, the inventor of the telephone, knew a good thing when he saw it. He and his wife Mabel had come to Baddeck for a vacation in 1885, mainly to escape the oppressive summer heat of their home in Washington, D.C. They were so captivated by the area and its Scottish inhabitants that they bought half a mountain, on which they built a very large summer home, *Beinn Bhreagh* (Gaelic for beautiful mountain). For the next 37 years until his death in 1922, Alexander never missed a season.

Situated on the shores of the Bras d'Or Lakes, Baddeck enjoys an international reputation for its superb location, its comprehensive boating facilities, and the many attractions that this village of less than 1,200 has to offer. Many come to visit The Alexander Graham Bell National Historic Site, while others want to play the new 18-hole golf course, or take part in the annual sailing regatta that has been held every August since 1904. Nearby attractions also include a nine-hole golf course at Forks Baddeck, and a

The Bras d'Or Yacht Club in Baddeck is protected by a natural breakwater formed by Kidston Island, shown here with its photogenic lighthouse.

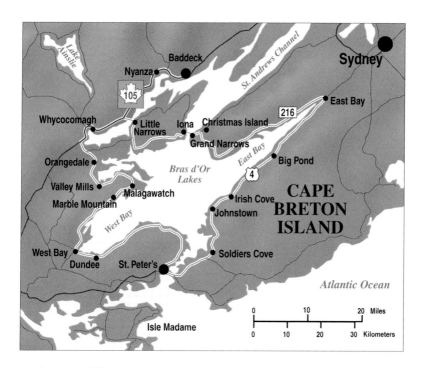

50-foot waterfall at Uisge Ban Park. Hunter's Mountain also provides access to hundreds of miles of recreational trails in the interior of the Cape Breton Highlands.

The Bras d'Or Lakes, considered one of the world's great sailing areas, are also known as Canada's Inland Sea. Covering an area of approximately 1,100 sq km (450 sq mi), the lakes are in reality an arm of the Atlantic Ocean, and almost divide the island in two.

The name *Bras d'Or* is most likely a corruption of the Portuguese word Labrador—a term used by 16th-century Portuguese fishermen when referring to parts of Nova Scotia. (Later French settlers translated it as "Arm of Gold.") This irregularly shaped lake system, approximately 100 km (60 mi) long by 50 km (30 mi) wide, is made up of several distinct bodies of water: Bras d'Or Lake (the main lake), West Bay, with its many islands, St. Peter's Inlet, East Bay, St. Andrews Channel, St. Patrick's Channel, and River Denis Basin.

Leaving Baddeck head west up the Trans-Canada Highway/Route 105, passing through Nyanza (named after Lake Victoria Nyanza in Africa—the origin of the Nile River), the first of four Mi'kmaq reserves that you will encounter on this trip around the Bras d'Or Lakes. Mi'kmaq Indians have lived along these shores since time immemorial. Using the lake as a source of

The Route from Baddeck

0 km (0 mi) From Baddeck head west on the Trans-Canada
Highway/Route 105.

43 km (26.7 mi) Turn left at Exit 4 to Orangedale.

49 km (30.4 mi) Arrive Orangedale, continue to Valley Mills.

56 km (34.8 mi) At Valley Mills turn left on Marble Mountain Road.

93 km (57.8 mi) Arrive West Bay. Continue on to Dundee
and St. Peter's.

135 km (83.9 mi) Arrive St. Peter's. Take Route 4 to East Bay.

201 km (124.8 mi) Arrive East Bay. Turn left on Route 216.

243 km (150.9 mi) Arrive Christmas Island. Turn left on Route 223.

246 km (152.8 mi) Arrive Grand Narrows. Cross bridge
and continue to Little Narrows.

272 km (168.9 mi) Arrive Little Narrows. Take ferry across
St. Patricks Channel.

274 km (170.2 mi) Turn right on Trans-Canada Highway to Baddeck.

300 km (186.3 mi) Arrive Baddeck.

food and transportation, they traveled far and wide to trade with other Algonquian tribes throughout Atlantic Canada and the state of Maine.

Ten minutes later you will arrive in the little village of Whycocomagh, a rather unique place that is home to two distinct cultures. One side of the Skye River contains a little community that was settled by immigrants from the Isle of Skye and the Highlands of Scotland. They arrived around 1823, and in less than 10 years had established a flourishing lumber trade with the British Isles. On the other side of the river is the Mi'kmaq Indian reserve from which the village takes its name, an aboriginal word that translates as "head of the waters."

Whycocomagh provides the usual tourist facilities, as well as several shops that offer an extensive line of traditional Mi'kmaq crafts. There are four service stations, a pharmacy and liquor store, as well as Vi's Restaurant, one of my favorite places to eat along this stretch of highway. Great homemade food!

Soon after leaving the village, at Iron Mines, turn left at Exit 4 and drive about 6 km (4 mi) to the tiny lakeside community of Orangedale, named after a Protestant fraternal order called the Orangemen. It has one of the oldest surviving General Stores on the island, offering everything from food to furniture to automobile tires. The Orangedale Station is the only remaining example of the twelve original Intercolonial Railway Stations built in Cape Breton between 1880 and 1900. In addition to providing shelter and services to the traveling public, the station was a busy shipping point for lumber, potatoes, Christmas trees, and fish and oysters from the Bras d'Or Lakes.

The Orangedale Station was built in 1886 in the "Railway Queen Anne" style, with squared timbers stacked one upon the other. When passenger rail service in Cape Breton came to an end in 1990, a group of concerned locals formed the Orangedale Station Association, which through a long difficult process was able to preserve the Orangedale Station and turn it into a lovely little museum. The first floor contains the ticket office, waiting room with wood burning stove, and freight shed. On the second floor is the original station agent's living quarters, furnished as the family home it once was in the years before World War I. Outside the station are four pieces of original rolling stock: a bright-red caboose; a crew van; a box car that had been converted to a small craft shop; and a Russell snowplough. This latter item, which was attached to the front of a steam engine, was the size of a box car, with a primitive control room for two "operators'" whose primary function was to operate the two wing plows.

Although no passenger trains have stopped at Orangedale Station since 1990, at least two freight trains a week pass by on their way from Sydney to Halifax, on the mainland. Freight traffic on this line is expected to increase dramatically, when a new coal mine on the east side of the island opens within a few years.

Alexander Graham Bell 1847–1922

Though Alexander Graham Bell is known for inventing the telephone, he also designed and built the world's fastest hydrofoil, was the driving force behind the first powered flight in the British Empire, and was one of the first people in the world to investigate the difficult problems associated with the teaching of the deaf. The son and grandson of speech experts, he had an intimate knowledge of the possibilities of sound. Also, as the son of a deaf mother, he had a true appreciation of the effort required by a deaf person to live in a hearing world. These two factors would provide the prime motivation for his upcoming invention of the telephone.

The actual invention of the telephone grew out of improvements Alexander had made to the electric telegraph. While working in Boston, Massachusetts, he had developed a device known as the "harmonic telegraph," which could send more than one message at a time over a single telegraph wire. He also thought that it should be possible to pick up all the sounds of the human voice using an adaptation of his harmonic telegraph. In 1875, along with his assistant Thomas A. Watson, Alexander constructed instruments that transmitted recognizable voice-like sounds.

Bell's first telephone patent was granted on March 7, 1876. Three days later he and Watson, located in different rooms, were about to test the new type of transmitter described in his patent. Watson heard

Bell's voice saying, "Mr. Watson, come here. I want you." Bell had up-set a battery, spilling acid on his clothing. He soon forgot about the ac-cident in his excitement over the success of his new telephone transmitter.

After the telephone Bell continued his experiments in communica-tion. His next invention was the "photophone-transmission" of sound on a beam of light, the forerunner of fiber-optics. He also vastly im-proved the techniques for teaching speech to the deaf. He also worked on the development of the photo-electric cell, the iron lung, and an un-successful attempt to invent the phonograph. After hearing of ship-wrecked sailors who died because of a lack of fresh water, he devised a process to produce fresh water from salt water.

In 1907 he set up the Aerial Experimental Association to examine the possibility of manned flight. After many experiments with man-lift-ing kites, he switched his attention to engine-powered craft. In Febru-ary, 1909, his Silver Dart made the first powered flight in the British Empire, from the frozen surface of Baddeck Bay. In an attempt to in-crease the speed of a boat, he developed a design that lifted the hull out of the water. In 1917, after many years of testing, his hydrofoil boat set a world water speed record of 114 km (68 mi) per hour. The huge, record setting, 60-ft-long, HD-4 Hydrofoil is on display in the Alexander Graham Bell Museum in Baddeck.

Alexander Graham Bell, one of the greatest inventors of the last 200 years, died in Baddeck on August 2, 1922. Both he and his devoted wife Mabel are buried on top of his lovely mountain.   ■

A recreational "Sea-Doo" heads for the surviving timbers of the former shipping pier at Marble Mountain. In the lower right of this picture you can see rough stone from the quarry, while the shoreline and shallow water is littered with white marble chips from the polishing process, which took place along the shoreline.

Returning to the junction on the outskirts of the village, turn left and head for Valley Mills, only a short distance away. After a few miles the paved road suddenly turns into a well-maintained gravel road that crosses two single-lane, iron bridges. At the T-intersection turn left, and the easy-going gravel continues until the pavement is regained at *Malagawatch* (Mi'kmaq for a triangular piece of land).

As you skirt the shore of Denys Basin, you pass through several picturesque little inlets and coves that provide a secure habitat for bald eagles, osprey, and many other types of waterfowl. The Cape Breton Smokehouse & Restaurant is a few miles down the road and hidden away just off the pavement. Owned by a German family, it offers waterfront dining, with superb seafood and various types of German cuisine and makes a great stop.

Two miles farther on you will arrive at a mountain of marble. From the look-off below the abandoned quarry, the panoramic scene takes in the full immensity of West Bay and it's many little islands. These appear as idyllic green sanctuaries, set against the deep blue of the surrounding water, and at least one is reputed to be the site of pirate treasure, buried by none other than the infamous Captain Kidd himself!

Off to the right, across the Bay, the carefully manicured greens of the golf course at the Dundee Resort stand out vividly from the surrounding forest cover. To the left the full expanse of the Big Lake extends into the far reaches of East Bay. The beach below this look-off is made up of hundreds of thousands of marble chips, all that remains of a once thriving industrial operation.

The marble quarry operated between 1869 and 1921 and transformed what had previously been a sleepy little settlement on the north shore of West Bay into a major industrial site that by 1900 employed well over 1,000 men. Marble was shipped to markets in eastern Canada and the Boston States (New England). A short walk uphill from the look-off will take you to the abandoned quarry. The year-round population of Marble Mountain today is about 75. A delightful little museum, located in the village's original one-room school and open during July and August, contains a wealth of information on the settlement, along with intriguing pictures of the village

The Dundee Golf Resort is also a haven for recreational boaters, and a nearby marina caters to various types of pleasure craft, large and small.

and the quarry. It gives a wonderful look at the major industrial complex that existed here in the years before World War I.

West Bay, the large body of water from which the next community takes its name, forms the western extremity of the Bras d'Or Lakes. It is rectangular in shape, 19 km (12 mi) long and 8 km (5 mi) wide, and is enclosed on both sides by high hills or mountains that reach a height of more than 230 m (750 ft).

From West Bay, bear left for a short distance to a small T-intersection, then bear left again and head for the resort and marina at Dundee, just 6 km (3.5 mi) up the road. After a stretch in the woods, you find yourself back close to the shoreline, with wonderful sweeping views out across the island dotted waters of West Bay.

Just before a one-lane bridge, a sheltered little cove on the left is home to Dundee Marine, a nice place to stop for a picnic, or perhaps enjoy a meal of local seafood at the rustic restaurant located on site. A little farther on is the full-service Dundee Resort and Golf Club, offering a championship 18-hole golf course, and premier accommodation consisting of 38 charming cottages, along with 60 traditional hotel rooms.

The St. Peter's Canal allows sailboats and small motor yachts easy access to the Bras d'Or Lakes from the Atlantic Ocean. It is often used by visiting American sailors from the coast of New England, who come to explore the many inlets and coves of Canada's Inland Sea.

Unlike most conventional lighthouses this charming beacon at Battery Provincial Park has a fixed red light, rather than a flashing white beam. Visible up to eight nautical miles, it warns approaching vessels of numerous rocky shoals around the entrance to St. Peter's Canal.

The road continues to follow the unspoiled shoreline of West Bay, with its many little coves and inlets. At one point, on the other side of the bay, you can plainly see the scar formed by the marble quarry on the side of Marble Mountain.

St. Peter's, a small village of 750 is situated on a narrow strip of land that separates the Atlantic Ocean from the Bras d'Or Lakes. Since time immemorial local Mi'kmaq Indians had used this site as a place to portage their canoes from the open waters of the Atlantic to the sheltered coves and inlets of the Bras d'Or Lakes.

In 1650 a Frenchman by the name of Nicolas Denys established a fishing and trading post on this narrow isthmus. Later, during the First Siege of Louisbourg (1745), soldiers from the New England Colonies captured the post and expelled the French inhabitants. The United Empire Loyalists who replaced them decided to fortify the location, and by 1787 Fort Dorchester had been built. Located on the highest point of land, this small bastion consisted of several cannons, a guardhouse, and a powder magazine.

Construction of a canal to link the Atlantic Ocean with the Bras d'Or Lakes took from 1854 to 1869 to complete. The 91-meter-long (300 ft)

The small, rural post office in Iona identifies itself in three languages: English, French, and Scots Gaelic, while the multi-lingual sign at the nearby harbor (inset photo) welcomes visiting boaters in four languages: Mi'kmaq, French, Gaelic, and English.

canal, a National Historic Site, is a tidal-lock canal, whose design compensates for the constant change in water levels due to the ocean tides.

The Nicolas Denys Museum, on a small hill overlooking the canal, is located on the site of the original trading post and contains local historical displays. The Battery Provincial Park, located on the other side of the canal, is a great picnic spot and place to watch boats passing through the canal. There is a photogenic little lighthouse, along with a campground and archaeological ruins dating back to Fort Dorchester.

The MacAskill House Museum in St. Peter's honors Wallace MacAskill (1890–1956), a famed Canadian photographer, whose picture of the famed Grand Banks fishing schooner Bluenose graces the back of the Canadian dime. The museum contains more than 100 of his photographs, along with a small but growing collection of cameras and a display of local handcrafts.

Leaving St. Peter's follow Route 4 north to Chapel Island First Nations Reserve. In the early 1750s, a Roman Catholic missionary converted the local Indians and built a small chapel on an offshore island. Chapel Island has been the historic religious center of the Mi'kmaq First Nation ever since, and was declared a Canadian National Historic Site in 2005. An annual gathering takes place each summer, attracting Mi'kmaq from all parts of Atlantic Canada and the state of Maine.

The name of the next little hamlet, Soldiers Cove, has an intriguing history. During the War of 1812, two British "Scottish" Regiments helped to defeat American forces that tried to invade Upper Canada (Ontario) and Lower Canada (Québec). After the war most of the Highland soldiers were discharged, and offered land grants in various parts of eastern Canada. At least three of these veterans made their way to Cape Breton Island and received 100-acre land grants on the southern shore of the Bras d'Or Lakes. Soldier's Cove is a lovely little spot, and there are usually one or two small boats swinging at anchor in the inner reaches of this inlet.

Just a few miles away is the tiny community of Johnstown, with its Sacred Heart Catholic Church strikingly situated on the top of a small hill. First opened in 1891, this charming building not only has a breathtaking view out over the Bras d'Or Lakes, but also has a unique shrine located on the church grounds. Back in 1946 Monsignor Ronald MacLean, a chaplain in the Royal Canadian Navy, visited the shrine to Our Lady of Guadalupe in Mexico. He was so impressed with this Catholic Patron of The Americas that upon his retirement he built a smaller version in his native Cape Breton. Inside the church are 12 paintings that depict the story of Our Lady of Guadalupe. The art work is a mixture of Mexican, Gaelic, and Mi'kmaq styles.

Later, as the winding road reaches the summit of the mountain at Irish Cove, the full splendour of the Bras d'Or Lakes is laid out in front of you. There is a superb look-off and picnic site on the left, which provides the most scenic views on the southern side of this inland sea.

Big Pond is the home of Rita MacNeil, one of Canada's most beloved singer/songwriters. Rita's Tea Room, in the former one-room school, offers a relaxing setting for a tea break, along with other light dining possibilities. The cozy building also houses an interesting outline of the singer's remarkable career and accomplishments.

At East Bay make a left turn, and follow Route 216 along the north side of East Bay to the largest First Nations Community in eastern Canada. Stretched out along the shore of the lake, and nestled in the lee of the Boisdale Hills, Eskasoni (Mi'kmaq for still water) is about 8 km (5 mi) long with a population of 3,200. Two gas stations and a small supermarket can be found in the village, along with several small stores.

After skirting the edge of the lake to Benacadie Pond, the road turns

The century-old General Store in Little Narrows continues to offer locally grown food, and other supplies to ferry passengers as well as residents of the tiny community.

inland for a few miles until you reach Christmas Island, where a left turn on Route 223 takes you to Grand Narrows, the site of the longest railroad bridge east of Montréal. With the arrival of the Intercolonial Railroad in the early 1890s, the village was transformed into a thriving little community with three stores, two restaurants, and two canneries, as well as a post office, blacksmith shop, and a boat yard. There was also a customs office to handle the increasing number of tourists who would arrive by train, before transferring to several small lake steamers, which would transport them all over the Bras d'Or Lakes.

The Grand Narrows Hotel was built in 1887 to handle this influx of people. One such person was Alexander Graham Bell, who first stayed there in the summer of 1889, while waiting for a boat to Baddeck, on the other side of the lake. This historic hotel has recently undergone a complete restoration and now operates as a Bed and Breakfast.

A modern road bridge crosses the Barra Strait, named after the first settlers in this area who came from the Isle of Barra in Scotland. On the other side is the small community of Iona, with its Highland Village, a living museum that recreates the history of the immigrants who arrived from the Highlands of Scotland and the Hebrides.

Enjoy the lovely coast ride along the Big Lake to Little Narrows, where a quaint little cable ferry ($5.00 fee) takes you back to the Trans-Canada Highway. From the T-intersection it is only 26 km (16 mi) back to Baddeck.

Highland Village Museum

If Scottish blood flows in your veins, or even if it doesn't, a visit to this living history museum and Gaelic cultural center in the tiny village of Iona (pop. 131) could be one of the highlights of your visit to Cape Breton.

Spread across the side of a hill, with spectacular panoramic views on all sides, this fascinating site contains 11 historic buildings such as a school, general store, and blacksmith shop, all staffed by costumed animators. Nine of these are original structures built by the early Scottish settlers, which were moved to this location from other parts of the island over the last 50 years. The last move only took place in 2003, when the large wooden church was placed on a barge, floated across the Bras d'Or Lakes, and towed up the steep hill by a team of bulldozers!

From a simple log cabin, very basic and plain, to later two-story family dwellings that were actually quite comfortable, this 43-acre site also has the only replica of a Hebridean-style "black house" to be found outside of Scotland. Made of field stone, with 6-ft-thick walls and a sod roof, this primitive structure was home to our Scottish ancestors before they crossed the Atlantic ocean. Be sure to ask an animator how it got it's name!

In addition to daily demonstrations in the Gaelic language and Celtic crafts, the museum has a Cape Breton Genealogy & Family History Centre, as well as a well-stocked gift shop, with all manner of all things Celtic.

The Highland Village Living History Museum is open daily from June 1 to October 17.   ■

Trip 27 Isle Madame Route

Distance: *82 km (50.7 mi)*
Highlights: *Isle Madame is a relatively flat, but fascinating coastal island, with numerous little coves and inlets, and several nearby small islands. You can easily spend a very enjoyable afternoon, or even a full day, exploring its many unique attractions.*

We start our exploration of Isle Madame from Route 104, built to Trans-Canada Highway standards. Take the exit for Isle Madame. This will put you on Route 320, which takes you over the small Lennox Passage Bridge to the captivating beauty of Isle Madame.

Along the way is Babin's Service Centre, a full service motorcycle shop that specializes in Yamaha, Suzuki, and Kawasaki. Although the owner and his family are French-Acadian, they are fully bilingual, and only too happy to meet with visiting bikers from all over eastern North America. One of my favorite stops!

Like many Acadian communities on rocky Isle Madame, the inhabitants of Sampson Cove depend on the fishery, rather than agriculture, to make their livelihood.

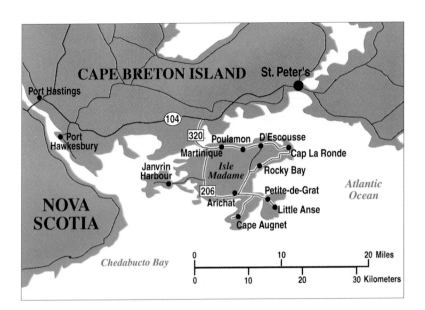

Named in honor of the Queen of France (the wife of Louis XIV), Isle Madame was one of the first parts of Nova Scotia to be settled by Europeans. Fish merchants from the Channel Islands, off the north coast of France, were engaged in fishing operations around this 17-sq-mi island as early as 1722.

The relatively flat island is dotted with many charming little fishing villages, whose French-speaking inhabitants are very proud of their Acadian

Isle Madame Route

0 km (0 mi.) From Route 104 take the Route 320 exit for Isle Madame.

5 km (3.2 mi) Cross the bridge and stay left on Route 320.

14 km (8.9 mi) Arrive D'Escousse. Continue straight to Poirierville and Cap La Ronde.

21 km (13.4 mi) Arrive Cap La Ronde. Continue along shore.

30 km (18.7 mi) Rejoin Route 320 and turn left to Arichat.

34 km (21.2 mi) Arrive Arichat. Take Route 206 to Petit-de-Grat and Little Anse.

43 km (26.6 mi) Arrive Little Anse. Return to the junction and turn left to Cape Augnet.

55 km (34.1 mi) Arrive Cape Augnet. Return to Arichet and continue on Route 206.

71 km (44.2 mi) Junction with road to Janvrin Island.

Side trip to Janvrin Harbour: 18 km (10.9 mi) round trip.

82 km (50.7 mi) Return to Route 104.

This tiny home, at the end of the road in Cape Augnet, reflects the simple decorative style often found in Acadian regions of Atlantic Canada.

heritage. A 45-km (28 mi), circular road that follows the perimeter of the island makes it a most enchanting place to spend a sunny afternoon, especially on a motorcycle!

After crossing the bridge, continue left on Route 320. This will take you through delightful little Acadian communities like Martinique, Poulamon (French for "small codfish" or "tomcod"), and D'Escousse (named after a French officer at Fortress Louisbourg, pop. 250). Along the way is the Lennox Passage Provincial Park, with a small lighthouse, a sandy beach, and picnic facilities.

From D'Escousse you have the option of turning right, and following Route 320 straight across the island to Arichat. However, I prefer to continue straight on a paved side road to Poirierville and Cap La Ronde (both named after early French settlers). At the top of a steep little hill a paved road will lead sharply to the right. Continuing straight leads to a dead end with little room to turn a heavy touring bike around. The road to the right, though a little rough in spots, will take you south along the very picturesque shore of Rocky Bay until you rejoin Route 320, not too far from Arichat (Mi'kmaq for "campground").

Blessed with a well-protected harbor, and close to prized fishing grounds, Arichat (pop. 900) in the 17th and 18th centuries was one of the busiest seaports on the entire Atlantic seaboard of North America. This delightful village, full of Acadian charm and character, has both a high road and a low road. The view over Chedabucto Bay from either is quite spectacular. The cozy L'Auberge Acadienne Inn (877-787-2200), which is open year round, is located on the high road.

Either road will take you to Our Lady of Assumption Cathedral, built in 1837. Now designated a Provincial Heritage Structure, the church is a fine example of early Acadian architecture in Cape Breton. Associated with the church was the Arichat Seminary (1853), which was set up to provide Catholic priests for the Diocese of Antigonish (Cape Breton and part of mainland Nova Scotia). Only two years later, the Seminary was moved to the small town of Antigonish on the mainland, and was renamed as St. Francis Xavier University.

Since the collapse of the Atlantic cod fishery in 1992, many fishing boats on Isle Madame, and elsewhere in Atlantic Canada, have been retired from the industry. They now sit idle in local shipyards, such as this one at Petit-de-Grat.

Directly below the church are two ancient cannons, which point out over Arichat Harbour towards Jerseyman's Island. A little memorial contains the following plaque, which pretty well sums up the history of this little Acadian village:

"In the 18th century, Arichat was a very prosperous port of call for cargo ships from around the world. Five shipbuilding enterprises and factories lined its waterfront. Jersey traders, who were French-speaking British citizens, settled on Jerseyman's Island off Arichat in the late 18th century. The island was later attacked by American privateer John Paul Jones, forcing the inhabitants to move to Isle Madame. The trading post of Robin, Jones and Whitman was relocated on Kavanaugh's Point to the east of the harbor. The twin cannons remain an historical landmark of this period."

The LeNoir Forge Museum is located on the lower road. Built during the days of great sailing ships, the Forge provided a much-needed source of materials and expertise for the repair and maintenance of the many national and international vessels that would stop in for supplies or repairs. Over the last two and a half centuries it had also seen service as a tavern, a bonded warehouse, a shed for storing coal and ice, and perhaps even as a bordello. (Back in 1764, male fishery workers from the Channel Islands, who came to Isle Madame on five-year contracts, were not allowed to bring their wives or families with them.) An Acadian style stone structure, which had fallen into disrepair, the LeNoir Forge was extensively rebuilt beginning in 1967, and designated a National Heritage Property.

From Arichat Route 206 continues east to the island of Petit-de-Grat (Basque French for "little fishing village"). First settled in 1714, and a favorite of photographers and artists, this picturesque little settlement (pop. 450) is an excellent example of a typical Acadian fishing community. The cultural center La Picasse, and a modern softball field with lights, are on your left as you enter the village.

A left turn when you cross the bridge will take you to one of my favorite little out-of-the-way places on Cape Breton Island. After passing through rugged Sampson Cove, the narrow, winding road, comes to an abrupt end at Little Anse (little cove, pop. 220), with beautiful views out over Rocky Bay and the Atlantic Ocean. A short hiking trail leads to Cap Rouge (Red Cape), with striking views of the lighthouse on Green Island, which guards the entrance to the Strait of Canso.

After returning to the Arichat junction, bear to the left for a short distance, and take the first road on the left, to Cape Augnet. This 5-km-long (3 mi) diversion is a real Acadian roller-coaster of a ride that ends at a small lighthouse, with a great view of Arichat Harbour and Jerseyman Island.

Little Anse, one of the most photogenic communities on Isle Madame, is at the road's end.

This is a slow road, and for most of it you will not get out of 2nd or 3rd gear. But it is a joy to ride!

Upon your return to the junction, a left turn will take you back to Arichat along the scenic lower road. After passing through the village, which has most of the usual tourist facilities, you will rejoin Route 206, as you make your way to West Arichat (pop. 425).

Here, if you have the time, you might want to take a left turn at a junction, and head for Janvrin Island, which is connected to Isle Madame by a small bridge. It is an interesting little side trip, with some unspoiled land and seascapes. The island is also home to Vollmer's Island Paradise, a secluded little resort with several rustic log cabins, and a maximum capacity of 16 guests.

On your return to Route 206, a left turn will take you back to Route 320 and the bridge over Lennox Passage. From there it is only a few kilometers to Route 104, which will take you back to St. Peter's, or on to the Strait of Canso and Port Hawkesbury.

Trip 28 Colliery Route and Marconi Trail

Distance; *135 km (83.6 mi)*
Highlights: *A scenic coastal highway, with panoramic views of Sydney Harbour, and out over the Atlantic Ocean.*

Although there are no coal deposits in Sydney itself, the extensive reserves in the surrounding towns and villages, on both sides of the harbor, are collectively known as The Sydney Coalfield. It is about 50 km (31 mi) wide, and extends under the ocean for about 145 km (90 mi), almost reaching the south coast of Newfoundland! For more than two centuries, from approximately 1750 to 1950, this area was the largest coal-producing region in Canada, with more than 70 mines in operation over that period of time. The highest yearly output in the Sydney Coalfield was in 1913, when an astonishing 5.7 million tons were mined. Even as late as 1960, it still provided one-third of the annual coal production in the country.

These guns and searchlights are part of the defenses of Fort Petrie, one of seven coastal-defense batteries guarding the entrance to Sydney Harbour during World War II.

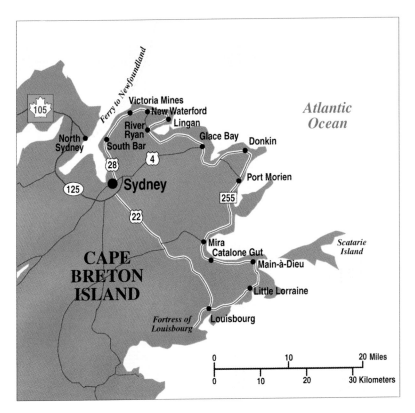

Over the years it is estimated that more than 300 million tons of coal have been removed from the Sydney Coalfield. Even so, the Government of Canada has estimated that more than one billion tons of coal remain, enough to produce several million tons per year for the next 200 years!

The Colliery Route begins where Route 28 leaves Sydney. From points outside Sydney follow the Trans-Canada Highway/Route 105 east to the outskirts of North Sydney. Take Route 125/Sydney Bypass around the city to a junction with Route 4 at Grand Lake Road. Go straight through the intersection, past the Walmart, and follow the new SPAR Road for a short distance to a traffic light. A right turn here, followed by a left turn, will take you to Route 28, which begins in the Sydney suburb of Whitney Pier.

After leaving Whitney Pier, the site of the former steel plant, the Colliery Route (Route 28) follows the east side of Sydney Harbour north toward the Atlantic Ocean. Along the way are panoramic coastal views of North Sydney, with its Newfoundland Ferry Terminal, the coal- and fossil-bearing cliffs of Sydney Mines, and off in the far distance the eastern flank of the Cape Breton Highlands and Cape Smoky.

The Route from Sydney

0 km (0 mi) Start in Sydney. Take Route 28/The Colliery Route to Glace Bay.

36 km (22.5 mi) Arrive Glace Bay. Take Route 255/The Marconi Trail to Louisbourg

103 km (63.8 mi) Arrive Louisbourg. Take Route 22/Fleur-de-Lis Trail to Sydney

135 km (83.6 mi) Arrive Sydney

Passing through South Bar, named after a nearby sand bar, you soon arrive at Victoria Mines, with its historic Fort Petrie standing guard on the edge of the cliff. Blessed with one of the finest natural harbors in the world, Sydney played a very strategic role in both World Wars. As an assembly port for wartime convoys bound for Britain, Sydney Harbour often accommodated more than 100 ships at a time!

With the outbreak of World War I (1914–1918) the defenses of both Sydney and Halifax Harbours were quickly upgraded to provide secure gathering places for civilian ships, as well as protection from enemy ships and submarines. During World War II (1939–1945) the convoy system was split into two distinct components. The "fast" convoys, containing ships, which could maintain a speed of at least 10 knots, sailed from Halifax. The "slow" convoys, with ships that traveled at a slower speed, left from Sydney.

Fort Petrie was one of the largest of the seven coastal-defense batteries built around the inner perimeter of the harbor, which also included Fort Petrie's "twin" battery on the other side of the harbor entrance, at Chapel Point in Sydney Mines. Fort Petrie contained two very large gun emplacements, an observation tower, searchlight facilities, and extensive underground areas for workshops and ammunition storage.

There has been a fort on this site since 1740, when a small bastion was built to protect the harbor. One year later a modest naval battle took place just outside the harbor entrance, between French ships and privateers from the New England colonies.

Fort Petrie, a National Historic Site, was extensively restored during the 1990s. Today visitors can learn about the history of the convoy system, and tour the fascinating facilities both above and below ground. It is also a great spot to have a picnic.

Continuing on, with the Low Point Lighthouse on your left, Route 28 bears right at the harbor entrance to the town of New Waterford (pop. 7,705). Named after the port of Waterford in Ireland, which sent many Irish immigrants to Cape Breton, the first coal was mined here in 1854.

The 15 flags at the Miner's Memorial in New Waterford reflect the wide range of nationalities that made the Sydney Coalfield one of the most cosmopolitan "working-class" regions in eastern Canada.

Over the years a total of 11 undersea mines operated in the vicinity, with the last one closing in 1999.

On your right, as you enter the town, the Colliery Lands Park pays tribute to the 298 men and boys killed in the local collieries. The largest loss of life occurred in No. 12 colliery on July 25, 1917, when 65 individuals ranging in age from 14 to 65 were killed in a massive explosion caused by an accumulation of coal dust. There were 205 survivors. The park, which is home to the New Waterford Historical Society, features an exposed coal seam, equipment displays, and a memorial with 15 flags, representing the various nationalities of the people who lost their lives underground, or under the ocean.

After a left turn at the Kentucky Fried Chicken outlet in town, the Colliery Route continues to the tiny community of Lingan, home to the Lingan Generating Station, the largest power plant in the province of Nova Scotia. Opened in 1979, at the height of the 1970s oil crisis, it was designed to burn coal from the nearby mines. With the end of mining on Cape Breton, the plant now burns imported coal from the United States and South America. It provides 25 percent of Nova Scotia's electrical power.

Nearby, a more environmentally friendly form of power generation came on line in 2007 with the construction of nine large wind turbines. Capable of producing enough electricity for 4,000 homes, these wind turbines may indicate the future of sustainable clean electrical power on the island.

At River Ryan, a left turn will take you through Gardiner Mines (guess what industry?) to Dominion (pop. 2,142), another former coal mining village. A small museum, in a restored one-room schoolhouse (c. 1888), gives the history of the early mines. There is a nice park and recreational area on the shore of the bay.

Just a short distance away Route 28 enters Glace Bay (pop. 16,984), at one time the location of the largest submarine coal mining operation in the world. For many years it was the heart of the coal industry in Cape Breton, with as many as 11 collieries in operation at any one time. Today the town has the usual tourist facilities, with one glaring exception. It has no hotels or motels. However, there are several Bed and Breakfast homes in the immediate vicinity.

Early French fishermen, noticing the spring pack ice in the harbor, named the spot Glace Bay (Ice Bay). When the British occupied Cape

At 505 feet, the twin stacks of the Lingan Generating Station tower over the surrounding countryside. At center right, the tops of two wind turbines are just visible above the thick fog bank. The lack of smoke from the Lingan smokestacks indicates that the multi-million dollar "scrubbers" recently installed at the plant are doing their part to protect the local environment.

Cape Breton Miners' Museum

Situated on a 15-acre site, overlooking the Atlantic Ocean, this wonderful complex pays tribute to the 250-year-old story of coal mining on Cape Breton Island. Featuring descriptive displays, and historical artifacts, the highlight of any visit is the 20-minute underground mine tour, guided by retired coal miners. (Because of a low roof, this tour may not be suitable for people over six-feet tall.)

The museum grounds also include a historic miner's home and a general store, both outfitted as of the year 1900. A cozy restaurant, with kerosene lamps and a large brick fireplace, offers homemade chowders and soups, along with various other menu items.

If you are lucky, your visit might coincide with a performance by the Men Of The Deeps, an internationally renowned chorus made up of former coal miners. Their concerts take place in an intimate, 150-seat theatre that is part of the main exhibition hall.

The Cape Breton Miners' Museum is located on Birkley Street (off South Street), less than two kilometers from downtown Glace Bay, and is open year round. (www.minersmuseum.com, 902-849-4522.) ■

Breton, after the First Siege of Louisbourg (1745), they built a fort in Glace Bay in order to protect their mining and fishing interests in the area. The town's first commercial mine opened in 1857, and the last one closed in 2001. Caledonia Colliery, in continuous operation from 1865 to 1961, set production records that were not equaled by any coal mine in Canada. Today the mines are long gone, but a fascinating Miners' Museum offers visitors a chance to put on a hard hat, complete with lamp, and make the descent into the depths of an actual mine.

Back in 1902 the inhabitants of Table Head, a Glace Bay suburb, were more than a little perplexed when four enormous wooden towers, each 215 feet high, were erected on a point of land overlooking the Atlantic Ocean. When told that the towers were designed to transmit a radio signal, west to east across the ocean to England, many shook their heads in disbelief. However, Italian inventor Guglielmo Marconi knew exactly what he was doing, and on December 15 of that year the historic message was sent, and received. The event was headline news around the world. Five years later a second transmitting station was added, followed in 1913 by a receiving station in the little fishing town of Louisbourg, about 64 km (40 mi) up the coast.

Fortress of Louisbourg

"We won! But who remembers the first major military victory in American history? It made England rejoice, France despair and set the wheels in motion for an American Revolution three decades after. And it all started here."

When J. Dennis Robinson wrote this introduction to his 2002 illustrated on-line essay, the writer and historian from New Hampshire was referring to the 1745 siege of the Fortress of Louisbourg. His work "4,000 Yankees Attack Canada," chronicled the logistics of assembling "the largest colonial militia ever assembled in the New World to that date," and explains why the assault was successful.

At that time Louisbourg was the largest fortified town in North America, enclosing an area of 57 acres within masonry walls 6 m (20 ft) thick. After a seven-week siege the Fortress was captured and occupied, by a combination of British Royal Marines and American militia from New England. Three years later a peace treaty returned Louisbourg to France.

In 1758 another war broke out between England and France, and Louisbourg once again came under attack, this time by the Royal Navy and Marines. This Second Siege of Louisbourg also lasted for seven

weeks, but the outcome was the same. Following it's capture the
French garrison and civilians were expelled, the Fortress was demol-
ished, and for the next 200 years nothing remained except a few ruins.

Today, the largest historical reconstruction in North America invites
visitors to step back in time to the summer of 1744, one year before
the First Siege. More than 60 buildings, many with costumed animators, give a fascinating glimpse into the daily life at this bustling seaport, which guarded the entrance to the Gulf of St. Lawrence, and the
approach to central Canada and Québec.

Highlights include: the quay (waterfront area), with self-guided
tours of historic buildings and daily demonstrations of musket and cannon fire; a bakery and three restaurants, which offer visitors a unique
chance to try 18th-century food and drink; and the King's Bastion, a
fort within a fort, where you find the Governor's Residence, Royal Chapel, and soldiers' barracks. In 1744 this Bastion was the largest building
in North America.

You should allow a minimum of four hours on site, which is open
from May 16 to October 15. Free parking is available at the Visitor
Centre and visitors will be transported to the Fortress by bus. Wear
comfortable shoes, carry a sweater or light jacket, and be sure to bring
a camera!   ■

*As part of the annual Cape Breton BikeFest, held in July, 250
motorcycles are allowed to drive into the Fortress of Louisbourg.
Space is limited, so apply early if you wish to take part in this event.*

A full moon rises over the fishing village of Port Morien, while a solitary lighthouse on nearby Flint Island prepares to cast its beam over the calm waters.

The Marconi National Historic Site honors his role in the early development of global communication. The cozy little museum has a Wireless Hall of Fame, and you can see the concrete foundations of the original towers. Located on the edge of 60-foot cliffs, it also offers impressive panoramic views up and down the rugged coastline. Not to be missed! (The site, which has no admission fee, is situated on a barren neck of land off Timmerman Street, and is open daily, 10 a.m. to 6 p.m., from June 1 to September 15. As you enter the town on Route 28, signs make it easy to find the little museum.)

Today, the appropriately named Marconi Trail (Route 255) enables visitors to follow in his footsteps from Glace Bay to Louisbourg. For 67 km (41 mi) the trail passes through picturesque little communities that hug the rugged Atlantic coastline. Within a few miles you reach a junction, with a tiny gas station/store on the left. Continue straight ahead to the village of Donkin, where an undersea coal mine was built in 1979, as a result of high oil prices around the world. When the price of oil returned to normal, the mine's two tunnels were allowed to flood. In 2008 a Swiss mining company drained the water from the tunnels, and the mine is on the verge of going into production. It has an estimated potential of up to 400 million tons of coal!

Just a few miles away is the village of Port Morien (pop. 578), the site of the earliest coal mine in North America. Beginning in 1720, coal was extracted from exposed seams in the side of ocean cliffs, and used to heat the new Fortress of Louisbourg. Port Morien, an active fishing community, was also home to the first Boy Scout troop in North America, back in 1908.

The Marconi Trail continues on around the shore of Mira Bay, through Mira Gut and Catalone Gut, to Main-à-Dieu (pop. 375), a very picturesque fishing village whose Acadian name translates as "Hand of God." This little community overlooks the uninhabited island of Scatarie, which was first settled in 1713. At one time the three-mile-long island had a population of 106, with its own school and a Catholic church. It is now a provincial wildlife sanctuary.

After passing through Little Lorraine (pop. 106), the Marconi Trail continues on through barren stretches of stunted spruce trees until it reaches Louisbourg (pop. 1157), the location of the largest historic reconstruction in North America. Although only one-quarter of the original fortified town has been rebuilt, the Fortress of Louisbourg National Historic Site is the jewel in the crown of Parks Canada.

The small town of Louisbourg, which is a 30-minute drive on Route 22 from the city of Sydney, has restaurants and accommodation, but no gas station. However, gas is available a few kilometers up Route 22 in Catalone.

Port Morien is proudly displays its place in history.

The Sydneys

With a population of approximately 26,000, **Sydney** is the industrial and economic center of southeastern Cape Breton. As such it provides a wide range of facilities for visitors, including a recently enlarged public wharf to accommodate the increasing number of cruise ships that visit the city each year. It has an historic North End that contains many historic buildings, and the oldest stone church on Cape Breton Island.

From 1784 to 1820, Cape Breton Island was not part of Nova Scotia, but a separate colony under the British crown, with Sydney as its capital. After the American Revolutionary War, many United Empire Loyalists came to Sydney and were soon joined by immigrants from Scotland. With the advent of railways in the latter part of the 19th century, Sydney became more important as a seaport, especially for the shipping of coal. Taking advantage of Cape Breton's extensive coal deposits, a state-of-the-art steel plant was built in 1901 and marked the beginning of a period of economic prosperity, which resulted in a rapid increase in population. By the start of World War I the Sydney Steel plant was making nearly half of all the steel produced in Canada. During World War II, with a workforce of more than 4,000 men, it produced one-third of all the steel for Canada's war effort. After a century of steel making, the Sydney Steel plant closed in 2001, a victim of obsolete technology, and the worldwide influx of much cheaper steel from China, India, and Japan.

The Trans-Canada Highway/Route 105 will take you directly into the Marine Atlantic ferry terminal in North Sydney, which is on the north side of Sydney Harbour, a half-hour drive from Sydney. The ferry service to Newfoundland and Labrador is an extension of the Trans-Canada Highway providing a vital link in Canada's interprovincial transit system. Ferry service to Newfoundland started in 1898, with three sailings each week, weather permitting. Now there are several sailings a day to Newfoundland, which transport almost half a million people annually, with 80 percent of these traveling between early June and the end of September. Reservations are mandatory, and the earlier you make them, the better! (Marine Atlantic reservations: 800-341-7981, www.marine-atlantic.ca).

As befits a major port, **North Sydney** (pop. 7,681) offers a wide range of facilities for the traveling public. A yacht club, with protected anchorage, welcomes visiting sailors, while an 18-hole golf course entices players with splendid views over the inner harbor. The North Sydney Historical Museum is just a short walk from the ferry terminal. The Clansman Motel & Restaurant (800-565-2668), owned by motorcycle enthusiasts, the Allen family, offers 44 rooms, and is near the

On a late April day, fishing boats make their way through pack ice to their sheltered berths in North Sydney. The pack ice arrives around mid-February, and often remains until early or mid-May.

Newfoundland Ferry terminal, and has a special motorcycle shelter and wash station, and emergency bike storage (in a secure building).

Sydney Mines with its extensive coal deposits, was first mentioned in a book written in 1672. By 1724 coal from local mines was being shipped to Boston and New York, as well as several islands in the Caribbean. In 1902 a steel plant and blast furnace were built, and an era of economic prosperity followed. By 1920, however, the steel-making facilities were dismantled and the town was forced to rely on its extensive coal reserves. Today, the town's historic post office, lovingly restored, forms the centerpiece of a major downtown renewal project. The former railroad station is now the town's historical museum. Next door is the new Cape Breton Fossil Centre (902-544-0992), where you can examine 300-million-year-old fossilized ferns and plants from the Sydney coal fields. Guided tours in search of fossils under the ocean cliffs are available several times a week.

In the old days, folks in the rural parts of Cape Breton Island used to refer to the three towns that border Sydney Harbour as "The Sydneys." The name was used affectionately, and perhaps even with a bit of envy, for the Sydneys were where the action was. In the years before World War I, there were two steel plants in the Sydneys, along with numerous undersea coal mines, and a vibrant seaport with an international connection to Newfoundland and Labrador—at that time an independent Dominion of the British Empire. The Sydneys were also the eastern end of the Canadian trans-continental railroad system. There was much more shopping and entertainment in the Sydneys than could ever be found in small rural communities. If you wanted a relatively good-paying job, then you went to the Sydneys. ∎

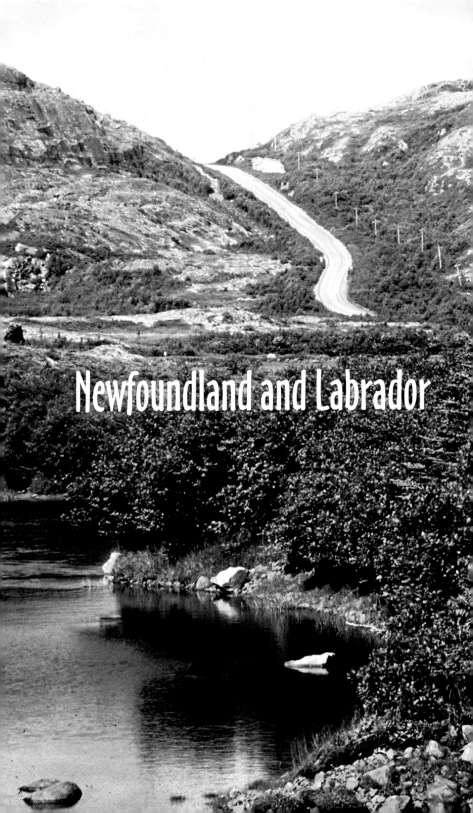

Newfoundland and Labrador

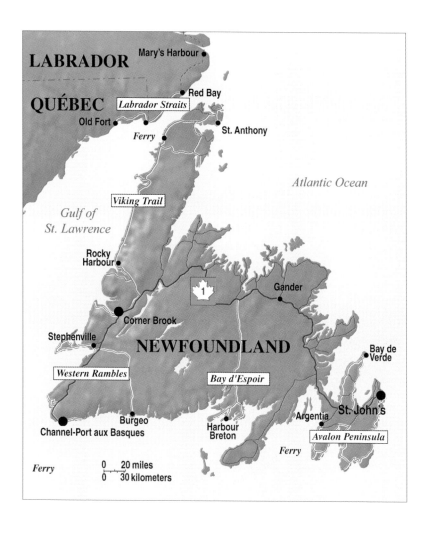

Newfoundland and Labrador

By Rannie Gillis

Situated on the extreme eastern edge of the continent, Canada's newest province is a unique place, unlike any other in this country, or the United States for that matter. Not only is it closer to Europe than any other part of North America, it also has its own dictionary and encyclopedia, its own "Royal" police force, and even its own time zone!

It also, as the name implies, consists of two parts: Newfoundland (pop. 479,105) is the 15th-largest island in the world, with an area of 43,031 sq mi. Labrador (pop. 26,364) is part of mainland Canada, and shares a common border with the French-Canadian province of Québec. It has an area of 113,640 sq mi. If it were part of the United States the province would rank fourth in size after Alaska, Texas, and California.

Today you will find nearly 750 communities, most of them quite small, a far cry from the 1,450 that existed at the time of confederation with Canada (1949). Thanks to government policy over the last 60 years, almost 700

The rugged shoreline of Trepassey Bay is typical of the coastal regions of Newfoundland and Labrador: high cliffs, coastal barrens, jagged rocks and shoals, and a stark beauty all its own. No wonder the province's unofficial nickname is "The Rock."

settlements have been abandoned. The vast majority of these were remote coastal outports, and their inhabitants were reluctantly relocated to larger centers.

The American Connection

During the Second World War more than 750,000 U.S. servicemen (and women) passed through Newfoundland and Labrador on their way to the battlefields of Europe. Of these, about 100,000 were actually stationed in the province, usually at American bases in Stephenville, Gander, Argentia, Goose Bay (Labrador), and Torbay (St. John's).

In the four years between 1941 and 1945, American servicemen married more than 25,000 Newfoundland and Labrador ladies. With the end of hostilities, almost all of these newlyweds returned to their husband's homes in the United States. Ever since there has been a special rapport between Newfoundlanders and Americans.

The arrival of the Cold War brought a renewed American military presence in Newfoundland and Labrador. In addition to the major bases, many other smaller facilities like early warning radar stations were built around the perimeter of the province and the coast of Labrador.

Argentia Naval Air Station (1941–1994) was the last American military presence in the province. The last servicemen left in 1994, more than 50 years after it first opened.

Picturesque homes and fishing sheds, many on stilts, line the shore of Rose Blanche Harbour.

The wonderful, winding road to Hermitage, on the island's south coast, is one of the gems of the Bay d'Espoir region.

A few tips on driving in Newfoundland and Labrador:
Never drive at night! The province averages 700 collisions each year, between moose/caribou and motor vehicles. Ninety per cent of these occur after dark, and 70 percent between May and October.

Take cool-weather clothing. In July and August the average daytime temperature is only 64 degrees. At night, especially in Northern Newfoundland and Labrador, it will often drop below freezing!

Because of snow or cold conditions, you really only have a six- or seven-week window (mid-July to early September) to bike in Newfoundland and Labrador.

Tank up often. Even on the Trans-Canada Highway there can be long stretches between service stations. If you leave the Trans-Canada be prepared to be self-sufficient and know just how far you can go on reserve.

Newfoundlanders are some of the most hospitable people you will find, but they have a natural shyness and reserve, especially around strangers. Go out of your way to introduce yourself, or strike up a conversation, and you will quickly be made to feel at home.

Be flexible in your travel plans. This is a very relaxed place, and life in the outports is far removed from the hustle and bustle of contemporary life. Keep in mind that the schedules for both large and small ferries depend on the weather.

Trip 29 Western Rambles

This chapter presents several riding options in the southwestern part of the Island of Newfoundland. One or more of these would be ideal for someone who only wanted to spend a short time in the province.

Port aux Basques (pop. 4,634) is a lively little full-service town located at the extreme southwestern tip of the province. With a natural, deep-water harbor, it was given its name in the early 1500s, by fishermen from the Basque regions of France and Spain.

Today, more than 65 percent of all freight entering Newfoundland and Labrador arrives at this port. It is also the main terminal for the Marine Atlantic ferries that provide year round service between this province and The Mainland, which is the term Newfoundlanders use to refer to the rest of Canada.

A word of advice for first time motorcyclists arriving in Port aux Basques: Within minutes of each ferry's arrival, especially in the summer months, several hundred vehicles will exit the boat and head straight out of town on a modern four-lane highway. Unfortunately, the four lanes do not last. Within 5 km (3 mi) the four lanes merge into two, and then the jockeying begins for space on the now-congested roadway. Large tractor-trailers vie

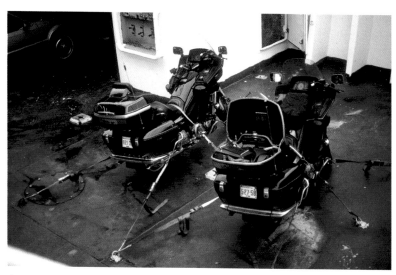

Our motorcycles, properly secured and strapped down, arrive safely in Port aux Basque, after the six-hour crossing from North Sydney, Nova Scotia.

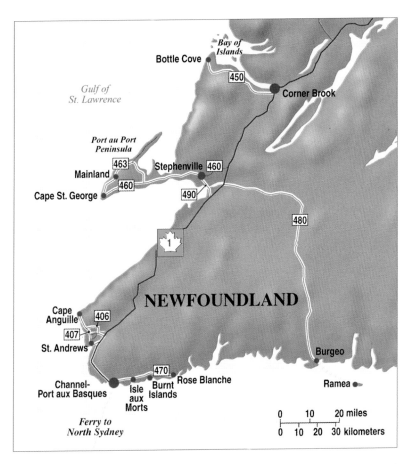

for space with family sedans, trucks with trailers, SUVs, motorbikes, and pedal bikes. It has been compared to an old-time Roman chariot race! Give yourself a break.

When I leave the ferry, I like to linger for a short while either at the ferry terminal, or at a cozy little provincial tourist bureau about a mile up the road. All it takes is 15 or 20 minutes. By then the majority of the ferry traffic will have moved off down the highway, and you can set out and travel at your own speed. Believe me, it makes your first few hours in Canada's newest province a lot easier.

Second word of advice: Never ever, if at all possible, travel after dark in Newfoundland and Labrador. The roads are alive with the silent presence of moose and caribou. (There are no deer in Newfoundland.) A chance encounter with one of these magnificent animals usually results in fatalities.

If you arrive in early or late afternoon, and decide to take the

Trans-Canada Highway, remember that the first major town with full facilities is Stephenville (pop. c. 8,000), a driving distance of 166 km (103 mi). The city of Corner Brook (pop. 20,083) is 219 km (136 mi) from the ferry. Pre-booking accommodations in both of these places is highly recommended in the summer months.

If staying overnight in Port aux Basques, you have your choice of two full-service hotels. St. Christopher's Hotel (800-563-4779) has 83 rooms and is situated on a hill overlooking the harbor. Hotel Port aux Basques (877-695-2171) has 49 rooms, and is also very close to the ferry. There are also several Bed-and-Breakfast homes, and a five-room Inn in the immediate area.

About 11 km (7mi) from Port aux Basques, on your right, is the aptly named Table Mountain, a flat-topped peak with a height of more than 500 m (1,500 ft). During World War II the United States built a radar station and small airstrip on top of the mountain. The very steep trail to the top is still used by off-road vehicles. Table Mountain is part of the Long Range Mountains, a chain of peaks and plateaus that extend up the west coast of Newfoundland to the top of the northern peninsula. They are, along with the Cape Breton Highlands, a northern extension of the Appalachian Mountain system, which begins in central Alabama and extends as far north as the Torngat Mountains in Labrador.

A few miles up the road is Wreckhouse—a large, open expanse of flat land between the mountains and the sea. It is notorious, under certain weather conditions, for the extremely high winds that come roaring down the mountain gullies, often with hurricane force velocity. So strong, in fact, that trains that ran on the nearby narrow-gauge railroad were often blown off the tracks. It still poses a significant hazard to high-sided tractor-trailers.

In 1939 the Reid Newfoundland Railroad hired a local farmer to help alleviate this problem. Lochie MacDougall seemed to have an uncanny ability to predict adverse wind conditions, and would phone up the line to stop any advancing trains if the winds got too high. Known locally as the "human wind gauge," he delayed hundreds of trains in the years up to his death in 1965. His wife continued the tradition until 1972.

An Environment Canada anemometer now provides remote wind data to the local Royal Canadian Mounted Police (RCMP) detachment, who will often stop highway traffic until the winds abate. The good news is that these gale force winds usually happen in the late fall and winter months. However, just a few years ago, I drove through Wreckhouse on my bike in mid-July, in 80-km/h (50 mph) winds, with heavy rain. Needless to say, it was an unnerving experience!

The restored, 1871-vintage lighthouse at Rose Blanche is built with granite from a local quarry.

Rose Blanche

Distance: *84 km (52.6 mi)*
Highlights: *A great introduction to Canada's newest province. Lots of twists and turns, barren but rugged coastal scenery, and seven quaint little outport communities with intriguing names like Fox Roost, Harbour Le Cou, Burnt Islands, and Isle aux Morts (Deadman's Island). Picturesque Rose Blanche boasts a charming little harbor and a lovely restored granite lighthouse, one of the oldest in eastern Canada.*

If you decide to remain close to the ferry, and if you still have a few hours of daylight, then I highly recommend this side trip to the end of the paved road in Rose Blanche (pop. 618). Situated in a well sheltered harbor, on the east side of a small bay, its name is a corruption of the French *roche blanche*

Route from Port aux Basque

0 km (0 mi) Depart Port aux Basque on Route 470.
42 km (26.3 mi) Arrive Rose Blanche. Turn around.
84 km (52.6 mi) Arrive Port aux Basque.

The town of Rose Blanche, nestled on the rocks around an inner harbor, has hardly a level piece of ground.

(white rock), a reference to several outcrops of white quartz in the area.

After Confederation with Canada in 1949, Rose Blanche remained the site of an abundant fishery, carried on year round because of the absence of winter pack ice. By 1960, when a fresh-frozen fish plant was established, the community was one of the most prosperous on the Southwest Coast. In 1961, after several years of construction, a primitive gravel road was completed between the outport and Port aux Basques.

Years ago Rose Blanche was my first port of call when I joined the S.S. Burgeo, with the Newfoundland and Labrador coastal boat service, during a vacation from university. I still vividly remember the ruins of a derelict lighthouse greeting us at the harbor entrance. Known as "The Stone Lighthouse," it was built in 1856 of white/grey granite from local quarries, and was one of the first lighthouses in eastern Canada. Today the lighthouse has been restored, and is open to the public in the summer months. Close by is a cozy little four-room Bed & Breakfast in a restored fisherman's cottage (Hook, Line, & Sinker, 709-956-2005).

Cape Anguille and the Codroy Valley

Distance: *120 km (74.6 mi).*
Highlights: *A gentle ride through some of the best agricultural land in the province, ending in wonderful coastal views from the lighthouse at the most westerly point on the Island of Newfoundland.*

Another option for a short day trip is the ride to the lighthouse at Cape Anguille, by way of the Codroy Valley. Nestled between the Anguille Mountains to the west, and the Long Range Mountains to the east, the valley extends inland from the sea for a distance of about 40 km (25 mi). It is about 16 km (10 mi) wide at the coast, and becomes progressively narrower as it moves inland.

Home to 15 little communities, the Codroy Valley contains the best agricultural soil in Newfoundland and Labrador. As well, the area is drained by two rivers—the Little Codroy, and the Grand Codroy. Both provide some of the finest salmon fishing to be found anywhere along the eastern seaboard. It is also home to the Grand Codroy Estuary, a wetland of international importance, which would be of interest to birdwatchers, naturalists, and photographers.

Although originally settled by Mi'kmaq Indians from Cape Breton Island, the first European settlers arrived in the first half of the 18th century. They came from the south of England and the Channel Islands, and were later joined by immigrants from Ireland, Scotland, and displaced French-Acadians from the Maritime Provinces.

From Port aux Basque take the Trans-Canada Highway/Route 1 for 35

Route from Port aux Basque

0 km (0 mi) From the ferry terminal take the Trans-Canada Highway/Route 1.

35 km (21.9 mi) Turn left on Route 407.

40 km (25.2 mi) In St. Andrews turn right to stay on Route 407.

50 km (31.4 mi) Join Route 406 and continue to Cape Anguille.

59 km (36.9 mi) Arrive Cape Anguille. Retrace path to junction with Route 407.

68 km (42.3 mi) Continue on Route 406.

82 km (50.7 mi) Turn right on the Trans-Canada Highway/Route 1 to return to Port aux Basque.

120 km (74.6 mi) Arrive Port aux Basque.

This sign says it all, with regard to the lonely stretch of road between the Trans-Canada Highway and the town of Burgeo.

km (21.9 mi) and turn left on Route 407. The paved road ends at Cape Anguille, the most westerly point on the island of Newfoundland, which rises steeply from sea level to a height of more than 180 m (600 ft). Along this coast is a narrow strip of flat land, where the first settlers built their homes. The present lighthouse dates from 1905, while the restored, century-old light keeper's home is now a quaint little inn, with no telephones or television in the rooms—a chance to get away from it all (Cape Anguille Lighthouse Inn, 877-254-6586).

Retrace your route, but take Route 406 back to the Trans-Canada Highway.

The exhilarating ride along the Burgeo highway is strikingly beautiful, even in the fog.

The Burgeo Road

Distance: *150 km (93.5 mi) one way*
Highlights: *Three distinct geological landforms including: thickly forested mountains; vast, wide-open, caribou barrens; and glacially scoured coastal landscapes that have not changed since the end of the last ice age. At the end of the road is one of the most isolated and photogenic outports in all of Newfoundland. To get the most out of this trip, an overnight stay in Burgeo is highly recommended.*

Route 1, the Trans-Canada Highway, runs for 909 km (564 mi) from Port aux Basques on the west coast to the capital city of St. John's on the east coast. For most of its length it follows the route of the former Newfoundland railroad, and passes through the heavily forested interior portions of

The Burgeo Road

0 km (0 mi) Turn east off the Trans-Canada Highway/Route 1 on Route 480, 153 km (94.8 mi) from Port aux Basque.

150 km (93.5 mi) Arrive Burgeo.

This pair of caribou in the road illustrate why drivers in Newfoundland and Labrador must stay vigilant, and stay within the 80 km/h (50 mph) speed limit.

the province. Because of the nature of this two-lane road, with few passing places, it is a mostly boring two-day drive.

I always tell tourists that if you want to experience the "real" Newfoundland, then you have to get off the Trans-Canada Highway, and visit some of the more than 600 outport communities that are found around this province's coastline. And there is no better place to start than by taking a trip down Route 480, the Burgeo highway. Located only an hour and a half up the Trans-Canada from Port aux Basques, it is a unique experience that provides a fascinating introduction for any first-time visitor to the province.

Known as The Caribou Trail, this 150-km (93.5 mi) highway has no facilities of any kind. There are no service stations, no homes, and no telephones. What you will find instead, however, is a pristine wilderness area, with plenty of moose and caribou, and three very distinct types of scenery.

Route 480 leaves the Trans-Canada Highway/Route 1 153 km (94.8 mi) from Port-aux-Basque. For the first 50 km (30 mi) on Route 480 you traverse the thickly forested Long Range Mountains from west to east. As you pass through this section of primeval forest, the many signs of recent logging activity testify to the fact that this is one of the main timber producing regions of the province.

The mountains slowly give way to rolling foothills, and for the next 50 km you find yourself on the aptly named Caribou Barrens. This is the home of one of the largest herds of migratory caribou in eastern North America, and it is not unusual to see caribou licking winter road salt from the rocks along the sides of the highway. For the last 50 km you cross a boulder-strewn landscape that would not look out of place on the far side of the moon. You would think that the last glacier had left only a few months before.

At scattered locations along the Burgeo road you will come across examples of a very unique Newfoundland custom, one that I have not found in other parts of Atlantic Canada—gravel-pit campers. The gravel pits, or quarries, originally provided material for the construction of the road. Now, many of them provide a rather peculiar year-round location for travel trailers and other forms of mobile campers. Some gravel pits are home to only one trailer, tucked up against a sheer rock wall for protection from the elements. Others may have three or four, usually representing members of one family. One gravel pit has more than 50!

The gravel pits are usually in close proximity to ponds or lakes, and they provide easy access to hunting and fishing grounds. Many have neat little

The quaint custom of gravel-pit camping is found only in Newfoundland and Labrador.

The outport community of Burgeo is the regional service center for several tiny villages along the isolated southwest coast of Newfoundland.

gardens, fenced off to keep them from providing a free lunch for the many moose and caribou that roam freely over the countryside. Best of all, the gravel pits are free. You don't need reservations, and you can leave your camper or mobile home there, year round, and it will not cost you one single penny. In addition, there are none of the restrictions and regulations that you would find in commercial campgrounds.

At the end of the road is the very photogenic outport of Burgeo (pop. 1,627). Located on a small island that is connected to the mainland by a short causeway, its splendid harbor is backed by a striking panorama of rugged and majestic mountains.

First settled in 1798, the town's name is a corruption of the Portuguese word *virgeo* (virgin). This referred to the fact that there were no aboriginals living in the immediate area when the first permanent settlers arrived. It was truly "virgin" territory. Aside from its spectacular location, Burgeo has one other feature that you will not find in any other part of Newfoundland—sand dunes! The aptly named Sandbanks Provincial Park is considered to be one of the finest in the province, and rightly so.

With miles of stunning beaches, and striking sand dunes, the park is a little gem, virtually unknown, even to most Newfoundlanders. There are 25 sites available for travel trailers, as well as numerous facilities for tenting and camping. For those who might not prefer to swim in the ocean, there is even a fresh water pond, with a sandy bottom.

Until the completion of the road in 1979, the community's only link with the rest of Newfoundland was by sea. Passengers, freight, and the Royal Mail, would arrive once a week on the Marine Atlantic coastal boat. Needless to say, the arrival of the vessel in the sheltered harbor was an event that was eagerly awaited by the local inhabitants.

The Matthew

Although Christopher Columbus discovered the New World, he never set foot on the North American continent. That honor fell to John Cabot, whose voyage of exploration was funded by the King of England. An historical replica of John Cabot's 15th-century ship, the Matthew, was built in Bristol, England, and sailed across the Atlantic Ocean to commemorate the 500th anniversary of John Cabot's discovery of Newfoundland in 1497. I had the opportunity to spend three days on the Matthew as a volunteer seaman as she sailed from Stephenville to Corner Brook, on the west coast of the island.   ■

Since the loop around the Port au Port Peninsula is never far from the coast, you are constantly treated with views of the spectacular rugged coastline.

Burgeo is a full-service community, with a hospital, RCMP detachment, restaurants, and a nine-room motel (Gillett's Motel, 709-886-1284). Time and weather permitting, you can also take the one-hour coastal ferry to the offshore island of Ramea (pop. 1,200). Although accommodation is available, there are only 6 km (4 mi) of road on Ramea.

Burgeo, and the several little islands that surround it, are geographically little changed since the end of the last Ice Age about 10,000 years ago. The retreating glaciers did a real good job of scraping the entire area clear of any topsoil. This is definitely not the place to try to plant a garden, or to grow a lawn in front of your house. The small homes, however, are typical outport dwellings. Neat, tidy, usually immaculate, and painted in a wide range of bright colors.

The streets in Burgeo are extremely narrow and meandering, following the convoluted contours of the surrounding terrain. The newest of them have literally been blasted from the primeval rock. In terms of town planning the layout of Burgeo's streets is far from rational, but that makes it a wonderful place to walk around. For one thing, the lay of the land, with its many hills and rocky outcrops, is such that you can't see where you're going. As a result, a different scene greets you at each twist and turn in the road. (It is virtually impossible for any first time visitor to the town to go for a walk without getting lost—not once, but several times!)

Port au Port Peninsula

Distance: *135 km (84.3 mi)*
Highlights: *Historic Acadian-French culture, outstanding coastal views that include towering ocean cliffs and interior barrens, and a huge Catholic Church that is the largest wooden structure in the province.*

Whether you are heading north or south on Route 1, the town of Stephenville is an easy 22 km (14 mi) ride via Route 490 or 31 km (19.3 mi) via Route 460 from the Trans-Canada Highway. Originally called the Acadian Village, after the French-speaking fishermen who lived there, Stephenville really came into its own during the early years of World War II, when the United States government decided to build the largest airbase in Atlantic Canada. At that time the little fishing village had a population of about 500. Today it is the service center for the Port au Port Peninsula, with a population of 8,000. Although not actually part of the peninsula, the town is connected to it by a small isthmus, which makes it an ideal place to start a tour.

There are about 20 tiny outport communities on this circuit, known originally as "The French Shore," and most of them have retained their unique language and culture. The French spoken here is different in many ways from Québec French, or the Acadian French of the Maritime Provinces.

At no point in this lovely little ride are you far away from the water; in fact, if any ride in this province could be called a "coastal ride" this would be it. Your tour starts out on Route 460 following the northern coastline of St. George's Bay, with the road clinging to the tops of the rugged coastal cliffs, until you reach the southwestern tip of the peninsula. Then you head north, and up, on Route 463 as the highway climbs to a little plateau at the extreme western edge of this triangular shaped remnant of the last glacial ice age. Before long you return to sea level, with your descent enhanced by stunning views out over the Gulf of St. Lawrence, as you make your way back to your starting point.

Highlights of this tour, apart from the panoramic views and wonderful coastal scenery, would include Our Lady Of Mercy Church, the largest

Route from Stephenville

0 km (0 mi) Depart Stephenville west on Route 460.
57 km (35.7mi) Arrive Cape St. George. Follow Route 463 along coast.
107 km (66.5mi) Turn left on Route 460
135 km (84.3mi) Return to Stephenville.

wooden building in Newfoundland and Labrador. This Provincial Heritage Structure opened in 1925, and can seat more than 1,000 people. Its construction was a tribute to the intense Catholic faith of the French inhabitants of this peninsula. Cape St. George is a very rugged headland, which marks the western end of St. George's Bay, and the Port au Port Peninsula. It is a great place to take a walk, take some pictures, or just take a break. A real surprise is the presence of a modern and very comfortable 14-room inn, with some fantastic coastal views. A great place to spend the night! (Inn At The Cape, 888-484-4700). Mainland is a 200-year-old, former French fishing station. The striking offshore island was named Red Island in 1767 by Captain James Cook, because of its vibrant red cliffs.

Ernest Harmon Air Force Base

In the early years of the Second World War, Newfoundland and Labrador were still part of the British Commonwealth, and in 1941 a "Destroyers for Bases Deal" was struck between the United States and the United Kingdom. The Royal Navy received 50 old American destroyers for their war effort, while the United States, still at peace, was given permission to build military bases on British territories throughout the world. The small village of Stephenville was chosen as one of these, because of the excellent flying conditions in the area, and it's strategic location on the Great Circle Route between North America and Europe.

Early in 1941 construction started on what would later be called Ernest Harmon Air Force Base, at that time the largest military airfield outside the continental United States. From 1943, until it closed in 1966, "Harmon Field" became an important international stopover for military and civilian aircraft flying between North America and Europe. When the Americans left, 400 buildings and a 3,350 m (11,000 ft) runway were turned over to the Canadian government, and later to the province of Newfoundland and Labrador.

Today most of these buildings are still in use by the town of Stephenville. Two former barracks now house a seniors' complex and the College of the North Atlantic. The former "PX Store," a small scale department store, is now the Harmon Mall, and the former base chapel is now the Zion Pentecostal Church. A former officers' quarters is now the Stephenville Hotel (24 rooms, 709-643-5176). There is also a Holiday Inn available in town (47 rooms, 800-465-4329). The airfield remains one of the largest in Atlantic Canada. ∎

Bottle Cove on the Bay of Islands is a perfect gem of an outport, far from the highway.

Bay of Islands

Distance: *50 km, one way (31 mi) from the Trans-Canada Highway at Corner Brook to Bottle Cove and Little Port via Route 450.*

Highlights: *An exhilarating, picturesque ride, through a series of small outports, culminating in a short side trip to Bottle Cove and Little Port, two of the best-kept secrets in the province. These tiny, end-of-the-road fishing villages are really something special. And the rugged, mountain scenery? Well, you just have to see it for yourself!*

This 100-km (62 mi), roller-coaster side-trip, is one of my favorite rides on the Island of Newfoundland. As soon as you leave Corner Brook on Route 450, you pass through a succession of delightful little villages that line the western shore of Humber Arm.

On your left are the Lewis Hills, a vast remote wilderness region that form a western offshoot of the Long Range Mountains. As such, it is an

Route from Corner Brook

0 km (0 mi) Depart from Corner Brook on Route 450.
50 km (30.8 mi) Arrive Bottle Cove and Little Port. Turn around.
100 km (61.6 mi) Arrive Corner Brook.

The view north from Bottle Cove on the Bay of Islands is one of a dramatic, rugged coastline.

extension of the Appalachian Mountain Range, and contains the highest point on the Island of Newfoundland, the uniquely named The Cabox, elevation 814 m (2,671 ft). At the northwestern extremity of these impressive mountains is the small Blow Me Down Provincial Park, with 28 campsites.

Nearby are Lark Harbour, Bottle Cove, and Little Port, three remote outport communities that did not have road access to Corner Brook until 1961. Beginning in the 15th century, all three were used as seasonal fishing stations by Basque fishermen from France and Spain.

At Bottle Cove and Little Port you will also find unique geological formations known as wave-cut platforms. These date back to the end of the last ice age, about 10,000 years ago. As the glaciers receded, wave action and coastal erosion cut these horizontal platforms, that were later raised above sea level, when the weight of the glaciers disappeared.

Corner Brook

Corner Brook (pop. 20,083), the largest population center on the west coast of Newfoundland, serves as the service center for the entire west coast of the province. Situated at the mouth of the Humber River, 25 miles inland from the Gulf of St. Lawrence, and at the base of the Long Range Mountains, Corner Brook has a spectacular setting, extending out along the exposed flanks of this large river valley.

The city can trace its origins, and its name, to the opening of a small sawmill in 1864. Built at the "corner" of a local brook, to take advantage of the vast forest resources around the Humber valley, by the mid-1920s the sawmill had been replaced by one of the world's largest pulp and paper companies. Today the local forest industry employs more than 1,500 people. Other small enterprises include a cement plant, a facility for making gypsum wallboard, and three fish plants. The city is also home to Sir Wilfred Grenfell College, and the College of the North Atlantic.

Points of interest include the Corner Brook Museum & Archives, and the Captain James Cook Monument, which offers stunning panoramic views out over the city, the Humber River Basin, and the Bay of Islands. Railroad buffs would enjoy a visit to the Railway Society of Newfoundland, which has a small collection of vintage rolling stock, and artifacts relating to the legendary Newfie Bullet, the famous trans-province train that ran between St. John's on the east coast, to Port aux Basques on the west side of the island. You can also take a spectacular ride through the Humber River Gorge, beneath towering cliffs, along the most famous Atlantic-salmon river in Eastern Canada. A modern ski and summer resort offers various recreation activities. A wide range of lodging options are available in Corner Brook. ∎

Trip 30 Bay d'Espoir & Connaigre Peninsula

Distance: _586 km (364 mi) Allow at least 2 days, and preferably 3 or 4._
Highlights: _A lonely highway through uninhabited forest and vast caribou barrens to the coast with spectacular fiords, steep cliffs, and mountains that rival those of Norway, dotted with tiny outport communities clinging to the shore._

After you turn off the Trans-Canada Highway/Route 1 on Route 360 south, there are no facilities of any kind for the next 142 km (88 mi). There are no service stations, no homes, no telephones, nothing but mile after mile of primeval forest and vast caribou barrens. But once you arrive at the little village called Head of Bay d'Espoir, you will find yourself in an incredible land of fiords and mountains, with many little outport settlements, all along the coast.

The speed limit on this deserted stretch of highway is only 80 km/h (50 mph). It seems absurdly low, especially since there is virtually no traffic and almost no chance of your being pulled over for speeding. (The RCMP do patrol the highway at least twice a day, but not after dark, if they can help it.) I found out why the speed limit is 80 km/h when I came around a turn

At Head of Bay d'Espoir you leave the stunted forest and vast caribou barrens behind, and enter an enchanted world of fiords and mountains, that will take you to some of the most remote outport settlements in coastal Newfoundland and Labrador.

at 90 km/h, and without any warning had a 1,500-lb moose come jogging out of the woods, up over the shoulder of the road, and stop directly in front of me. It was the best PANIC STOP that I ever made in more than 30 years of touring by motorcycle. I was literally standing up straight, by the time I got my big, 900-lb Yamaha Venture stopped, less than 20 feet from that moose. The enormous animal just stood there, majestic and stern, staring me straight in the face and almost daring me to do something about it. I settled back on the seat, put both feet flat on the ground, and tried to regain my composure, while the moose made up its mind as to its next move. As he

Bay d'Espoir from the Trans-Canada Highway

0 km (0 mi) Turn off the Trans-Canada Highway/Route 1 on Route 360.
129 km (80.1 mi) Turn right on Route 361.
142 km (88.2 mi) Arrive Head of Bay d'Espoir.
 To end of paved road in St. Albans is an additional 16.6 km (10.3 mi).
155 km (96.3 mi) Return to Route 360 and turn right.
194 km (120.5 mi) Turn left on Route 362.
222 km (137.9 mi) Turn left on Route 363.
231 km (143.5 mi) Arrive Belleoram. Turn around.
240 km (149.1 mi) At junction with Route 362 stay on Route 363.
245 km (152.2 mi) Arrive English Harbour West. Continue on Route
 363.
258 km (160.2 mi) Arrive Coomb's Cove. Turn around.
276 km (171.4 mi) Turn left on Route 362.
303 km (188.2 mi) Turn left on Route 360.
338 km (209.9 mi) Arrive Harbour Breton. Turn around.
361 km (224.2 mi) Turn left on Route 364.
383 km (237.9 mi) Arrive Hermitage. Return to Route 360.
 To end of pavement at Seal Cove is an additional 14.7 km (9 mi).
405 km (251.5 mi) Turn left on Route 360.
586 km (364.0 mi) Arrive Trans-Canada Highway/Route 1.

stood there, twitching and glaring, it suddenly dawned on me that the bottom of the animal's stomach was just about level with the top of my windshield. That would be four or five feet off the ground!

A startled moose is a very unpredictable animal, and will charge a motor vehicle without warning. The worst thing you can do is sound your horn. In this case, the animal turned and loped down over the shoulder of the road. It then stopped, and with a last glance back over its shoulder, disappeared into the woods. (Moose have very tall and lanky legs. If hit by a car, the legs give way, and the body of the animal is propelled up the hood and into the passenger compartment, usually with fatal results. If hit by a motorcycle, well?)

A visit to this part of Newfoundland's south coast is like stepping back in time to the early years of the 20th century. Back then there were no roads, and people were isolated from each other, and from basic services. It's still very much like that on the south coast, and the people who live there wouldn't move for love or money. (The first rough-gravel road to Bay d'Espoir was not completed until 1971. Before that you arrived, and left, on the coastal boat.)

This virtually unknown region called Bay d'Espoir (Bay of Hope), was given its name by fishermen who came over from France in the early 15th century. The locals refer to it as "Bay Despair," though it is anything but—in spite of the depressed state of the local fishery.

It will take at least two hours to travel from the Trans-Canada Highway to Head of Bay d'Espoir (pop. 865). There are two nice little motels in this charming village—Motel Bay d'Espoir Cottages with 7 cottages (709-882-2766) and Vancor Motel and Restaurant with 20 units (709-882-2766).

Just a few miles away is a hydroelectric plant, open to visitors, that produces almost half of all the electricity used on the island of Newfoundland. Nearby communities with accommodations include in Milltown, The Bear Sleeps Inn with three rooms (709-882-2841) and in St. Alban's, the St. Alban's Inn and Dining Room with 13 rooms (709-538-3885). Any of these places would make an ideal spot to use as a touring base.

Should you come down from the Trans-Canada Highway in the morning, there is the option of having lunch at Head Bay, and continuing on down Route 360 to the Connaigre Peninsula. Approximately 39 km

Question: "How do I get one of those bikes?" Answer: "Stay in school and graduate." Wherever we went in the Bay d'Espoir region, Newfoundland youngsters were amazed at the size of our motorcycles. While smaller bikes and ATVs are common, most touring rigs never venture this far from the Trans-Canada Highway.

On the Hermitage road there is no traffic, no stop signs, no divided highways—just mile after mile of magnificent, uncluttered scenery.

(24 mi) down, take Route 362, which bears left through a barren, desolate landscape with a strange and mysterious beauty all its own. It is a lunar landscape that appears not to have changed much since the glaciers left. This spectacular drive leads to picturesque little outport communities, such as Pool's Cove, Belleoram, English Harbour West, and Coombe's Cove, which hug the western shore of Fortune Bay. This is one of the largest bays on the south coast of Newfoundland, and the name first appeared on an old Portuguese fishing map dated 1527! Accommodation is available at English Harbour West at the Olde Oven Inn with four rooms (709-888-3456).

Returning to the junction with Route 360 and turning left will take you on to Harbour Breton, the commercial center of the region. The road to Harbour Breton is one of those roller coaster rides found only in Newfoundland that sweeps you from sea level to over 300 m (1,000 ft) on at least six occasions. It starts out on an upland plateau, and quickly evolves into a ride that traverses several mountains and descends into spectacular glacially carved valleys. One minute you are 300 m (1,000 ft) above sea level, the next you are at sea level, and looking directly ahead at a stretch of highway that seems to head straight up into the clouds!

Located on a superb, land-locked harbor, at the end of a broad peninsula, Harbour Breton (pop. 2,079) is one of the oldest fishing centers on the south coast of Newfoundland. First visited by Breton fishermen from Brittany in northern France, Harbour Breton became the headquarters for the many English fishing fleets that operated in Fortune Bay in the 17th century. When Captain James Cook surveyed the south coast of Newfoundland for the British Admiralty in 1776, he pronounced Harbour Breton to be the finest harbor in all of Fortune Bay, and one of the finest in Newfoundland.

Above the ice-free harbor is a range of high mountains and steep cliffs, which made any form of agriculture virtually impossible. On August 1, 1973, one of those steep cliffs collapsed without warning, destroying four homes and taking the lives of four young children.

Thanks to its splendid location with regard to the Grand Banks fishing grounds, Harbour Breton was the dominant port along this stretch of the south coast, as well as a center of trade and commerce for many nearby outports. As such, it offers a good selection of tourist facilities which include a modern medical center, gas and service stations, fast food and convenience outlets, a bank, a restaurant, and the Southern Port Hotel and Dining

A 90-minute hiking trail leads to fantastic views from the top of Iron Skull Mountain in Belleoram.

Room with 16 rooms (709-885-2283). There are also campsites available at Deadman's Cove Park (709-885-2354).

A 23 km (14.3 mi) ride back up Route 360 will take you to the junction with Route 364, which leads to Hermitage, and the end of the pavement at Seal Cove. This is a wonderful ride, with plenty of sweeping curves, lots of hills, and wonderful panoramic views out over the surrounding countryside.

Hermitage (pop. 499) offers food, gas, the four-unit Sandyville Inn (709-883-2383), and a 20-minute ferry ride that gives you the opportunity to visit one of the few remaining authentic outport communities on the Island of Newfoundland. Authentic in the sense that there are no roads leading to it, and the only way to get there is by boat.

Gaultois (French for sharp pinnacle) is located on Long Island, an off-shore island in Hermitage Bay. Eighteen kilometers (11 mi) long, and 34 km (21 mi) in circumference, Long Island used to have several self-sufficient outports. Gaultois is the only one remaining, after the Newfoundland government forced the others to close in the 1960s and 70s. Ever since the 18th century, this virtually land-locked harbor has been an important fishing station, mainly because of its ice-free location and proximity to some of the finest fishing grounds in the Grand Banks.

Gaultois (pop. 450), located on steep cliffs around the harbor, has no roads except for one, short, dirt lane—The High Road—along which supplies are hauled from the local wharf by four-wheel, off-road motorbikes. In the winter months, the bikes are replaced by snowmobiles. There are wooden walkways built on stilts over the water, clinging to the sheer cliffs and ringing the harbor. They function not only as sidewalks, but even more importantly, as public meeting places. Kids even ride their bicycles on them. There is a church, a new school for 29 students (grades 1–12), and an old-fashioned general store that has changed very little since it first opened in 1929.

On my last visit to this region, we left our bikes on the side of the road in Hermitage (try doing that in mainland Canada or the United States). Our plan was to spend one night in Gaultois, but we ended up staying for two, when Calvin Hunt, a retired air force pilot decided that he would take us for a boat cruise. It was too good an offer to turn down. We spent the better part of six hours visiting three of the abandoned outport communities that lay in secluded coves and inlets around the back of the island. They were a tragic and stark reminder of the Newfoundland government's misguided attempt to resettle small outport communities in the 1960s.

This offer of a boat cruise was a typical Newfoundland thing to do. On

The only sidewalk in Gaultois leads to the general store, fish plant, and the ferry wharf.

the spur of the moment a Newfoundlander may ask you in for tea, or perhaps a meal, or even a cruise on a small boat. It is an opportunity not to be missed! The more isolated the community, the happier they are to see you, since most tourists don't travel too far from the security of the Trans-Canada Highway.

If at all possible, I strongly recommend a visit to this fascinating little village, if only for a short day trip. For those who would like to overnight, Bed and Breakfast accommodation is available: Annie Fudge (709-841-3421) and Judy Mayo (709-841-4531).

Once you are back in Hermitage you have a 200-km (126 mi) ride to return to the Trans-Canada Highway.

Trip 31 The Avalon Peninsula

Distance: *450 km (280 mi) From Argentia along the coast to St. John's*
290 km (180 mi) Baccalieu Trail/Bay de Verde loop
Highlights: *The eastern edge of the New World, one of the oldest cities on the continent, vast caribou barrens, and historic fishing outports that date back 500 years.*

Because of its remote location, jutting out into the North Atlantic Ocean, the Avalon Peninsula is the closest part of North America to Europe. It was also the closest part of North America to the fabled fishing grounds that make up the Grand Banks of Newfoundland. Only 5 km (3 mi) wide at its narrowest point, the Avalon region is approximately 180 km (112 mi) long, and about 100 km (62 mi) wide. Thanks to it's provincial capital of St. John's, it also contains almost half of the province's population. However, most of the peninsula is sparsely inhabited, unless you count the vast herds of wild caribou that roam the barrens.

Almost hidden by the surrounding mountains, the very narrow entrance to St. John's Harbour is indicated by Cabot Tower on Signal Hill, at the top right of this photograph.

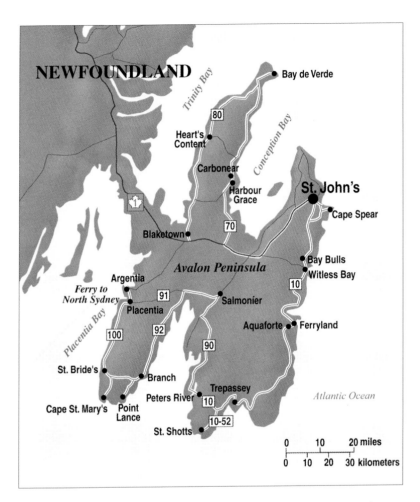

A significant portion of the first permanent settlers in this part of New-foundland were of Celtic descent, especially those fishermen and settlers who came from the south and west coasts of Ireland. The descendants of these early Irish settlers can still be found along the Irish Shore, the coastal region that stretches from St. Bride's to St. John's, and on to Conception Bay. The names on the mailboxes give them away—Fitzgerald; Power; Kennedy; Doyle; Coffey; and McGrath.

Not much has changed along this coast since the first permanent settlers arrived. It is still a wonderland of rivers, lakes, silent hills, and immense caribou barrens. Here you will find brightly painted houses, quaint old churches, and a lifestyle that is remarkably similar to that which you would encounter in the more remote corners of western and southern Ireland.

The Route from Argentia

0 km (0 mi) Arrive Argentia. Take Route 100 south.

6 km (3.9 mi) Arrive Placentia.

55 km (34.0 mi) Arrive St. Bride's

59 km (36.7 mi) Turn right to Cape St. Mary's.

72 km (44.7 mi) Arrive Cape St. Mary's. Return to Route 100.

85 km (52.7 mi) Turn right on Route 100.

94 km (58.5 mi) Turn right on Route 100-17.

105 km (65.1 mi) Arrive Point Lance. Return to Route 100.

115 km (71.7 mi) Turn Right on Route 100.

120 km (74.4 mi) Arrive Branch. Take Route 92 north.

171 km (106.6 mi) Turn right toward Salmonier.

190 km (117.7 mi) Arrive Salmonier. Take Route 90 south.

248 km (153.8 mi) Arrive Peter's River. Continue on Route 10.

264 km (164.0 mi) Junction with Route 10-52 to St. Shotts.
 Side trip to St. Shotts 14 km (8.8 mi) one way

281 km (174.5 mi) Arrive Trepassey. Continue on Route 10.

346 km (214.7 mi) Arrive Aquaforte. Continue on Route 10.

351 km (218.1 mi) Arrive Ferryland. Continue on Route 10.

392 km (243.6 mi) Arrive Witless Bay. Continue on Route 10.

397 km (246.7 mi) Arrive Bay Bulls. Continue on Route 10.

414 km (257.5 mi) Turn right on Petty Harbour Road to Cape Spear.

431 km (268.3 mi) Arrive Cape Spear. Return to Route 11 and continue
 to St. John's.

448 km (278.8 mi) Arrive St. John's.

Picturesque little villages, like St. Mary's and St. Bride's, are perfect examples of just how well the traditional music and culture of Ireland has been preserved and handed down from generation to generation. Here you will find songs, dances, fiddle tunes, and a tradition of story telling that harks back directly to the Emerald Isle.

The Marine Atlantic ferry crossing from North Sydney, Nova Scotia, to Argentia (pop. 450), on the west side of the Avalon Peninsula usually takes 14 hours, depending on weather conditions. From here a modern two-lane highway leads directly to the capital city of St. John's, a distance of 134 km (83 mi) via Route 100 and the Trans-Canada Highway (Route 1). But for this journey we will take the much longer coastal route to St. John's.

A short distance south of the ferry landing is the town of Placentia, situated on a low-lying stretch of land surrounded by a coastal forest. In the early days of the 17th century it was the French capital of Newfoundland, first settled in 1662. Aware of its strategic location, the French forces built a fort on a nearby hilltop in order to protect the settlement from attack by English raiders (Castle Hill National Historic Site). In 1713 when the treaty of Utrecht gave all of Newfoundland to England, the French abandoned their settlement in Placentia and moved to the tiny French fishing village of Louisbourg on Cape Breton Island. There, in the summer of 1720, they began construction of the great Fortress that was to play such an important part in the colonial wars between the French and the English for control of Canada. Placentia has one, 17-room Hotel, Harold Hotel (877-227-2107), several small Bed and Breakfasts, and the usual tourist facilities.

Take Route 100 south for a roller-coaster type of ride of 48 km (30 mi) over several mountains to St. Bride's (pop. 386). Located at the southern tip of Placentia Bay, the village is a relaxing place to stay while visiting one of the world's great ecological reserves. Most visitors stay at the Bird Island Resort (888-337-2450), a charming little complex of 15 housekeeping units, five motel rooms, and one bridal suite.

It is only a short ride, on a paved road, to Cape St. Mary's Ecological Reserve, an awe-inspiring seabird colony. Here you will be able to observe nesting seabirds, often as close as only 10 m (33 ft) away. Located on the edge of steep ocean cliffs, the reserve is home to thousands of gannets, kittiwakes, razorbills, and great cormorants, among others. Note that the observation point is a 30-minute walk from the Interpretative Centre, which is run by the Wildlife Division in one of the lightkeeper's cottages.

The remote outport community of Point Lance (pop. 150) is about 24 km (15 mi) from St. Bride's, on Route 100–17. Located at the end of a broad valley, with rolling hills on each side, the tiny outport was given it's name because the western hills end in a point of land that resembles the tip of a spear, or lance. One of the most isolated outports on the Avalon Peninsula, the only way in or out of Point Lance was by boat, until the first primitive gravel road to the outside world was opened in 1950. Electricity arrived in 1966, followed by the first telephone service in 1972. Today the access road is paved, which makes it easy for visitors to experience this charming little community.

For the last 50 years, the fiercely independent fishermen of Point Lance have resisted all attempts by the provincial government to relocate the residents, and close the outport. Their Irish ancestors have been there for more than 200 years, and it looks like their descendants will remain.

Should you visit, be sure to stop in at Careen's Store, the social and retail center of this little community. As with other tiny outports along this coast, visitors are few and far between, and thus receive a genuine and enthusiastic welcome.

Local children were fascinated with the first touring motorcycles they had ever seen at the end of the road in Point Lance, ten paved kilometers from the main highway.

It is only 15 km (9.3 mi) from Point Lance to Branch (pop. 400), where Route 100 becomes Route 92. The road now heads northeast, and for the next 51 km (32 mi) passes through a primeval wilderness of lakes, rivers, and coastal barrens. At its northern end a short gravel road (Route 91) leads to Cataracts Provincial Park, a great place to picnic. A deep gorge and two cascading waterfalls are easily accessible, and make for some great photos.

A short paved section of this road leads to Salmonier, where you join Route 90. Here you have two options. If you take Route 90 north, it is only 80 km (50 mi) to St. John's. But to continue the coastal route follow Route 90 south to Peters River, where it becomes Route 10, and continue on to Trepassey, a leisurely 90 km (56 mi) from the junction at Salmonier.

About 16 km (10 mi) from Peters River Route 10–52 leaves to the right and leads to St. Shotts (pop. 109), another one of the former isolated outports along this Irish Shore. This makes an interesting side trip if you want to take the time.

Trepassey (pop. 889), is a formerly vibrant fishing community that was laid low by the Cod Moratorium of 1992. It takes its name from the French word for "dead men," a reference to the many lives lost due to shipwreck along this coast. Though originally visited by fishermen from France, Spain, and Portugal, the population had become mostly Irish by the latter part of the 18th century. Since Trepassey is approximately half way between

Argentia and St. John's on the coastal route, many visitors choose to make this an overnight stop. For those who do, lodging options include the Northwest Lodge, a four-room Bed and Breakfast (877-398-2888); and the 10-room Trepassey Motel & Restaurant (888-439-2934).

In 1919, three "flying boats" (seaplanes) of the United States Navy took off from Trepassey Harbour and flew to Portugal, by way of a refueling stop at the Azores. It was the first successful flight across the Atlantic Ocean. (Charles Lindberg made the first solo trans-Atlantic flight in 1927.) Then, in 1928, American aviatrix Amelia Earhart became the first woman to fly the Atlantic, when she took off from a local meadow and flew as a passenger to Wales, in the United Kingdom. The flight, with two men on board, lasted 20 hours.

The coastal route from Trepassey to St. John's is a 167 km (104 mi) journey, which will probably take you the better part of three or four hours, especially if you stop in one or more of the fascinating little outports.

A short distance after leaving Trepassey Route 10 heads northeast across vast, wide-open spaces. At one point, on a stretch known locally as the Caribou Barrens, we stopped to photograph a herd of caribou. I stopped counting when I got to 100, and there were many more. We were able to approach to within 10 m (33 ft) of the animals, as they seemed to have little

The landscape near the Avalon Reservation is vast, empty caribou barrens.

fear of humans, or at least those humans wearing leather jackets and motorcycle helmets.

Later that same day, in the tiny outport settlement of Aquaforte (pop. 103), we literally rode back in time when we came across the square-rigged sailing ship H.M.S. Rose, tied up at the local wharf. A full-size replica of a 16th-century British Man-of-War, she was part of a fleet of Tall Ships from around the world that were visiting St. John's. The ship later appeared in the 2003 movie *Master and Commander: Far Side of the World*, starring Russell Crowe.

Ferryland (pop. 529) was once a popular fishing harbor on the east coast of Newfoundland. In 1621 a small group of settlers arrived from England, in the company of the first Lord Baltimore. (His son would later settle, and give his name to Baltimore, Maryland.) Before long, King James I granted him title to the Province of Avalon. At the fascinating Colony of Avalon Interpretation Centre visitors are able to observe archaeologists as they excavate the extensive ruins of the original settlement. There are many informative exhibits, as well as 17th-century gardens, and a small,

Discovering the H.M.S. Rose, a full-size replica of a 16th-century Man-of-War in Aquaforte was one of those chance occurrences that make a trip memorable.

The lighthouse at Cape Spear is the most easterly light on the North American continent. There is nothing between here and the west coast of Ireland except the vast expanse of the North Atlantic Ocean.

living-history museum is located in the courthouse, which overlooks Ferryland Downs.

From Ferryland it is 41 km (25.5 mi) to Witless Bay (pop. 1070). Named after a certain Captain Whittle, from Dorsetshire, England, it was originally called Whittle's Bay. However, after the good captain and his family left, it became Whittle-less Bay, which quickly morphed into the present name.

Nearby Bay Bulls (pop. 1,200), one of the oldest communities in North America (1592), offers boat tours to observe either whales or icebergs, or both, depending on the season.

A short detour will take you to Cape Spear National Historic Site, the most easterly point of land in North America. The lighthouse, in service from 1835 to 1955, is the oldest still standing in Newfoundland and Labrador, and is now a lifestyle museum (c. 1839). Cape Spear is the place on the continent where the sun shines first, and from the top of the 100-meter (328 ft) cliffs you can wave to your relatives in Europe, only 3,000 km (2,000 mi) away!

St. John's

First settled in 1546, this historic East Coast port is the oldest English speaking city on the continent, with the oldest street (Water Street). It is home to the oldest annual sporting event, the Royal St. John's Regatta, which has been held every summer since 1816; Signal Hill was the place where Guglielmo Marconi received the first trans-Atlantic wireless message on December 12, 1901; and the first non-stop trans-Atlantic airplane flight (Newfoundland to Ireland), piloted by Alcock and Brown, took off from a local field on June 14, 1919.

Situated on steep slopes, overlooking a well-protected harbor, St. John's has often been compared to San Francisco. Like that famous West Coast American port, it also has a vibrant artistic and cultural life, dominated by a very lively traditional music scene. In fact, George Street claims to have the most pubs and bars per capita of any city in North America!

The city has much to offer any visitor. Among the points of interest is the Signal Hill National Historic Site. Over the centuries signal flags were raised on this spot to tell local merchants what cargo or fishing vessels were approaching the harbor entrance. Though Signal Hill has been the location of numerous military fortifications, it is dominated today by the century-old Cabot Tower, built to commemorate the discovery of mainland North America by John Cabot.

The Newfoundland Museum on Duckworth Street has a wide range of historic artifacts and information, especially with regard to Newfoundland's original inhabitants, the Beothuck Indians (now extinct), and the city's important role as a fishing port, seaport, and vital wartime convoy assembly point.

The Railway Coastal Museum on Water Street is located in the original 1903 Victorian railroad station. This fascinating transportation museum chronicles the important role the railroad and coastal boat service played in the settlement and development of this former British colony. It is also the site of the Mile Zero Marker, for the Trans-Canada Trail. When completed this 17,600 km (11,000 mi) multi-use corridor—most of which follows abandoned railway lines—will be the longest recreational trail in the world!

The Rooms on Bonaventure Avenue is a striking new cultural facility, with panoramic views of the historic harbor that houses the Provincial Archives, Art Gallery, and Museum.   ■

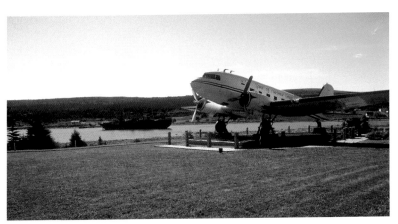

On May 20, 1932, Amelia Earhart took off from Harbour Grace and became the first woman to fly solo across the Atlantic Ocean. The aircraft is a fully restored Douglas DC-3, built in California in 1943. After military service in North Africa, the aircraft flew in various parts of northern Canada, before being donated to the town of Harbour Grace in 1993.

The grounds are open year round, but the lighthouse and Interpretation Centre are only open from mid-May to mid-October. You will also find a coastal defense battery from World War II at the Cape, equipped with two, 10-inch guns designed to protect St. John's Harbour from German warships and surface raiders.

About 17 km (10.5 mi) from Cape Spear is downtown St. John's (pop. 181,113), the capital and largest city in the province. The downtown area is quite hilly, with many streets that are steep and narrow, and full of traffic. If you are not comfortable with maneuvering a loaded touring bike under such conditions, it would be better to book accommodation on the outskirts of the city. As befits the capital city of Newfoundland and Labrador, there is a wide selection of accommodation available with many of the brand-name hotel chains represented.

The Baccalieu Trail – Bay de Verde loop

0 km (0 mi) From St John's take Route 1.
68 km (42.1 mi) Take Exit 31 to Route 70 north.
102 km (63.4 mi) Arrive Harbour Grace. Continue on Route 70.
174 km (108.1 mi) Arrive Bay de Verde. Return on Route 70.
185 km (115.0 mi) Take Route 80 to Heart's Content.
230 km (142.6 mi) Arrive Heart's Content. Continue on Route 80.
290 km (180.2 mi) Arrive Trans-Canada Highway/Route 1.

Waiting to go on a whale watching cruise, with the town of Bay de Verde on the hill in the background.

For those who would like to spend another day on the Avalon Peninsula, I would recommend the roughly 220-km (140 mi) loop around the Bay de Verde peninsula known as The Baccalieu Trail. Named after an old Spanish name for codfish, this route offers more than 60 outport communities, including several that are of great historical significance, and offers magnificent coastal views out over Conception Bay and Trinity Bay.

From St. John's follow the Trans-Canada Highway/Route 1 west for approximately 68 km (42 mi) to Exit 31. From here follow signs for Bay Roberts/Carbonear. It is about 34 km (21 mi) from Route 1 to Harbour Grace, by way of Route 70.

Harbour Grace (pop. 3,074) was founded by French fishermen in 1517, and is one of the oldest towns in Canada. Situated on a large harbor, it became well known for it's fishing and shipbuilding, and gained international recognition in the early 20th century for its part in the history of Trans-Atlantic aviation. On May 20, 1932, Amelia Earhart took off from here and became the first woman to fly solo across the Atlantic Ocean.

Harbour Grace to Carbonear is only 9 km (5.6 mi). Carbonear (pop. 4,723), and it's nearby island of the same name, played an important part in 17th-century conflicts between England and France for control of the lucrative fishing grounds around Newfoundland and Labrador. It was also frequented by various pirates, especially Peter Easton, and was attacked by American privateers during the Revolutionary War. It has a lovely little museum in the former railroad station.

Continue along the Baccalieu Trail for 63 km (39 mi) to Bay de Verde (pop. 470). The town was given its name by Portuguese fishermen who set up seasonal shore stations in the early 16th century. Permanent settlers from England arrived in 1662, and the outport became very prosperous over the next few centuries. A very steep, but paved road, leads to the picturesque harbor, home to Quinlan Fisheries, one of the few remaining fish processing plants on the Island of Newfoundland. Baccalieu Island, just a few kilometers offshore, is a designated Ecological Reserve, known for its seabird colonies.

Continue to follow the Baccalieu Trail down Route 80 along the coast of Trinity Bay to Heart's Content. With it's large sheltered harbor, Heart's Content (pop. 495), achieved international recognition in 1866 when the first Trans-Atlantic telegraphic cable was landed there. Telegraph messages from Ireland, 3000 km away, could now be received in minutes, instead of waiting six to eight weeks for a sailing ship to arrive from Europe. The old Cable Station is now a Provincial Historic Site, containing a fascinating display of early telecommunications equipment, and other historical artifacts.

From Heart's Content it is 60 km (37 mi) to Blaketown and the Trans-Canada Highway/Route 1.

The road around the Bay de Verde peninsula offers many scenic viewpoints, such as this one on the outskirts of the outport also called Bay de Verde.

Whale watching

One time when I was in Bay de Verde I had the opportunity to go out on a 38-foot yacht to visit a pod of humpbacked whales. After manoeuvring around small boats and clearing the breakwater, we headed out into the bay. A large rocky headland, with near-vertical cliffs reaching several hundred feet into the air was on our left. Directly ahead, across several miles of open water, was the long, low outline of Baccalieu Island.

Suddenly a huge black shape reared from the water less than ten feet from the bow. It was a humpback whale, majestic and awesome, and as long as the boat! We were startled and astonished, to find ourselves so close to one of the largest creatures on the face of the earth. I was so startled that the camera I held at the ready went unused. My first thought was that the bow of the boat would crash into the glistening ebony form that marked the back of this incredible animal. Then, as suddenly as it appeared, it was gone. Sunk out of sight directly in front of our eyes. The last glimpse we had was of the massive tail slipping silently under the surface.

Humpbacked whales are an endangered species. Up until the early 1960s, they, along with other species, were hunted almost to the point of extinction. Finally, in 1972, the federal government banned all commercial whaling activities in Canadian waters. Actually, by that time the available whales were so few in number that there were only three whaling operations remaining—two in Newfoundland and one in Nova Scotia.

Though we were startled by the whale, the captain was not, and told us not to worry. "He knows what he is doing. He just came up to welcome us."

As the captain throttled back the engines and slowed to a crawl, we were suddenly surrounded by at least a dozen humpback whales, cavorting on all sides of our vessel. There was a breaching pair on our left side. I tried to photograph the three that had just surfaced directly in front of us. Another, less than six feet away from my spot on the flying bridge, appeared to look me directly in the eye before submerging in a spray of foam.

These animals, weighing 20 to 40 tons and many longer than the yacht, caused me to wonder what would happen if one decided to come up directly under the boat. The captain admitted that they could easily flip the boat over. "But that won't happen," he assured us. "They know my boat. They know the sound of my engines. They know the sound of each engine on every boat that enters or leaves this bay. Humpbacks are very intelligent, and also very friendly. They like to socialize, that's why you see so many of them together. They also have nothing to be afraid of, aside from man that is."

By this time we had coasted to a stop, and rocked gently to and fro as the engines continued to turn over in neutral. Other humpbacks had joined the party, so many so that I stopped counting at 32. It was just too difficult to keep track of them as they went through their paces around us. Water spouted from their vent holes, in some cases creating exquisite little rainbows that lingered for only a few seconds before dissolving into nothingness. Some appeared to be playing follow the leader, or tag, as they frolicked around the yacht, obviously taking great glee in creating surges of water that would rock the stationary boat and force us to hang on to the vessel, or to each other.

Somewhat reluctantly, the captain put the engines back in gear and we slowly started to make headway. As if realizing that our visit was over, some of the whales headed off in other directions, while a half-dozen or so continued to follow us for quite some time. Then they too were gone, as we returned Bay de Verde, still marvelling at the wonderful spectacle we had just witnessed. ∎

Trip 32   Viking Trail

Distance: *817 km (508 mi) This trip from Deer Lake to St. Anthony, with side trips will take at least five days. Adding the Labrador Straits tour could easily increase the trip to seven to eight days.*
Highlights: *A flat mesa where nothing grows, a glacial fiord with cliffs 600 m (2,000 ft) high, a roller-coaster ride around a beautiful bay, and two United Nations World Heritage Sites.*

Without warning, you round a sharp bend in the road and come face to face with this orange-tan colored mountain. This strange apparition, which appears at first glance to be a transplanted mesa, belongs in the "Cowboy and Indian" territory of the southwestern United States—not in Newfoundland and Labrador. But there it is, directly in front of you. You almost have to pinch yourself, to see if you have somehow been transported to the wilds of Colorado or Arizona!

Welcome to the Tablelands, and Gros Morne (French for "Great Peak") National Park, one of the most spectacular of the 38 National Parks in Canada. Located on the west coast of the province, and only 32 km (20 mi) from the Trans-Canada Highway at Deer Lake, the park provides a sublime introduction to the many wonders of The Viking Trail.

This is your first good view of the the northern edge of the Tablelands.

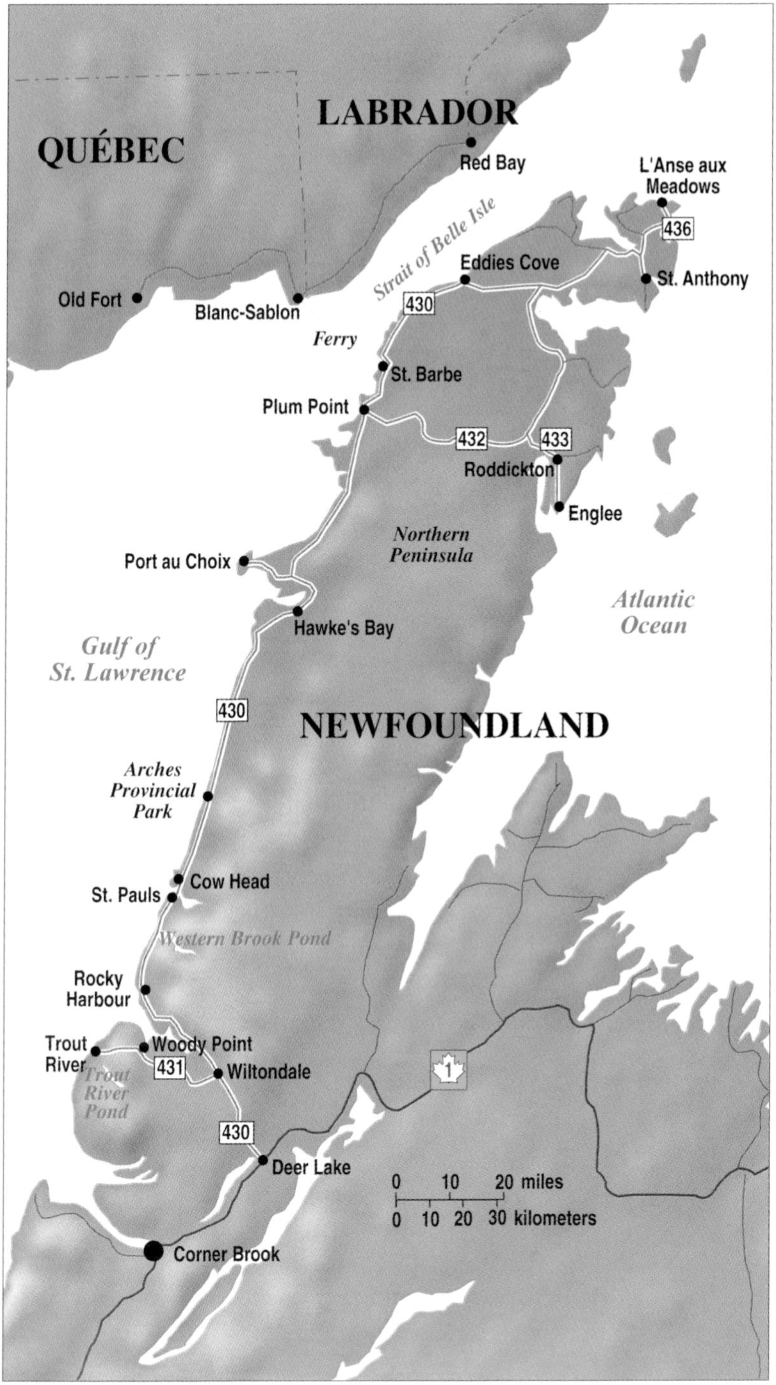

QUÉBEC

LABRADOR

Red Bay

L'Anse aux Meadows

436

Strait of Belle Isle

Old Fort

Blanc-Sablon

Eddies Cove

St. Anthony

430

Ferry

St. Barbe

Plum Point

432   433

Roddickton

Englee

Port au Choix

Northern Peninsula

Atlantic Ocean

Hawke's Bay

Gulf of St. Lawrence

430

NEWFOUNDLAND

Arches Provincial Park

Cow Head

St. Pauls

Western Brook Pond

Rocky Harbour

Trout River

Woody Point

431

Wiltondale

Trout River Pond

1

430

Deer Lake

0   10   20 miles

0   10   20   30 kilometers

Corner Brook

Route from Deer Lake to St. Anthony

0 km (0 mi) Take Route 430 north from the Trans-Canada Highway/Route 1 at Deer Lake.

30 km (18.6 mi) In Wiltondale turn left on Route 431.

63 km (39.3 mi) Arrive Woody Point. Continue on Route 431.

81 km (50.2 mi) Arrive Trout River. Return to Route 430.

131 km (81.3 mi) Turn left on Route 430.

169 km (104.8 mi) Arrive Rocky Harbour. Continue on Route 430.

215 km (133.1 mi) Arrive Cow Head. Continue on Route 430.

318 km (197.4 mi) Turn left on Route 430–28 to Port au Choix.

331 km (205.4 mi) Arrive Port au Choix . Return to Route 430.

343 km (212.8 mi) Turn left on Route 430.

390 km (242.4 mi) Arrive Plum Point. Continue on Route 430.

411 km (255.6 mi) Arrive St. Barbe. Continue on Route 430.

529 km (329.2 mi) Arrive St. Anthony. Return on Route 430.

540 km (335.9 mi) Turn right on Route 436.

569 km (353.8 mi) Arrive L'Anse aux Meadows. Return to Route 430.

598 km (371.7 mi) Turn right on Route 430.

638 km (396.2 mi) Turn left on Route 432.

694 km (430.8 mi) Turn left on Route 433.

713 km (442.4 mi) Arrive Roddickton. Continue on Route 433.

729 km (452.7 mi) Arrive Englee. Return to Route 432.

764 km (474.6 mi) Turn left on Route 432.

817 km (507.8 mi) Arrive Route 430.

Formed over a period of millions of years, and scoured by at least ten separate ice ages, Gros Morne is a primeval landscape of fiords, mountains, and spectacular ocean scenery. In fact, this region has not changed much since the retreat of the last glaciers about 10,000 years ago. Park Wardens at the visitor center can show you proof of continents in collision, signs of undersea avalanches and prehistoric volcanos, and the fossilized remains of ancient sea creatures, many of them quite bizarre, that swam in our oceans more than 500 million years ago.

The Viking Trail/Route 430 follows the exposed western edge of the Northern Peninsula all the way to the Strait of Belle Isle, at the extreme northern tip of the Island of Newfoundland. Once you leave Gros Morne National Park, you will travel on a low coastal plain, with the calm waters of the Gulf of St. Lawrence on your left, and the massive bulk of the Long Range Mountains off to your right. It is, by its very nature, a relatively slow drive, but with scenery like this who wants to drive fast!

Route 430 begins at Deer Lake (pop. c. 5,000), which has all the tourism

On the right is the bizarre, barren, transplanted mesa known as the Tablelands, while on the left is the thickly forested bulk of the Lookout Mountains.

amenities, including two motels and numerous Bed and Breakfasts. (Deer Lake Motel, 56 rooms, 800-563-2144; and The Driftwood Inn, 25 rooms 888-635-5115).

It is a relatively easy 32 km (20.7 mi) drive to the junction at Wiltondale. (Remember it is moose country!) When I travel to Gros Morne, I often stay at the Frontier Cottages in this charming little village (800-668-2520). With seven two-bedroom log cabins, a restaurant, and a convenience store, it makes an ideal place to tour the south side of Bonne Bay (French for beautiful bay), and take a boat tour of Trout River Pond.

The 50 km (31 mi) of Route 431, from Wiltondale to the end of the road at Trout River, is a wonderful, roller-coaster type of ride, one of the best and most breathtaking in the province, packing a gorgeous variety of scenic splendor into a short distance. This lovely road will also give you the opportunity to visit two charming outport communities.

Woody Point (pop. 400) is a photogenic little town, with an historic waterfront, and four Provincial Heritage Structures, including the Woody

The waters of Bonne Bay are tranquil on this quiet summer day in Woody Point.

Point Theatre. Built in 1908, the former Lord Nelson Orange Lodge is now home to a thriving summer festival. The town, a haven for artists, musicians, and photographers, has several Bed and Breakfasts, and a nine-room motel (Woody Point Motel, 866-453-2515).

Trout River (pop. 688) was first settled in 1815 by George Crocker, a fisherman from the south coast of England. Until 1880, he and his family were the only people in the isolated outport. Today, with several scenic hiking trails and the boat tour of Trout River Pond, it captivates all who visit, especially those who enjoy the fresh seafood available at local restaurants. Rustic accommodation is available at Crocker Cabins (877-951-3236) and the Tableland Resort (877-451-2101).

Lying between Woody Point and Trout River are the Tablelands, a unique geological feature, which in 1987 was one of the main reasons Gros Morne National Park received United Nations designation as a World Heritage Site. The Tablelands consist of a 20-km-long (12 mi), orange-colored barren mountain made of a rock known as periodite. This rock is very low in calcium, very high in magnesium, has few of the nutrients needed to sustain plant life, and has toxic amounts of heavy metals. The rusty color of the Tablelands is due to the high levels of iron in the rock. The Tablelands are totally devoid of vegetation of any kind, except for a form of scrub grass and stunted brush that grows in the wind-blown fertile soil around its base. This particular block of peridotite was thrust up from an estimated 30–40 km (20 mi) beneath the ocean, during a cataclysmic event that happened about 300 million years ago. Geologists tell us that its formation was a result of a collision between the American and European tectonic plates, and took place during a time when the continents were being formed and the earth's crust was starting to cool.

What makes this site even more impressive is its stunning location. As you approach, the Tablelands are hidden from view behind the other peaks of the Long Range Mountains. These peaks, with their thick cover of natural forest, are a northern extension of the Appalachian Mountain Range that is found in the northeastern United States. As you come over a ridge you find yourself in a narrow valley. On the left side loom the barren, bleak, and desolate contours of the Tablelands. On the right, the thickly forested, primeval looking, massive bulk of the Lookout Hills. It is definitely a study in contrasts, a bizarre image that once seen will continue to haunt your mind for a long time to come.

From Trout River you can take a two-hour boat tour to the inner reaches of Trout River Pond, which takes you behind the Tablelands. During the summer the trip is usually available at least twice a day.

The mist gives the cliffs that tower over Western Brook Pond an atmosphere of foreboding.

When you return to Route 430, head north through the park. This road is an awe-inspiring ride as it sweeps you up and over the majestic Long Range Mountains that straddle both sides of historic Bonne Bay. You are presented with one stunning vista after another.

Rocky Harbour (pop. 1,068) is the largest town in Gros Morne National Park, and the commercial hub of the region. With all the essential facilities, it also provides a central location for touring. (Western Brook Pond is 30 km (18.6 mi) north, and Trout River Pond is a slow 87 km (54 mi) south.) There is a wide range of accommodation, including the 40-room Fisherman's Landing Inn (866-458-2711) and the 52-room Ocean View Motel (800-563-9887).

The Gros Morne National Park Visitor Centre is located on Route 430, 4 km (2.5 mi) south of Rocky Harbour and open from May 21 to the end of October. The new Discovery Centre on Route 431 near Woody Point is open from May 21 to October 11.

The second boat tour available in Gros Morne National Park is a spectacular trip up Western Brook Pond, located in the northern part of the park. In a perfect example of Newfoundland understatement, calling Western

The lonely ride up the Northern Peninsula on Route 430 gives you plenty of time to contemplate your place in the universe.

Constant wind and wave erosion has carved three natural arches in the exposed piece of coastal limestone at Arches Provincial Park.

Brook a "pond" would be roughly equivalent to calling the Grand Canyon in Arizona a "ditch!" The pond is actually a 16 km (10 mi) landlocked fiord, the equal of anything to be found in Norway or New Zealand. With an average depth of 180 m (600 ft), Western Brook has the highest cliffs found anywhere in North America. At their loftiest point these near-vertical cliff faces extend 670 m (2,200 ft) above the water!

In contrast to the Trout River Pond tour where the parking lot is next to the boat launch, the parking for the Western Brook Pond tour is a 30 to 40 min. walk from the dock where the two boats tie up.

Route 430 north from Rocky Harbour follows the exposed coastline to St. Pauls and Cow Head (pop. c. 500), both of which offer the closest accommodation to Western Brook Pond. The Gros Morne Resort in St. Pauls has 20 rooms (888-243-2644).

Cow Head is home to one of the best sand beaches in Newfoundland, has several unique geological features, and a fantastic view of the Long Range Mountains. The 60-unit Shallow Bay Motel (800-563-1946) is also home to the Gros Morne Theatre Festival, which offers "a lively mix of drama, dinner theatre, and Newfoundland good times!"

From Cow Head Route 430 hugs the coast as it makes its way north for 99 km to Hawke's Bay (Torrent River Inn, 29 rooms, 800-563-8811). A nice stop along the way is the Arches Provincial Park, where erosion has cut three large arches through a type of stone called dolomite. It is an excellent spot for some rather unique photographs.

A short detour west from Hawke's Bay will take you to Port au Choix National Historic Site, one of the richest archaeological venues in North America. Here, beginning in the 1960s, researchers discovered the remains of a small village, including three cemeteries that date back to the Maritime Archaic People who occupied the site about 3,700 years ago. A total of four different aboriginal cultures inhabited this site. The nearby town (pop. 1,010) has a Parks Canada Visitor center, a Heritage Museum with relics of The French Shore, and the usual tourist facilities, including the 30-room Sea Echo Motel (709-861-3777).

The drive from Port au Choix to the Labrador ferry passes through Plum Point (Plum Point Motel, 40 rooms, 888-663-2533). The ferry terminal at St. Barbe also has accommodations, the 20-room Dockside Motel (877-667-2444). Either community is a good choice for those who need overnight lodging before taking the ferry across the Strait of Belle Isle.

From St. Barbe to the end of the road in St. Anthony (pop. 2,476) is 118 km (73.6 mi). At Eddies Cove the highway leaves the coast, and heads inland across a unique landscape of barren muskeg and glacially scoured rock formations. You could be on the backside of the moon!

Local bikers in Roddington check out our touring machines for size.

Many large trucks have this $4,000 accessory to prevent expensive damage to the engine, vehicle and driver in the event of a collision with a moose or caribou.

First settled in the early 1500s by Basque and French fishermen, the town of St. Anthony is the commercial center of the Northern Peninsula. During the Cold War the town also served as a radar site for the U. S. military, with more than 250 servicemen stationed there.

In addition to several Bed and Breakfasts, St. Anthony has three larger accommodation options. The Grenfell Heritage Hotel has 20 newly renovated rooms (888-450-8398); while The Haven Inn has 38 rooms

From a distance, these look like they could be the original Viking dwellings, instead of modern day reconstructions. The original earthen foundations are just to the left of this historic site.

L'Anse aux Meadows National Historic Park

L'Anse aux Meadows National Historic Park, open from early June to the first week in October, is the only authenticated Norse site in the New World. Because of its unique significance, it was declared a United Nations World Heritage Site in 1978.

Around the year 1001 A.D., Leifr Eiriksson (Old Norse for "Leif, son of Erik the Red") decided to set sail from Greenland in search of unexplored lands to the west. As Norse navigators could not accurately determine latitude, Leif and his crew of 35 were forced to hug the coastline whenever possible. They also made note of any prominent landmarks that would be helpful on their return journey. Leaving the coast of Greenland behind, they traveled west to Baffin Island, and then on to northern Labrador. They then sailed south along the coast of Labrador until they reached the Strait of Belle Isle. Once they entered the Strait, they could plainly see the coastline of Newfoundland's

Great Northern Peninsula. It was now less than ten miles to the sheltered little bay at L'Anse aux Meadows, which they named Vinland. Their long and hazardous voyage was now over. After further exploration in the immediate vicinity, Leif and his men returned to L'Anse aux Meadows. Here, in an open meadow close to the shore, they set up camp and prepared for the coming winter. As soon as ice conditions permitted, in late spring or early summer, they set sail for Greenland, and arrived without incident.

Over the next ten years at least four other expeditions sailed from Greenland to northern Newfoundland. The third of these (1006 A.D.) also included the first women, one of whom gave birth to the first child of European descent born in the New World. She was named *Snorri* (Snor's Daughter), after her father.

After 1010 A.D., there are no further references to Vinland in the Norse Sagas, and the early explorations passed into legend.   ■

Costumed animators help you understand what life was like more than 1,000 years ago, and illustrate all the chores that had to be done as the Norse settlers tried to survive in this new land.

Because of the very poor soil conditions in Newfoundland and Labrador, many residents will create little vegetable gardens, wherever they might find a bit of fertile soil. These tidy gardens, which might be 15 to 20 km (10–12 mi) from town, are always fenced, in an often futile attempt to prevent moose from having a free meal.

(877-428-3646); and the appropriately named Vinland Motel offers 43 rooms (800-563-7578).

Unless they were going to Labrador, most visitors to the west coast of Newfoundland would not make the long trip up (and down) the northern peninsula were it not for the chance to visit what might be the most important archaeological site in North America!

L'Anse aux Meadows National Historic Park, at the very tip of the Northern Peninsula, is 40 km (24.6 mi) from the town of St. Anthony. It was here, 500 years before Columbus, that the Vikings established the first European settlement in North America, about the year 1000 A.D. A reconstruction of their six sod huts, and a stunning Interpretation Centre, tell the story of these hardy adventurers who braved the stormy waters of the North Atlantic in their small boats.

For a nice detour before returning back down the Northern Peninsula, I recommend taking Route 432 south from the St. Anthony airport. The junction is 51 km (31.2 mi) from town, and this relatively new road will take you to two little communities that until very recently were among the most isolated outports in the entire province. The road from the airport to Roddickton (pop. c. 1,000) passes through isolated wilderness, with very little traffic, and a very good chance of meeting moose or black bear. This region contains some of the best hunting and fishing opportunities in the province. It is also not a road to drive fast!

The Mayflower Inn in Roddickton (866-218-4400), which promotes itself as the "Moose Capital of the World," offers 23 rooms and 9 cozy cottages. Seasonal guides are also available for those who would like to hunt or fish.

Another 16 km (10 mi) will take you to the end of Route 433 in Englee (pop. 694), a tidy little outport that provides some great photo opportunities. It is a great place to park your bike, and just take a walk around. Be aware that large touring motorcycles are not common in places like Englee, so you will probably find yourself, and your bike, the center of attraction.

From Englee it is a 35 km (22 mi) ride back to the junction with Route 432, and another 53 km (33.2 mi) run directly west to the main coastal road at Plum Point. This is also a pure wilderness experience, where speed is not of the essence. Believe me, I have had moose come up on the road, seemingly from nowhere, and it can be an unnerving experience. My advice would be to slow down, and enjoy the scenery.

By the way, the little roadside gardens that you pass belong to residents of either Roddickton or Englee, where the soil is too poor, and too rocky, to allow vegetables to grow!

(From the main coastal road at Plum Point to the ferry terminal at Port aux Basques is 545 km (338 mi), a seven-hour drive, not-stop!)

Trip 33 Labrador Straits

Distances: 72 km (44.7 mi) from Blanc-Sablon to end of the pavement
  at Old Fort, Québec.
  82 km (50.9 mi) from Blanc-Sablon ferry terminal to end of the pavement
  at Red Bay, Labrador.
  335 km (208 mi) (one way) gravel road from Red Bay to Cartwright.
  391 km (242.8 mi) (one way) gravel road from Cartwright to
  Happy Valley-Goose Bay.

Highlights: An extraordinary touring experience that is unique in eastern North America. The oldest burial site in North America, the earliest
industrial site in the New World, the tallest lighthouse in Atlantic Canada, vast treeless barrens, primeval wilderness, and 10,000-year-old
icebergs in July.

Before you come to Labrador you need to do some serious planning, and
make some advance reservations. This is especially important in the summer months, as there is only so much vehicle space available on the ferry,
and accommodations tend to sell out several months in advance. At least

The barren, rocky coastline around the ferry terminal at Blanc-Sablon, Québec, may seem
intimidating to first-time visitors. But there is a world-class adventure awaiting anyone
who visits these coastal regions of Québec and Labrador.

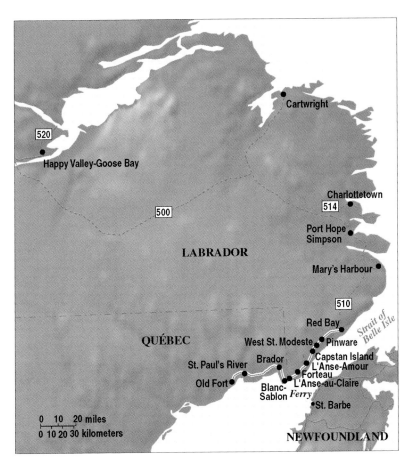

you don't have to worry about getting lost, as there is only one paved road, and it follows the coast—both in Labrador and on the Québec side, where it comes to a dead end 72 km (44.7 mi) from the ferry terminal. In Labrador the paved road ends at Red Bay, 82 km (50.9 mi) from the ferry. The road beyond Red Bay to Cartwright and to Happy Valley-Goose Bay is gravel and not recommended for touring motorcycles, although dual-sport machines with suitable tires should not have any problem.

The Strait of Belle Isle separates Newfoundland's Great Northern Peninsula from Southern Labrador and the French-speaking province of Québec. Only 16 km (10 mi) wide at its narrowest point, winter ice conditions usually make it impossible to cross from early December to the end of May. There is a seasonal, 90-minute ferry service between St. Barbe, Newfoundland, and Blanc-Sablon, Québec, which is less than three kilometers from the Labrador border.

This village is typical of those found on Québec's Lower North Shore. Notice the absence of trees, and the bleak landscape that was scraped bare by the glaciers of the last ice age.

Whenever I visit the Labrador Straits, I make my base in L'Anse-au-Claire (pop. 264) at the Northern Light Inn (800-563-3188). It is the closest full-service motel to the ferry, with 54 air-conditioned (!) rooms, and five housekeeping cottages that will sleep five or six. It is also just about midway between the ends of the paved road on the Québec side, and the Labrador side, which makes it ideal for touring. The community name is French and translates as "Clair's Cove."

This full-service village is also home to the Labrador Visitor Centre, located in the community's first church (1909). Various exhibits and displays explain the historical and cultural heritage of the Labrador Coastal Drive, while the young staffers can offer help and advice with regard to your stay. (Open mid-June to early October, admission free.)

Weather conditions can vary considerably along the Labrador Straits. The summers are brief, from mid-July to the end of August, but usually warm. Coastal fog is often present, but will usually burn off by 10 a.m. The average daylight temperature during this period can range from 12 to 24 C (56 to 80 F). However, the temperature can drop below freezing overnight, something that you may want to consider if you plan to camp.

Another thing to be aware of, and not just for camping, is the distinct possibility of being attacked by vicious swarms of biting black flies. They are, however, usually only a problem when the air is calm and warm. How much of a problem?

My good friend Tom Dunn estimated that on one trip to Labrador we had only 40 seconds to get from our cabin to our bikes, with our helmets already on, before we were assaulted by these ferocious creatures. Believe me, unless you are in motion, they will get inside your helmet, your ears, your nose, etc., etc. But if you are lucky enough to wake up to a sunny, dry day, with a light breeze, then you have the opportunity to travel unassaulted through this amazing primeval wilderness, a region that has remained basically unchanged since the end of the last ice age over 10,000 years ago.

On your first morning, after filling your gas tank, you should head back 5 km (3 mi) to the ferry at Blanc-Sablon ("White Sands," pop. 325), and follow Route 138 into Québec, until you reach the end of the road at Old Fort (pop. 347). This lovely scenic highway runs for 72 km (44.7 mi) and is called the Jacques Cartier Trail, after the French explorer who first sailed this coast in 1534.

For most of this tour you will be on a vast, treeless plateau, where rocks the size of automobiles lay strewn about the bleak landscape, exactly where they came to rest when the last of the glaciers had finally melted away. These windswept caribou barrens, more than 300 m (1,000 ft) above sea level,

The massive boulders found all along the Labrador Straits are glacial erratics left behind by the receding glaciers 10,000 years ago.

stretch off to the horizon. Far to the north, you can just barely distinguish the slopes of towering mountains, massive peaks whose tops are usually hidden in mist or low-lying cloud.

Every so often the road will suddenly drop from the plateau to sea level, often in a vivid series of sweeping turns. When this happens you know that you have reached another little village, along this primitive coast. French interests built a primitive fort in Brador (pop. 136), around 1700. During the 18th and 19th centuries Bradore Bay served as a gathering place for fishing fleets from Newfoundland, Nova Scotia, the United States, and the Jersey Islands, off the coast of France.

In Middle Bay (pop. 52) Basque fishermen from France and Spain hunted whales during the 16th century. Archaeologists have discovered red roofing tiles along the shore, indicating that seasonal shelters were built to render whale blubber into oil that would be used to light the homes of Europe.

St. Paul's River (pop. 468), was originally known as Eskimo River, after the Inuit tribes who lived around the bay. Today it is known as the place where the cod trap was invented in 1871, by William Henry Whiteley—an

A distance of 457 km (285 mi) separates the end of the road at Old Fort, from the end of the road at Natashquan, farther down the Lower North Shore. The several small villages in between are only accessible by coastal boat, or by snowmobiles in the winter months.

Four motorcyclists, riding in formation, climb from sea level to the top of the 1,000-foot plateau along Québec's Lower North Shore.

American sailor from Massachusetts. This contraption revolutionized the fishing industry, and led to lower costs and a reduction in the amount of labor required to harvest this resource.

Old Fort (pop. 347) is the end of the road. Named after an early fur-trading fort (c. 1702), the sheltered bay of the same name is protected by steep hills and several offshore islands. Over the years settlers came from England, the Channel Islands, and Newfoundland.

It will take you at least two hours, depending on photo stops, to make the round-trip journey from Blanc-Sablon to Old Fort and back again. Be aware that this region, known locally as the Lower North Shore, is a remote wilderness. Once you leave Blanc-Sablon gas, food, and accommodation is usually not available at any of these outlying villages. It is best to fill your tank before you start.

After returning to the ferry, and if the weather holds, you could easily make the run to the end of the pavement at Red Bay, and be back to your motel before dark. However, I would recommend that you set aside at least one full day to explore this part of the Labrador Straits. Unlike the Québec side, which has little in the way of museums or easily accessed archeological sites, Route 510 in Southern Labrador has a great deal to offer the inquisitive visitor.

Between L'Anse aux Claire, and the end of the paved road in Red Bay, are six little communities, some of which offer full tourist facilities, while others have unique archaeological or historical sites. Forteau ("strong water," pop. 477) was at one time the largest British settlement on the Labrador Straits. It has a gas station, post office & liquor outlet, and the only Royal Canadian Mounted Police Detachment along this coast. There is also a hiking trail that leads to a wonderful look-out over Forteau Bay. Accommodations include the Grenfell Louie A. Hall B&B (five rooms, 709-931-2916) and Seaview Cabins (five units, 709-931-2842).

At L'Anse-Amour ("cove of love," pop. 8), located 3 km (2 mi) from Route 510 along a very good gravel road, archaeologists have uncovered a burial mound that is the oldest known funeral monument in North

This iceberg is one of six I saw during a July ride. In the sunlight the ice reflects a kaleidoscope of color with hues of white, blue, and green and every shade in between, depending on the position of the sun.

From the top of this light at Point Amour you can easily see the rusted remains of the Royal Navy battle cruiser littered along the shore.

America. The Maritime Archaic Indians buried a 12-year-old boy here, 7,500 years ago. Aboriginal people lived here as early as 9,000 years ago, on the edge of the retreating glaciers. A series of small campsites and burial grounds are all that remains of these early relatives of the Inuit and Eskimo caribou hunters of northeastern North America. The Lighthouse Cove B&B (three rooms, 709-927-5690) is only 1 km from both the burial site, and the Point Amour Lighthouse.

At a height of 109 ft (33 m) from the ground and 175 ft (53 m) above sea level, the Point Amour Lighthouse is the tallest light on the Atlantic seaboard. Built in 1854, the interior of this Provincial Historic Site has been restored to its original style, and an interpretation center has been added. The view from the top of the light, on a clear day, is vast and panoramic. You can easily make out the coast of Newfoundland's northern peninsula, on the other side of the Strait of Belle Isle. But there is also military history nearby.

Back in 1922, within sight of the lighthouse, the newest and most technically advanced battle cruiser in Britain's Royal Navy ran aground, at top speed and in heavy fog, while attempting to evade a large iceberg. The *H.M.S. Raleigh*—2,000 tons, 183 m (600 ft) long, and with a crew of more than 700—had tried to navigate the dangerous waters of the Strait of Belle Isle because her captain and officers had decided to go salmon fishing in a nearby river!

The British Admiralty was not pleased, especially when it was discovered that she could not be refloated. Four years later, after the locals had been told to remove everything they could carry (including 14,000 gallons of rum), the embarrassed British government sent over a team of explosive experts with orders to blow up the ship. Today her twisted skeleton lies in shallow water, only a few hundred yards from the lighthouse. The shoreline is still littered with some fairly substantial pieces of wreckage, while large signs warn of the danger of live, unexploded, naval shells in the vicinity.

L'Anse au Loup ("wolf cove," pop. 631) is a vibrant fishing community that was first settled by the French in the early 1700s. Later immigrants came from England, Scotland, and Ireland. It has gas stations, a bank, and a library with Internet access. Barney's B&B offers home-cooked meals, access to the kitchen, and has three rooms available (709-927-5634).

To mark a food cache or a hunter's burial site the Inuit erected stone figures called Inukshuks, which means "human likeness" or "someone was here."

Capstan Island (pop. 46) is a tiny fishing village in the lee of a very large and prominent precipice known as "The Battery." These steep cliffs have witnessed many tragic shipwrecks, and the area is said to be haunted. If you drive through here on a dark, windy day, you can easily understand why!

West St. Modeste (pop. 330) was named after a village in Normandy, France. Here you will find a gas station, campground, and two general stores. The Oceanview Resort Motel & Cottages offers 10 air-conditioned rooms, four housekeeping cottages, and a restaurant and lounge (709-927-5288).

Pinware (pop. 166) has some of the oldest archaeological sites in Labrador, dating back to the end of the last great ice age, some 9,000 years ago. It also has a gas station, grocery stores, and three salmon fishing lodges. Close by, is Pinware River Provincial Park, where you can examine the early geological history of this part of the Canadian Shield. Rocks in this park have been dated to 1.4 billion years ago, and have been sculpted and molded by the numerous glacial advances and retreats that have occurred over eons of time.

The Pinware River is also one of the finest salmon rivers in eastern Canada, and the impressive bridge that spans it is a great place to take a well-deserved break. From the bridge you can take photographs of the often-raging river, and its spectacular surroundings, and experience primeval wilderness up close.

At the end of the paved highway is Red Bay (pop. 264), a delightful little village with more tourist facilities than you would expect for a place of this size. It has a gas station, grocery stores, craft shops, hiking trails, and a wonderful restaurant. The Basinview B&B offers four rooms (709-920-2022), and if they are full, they can arrange other accommodation in the community. Red Bay also happens to be the location of the earliest industrial site in North America.

At the Red Bay National Historic Site archaeologists have discovered several shipwrecks from the period 1550–1600, when this was the whaling capital of the world. From late June to early December hundreds of whales were killed, towed ashore, and rendered into whale oil to light the lamps of Europe. During this short season, seafaring men from the Basque Provinces of France and Spain crossed the Atlantic Ocean to earn their fortunes in the New World. Many weren't so lucky. The bones of 140 men have been found, offering silent testimony to the unimaginable hardships of life at a 16th-century whaling station.

Beginning in 1978, a team of underwater archaeologists from Parks Canada started to explore the local harbor, on a seasonal basis. They quickly located a wrecked ship, which turned out to be the San Juan, a galleon that had been lost in a storm back in 1565. Six years of diving revealed the remains of the most complete 16th-century, ocean-going vessel found anywhere in the world. The ship was amazingly well-preserved because of the cold water. At a lovely little Visitor Orientation Centre you can watch a 30-minute film that documents the history of the site, and the restoration that took place at this 16th-century Basque whaling port. You can also take a self-guided walking tour of archaeological sites on nearby Saddle Island, or just stroll around the picturesque little fishing village, taking lots of pictures.

The Trans-Labrador Highway passes through a vast, awe-inspiring, uninhabited landscape.
© 2010 Adam Romanowicz | http://3scape.com

Trans-Labrador Highway (Route 500)

To travel the Trans-Labrador Highway (666 mi, 1075 km) is a major undertaking, rather like an expedition, through some of the most primitive wilderness regions in North America. Many do not complete their journey because they have overestimated themselves or their bikes, or underestimated the nature of the trip itself.

Most of this remote highway has a surface of loose rock and gravel, and can be difficult to drive, even under the best weather conditions. If the weather turns bad, which happens a lot, it becomes downright treacherous. It is really only suitable for heavy-duty industrial vehicles, or dual-purpose, adventure-style motorcycles.

On a motorcycle this four to six day ride is only possible from June to October. For the rest of the year this road would be impassable for bikes and most other vehicles because of extreme weather conditions. To confirm road conditions contact: Department of Works, Services and Transportation, Happy Valley-Goose Bay, (709) 896-3185.

The Trans-Labrador Highway consists of two sections: Western and Central Labrador (534 km/331 mi) from Labrador City on the Québec border to Happy Valley-Goose Bay, which opened in 1992. Eastern and Southern Labrador (541 km/335 mi) from Happy Valley-Goose Bay to Red Bay. It was not completed until December, 2009.

As of February, 2010, individuals traveling the Trans-Labrador Highway have access to emergency telephone service. A total of 65 satellite phones are available, free of charge, at the following locations (west to east): Wabush Hotel (Wabush); Midway Travel Inn (Churchill Falls); Hotel North Two & Royal Inn and Suites (Happy Valley-Goose Bay); Cartwright Hotel (Cartwright); Alexis Hotel (Port Hope Simpson); Town Office (Charlottetown).

To borrow a satellite phone Newfoundland and Labrador residents must provide their driver's license number, while non-residents are required to submit a valid credit card number. Phones may be dropped off at the end of the trip at any participating location.

Things to Know - Before You Go

- Large, "industrial-style" trucks, traveling at a relatively high speed, always have the right of way. These experienced drivers know the road, while you do not. They command your respect, because if you have an accident, or otherwise require assistance, they may mean the difference between life and death.
- Large trucks produce great amounts of blinding dust, as well as flying rocks and other debris, especially under dry conditions. Should you see an approaching dust cloud, it would be wise to pull over to the side of the road, and wait until the vehicle has passed and driving conditions have returned to normal (if normal is possible on the Trans-Labrador Highway!).
- Keep to the right at all times—especially under wet conditions— when approaching the top of a hill or rounding any curve, because of large trucks, traveling at relatively high speed.
- Slow down when traveling on loose gravel, especially when entering a turn. If you do not, you may find yourself exiting a turn and sliding off the road.
- Because you will be traversing very remote areas, gas up whenever possible. Primitive service facilities will be few and far between.
- Never travel after dark, because of moose, caribou, or other animals on the road. ■

Index

About the Authors

Ken Aiken is a motorcycling photographer and travel writer who has been behind a camera since his school days. He is the author of *Touring Vermont's Scenic Roads*, and has been a contributing editor for *Street Bike, CC Motorcycle News* and *Road Runner*. His features and product reviews have appeared in *Rider, Backroads, ThunderPress, Road Bike, Cruising Rider*, and other motorcycle touring magazines, and he has been a seminar speaker at Americade for more than a decade. For two years he was the Chief Scout and map developer for MAD Maps, Inc. where he developed regional, city, and rally maps that include the popular Harley-Davidson Great Roads series. Currently he is the U.S. representative for motorcycle tourism for the Charlevoix region of Québec. Some of Aiken's work can be seen on NaturalTraveler.com. He divides his time between Montréal, Vermont, and being on the road.

Ken Aiken at the end of the road in Natashquan, Québec.

Rannie Gillis out for a ride with Ann MacLean.

Rannie Gillis, a native of North Sydney, Cape Breton Island, is a writer and photographer who specializes in the Celtic World (Scotland, Ireland, Nova Scotia, Newfoundland, and Labrador). He has toured both in Europe and in the United States by motorcycle. The author of several books, he has also had numerous travel articles published in various Canadian and American motorcycle magazines, and for the past 18 years he has written a weekly travel column for the *Cape Breton Post*. A retired teacher and guidance counselor, he lives in North Sydney, less than one mile from the Newfoundland ferry terminal.